Study Skills for PTLLS

Study Skills for PTLLS

Jacklyn Williams
Editor: Ann Gravells

Learning Matters

First published in 2010 by Learning Matters Ltd

British Library Cataloguing in Publication Data
A CIP record for this book is available from the British Library.

ISBN: 978 1 84445 459 4

This book is also available in the following ebook formats:
Adobe ebook ISBN: 978 184445 701 4
EPUB ebook ISBN: 978 184445 700 7
Kindle ISBN: 978 184445 991 9

Cover design by Topics – The Creative Partnership
Project management by Deer Park Productions, Tavistock, Devon
Typeset by Pantek Arts Ltd, Maidstone, Kent
Printed and bound in Great Britain by Bell & Bain Ltd, Glasgow

Learning Matters Ltd
33 Southernhay East
Exeter EX1 1NX
Tel: 01392 215560
info@learningmatters.co.uk
www.learningmatters.co.uk

CONTENTS

ACKNOWLEDGEMENTS

I would like to thank the following for their patience, encouragement and support whilst writing this book.

Hilary Allen
Ann Gravells
Amy Thornton
Christopher Williams
Helen Williams
Max Williams

Every effort has been made to trace the copyright holders and to obtain their permission for the use of copyright material. The publisher and author will gladly receive any information enabling them to rectify any error or omission in subsequent editions.

THE AUTHOR

Jacklyn Williams has been teaching since 1995, developing, managing and teaching adult education programmes in business education, skills for life, key skills, and teacher training. She has worked in sectors including further education, personal and community development learning, family learning, the prison service, and work-based learning. She also works nationally as a trainer and consultant in lifelong learning, is an external verifier for City & Guilds and is an NLP Master Practitioner, which she says brings an added dimension to her teacher training.

Jacklyn holds QTLS status, and has postgraduate qualifications in education, teaching and learning, and coaching and mentoring, together with specialist qualifications in ESOL, literacy, numeracy and e-learning.

The structure of the book and how to use it

The purpose of the book

The book has been specifically written for anyone who is working towards the Preparing to Teach in the Lifelong Learning Sector (PTLLS) Award at either level 3 or level 4. You might not yet be teaching (known as pre-service), but are hoping to embark on a career in post-compulsory teaching or training – known as the Lifelong Learning Sector. Or you might already be an experienced teacher (known as in-service), who needs to obtain a suitable teaching qualification. You might be returning to study after a long break, or be taking the PTLLS Award alongside another qualification. The book has therefore been designed to provide an easy-to-use guide to the academic skills needed to:

- use study time efficiently;
- develop effective learning strategies;
- work towards meeting the PTLLS Award learning outcomes and assessment criteria.

The book is intended to take you on a journey from when you commence your PTLLS Award (or even before, while you consider whether it is right for you), through the various stages of gaining the skills, knowledge and understanding needed to meet deadlines and produce the required work in a well-organised, attractively presented portfolio.

Even if you decide that you do not wish to complete the PTLLS Award at this stage, the information in the book will prove invaluable in guiding you through a range of strategies to enable you to study and learn more effectively.

Content and Structure

The book is confined to study skills relevant to the PTLLS Award, the information in it being complementary to that in the companion text books by Ann Gravells, *Preparing to Teach in the Lifelong Learning Sector* and *Passing PTLLS Assessments*. These texts give specific information relating to the full process of teaching along with guidance to help you demonstrate and evidence your competence.

Each chapter contains relevant activities to enable you to engage with the content and identify its relevance to your own situation; there are also examples to help your understanding. At the end of each chapter is a list of textbooks, websites and other resources which will enable you to research relevant topics further.

For ease and speed of understanding, abbreviations and acronyms are expanded the first time that they are used in each chapter. This is something that you would also do within your own written work.

The appendices include answers to the formal activities in the chapters together with a list of useful books and websites.

The index will help you quickly locate topics if you are dipping into the book to find specific information, or want to check up on a particular point. Again, this is something you can do with any textbook to help you quickly find the information you need.

How to use the book

Each chapter stands alone and can be read independently. You may choose to read consecutively from Chapter 1 to Chapter 5, or to work through the chapters according to your requirements at the time. Alternatively, you may decide to use the book as a reference source and look up relevant aspects within the chapters as required.

The PTLLS Award can be studied in many different ways; for example, face-to-face, distance learning, and/or blended learning. It is delivered over varying time spans, from intensive one-week programmes to day or evening classes lasting ten weeks or more. Accreditation is through many different Awarding Organisations, each with their own assessment strategy. The content of the qualification is the same; however, it can be assessed differently as long as all the assessment criteria are met during the process. The PTLLS Award can be completed as a stand-alone qualification, or as part of the Certificate (CTLLS) or the Diploma (DTLLS) in Teaching in the Lifelong Learning Sector; the latter is also known as the Certificate in Education (Cert. Ed.) or Post Graduate Certificate in Education (PGCE).

Whichever route you follow to achieve your PTLLS Award, the study skills needed for successful completion will be the same. This book has been organised so that the necessary skills are presented in a way that is useful and accessible to anyone following any PTLLS Award programme.

The book should fully meet your requirements whether you are completing the PTLLS Award at level 3 or level 4, as you can pick and mix the pages that you study according to your needs at the time. If you are aiming to achieve at level 3, you might choose not to go into too much detail regarding research and referencing. If you are aiming to achieve at level 4, you will need to carry out independent research and write in an academic style, referencing your work to theorists. You will therefore find the pages around this topic particularly useful. Your assessor will be able to inform you of any particular awarding organisation requirements.

Further ways to reference other sources

Electronic sources

References for other electronic sources follow a similar pattern, with the medium – in the following example CD-ROM – shown in the square brackets occupied by *online* for an internet reference.

Surname, Initials of author/editor (Year) 'Article title' [medium] *Title of publication in italics, volume in italics* (issue number).

LSIS (2009) 'Equality, diversity and inclusion', [CD-ROM] *Resources for teacher educators,* Version 2.0.

DVD, film or video

***Title in italics.* (Year of distribution) [medium] Directed by Forename Surname, Place of Publication: Production company name.**

What's eating Gilbert Grape? (1993) [DVD] Directed by Lasse Hallström. USA: Paramount Pictures.

Printed learning materials

You should avoid direct reference to printed learning materials given to you during taught sessions, unless they have been issued in place of a textbook. Printed learning materials should be used as a guide to independent reading.

Missing information

Where an item has no author, it is ordered in the reference list by the first significant word of the title. Where an item has no date, it should be shown as (*date unknown*). Before using an undated source, however, it is worth thinking carefully about its relevance and value to your work.

Finding referencing details

Publishing information is usually:

- in a book, on the back of the title page;
- in journals, on the inside page;
- on CD-ROMs, DVDs and videos, on the sleeve or insert;
- in websites, in the web address and the web page being visited. (For more information about website addresses, see Chapter 3.)

Keeping a log of information sources is a good practice to develop from the start of your PTLLS Award programme. You will save a great deal of time and work by noting referencing information as soon as you access it or first read a publication. As you work towards your assessment, keep an ongoing table of references used.

If you are using a word processor you could enter an electronic table on the final page, or use a separate document. This has the advantage that, if correctly set up, it can be automatically sorted later into alphabetical and date order. Minimum column headings you will need are: Surname, Initials, Date, Title, Place, Publisher. If you prefer, you could enter your references by author surname or first significant title word into an A-Z notebook, or a binder with A-Z dividers, or you could use a voice recorder to keep an audio file of the details. Keeping an up-to-date list as you progress will save time later on.

Activity

Practise your referencing skills

Question 1. This is the reference for Gravells' book in John's bibliography. Tick or cross the correct number for each part of this reference in the table below.

Extract from John's assessment

Gravells (2008: 23) states that *using the senses – sight, hearing, touch, smell and taste – will enable you to learn and remember.*

1	2	3	4	5	6
Gravells,	A.	(2008)	*Preparing to teach in the lifelong learning sector*, 3rd edn.	Exeter:	Learning Matters.

	1	2	3	4	5	6
Surname of the writer of the book	☐	☐	☐	☐	☐	☐
Publisher's name	☐	☐	☐	☐	☐	☐
Name of the book	☐	☐	☐	☐	☐	☐
Place of publication...	☐	☐	☐	☐	☐	☐
Year of publication	☐	☐	☐	☐	☐	☐
The writer's initial(s)	☐	☐	☐	☐	☐	☐

Question 2. Emma has used the internet to research her assessment. Tick or cross the correct number for each part of the reference in the table below.

1	2	3	4	5	6
Petty,	G.	(2004)	*Active learning* [online]	available at www.geoffpetty.com/activelearning.html	[accessed 2 June 2010].

Learning styles

Learning styles relate to a person's preferences for receiving information and problem-solving. Being aware of your learning style will help you to get the most out of learning opportunities and to identify areas for personal and professional development.

Perhaps the most widely-used learning styles model is VAK (visual, auditory, kinaesthetic), or learning through seeing, hearing and/or doing. If you don't already know your learning styles, access one of the websites listed at the end of this chapter and complete a questionnaire. Once you know your learning preference, you can adapt information and materials either to complement your strengths or to develop less active styles. Always inform your teacher of your learning style as this will enable them to adapt their teaching methods to suit your needs.

Activity

Now you have identified your learning preferences, take a few moments to think how you could make use of this information to:

a. adapt learning material to make it easier for you to understand and learn;

b. develop strengths where your skills are less well established.

Look at the following checklist and tick the things you feel you do well. Are there items on the list that you would like to include as personal goals for development? What about anything that is not on the list, but that you might like to add?

	Do well	Could improve
Visual/seeing		
Reviewing an activity by looking at something in print.		
Checking your notes are copied down accurately.		
Being sure to use upper and lower case letters (rather than capitals) and looking at the shapes/patterns that they make.		
Looking for words within words; for example, **format**ive.		
Using illustrations, charts and diagrams.		
Using highlighters to emphasise important points.		
Creating spray diagrams, spider diagrams, or concept maps.		
Turning your notes into a storyboard or cartoon strip.		
Finding pictures that support or replace text.		

Auditory/hearing		
Listening to tapes, podcasts, compact discs, to help you learn.		
Paraphrasing new learning to explain it in your own words.		
Discussing your ideas with peers or friends and family.		
Creating your own podcast explaining new information.		
Repeating words or phrases silently to yourself.		
Splitting words or phrases into syllables or chunks and exaggerating the sounds.		
Chanting words and phrases to music.		
Making rhymes from information you need to remember.		
Using active listening skills including questioning and summarising.		
Kinaesthetic/doing		
Carrying out a practical activity to review learning.		
Writing things out as a step-by-step account.		
Producing a written account paraphrasing new learning into your own words.		
Turning your notes into a storyboard or cartoon strip.		
Finger-tracing keywords while saying them out loud.		
Writing down key information from memory.		
Using joined-up writing, rather than printing to help with flow.		
Typing or word processing to increase speed and help with flow.		

VAK is only one learning styles model. The BBC, in conjunction with the Open University, offers a model that adds two further processes of feeling/belonging and reflecting/evaluating. Fleming's (2005) VARK model adds a read/write process. Honey and Mumford (1992) identify four different styles of reflectors, theorists, activists and pragmatists, while Gardner's (1983) multiple intelligence theory recognises eight different intelligences, namely:

- verbal/linguistic – an ability with words and language;
- mathematical/logical – an aptitude for logic, reasoning and mathematical tasks;
- musical – an aptitude for music, rhythm and composition;
- inter-personal – a capacity for empathy and social awareness and involvement;
- intra-personal – reflective and self-aware, an ability for personal organisation;
- visual-spatial – an ability to think three-dimensionally and judge spatial relationships;
- kinaesthetic – a capacity for dexterity and a keen sense of body awareness;
- naturalist – an ability to recognise and categorise environmental elements, an affinity with nature.

Recognising your preferred learning styles, and carrying out activities to strengthen other styles, can help you to become a more effective learner. For example, if you are an activist, tending to jump in with both feet first, you could consider spending some time reflecting on previous experiences and identifying relevant theories before taking action.

Memory techniques

Memory is the ability to store and recall information. All learning, regardless of learning style, is based on memory. Many things conjure up memories: sounds, sights, scents, touch, tastes, emotional feelings and physical movement. The more senses that are actively involved in an experience, the more likely it is to be remembered clearly. In addition to multi-sensory experiences, people generally remember things that are:

- of particular interest;
- first and last in a sequence;
- concrete, rather than abstract;
- linked or associated with something familiar;
- absurd, comical, vulgar, rude, or bizarre;
- in picture form;
- experienced when in a calm and confident frame of mind.

You can use this knowledge to help your memory.

Be, and act, interested

If you are not immediately interested in something, use your acting skills. Lean forward, listen, watch or read actively, as though you are studying the most fascinating subject in the world.

Make sure that you understand

Rephrase material in your own words. Write short notes about it. Make links and associations to other examples, drawing pictures or diagrams. Revisit your work at least three times; once after approximately 24 hours, again after a week, and again after three or four weeks.

Organisation, association and visualisation techniques

Organisation

This involves activities such as:

- linking things that are visually similar; for example, by colour, or shape, or size;
- sequencing, or arranging into a series; for example in alphabetical or date order;
- categorising, or putting items into groups with similar characteristics.

Example

Max needs to remember a list of 15 successful people with dyslexia for his micro-teach session. He is interested in the reasons for their success and fame, he finds out a little about them, and arranges his list as follows:

Entrepreneurs/business leaders:
Sir Richard Branson
William Hewlett
F. W. Woolworth

Athletes:
Muhammad Ali
Sir Steve Redgrave
Sir Jackie Stewart

Political Leaders:
Winston Churchill
Michael Heseltine
John F. Kennedy

Actors:
Orlando Bloom
Keira Knightley
Keanu Reeves

Comedians:
Jay Leno
Robin Williams
Eddie Izzard

(Griggs, 2010)

Now, instead of having a long list of 15 unconnected names to remember, Max has five sets of meaningful categories, with just three names in each.

Association

The more that one item or fact can be associated with others, the better it will be remembered. For example, if you need to remember to take an electrical cable safety cover to a teaching session, think about how and why you are going to use it. Imagine using it, ten times as large as life, to cover a gigantic cable that is writhing across the room like a snake. Having made a clear association between the cable and the safety cover, you are much more likely to remember it.

Visualisation

Picturing a mental image which is connected to the item will help you remember it. Try to apply techniques such as:

- exaggeration – make it much larger than life;
- contraction – make it much smaller than it is in reality;
- absurdity – make it as nonsensical and bizarre as possible;
- colour – use strong, vibrant colours;
- movement – animate it;
- involve all the senses – try to imagine not only how it looks, but also sounds, smells, tastes and feels.

The link system

The link system is useful for memorising notes. Extract a key word from each main point of your notes, and then, thinking of the points carefully, form a vivid mental image for each one, remembering to use the visualisation techniques above. Link or associate the first one to the next, and so on, in turn, until you come to the last one.

Example

Dan is going to deliver his micro-teach on readability. He wants to remember to talk about:

- ***white space;***
- ***leading (the spacing between the lines);***
- ***font choice and size;***
- ***use of upper and lower case;***
- ***illustrations and overprinting;***
- ***page layout and page breaks;***
- ***paper choice;***
- ***readability.***

Example

First, he closes his eyes and creates a vivid and striking image of another planet where all around is bright, dazzling white space.

He then links the next item on his list, leading, to the white space. He visualises aliens on the roof of a building in the white space, stealing lead from a building roof.

He then forgets the white space, and links the aliens taking lead from the building roof to the font, or starting place, on a race track where there are alien horses with wings ready to start a race.

Next he forgets the lead on the roof, and links the font to a huge case with the words 'First Prize' written on it, and a bright ribbon around it.

Dan continues this until the end of his list of eight items. He is then able to remember them all during his micro-teach session.

The story method

In this variation of the link system, the items to be remembered are visualised in the same way, and then woven into a story. It can be more difficult, especially with a longer list, to successfully link all the items together into one flowing and memorable story.

Activity

Think of an occasion when you will need to memorise a list or a series of notes. For example, you may have a list of eight or ten points that you want to make in a presentation, or include in your micro-teach. Use the link system or the story method.

Once you have linked your items, or woven them into a story, cover your list and try to write down the main points in the right order. As you recall the linking words, you should also be able to remember what you wanted to say about each one.

The room system

This memory technique involves identifying a mental image for the item to be remembered, and then linking it to a chosen place or location.

Example

Jenna is attending a PTLLS Award class this evening and has five tasks that she wants to remember to do in readiness: make an entry in her reflective learning journal; print out an assessment task; return a book to the library; get a bottle of water; and get some petrol for her car.

She thinks of her house, and chooses a room that contains as many different objects as possible. Deciding on the kitchen, she takes a slow, mental walk around it. Using all her senses (sight, sound, touch, taste and smell), she takes in all the details of the room and its contents. She then thinks of the tasks to be remembered, in order, linking each task with an individual object in the room, making a vivid mental picture of each as she does so.

When all the tasks to be remembered are linked in her mind to the various objects, she can go through her mental walk around the kitchen, recalling the tasks she has placed along the way.

1. ***Object:*** ***Kitchen table***
   Task: ***Reflective learning journal (RLJ) entry***
   Image: ***Kitchen table with a giant RLJ as a tablecloth.***
2. ***Object:*** ***Microwave***
   Task: ***Printing assessment***
   Image: ***Printed paper pouring out of the microwave.***
3. ***Object:*** ***Washing machine***
   Task: ***Return book to the library***
   Image: ***A bright red book spinning in the washer/drier.***
4. ***Object:*** ***Kitchen sink***
   Task: ***Get a bottle of water***
   Image: ***Bottles of water popping out of the taps.***
5. ***Object:*** ***Refrigerator***
   Task: ***Buy petrol***
   Image: ***The refrigerator in the shape of a petrol can.***

Using the techniques in this chapter will help you become a more effective learner which should help towards successful achievement of your PTLLS Award.

Summary

In this chapter you have learned about:

- meeting the Lifelong Learning UK standards;
- referencing your work;

- interpreting the skills needed for the PTLLS Award;
- becoming an expert learner.

Theory focus

Books

Desforges, C. (ed) (1995) *An introduction to teaching*. Oxford: Blackwell Publishers.

DfEE (1999) *Improving literacy and numeracy: A fresh start: The report of the working group* (Chairman: Sir Claus Moser). London: DfEE Publications.

Fleming, N. (2005) *Teaching and learning styles: VARK strategies*. Honolulu: Honolulu Community College.

Gardner, H. (1983) *Frames of mind*. New York: Basic Books.

Gravells, A. (2008) *Preparing to teach in the lifelong learning sector*, 3rd edn. Exeter: Learning Matters.

Gravells, A. (2010) *Passing PTLLS assessments*. Exeter: Learning Matters.

Gravells, A. and Simpson, S. (2009) *Equality and diversity in the lifelong learning sector*. Exeter: Learning Matters.

Honey, P. and Mumford, A. (1992) *The manual of learning styles*, 3rd edn. Maidenhead: Peter Honey Associates.

Kirkup, G. and Jones, A. (1996) 'New technologies for open learning: the superhighway to the learning society?', in P. Raggatt, R. Edwards and N Small (eds) *The learning society: challenges and trends* (Chapter 17, 272–291). London: Routledge.

Scheurich, J.J. (1994) 'Policy archaeology: a new policy studies methodology', *Journal of Education Policy*, 9 (4): 297–316.

Vella, J., Berardinelli, P. and Burrow, J. (1998) *How do they know they know?* San Francisco: Jossey-Bass Publishers.

What's eating Gilbert Grape? (1993) [DVD] Directed by Lasse Hallström. USA: Paramount Pictures.

Williams, J. (2010) *Study skills for PTLLS*. Exeter: Learning Matters.

Websites

DRC (2007) *Understanding the Disability Discrimination Act – a guide for colleges, universities and adult community learning providers in Great Britain* [online] available at **www.lluk.org/documents/d_r_c_guidance__2007.pdf**

Griggs, K. (2010) *Famous celebrity x's* [online] available at **www.xtraordinary people.com/celebrity**

Institute for Learning – **www.ifl.ac.uk**

Learning Styles:

BBC/Open University (2004) *Learning Styles* [online] available at **www.open2.net/survey/learningstyles**

Fleming, N. (2009) *VARK – A Guide to Learning Styles* [online] available at **www.vark-learn.com/english/page.asp? p=questionnaire**

Gardner, H. *'Multiple Intelligences'* (date unknown) from *The Distance Learning Technology Resource Guide, by Carla Lane* (Howard Gardner) [online] available at **www.tecweb.org/styles/gardner.html**

Honey and Mumford (1992) – *Learning styles* (2004) [online] available at **www.brainboxx.co.uk/A2_LEARNSTYLES/ pages/learningstyles.htm**

(VAK) *Discover your preferred learning style* (2004) [online] available at **www.brainboxx.co.uk/A3_ASPECTS/pages/VAK_quest.htm**

LLUK (2007a) *Further education workforce reforms* [online] available at **www.lluk.org/feworkforcereforms.htm**

LLUK (2007b) *New overarching professional standards for teachers, tutors and trainers in the lifelong learning sector* [online] available at **www.lluk.org.uk/documents/professional_standards_for_itts_020107.pdf**

LLUK (2008) *About LLUK* [online] available at **www.lluk.org/2818.htm**

LSIS (2009) 'Equality, diversity and inclusion', *Resources for teacher educators,* [CD-ROM] *Version 2.0.*

Petty, G. (2004) *Active learning* [online] available at **www.geoffpetty.com/activelearning.html**

Qualifications and Credit Framework **www.qcda.gov.uk/8150.aspx**

SVUK (2007) *Evidencing skills and qualifications*, [online] available at **www.standardsverificationuk.org/2924.htm**

CHAPTER 2
TAUGHT SESSIONS

Introduction

In this chapter you will learn about:

- getting the most from taught sessions;
- effective note-taking;
- keeping notes and information safely;
- making the most of group activities.

There are activities and examples to help you reflect on the above which will assist your understanding of getting the best out of taught sessions.

Getting the most from taught sessions

Taught sessions are those sessions where you receive information from your PTLLS teacher. This could be as part of a group, a one-to-one session or even electronically. As well as the time attending taught sessions, the PTLLS Award has a similar amount of time allocated for self-study, usually 30 hours. During this time, you will be able to carry out independent self-directed learning and research to help you to complete your assessments and to find out more about the areas that you find especially interesting or relevant.

Taught sessions may take place face-to-face as part of a group and may be held in a conventional classroom, community hall, room at work, or any other relevant setting. They may be spread over a number of weeks, or compressed into an intensive programme over a few days, either consecutively or as part of a day release programme. Learning could also be undertaken using a blended approach: partly face-to-face in a classroom and partly through distance or online delivery, using a virtual learning environment (VLE) such as Moodle, Blackboard, WebCT or Bodington. Using a VLE, the teacher can upload the learning resources for the online sessions via the internet, so that learners are able to access them from any computer with an internet connection. Learners and teachers are also able to communicate through discussion forums. In this way, learning can be supported 24 hours a day, seven days a week. You may even attend your taught sessions in a learning environment within a three-dimensional online world such as Second Life. If you have enrolled on a distance learning or online programme, where all the taught content is delivered electronically, you will study from home or another suitable environment such as an office, library or a cyber cafe and may meet other members of your programme only virtually, or even not at all. If you are currently teaching, you will need a mentor, someone in the same specialist subject area as your own, who can give you help and support as you progress.

No matter how you are studying for the PTLLS Award, or where your learning for the taught sessions takes place, it is important for you to prepare and organise yourself so that you can get the best out of this time.

In order to get the most from your PTLLS Award taught sessions, you need to think about how you learn best. Consider how you have approached different taught sessions in the past. Think about what worked well that you could re-use, and what you might need to change, and how. Make sure you are comfortable when you set out to learn: that you have had enough to eat; are dressed for comfort; and have all the tools you need around you, including spectacles (if worn), paper, pens and highlighters. Try to make sure that you leave any worries outside the learning environment and, if possible, arrive early so that you are not rushing. Allow yourself time to get to know the other learners on your PTLLS Award programme as you will also learn from their knowledge and experience.

You have needs as a learner, in exactly the same way that your learners will. Sometimes when struggling to keep up with work, personal commitments and study, it is easy to forget to meet personal learning needs.

Activity

Think about a programme of study you have followed in the past that was successful. Make a list of the things that you think contributed to this. Why was this and can you use these tactics to help you now?

Thinking back, in the list of things that contributed to a successful learning experience, you probably noted that the venue was accessible and comfortable, with adequate heating, good lighting and ventilation. There was, most likely, a good group dynamic where group members and teacher were respectful and supportive of each other in a safe environment. You were probably highly motivated to learn a subject, which you recognised was important and useful, and you probably experienced a real sense of achieving your goal.

Sometimes, if a subject seems interesting or relevant, or a goal is particularly important, feelings of loneliness or hunger might go unnoticed. When progress is not so good, however, attention might turn to 'comfort snacks'. Make sure that, for such times, there are some healthy, energy-providing food and drinks in the cupboard or fridge, or in your study bag.

Activity

Look at the following checklist to help you to get the best out of any learning environment. Tick the aspects that apply and consider what else you may need to do before attending your next taught session.

Do I always arrive on time for my sessions?	Whenever possible arrive on time or a little early for teaching sessions. This not only enables an organised and relaxed start to the session, but is considerate of others. It also allows time to get to know other learners.	☐
Do I always make sure I have enough to eat?	As adults, with busy lives, skipping meals often seems inevitable. Thinking ahead and planning meals and/or snacks can lead to an improvement in your comfort and your learning.	☐
Do I always make sure I have a bottle of water?	Keep drinking water with you (preferably in a sports bottle to prevent spillage). Most people need between six and eight glasses of water every day to: • regulate body temperature; • help the body to absorb nutrients; • convert food into energy. Moderate dehydration can cause headaches and dizziness, and thirst can cause memory, attention and concentration to decrease by about 10 per cent.	☐
Do I always remember all accessories and equipment?	Remember to take any accessories or equipment you need to be able to participate fully in the programme; for example, spectacles, pen and paper for note-taking, any coloured overlays needed for reading, etc.	☐
Do I make sure my teacher is aware of any specific needs I have?	Ensure that your teacher is aware of any specific needs that you might have, and that these can be met; for example handouts in a large font, on a coloured background, or available electronically.	☐
Do I try to attend every session if I possibly can? If I can't attend, for any reason, have I made study-buddy arrangements?	It is always difficult to catch up effectively with the content of missed sessions. Make sure that you have all the dates and times of your taught sessions displayed clearly in a prominent place, and keep a note of your study buddy's contact details somewhere easy to find, just in case.	☐

Study buddies

Although it is important to attend all the taught sessions of a programme so that you don't miss anything, sometimes it is not always possible. It is a good idea, on the first session of your attendance to find a study buddy. Study buddying is a two-way arrangement where, if you have to be away during part of or the whole of a session, your study buddy will collect handouts for you and create an extra copy of their session notes, which they will write with a little extra care because they know you are going to have to read them. If you can also arrange to meet up for half an hour or so before the next session, for a handover, so much the better. Study buddying makes it much easier to catch up on any missed material, and it can be enjoyable and productive spending a few minutes reviewing and catching up if time permits. It is also useful to keep in touch with them between sessions, perhaps discussing reading and research findings.

Activity

Consider a learning experience that was not so productive. What reasons can you identify for this and why did this happen?

In the less-productive learning situation, was perhaps the room too hot or too cold? Were you hungry or thirsty during sessions, with no facilities available on site to access refreshments? Maybe there was minimal group interaction, and/or a lack of feedback or support from your teacher?

Learning goals

It's important to have goals to work towards, to ensure you keep on track with your assessments. You will probably discuss these with your teacher early on in the programme. When you are identifying these, you might want to look more widely than developing your skills, knowledge and understanding of teaching. For example, you might want to develop some aspects of information communication technology (ICT) such as learning how to produce a computer-generated presentation, or you might want to acquire skills and techniques that help you overcome nerves when presenting to a group.

Activity

Look at the checklist overleaf. Is there anything on the list that you would like to include as a personal goal for development? What about anything that is not on the list, but that you might like to add? There are some blank spaces at the end for you to include your own ideas.

By the end of the PTLLS Award programme, I want to be able to:	
Gain the qualification.	☐
Decide whether teaching is for me.	☐
Develop the skills of an inspirational teacher.	☐
Use a range of different teaching and learning methods.	☐
Use different strategies to motivate learners.	☐
Manage and promote equality and diversity in the classroom.	☐
Plan a scheme of work.	☐
Write effective session plans.	☐
Assess learners effectively.	☐
Meet challenges with greater self-confidence.	☐
Use my own preferred learning styles effectively to improve the way I learn.	☐
Improve grammar, spelling and/or punctuation.	☐
Overcome nerves when presenting to a group.	☐
Critically and objectively reflect on, and revise, my own teaching practice.	☐
Give feedback appropriately and confidently.	☐
Receive and use feedback from others in a constructive way.	☐
Develop my ICT skills – word processing, presentations, spreadsheets, other.	☐
Improve my confidence.	☐
	☐
	☐
	☐

During your learning, take time to re-visit your personal goals regularly, noting your achievements and also areas where you might need to refocus. You might decide to allow yourself a small treat for each goal achieved to help your motivation. Remember that the PTLLS Award could change your life, both as a teacher and as a learner, if you identify and focus clearly on what you want to get out of it.

Example

Sally is following a PTLLS Award programme held in her local village hall; an old draughty building, with one teaching room that has an erratic heating system dependent upon a coin meter, and no social facilities. The teacher knows her subject inside out, and is enthusiastic, but provides little feedback to her group of 12 learners.

Sally determines to get the best she can out of this learning situation by:

- ***preparing a pre-packed snack, including a flask of hot soup, for the break mid-session;***
- ***making a point of arriving early for the session so that she can settle in comfortably and exchange views and ideas with some of the other learners;***
- ***taking a bottle of drinking water;***
- ***wearing several layers of clothing, so that she can easily and quickly adapt to the changing ambient temperature;***
- ***setting her own personal short-term goals and self-assessing her achievement, allowing herself a small reward for each goal achieved;***
- ***making notes of points on which she specifically wants the teacher's feedback, so that she remembers to ask;***
- ***keeping a reflective learning journal showing her progress towards her personal goals.***

Effective note-taking

Whatever system you use for note-taking, make sure that you always use one size of paper. This helps with easy filing and retrieval of your notes. A4 is generally a good choice (30 cm x 21 cm): it is available in a range of colours, with and without lines, fits into standard folders or binders, and is easy to manage. When note-taking, always leave a wide margin on the right-hand side to make additional notes and comments, and to follow up references and research. When hand-writing notes, be careful to write the date on each page, and number each page in order as you write it. If you are using a computer to make your notes, set up a footer (see Chapter 4) to automatically include this information at the bottom of each page. In this way, if your notes should happen to become mixed up later on, they are much easier to locate and re-file. If you are filing your notes using a session-by-session system, it is also helpful to make a note of the date on any printed learning materials you are given.

Activity

Think back to a time when you took notes from a learning session or a meeting. What were the positive and negative aspects:

- ***during the note-taking process itself?***
- ***afterwards when you reviewed the material?***

Often, note-taking can be a fraught activity. Frantic efforts to keep up result in feelings of frustration during the note-taking process itself, with much of the information being missed, and afterwards what is left can be illegible, unclear and without meaning.

It is important to make sure, when taking notes during a taught session, that you:

- continue to engage fully with the session, entering into any discussions;
- identify and make sense of the key points;
- capture enough detail for your notes to be meaningful and make sense.

Any attempt to write down exactly what is said or written is likely to result in a failure on all counts. Writing down key words or phrases, or making notes by missing out the vowels in words, will help speed up your writing.

After the session, it is important to review your notes as soon as possible, annotating and clarifying any unclear sections while the content is still fresh in your memory. When you come to revisit your notes, it is important that they provide enough detail to:

- revise and recall the material covered, for use in your assessments;
- direct you to further reading and research;
- enable you to accurately reference other authors' material.

Note-taking is an active form of learning: you actively engage with material that you would otherwise receive in a passive form through listening or reading; and by choosing the right note-taking methods and techniques you can transform your notes into a form that really suits the way you think and learn.

Activity

On a piece of A4 paper, note down at least five reasons why you might make notes during your PTLLS Award programme.

How many of the following reasons did you come up with?

1. Note-taking is an active process, which helps you to remember the content (even more so if you have strong kinaesthetic learning preferences).
2. Taking notes helps you to concentrate on the material you are learning.
3. Notes can be useful in comparing and contrasting different theories, principles and ideas.
4. Notes can be used to revisit key facts and theories quickly.
5. Putting notes into your own words can help you to understand difficult concepts.
6. Notes offer opportunities to revisit and revise material to aid learning.
7. Notes can make a large amount of information much more manageable.
8. You can personalise your notes to make them more memorable to you.
9. Notes are useful when planning and writing assessments and for later reference in a work situation.
10. Notes enable you to discuss your work with others; for example, your study buddy or peers.

Some tips for effective note-taking

- Be selective with your note-taking; make notes of the main facts only, not examples or anecdotes.
- When note-taking from a lecture or discussion, use the structure to work out what is important. Words or phrases such as 'a key point is...' or 'the main impact of this...' are important indicators, as is information being repeated, and the use of pauses for emphasis.
- When note-taking from written material, make use of features in the text itself, such as headings and sub-headings, emboldened text, larger font size, underlining, etc., to determine the key points.
- Listen, or read, actively, staying engaged with the material throughout the session, and pace your note-taking.
- Use symbols, abbreviations and keywords to reduce the amount you need to write. Some short forms already exist, such as + or & (and), = (equals), @ (at), e.g. (for example), and i.e. (that is). You can make up others for frequently occurring words or phrases; perhaps using 4 for 'for', L for 'learner', T for 'teacher', or 'SoW' for 'Scheme of Work'. Long words can often be shortened, without losing meaning; for example, assessment can be effectively reduced to 'assmt'. (It can also be a useful trick to use a short form for longer words or phrases when word processing your assessments, and then complete them in full by using the global search and replace facility (see Chapter 4).

- Use colours to identify different themes, styles or approaches. Make sure you have a set of highlighters or coloured pens with you.
- Review your notes as soon as possible after you have written them, and add any necessary clarification or expansion. This has two main benefits.
    1. You will be able to make sense of your notes much more easily while the session is still fresh in your mind.
    2. Reviewing learning helps transfer into long-term memory.
- Leave out words such as: *a, an, the, is, are, was, were, of,* and pronouns such as: *(s)he, it(s), this, that, these, those, them*. Be careful, however, not to leave out any words essential to meaning.
- Ignore spelling, punctuation and grammar when note-taking, unless the correct form is essential to meaning.
- If you are taking direct quotations from other people's work, remember to enclose them in speech marks and include the full reference straight away. If you are working at level 4, you will need to include quotations and citations (where you paraphrase another author's work) in your assessments. Making a table on the last page of your assessment, or keeping a separate document, where you enter reference details as you go along, is a good way of making sure all your sources are acknowledged. For example, the entry for this book would be as follows.

Surname	Initials	Date	Title	Place of Publication	Publisher
Williams,	J. K.	(2010)	*Study skills for PTLLS*	Exeter	Learning Matters

For further details about Harvard referencing, see Chapter 1.

Example

Aliya has taken notes from a workshop regarding schemes of work. She has used some of the tips to help her.

SoW – essential 4 groups. Do in advance.
Must include:
Overall:

- ***Who for***
- ***Subject***
- ***Content***
- ***Ordering, sequencing***
- ***Sessn lengths/times, room***

Example

- ***Each sessn:***
- ***Aims & objs or LO***
- ***Key topics***
- ***T activity***
- ***L -"-***
- ***Assmt***
- ***Resources***
- ***E&D, sustainability, ECM, func skills***

Sometimes you can highlight or underline material to draw out the key points on printed learning materials you are given, avoiding the need to create your own notes. You might also be happy to annotate textbooks, making comments and critical observations in the margins, whereas other learners will prefer to keep their books in original condition. Do not, however, make notes within books borrowed from libraries or other people.

Different types of note-taking

When you do have to create your own notes, the two main ways in which this can be done are:

1. by taking traditional linear, sequential, notes;
2. by taking nuclear or pattern notes, which can be added to in any order.

You can use various forms of these, depending upon your context, the final purpose of the notes, and your preferred learning style.

Linear note-taking

Linear note-taking (where notes are entered sequentially in order, as lines of text) is probably the most frequently-used note-taking method. This form of note-taking can be useful for analytical tasks where you separate a topic into its main parts or important features and consider their relationship to one another. Linear notes often follow a structure that is developed through sections and sub-sections, using increasing levels of indentation on the page. Ideas and information are classified together in hierarchies or sets, using only key words (see Figure 2.1).

Example

Zach has taken some linear notes during a session on learning styles. He has structured his notes in the order they were delivered in the session, leaving spaces between the headings so that he can go back and add any further details needed.

Learning styles *21 June 2010 – page 1*

Types

- Honey and Mumford
  - Activist
  - Pragmatist
  - Reflector
  - Theorist

- VARK
  - Visual
  - Aural
  - Read-Write
  - Kinaesthetic

- Howard Gardner
  1) Verbal/linguistic
  2) Mathematical/logical
  3) Musical
  4) Inter-personal
  5) Intra-personal
  6) Visual-spatial
  7) Bodily kinaesthetic
  8) Naturalist

Implications for teaching

- Mix of T&L methods
- Resources
- Group dynamics
- Learner response time

Figure 2.1 Linear notes

Nuclear or pattern note-taking

Many people prefer to take notes in a nuclear or non-linear way, working outwards from the centre. Spray diagrams, mind maps, spider diagrams and concept maps are all examples of nuclear or pattern note-taking, in which ideas or information can be presented through drawings and diagrams. Making notes in this way can help you to think more imaginatively, especially if you have a strong visual preference, i.e. prefer to learn by seeing. The visual representation, with the use of colour, pictures, drawings, symbols and arrows, can help to convey meaning by showing the relationship between concepts, and highlighting important points. Pattern or nuclear notes have the added advantage that information can be entered in any sequence, unlike linear notes for which there needs to be some structure in place from the outset.

Spray or spider diagrams are ideal note-taking instruments as they can be used to summarise other people's ideas. Mind maps and concept maps are useful for developing your own ideas on a subject; for example, to sort ideas after brainstorming sessions and to organise information when planning a report or assessment.

Figure 2.2 shows a spray diagram about ground rules. A spray diagram involves quickly jotting down all your ideas on a subject and then linking them up to make connections.

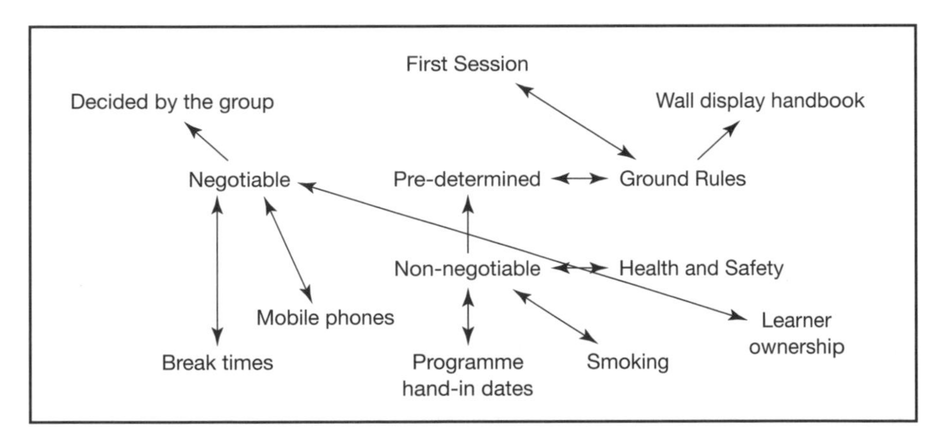

Figure 2.2 A spray diagram about ground rules

In a spider diagram, or concept map, the core topic is shown in the image or circle in the centre of the diagram. Main themes are linked by branches from this core. Some of these themes then have sub-themes that branch outwards from the main branches. The points closer to the centre are usually more general, with points to the outside of the diagram becoming more detailed and specific.

It can be really satisfying to draw a spider diagram or concept map. The best way to approach it is as follows.

1. Use a sheet of plain paper (A4 or larger). Using pre-lined paper can restrict the free flow of ideas;
2. Position the paper in landscape view, with the long edge at the top. This gives more space from left-to-right (as you write).
3. Use brightly coloured crayons or pens, draw an image or symbol that represents your core topic in the centre of the paper. This should be no more than 2" or 5cm high or wide.
4. Label this core image clearly.
5. Use different colours, draw main branches off the core image. Make the branches thicker near the core, and let them start to thin out towards the ends.
6. Label each of the ideas coming out from the core, using just one word, taking up the length of the branch.
7. Develop new ideas, shown by smaller branches coming out from each main branch, drawing pictures or symbols for each if you wish.
8. Remember to have fun with your creation. Use colour and dimension imaginatively. Exaggerate. Add a little humour and absurdity. Make visual associations to other relevant concepts and memories.

Drafting initial thoughts on sticky notes and then moving them around until you are happy with their final positioning can be an effective way to start a mind map or concept map, and works particularly well if you are mapping as part of a group exercise. In this way, the different concepts can be moved around, re-positioned and categorised several times until they reach optimum position. Refer to Buzan World at **www.buzanworld.com/Mind_Maps.htm** for examples of spider diagrams and mind maps.

Other note-taking resources

Remember that handwritten notes are not the only source of useful information. If you have a mobile phone with a camera, or a small digital camera, you can take photographs of some of the flipchart pages and graphic organisers resulting from group work. Using tape or digital voice recorders can also be a useful addition to your own note-taking; but do remember to ask first if everyone is happy for you to do this during the taught sessions. Sharing notes with peers is another way of enhancing the information that can be taken from a taught session. Any of these methods can be a useful addition to your own note-taking, but should never be used as an alternative, unless of course, you are unable to attend a session, in which case your study buddy can create a set of notes for you.

When you have taken your notes, you might like to make a 'Wordle' from them (see Figure 2.3, which shows a 'Wordle' of this chapter) and use this to remind you of the key points of the session. A wordle is like a doodle but contains key words to help you remember topics.

Figure 2.3 Wordle created from the contents of Chapter 2 using www.wordle.net

Keeping notes and information safely

You might receive a large amount of information while you are working towards the PTLLS Award. You will need to develop an effective filing system for:

- printed learning materials given to you by your teacher;
- notes you take during the taught sessions;
- notes you take during paired and group discussions and activities with your peers;
- notes made from your own reading and research;
- hard copies of other relevant materials.

Whichever way you decide to store your notes, it is important that you start your study with an appropriate filing system which is organised and to hand. Your system should enable you to divide your notes into easy-to-find categories or sections. Possibly the easiest way to store your notes is in a lever arch file, so that papers can be easily inserted, removed, and refiled or repositioned as necessary. Whatever your choice of container, you should include dividers to mark the partitions you have chosen, possibly:

- in date order, session-by-session;
- by assessment topic;
- divided into the five learning outcomes of the PTLLS Award:
    1. understand own role, responsibilities and boundaries of role in relation to teaching;
    2. understand appropriate teaching and learning approaches in the specialist area;
    3. demonstrate session-planning skills;
    4. understand how to deliver inclusive sessions which motivate learners;
    5. understand the use of different assessment methods and the need for record keeping.

Activity

Think about how you want to store and retrieve your notes and materials. Do you want to be able to find them session-by-session, by assessment topic or by each PTLLS Award learning outcome? What resources will you need to do this quickly and effectively?

Once you have acquired a suitable container and dividers, and decided on the structure of your file, you will need to ensure that it is quick and easy to keep up to date. Using note paper that is pre-punched to suit your folder will save time. You will be able to file your handwritten notes from sessions straight away, so that they are easy to find when you next need to refer to them. Taking along a small hole-punch to the sessions will mean you can file away printed learning materials as they are issued. Alternatively, you could invest in some A4 hole-punched plastic pockets, although if you do use these, make sure that all your notes can be seen without the need to remove pages from the pockets. Accidentally slipping a page of notes behind or between other notes in a plastic pocket is one of the easiest ways to guarantee hours of frustrated searching.

Remember that, as well as a file for your own notes and materials, you will need a file for your portfolio of evidence which will be submitted for formal assessment. The latter should only contain evidence of work produced to meet the PTLLS Award assessment criteria.

Making the most of group activities

The PTLLS Award is designed to meet the needs of learners who are not yet teaching (pre-service) and those who are practising teachers (in-service), across a wide range of subjects in a variety of teaching contexts and environments. The following are some examples of these.

Teaching contexts	Environments
Adult and community learning...	Community halls and schools
Further education ...	Colleges on campus sites
Offender learning ...	Prisons, probation centres
Third sector, for example: ... • voluntary and community organisations, • charities, • social enterprises, • co-operatives, • mutuals, • housing associations, etc.	Community centres and family centres Learning buses or lorries
Work-based learning ...	Various places of employment

If you are in a group where there is the opportunity to collaborate with others, taking advantage of this will help you to learn from your peers as well as your teacher. You can find out about various responsibilities, challenges, strategies and conditions in different organisations. You might also find it helpful to discuss and swap resources and learning materials.

Activity

Think about your strengths and teaching and learning experiences to date. Write a list of five key areas of skills, knowledge or understanding you could share with other group members. Consider your unique talents and abilities. What is it that you do especially well and enjoy doing that can be difficult for other people? How could you pass your skills on to others?

When you are working with others in your PTLLS Award group, remember to take notice of how they address different situations and challenges. You can then adopt any strategies you see that work, and avoid or adapt those that do not.

Activity

Having identified your key strengths, also think about two or three key areas that you would like to improve. How could you learn from others to help yourself?

The benefits of learning in groups are far wider than simply offering the potential to transfer skills, and knowledge. Consider the TEAM perspective:

Together
Everyone
Achieves
More.

Research has shown that co-operative groups perform better than independent individuals (Laughlin and Ellis, 1986). When working as a team, the results achieved are greater than the sum of the individual parts in terms of:

- quality of decisions;
- better judgements;
- motivation;
- speed of learning;
- support.

This does not happen straight away, though, and it will take time for you to feel comfortable working in group situations.

Group development

Groups take time to form. Initially all the group members may be apprehensive about the programme and its demands, and uncertain about discussing hopes and concerns with others, whether face-to-face or through the use of discussion forums in a blended or online programme. As the programme gets underway, however, everyone will start to find out more about each other. Icebreaker exercises are a good way to get to know others in the early stages of a programme and it is a good idea to play an active part in these, even if you do not normally enjoy them. Whether conducted face-to-face or online through discussion forums, etc., they are an opportunity to forge new friendships and develop new skills.

Soon the group should start to settle and effective group working will become the norm. Many contacts and friendships sealed during PTLLS Award programmes are maintained beyond, continuing, in some cases, through other programmes, and beyond.

Working effectively with others

Working with others can sometimes prove difficult. The points that follow might help.

1. Remember that each individual has their own beliefs, values and attitudes, to which they are entitled.
2. Recognise and value individual talents and skills.

3. Accept that everyone will be able to contribute positively to the group in some way.
4. Allow all members the opportunity to speak; respect their rights to their views and opinions and remember that their contributions are equally as valuable as your own.
5. Engage fully in all group discussion and activities, remembering not to speak over others.
6. Remember that conflict is natural within a group. Disagreements can highlight and explore different perspectives and approaches.
7. Disagreements should never become personal. If you find yourself challenging something that is said or done, remember to comment on the behaviour and not the person.

Example

During a session on equality and diversity, one of the group members uses the term 'coloured' instead of 'black'. Suneera is upset by this remark, but she is careful to challenge and confront it in a sensitive manner, using a three-step approach.

1. ***She states the behaviour that has upset her: 'When you refer to black people as coloured ...'***
2. ***She states the impact/effect of the behaviour: 'I feel very upset and hurt,'***
3. ***She goes on to state a preferred future behaviour: 'please use the term "black" in future'.***

When working within groups and carrying out joint activities, individuals will usually take up one or more roles and responsibilities. These roles and responsibilities might vary, depending upon the nature and size of the group and the tasks in question. For a group task to be successfully completed, its members will need to effectively share out roles and responsibilities for:

- leading and focusing group members;
- ensuring that there is no in-fighting and all members' contributions are valued;
- finding creative solutions to problems;
- making sure ideas are viable;
- acquiring necessary resources;
- planning and scheduling tasks;
- drawing the overall task to a successful and timely conclusion;
- ensuring that everyone in the group is, and feels, involved.

Activity

When you next undertake a group activity, note how you approached the different roles and responsibilities outlined. What approaches were taken up by the other group members? What were your own strengths and preferences? Were all of the roles taken up? Was the task effectively completed? This could form the focus of an entry in your reflective learning journal.

A great deal can be learned from observing how your peers approach tasks and situations. Depending upon their learning styles, beliefs, values, attitudes and life experiences, people will react to situations in different ways. When you are next with a group, consider whether you would naturally shy away from an activity and then try to overcome this by getting involved. You might also realise that you tend to take over in certain circumstances when it might be good to sit back and allow others space to develop their own skills.

Much can also be learned from peer evaluation, and from self-evaluation of your own actions and your work. Part of the PTLLS Award will enable you to develop strategies for giving constructive feedback to others, and, equally importantly, experience receiving feedback and acting on it constructively.

Reflecting on the PTLLS Award sessions

Part of the practical assessment for your PTLLS Award involves you demonstrating the qualities of a reflective practitioner. A way of doing this is to look back over each of the PTLLS Award taught sessions that you have attended, preferably soon after the event, and ask yourself some key questions.

- What were the main points I learned?
- How will/could these be useful?
- What else do I want to achieve as a result of this session?
- What did I do? How was I feeling? What was I thinking?
- How did others respond?
- What were the consequences?
- What does this teach me?
- What might I do differently in a similar session in the future, or in my own teaching?
- What impact will it have?

Not only will this reflection contribute towards the entries in your reflective learning journal, but it will also help you to get the best out of your experiences during the taught sessions. For more detailed information on reflective practice and writing reflective learning journals, see Chapter 3.

Summary

In this chapter you have learned about:

- getting the most from taught sessions;
- effective note-taking;
- keeping notes and information safely;
- making the most of group activities.

Theory focus

Books

Buzan, T. (1989) *Use your head*, 2nd edn. London: BBC Books.

Gardner, H. (1983) *Frames of mind*. New York: Basic Books.

Gravells, A. (2008) *Preparing to teach in the lifelong learning sector*, 3rd edn. Exeter: Learning Matters.

Gravells, A. (2010) *Passing PTLLS assessments*. Exeter: Learning Matters.

Honey, P. and Mumford, A. (1992) *The manual of learning styles*, 3rd edn. Maidenhead: Peter Honey Associates.

Laughlin, P. and Ellis, A. (1986). 'Demonstrability and social combination processes on mathematical intellective tasks', *Journal of Experimental Social Psychology*, 22: 177–189.

Websites

Buzan World	**www.buzanworld.com/Mind_Maps.htm**
Maslow's Hierarchy of Needs	**http://maslow.com**
Open University (study skills and other modules)	**http://openlearn.open.ac.uk**
VARK (learning styles)	**www.vark-learn.com/english/index.asp**
Wordle	**www.wordle.net**

CHAPTER 3
SELF-STUDY

Introduction

In this chapter you will learn about:

- researching using different media;
- choosing and evaluating texts and other resources;
- reading texts actively and critically;
- reflective practice and journal writing.

There are activities and examples to help you reflect on the above which will assist your understanding of how to study for your PTLLS Award.

Researching using different media

Libraries

A good starting place for research can be a library or learning resource centre (LRC). Depending upon where you live, this may be your local library or the library belonging to a college, university or other organisation where you are studying. Take the time to join any local libraries as soon as possible – and obtain a leaflet, or access their website, to gain information such as:

- their opening hours – these might be different in term times and during holidays;
- the types of items that are available;
- how many items you can borrow at any one time, and for how long;
- whether you can reserve books or other media, and, if so, whether this has to be in person, or can be via the telephone or internet;
- if there is a fine system for late returns, and, if so, how it works;
- if photocopies can be made and, if so, the charges and any restrictions.

Activity

If you haven't already joined or visited a library or LRC, make a list of all the products and services you might expect them to provide. Then, take time to visit and join and see what is available that could help with your PTLLS studies.

Some of the more commonly available products and services, besides books that you might find in a library include:

- academic journals and periodicals;
- CDs, DVDs and videos;
- computers with internet access (often giving free use);
- library services induction from experienced staff;
- media reservation service;
- newspapers and magazines;
- photocopying, laminating and binding equipment or services;
- quiet study areas with sockets and space for laptops and other equipment.

Finding information in the library

Books

Reference and textbooks are an excellent way of finding out information relating to the subject you are studying. You don't have to read the full book from cover to cover to find what you want; use the index at the back to locate relevant topics and their page number. Books are filed and displayed by subject, broken down into numerical sequence by *call number*, which is shown on the spine of the book. A call number tells you the exact location of the book title in the library, and can be found from the library catalogue which is often electronic. (Detailed information about carrying out electronic searches is included later in this chapter.) Usual catalogue systems are the Dewey Decimal Classification (DDC), which is the world's most common library classification system, used in 200,000 libraries worldwide (OCLC, 2009), or the Library of Congress (LC), system which is used in many college, university, and research libraries. The DDC system was devised by Melvil Dewey in the 1870s and has been owned by the OCLC (Online Computer Library Center) since 1988. Currently in its 22nd edition, it provides a logical, familiar and easily navigable system for organising library books and, because of this, is used in most public and school libraries (OCLC, 2009). Although not as easy to navigate as the DDC system, the LC system effectively handles large collections, hence its use in college, university and research libraries, which often have vast collections of books. Both DDC and LC call numbers are made up of general and specific subject codes, followed by a title code, and frequently include an author code and year of publication.

The DDC system is made up of ten main classes or categories between 000 and 900, each divided into ten secondary classes or sub-categories, each having ten subdivisions, as in the following example.

300	is *Social Sciences (main category)*		
	370	represents Education (sub-category); each sub-category is further sub-divided, e.g. 371 through to 379	
		371 school management, special education; 372 primary education; 373 secondary education; 374 adult education; 375 curricula; 376 education of women; 377 schools and religion; 378 higher education; 379 finance, supervision and control of public education.	
		370.7	Each of these subject areas continues to be further sub-divided into smaller and smaller sections, with the call number becoming longer as sections become more specific: represents *Education, research and related topics;*
			370.711 represents *teacher training;* 370.715 *Continuing Professional Development (CPD).*

Within the LC system, call numbers can begin with one, two, or three letters, the first letter representing one of the 21 major divisions of the LC system. For example, class L represents education. The second letter, B in the following example, represents a sub-class: Theory and practice of education.

Theory and practice of education:	LB
Together, the sub-class LB2395 denotes *Methods of study in Higher Education*	2395
The decimal indicates filing in decimal order, The alpha-numeric reference is usually derived from author's name.	M378
The final section of a call number is generally the year of publication	2008

LB2395.M378 2008 is the LC call number for:

Denby, N., Butroyd, R., Swift, H., Price, J. and Glazzard, J. (2008) *Master's level study in education: A guide to success for PGCE students*. Maidenhead: OUP.

It helps to find books if you already know the surname and initials of the writer(s) and the title of the book. If you have only sketchy details, entering the information you do have into the text search field of an online bookstore will often produce the desired results. Once you have this information, be careful to keep it safe and note the date of publication, city or town of publication and publisher's name, for your references list or bibliography. You should also make a note of the call number so that you can find the book again quickly and easily.

Activity

Identify and make a note of the classification system (or systems) used to categorise books in your local library or LRC. Find and look through the shelves of teaching and training books. Look in the index of some of the books to locate relevant topics for your PTLLS assessments; for example, resources. Start a reference log, noting the call numbers of books that you might want to refer to again.

Teaching and learning journals or periodicals

These are useful sources of reference for your assessments because they usually contain the most up-to-date research and developments in teaching. Most journal articles have an abstract at the front which gives you a brief summary of the content. Journals are usually published at regular intervals during the year, and numbered into volumes and issues. Often one volume will contain all the issues, or magazines, published during a calendar year, although issues might be organised into volumes spanning academic years, or other significant time periods. To find a particular journal article, you will need to know the:

- title of the journal, year of publication, and volume number;
- name and initials of the author(s);
- title of the article.

The above information, together with the issue number and the page numbers, will also be needed for referencing within your work. Again, make sure you keep the referencing details safe, together with any information you extract, and a note of the call number.

Indexes and abstracts

These are separate publications which give a brief overview of journal articles, including who wrote them, where they can be found, and the general idea of the content. Often, you may find that the information from the abstract is sufficient for use in your PTLLS assessment, without needing to read the original article in full. Again, be careful to keep all information safely for referencing.

Electronic information

An increasing amount of information is published electronically and available online. To access an electronic journal or article, you must first access the internet and type the uniform resource locator (URL) or web address into your computer's browser. (A browser is the computer program that makes it possible for you to read information on the internet. Most personal computers use Internet Explorer as standard, while Macs use Safari, although you can choose alternatives such as Firefox or Mozilla). A URL is made up of several parts. It is useful to understand these as they can help you gauge the relevance of the information on the website.

Example

Part of address	Meaning
http://	The first part of the web address is the protocol, which tells the web browser the type of server it will be talking to in order to reach the URL. This protocol http:// (short for Hypertext Transfer Protocol), indicates a hypertext document or directory. Remaining parts of the URL do vary depending on the protocol, but most servers use http://
www.	Indicates a page on the world wide web (sometimes www is missing, but where it is included, you can usually leave out http:// and it will insert automatically.
www.ifl.ac.uk	Together, these indicate the web server name, or fully qualified domain name.
ifl.ac.uk	The domain name, in this case, registered to an academic (.ac) organisation in the UK is the part of the name registered for exclusive use (see below for more details).
/iflonline	Finally comes the path through which the web page is retrieved. This part of the address signifies the start of the path indicating a directory or folder on the web server called iflonline and containing a set of related pages within the website.
/joinonline	A sub-folder called joinonline.
/personaldetails.html	A page called personaldetails.html. NB: Most web pages end in .htm, .html or .shtml.
Complete URL: **https://www.ifl.ac.uk/iflonline/joinonline/personaldetails.html**	

The final part of the *domain name* tells you the type of individual or organisation to whom the website is registered:

Address ending	Description
.co.uk	.co is for companies, and .uk is the country code. For example, www.amazon.co.uk denotes Amazon's UK site.
.com	.com indicates US organisations, but also international ones. (It is the most popular ending.)
.gov.uk	.gov.uk signifies a UK government organisation; for example, the government Department for Business, Innovation and Skills is found at www.dius.gov.uk.
ac.uk or .sch.uk .edu	In the UK universities and other educational establishments use .ac.uk while schools use .sch.uk. In the United States, they use .edu for academic institutions. For example, the IfL domain name is www.ifl.ac.uk and that of Harvard University is www.harvard.edu.
.net	This is usually for internet-related organisations or companies.

Activity

Look at the list of useful websites in Appendix 5. Select a couple that you would like to investigate further. Type in the URL for each of the sites and browse or look through the information that is displayed on the screen. If you want to keep a permanent record, or you find it difficult to read from the screen, you can print it out and read it from the hard (paper) copy. It's good to use a highlighter to mark the significant parts you might refer to in your work.

Search engines

Search engines such as Google, **www.google.co.uk**; Yahoo!, **http://uk.yahoo.com**; Alta Vista, **http://uk.altavista.com**; and Ask Jeeves, **http://uk.ask.com**, search the internet for keywords or phrases, and then display the results, which are unmonitored and unchecked. Searches might deliver huge quantities of information, much of which is out of date, biased, inaccurate, and/or irrelevant, so you need to judge the reliability of all results carefully. Just because someone has published an article on the internet, it does not mean that they have any real knowledge of the subject, or that their writing is impartial. It's also worth remembering that the same article or reference can turn up many times in the search engine results.

When searching you need to be specific with your topic.

- Place the main subject first in your criteria, as some search engines use the first word to establish relevance ranking.
- Structure your search carefully. If you want to:
  - look for all the words that you specify, simply type them into the search field, separated by spaces;
  - find an exact phrase, surround it in quotation marks; for example, 'scheme of work';
  - look for any one of the words you specify, type OR in between them; for example, 'session plan' OR 'lesson plan';
  - specify that a word or phrase must appear in any documents listed, put a (+) sign in front it; for example, '+motivation';
  - prevent a word or phrase from appearing, type it into the search field immediately preceded by a hyphen; for example, '-sports';
- Use the keyword *database* in your search: you may find a searchable database on your topic.
- Use more than one keyword, but no more than six to eight.
- Try different spellings; for example, American English, or common misspellings.

Example

Afra is researching for her assessment on equality and diversity. Firstly she defines the subject in a sentence.

Promoting equality is an essential role of the teacher in post-16 education.

She goes on to split this sentence into key concepts, discarding everything else: **equality, teacher roles, post-16.**

For each of these, she thinks of synonyms (words with a similar meaning) or related terms that would be useful, including:

- **equality, diversity, inclusion;**
- **teacher roles, teacher responsibilities;**
- **post-16, post-compulsory, FE, Lifelong Learning;**

When entering her search, she uses OR and +:
equality OR diversity OR inclusion +education.

When her first results set comes up, she finds she has a great many references to primary education, so she tries again: **equality OR diversity OR inclusion –primary +education.**

Her results this time are much more worthwhile.

The advanced search option provided by most search engines can also be used to make searches more specific. Instructions vary by search engine, but are generally straightforward to follow, with dedicated boxes often being provided for the functions outlined above. A useful additional feature is that of being able to restrict your search to a particular domain; for example, to just UK sites or to academic or government sites.

A limitation of search engines is that there is a quantity of invisible information that is hidden from them. Some of this more scholarly type information can be found through the search engine Google Scholar: **http://scholar.google.co.uk**, which searches materials from academic, professional and educational organisations. Because Google Scholar co-operates with publishers to reveal content which is normally inaccessible, it is likely to reveal useful information that is unavailable from the general commercial search engines. Not everything listed on Google Scholar is freely available, however, and you may find yourself unable to open or download certain resources.

Information gateways

One way of helping to ensure that the information you obtain from the internet is current and unbiased, and to cut down on the time you spend searching, is to use academic subject gateways instead of commercial search engines. These subject gateways (also called directories) provide direct links to more academic, reliable information, usually with a brief description of the resource. Maintained by experts in the different subject areas, they have strictly imposed quality criteria and therefore the sites listed on them can be relied on for consistent quality and accurate and trustworthy information. As a result of their focused coverage, you will also probably get a smaller number of 'hits' or results returned, which will save you a great deal of time filtering out those that are unsuitable for your purposes. Subject gateways and online libraries with resources linked to education that you may wish to try include those listed below.

BeCal – Belief, Culture and Learning	A learning gateway which supports citizenship education.	**www.becal.net**
BUBL Information Service	Aimed at higher education, but useful for further education, you can search by keyword or browse by subject.	**www.bubl.ac.uk**
Eurydice at NFER.	Part of the European information network on education.	**www.nfer.ac.uk/eurydice**
Excellence Gateway (LSIS)	Post-16 learning and skills resources, support and advice, and opportunities to participate and share good practice.	**www.excellencegateway.org.uk**
IngentaConnect	Access to online journal abstracts and articles, many free of charge.	**www.ingentaconnect.com**
Intute: Education	A free online service provided by a consortium of seven universities. Access to websites selected and evaluated by subject specialists.	**www.intute.ac.uk**
Pinakes	Links to major subject gateways.	**www.hw.ac.uk/libwww/irn/pinakes/pinakes.html**
Questia	A large online library with a broad selection of books and journal articles. There is no charge for searching, but a subscription is required to access publications.	**www.questia.com**

Social bookmarking

Social bookmarking sites are web 2.0 applications (web pages that allow visitors to interact with the web page content). You can use these sites to bookmark useful web pages so that you can record your journey around the world wide web. An advantage of the social bookmarking system, as opposed to bookmarking in a browser, or copying and pasting links into a table in a word processing package, is that because your bookmarks are held centrally, they are available from anywhere at any time, not just from the computer on which you made the bookmark. By giving descriptive tags (keywords) to your bookmarks, you can also make them much easier to manage and organise. Social bookmarking sites can be helpful, not only to keep an online record of web resources that you have found useful, but also to get ideas of other sites to visit, as you will be able to see other sites that are being visited by different people who have tagged some of the same sites as you. It is rather like being able to scan other learners' bookshelves for ideas, but on a worldwide scale. Useful bookmarking sites for studying include:

- Citeulike – **www.citeulike.org**
- Connotea – **www.connotea.org**
- Delicious – **http://delicious.com**
- Scholar – **www.scholar.com**
- H20 Playlist – **http://h2obeta.law.harvard.edu**
- 2collab – **www.2collab.com**
- LibraryThing – **www.librarything.com**
- Diigo – **www.diigo.com**

Activity

If you do not already use social bookmarking, choose and investigate one or two of the sites from the list. Look at the resources behind one or two of the most active tags or take a tour around the website.

If you are impressed, why not register? Remember to keep a note of your registration details.

Choosing and evaluating texts and other resources

Textbooks

When evaluating textbooks to help you study for your PTLLS Award, there is a number of important points to be considered. Referring to the '4As' (Williams, 2010) checking system will help you to spend your study time more effectively by helping you to choose and work from reliable, unbiased sources; or if you do use sources with a bias, accounting for this. The 4As are:

- **A**uthorship and provenance;
- **A**spect;
- **A**udience and extent;
- **A**ccessibility.

Authorship

- Does the text seem trustworthy? Who wrote it? What is their reputation?
- How does this text relate to other information on the same subject?
- When was the most recent edition of the book published? When was it last reprinted?

Aspect

- Is there an introduction setting out scope and purpose?
- Are the arguments logical and sound, or is there some dubious reasoning?
- Are the arguments supported by facts and evidence, and fully referenced?
- Are there any alternative explanations to those given by the author?

Audience and extent

- How comprehensive is the information?
- Who are the intended audience (specialists, experts, general public, learners, etc.)?

Accessiblity

- Are the level of language and depth and breadth of content accessible, and appropriate for use in your PTLLS assessments?

E-books

An e-book, or electronic book, is a book that you can read on screen instead of on paper. E-books are not limited to text; they can include pictures, sound clips, animated graphics and video. Many different things are given the label 'e-books'. Some are actually small dedicated computers, while others are computer programs which can be used on a personal computer, laptop or portable handheld device such as a personal digital assistant (PDA). Advantages of e-books include the ability to store a great deal of information effectively in much less physical space than their conventional counterparts, on a computer or other device. Portable e-books also have a much larger capacity than a conventional book of comparable size and weight. When using an e-book, you can mark your page with an electronic bookmark and automatically return to it upon reopening the book. You can also make notes on the text. Some e-books have built-in dictionaries enabling you to click on a word to find out what it means, and reference books which come with extensive collections of references and footnotes. On the downside, they are limited to the book formats supported by the manufacturers, who often try to lock the reader into only one format. They also have to be connected to a computer with a broadband or wireless link to download texts or manage libraries. The same rules govern their evaluation as those for conventional books.

CD-ROMs and DVD-ROMs

A great deal of educational content is available on pre-recorded CDs and DVDs which are now very cheap to mass produce and purchase. In terms of similarity, CDs and DVDs are both the same size and shape. The use of the affix '–ROM' in this case denotes read-only memory, meaning that data cannot be added or recorded over, it can only be read. Main differences are in the storage, with a CD-ROM having a storage capacity of 650 megabytes – roughly equivalent to 6,500 pages, and a DVD-ROM holding over six times the information with a capacity of 4.7 gigabytes. DVDs also access data much more quickly. CDs can be read by both CD and DVD drives, whereas DVDs can be read only by a computer with a DVD drive. The advantages of using CD and DVD discs rather than accessing information via the internet include the absence of connectivity issues and costs, and slow download times. Sound, large graphics, animations and video clips are available with complete user interactivity, and discs can also include outside links to complementary websites. These media should be subjected to similar scrutiny as textbooks and e-books.

Websites

As outlined earlier in this chapter, data on the web can be inaccurate, unreliable, out of date, and quite possibly biased (showing favouritism to one party or view). Once again, it is useful to use the 4As system as a check (Williams, 2010).

Authorship and provenance

- In the evaluation of information sources, provenance, from the French verb *provenir*, meaning 'to come from', is about origin and authenticity. Does the article or information have a stated author? If so, what is their educational or occupational background? Are they connected with a respected professional association, institution or publisher?
- Is the publisher or website well known in the field, and is it on the recommended reading list?
- Is the website from an official source? The final part of the domain name tells you the type of individual or organisation to whom the website is registered. Official websites such as those belonging to educational or government departments are more likely to be the source of up-to-date and reliable information, not least because they have their reputations to preserve. They usually end in .ac.uk or .gov.uk respectively.
- Does the article itself have a good references list or bibliography with working links to other reputable websites?
- Does the information appear to be accurate? How does it relate to other articles on the same subject?
- When was the information last updated? Is there a date given – for the original publication, and/or for subsequent updates?
- Wikipedia (**www.wikipedia.org**) contains a wealth of information which is usually presented in a format that is easy to read and absorb. It can often be a good place to start research into a new topic or new terminology. However, by the nature of its assorted authorship, it lacks the authority to be used as a citeable source.

Aspect

- From what aspect is the article written? Is there an introductory statement setting out its scope and purpose?
- How objective does the text appear? Is it biased to a particular personal or political viewpoint, and if so, which? Does this matter for your purposes?
- Is the language used informative, or persuasive?

Audience and extent

- How comprehensive is the information?
- What audience does it appear to be aimed at? The type of language used should help you to make an informed judgement here.

Accessiblity

- Do the level of language and depth of study match your needs?
- How accessible is the site and the material on it? Is the site straightforward to navigate? Can you find your way around the information easily?
- Are links to other pages obvious, and working?
- Can you easily print what you need?

Podcasts

The name 'Podcast' originates from 'iPod' and 'broadcast', as originally podcasts were audio programmes formatted to be played on an iPod, although now they can be downloaded to an iPod or an MP3 player. Some are free, and others are sold via the internet. Podcasts can be downloaded or used online (subject to adequate broadband and appropriate software and plug-ins).

Plug-ins are free computer software that let you receive information such as sound, video and animation, so called because they plug in to your browser the first time you download them onto your computer, generally installing automatically. If you visit a site that needs a plug-in, your browser will ask you whether you want to download it. Once installed, you will often have to restart your browser or even your operating system before the plug-in becomes active. Once active however, plug-ins engage automatically whenever they are needed.

Enhanced podcasts (audio podcasts that can display images and sound at the same time) are also now available, and can contain chapter markers, hyperlinks (links to other websites) and artwork. Enhanced podcasting is a very practical way to present information including lectures, slide shows, video clips, etc. Many podcasts are produced by professionals, although, as with website articles, many are also produced by amateurs. Again, the 4As (Williams, 2010) can be used to assess the suitability of podcasts.

Authorship and provenance

- Does the podcast have a stated author? If so, what is their educational or occupational background? Are they connected with a respected professional association, institution or publisher?
- Are sources for further information (websites and email) included in the podcast?
- Does the information appear to be accurate? How does it relate to other information you have found on the same subject?
- When was podcast last updated? Is there a date given – for the original publication, and/or for subsequent updates?

Aspect

- Is there an introduction setting out scope and purpose?
- How objective does the content appear?
- Is effective use made of the presenter, discussions and interviews?
- Is the content biased to a particular personal or political viewpoint, and if so, which – and does it matter?
- Is the language used informative, or persuasive?

Audience and extent

- How comprehensive is the information?
- What audience does it appear to be aimed at? Again, the type of language used should help you to make an informed judgement here.

Accessibility

- Do the level of language and depth of study match your own specific needs?
- Is the topic well structured and organised and presented in an interesting and imaginative way?
- Are vocals clear without background noise or popping, with the presenters able to be clearly heard above background music and effects?
- Are any audio effects used constructively to enhance the listening and learning experience?

Carefully-chosen podcasts can be an excellent source of information and learning. Audio podcasts have the advantage that they can be downloaded and listened to conveniently during time that might otherwise be downtime, such as when travelling on a train or a bus, or when walking or exercising.

Virtual learning environment (VLE) learning tools

Your PTLLS Award may be supported to a greater or lesser extent by the use of a virtual learning environment (VLE) such as Moodle, Blackboard, WebCT or Bodington (see Chapter 2). VLEs can be accessed from any computer with an internet connection, providing a flexible learning environment. If the timetable, activities and related materials are available on a VLE from the beginning of your studies, you can use this information to organise work, family commitments and plan time for studying. Using a VLE as part of a distance or blended learning programme can substantially reduce time and expenses travelling to and from classes. A VLE can provide opportunities for study at convenient times outside face-to-face sessions. If you find yourself unable to attend a session, and the learning materials are available via a VLE, you will be able to access them (subject to computer and internet access) and read through them before the next session, which will enable you to clarify anything that was unclear. Another big advantage of VLEs is that you can receive immediate feedback from simulations and quizzes, rather than having to wait for homework to be marked. Also, if you know that the all learning materials are available on the VLE, it makes it easier to listen, ask questions and engage fully in the face-to-face activities, without having to worry about taking detailed notes as you can access them later.

Reading texts actively and critically

Skimming

It is useful to skim texts (and other materials) to get a general idea of their content and usefulness. Skimming involves looking over a piece of information quickly to obtain its gist, purpose and tone. When skimming, you do not read the whole text word for word. If, as a result of skimming, you find that the content appears useful, you can allocate more time to examine it in detail. When skimming, use as many clues as possible to give you background information.

- Read the title and sub-headings.
- Note comments made in the introduction, abstract and summary.
- Identify the author(s).
- Establish when the text was written.
- Look at illustrations to predict the contents.
- Read the first and last sentences of each paragraph, which should introduce and conclude the topic or idea respectively.

Activity

Next time you visit the library, look at a textbook that you think might be helpful in your PTLLS studies and skim through it to establish its general idea, purpose and tone. Once you have done this, if the book appears promising, remember to make notes of the content, reference details and the call number so that you are able to use the information you have extracted, and find the book again quickly on a subsequent visit.

Scanning

Scanning has a different purpose, this time looking, not for the gist, but for detail. Texts are scanned for two purposes. The first is to glean specific information; for example, a name, or date, a particular reference or information. Once this information is found, the text can be disregarded without further investigation. The second purpose for scanning is to rapidly explore a text to see if it warrants skimming before more detailed inspection. You might, for example, scan for a keyword or heading. When searching through electronic texts, it is useful to identify two or three keywords that might supply the information you are looking for, and then enter these, one by one, into the find or search facility. In this way you can quickly see whether the text in question is likely to have the content you require.

Example

Ibrahim wants to quickly check out a website he has found on the internet that looks as though it might provide some useful information for his assessment task regarding embedding functional skills.

He decides on six key terms, which are:

- ***functional skills;***
- ***literacy;***
- ***numeracy;***
- ***ICT;***
- ***English;***
- ***maths.***

He quickly carries out an automatic search for each of these, noting the number of hits he gets.

His scanning exercise delivers only three hits, all for ICT, so he discards it as a potential reference source.

Previewing

Previewing a text is using as much advance information about it as possible to decide its contents and context. You can do this by looking through:

- the blurb, a short promotional description, usually on the back page;
- the abstract, if there is one;
- the index;
- contents pages;
- references list;

- bibliography;
- titles;
- headlines;
- illustrations.

This should give you a strong impression of the text, making subsequent detailed reading much more straightforward.

Active reading

When you are reading a document in detail, it can help to highlight, underline and annotate as you read. This stimulates visual and kinaesthetic pathways, and emphasises the information which you could review again later. It also helps to stop your mind wandering, keeping it focused on the material. If you are using an electronic source, or do not wish to mark the hard copy, it may be worth printing or photocopying the information first.

When reading difficult material with new terminology, photocopy or compile a glossary, keeping it beside you as you read. Note down the key concepts in your own words to help your understanding.

SQ3R reading technique

Rowntree (1998) suggests the *SQ3R* (**S**urvey, **Q**uestion, **R**ead, **R**ecall and **R**eview) approach to effective reading and note-taking.

1. Survey the chapter or book, leafing through to note the layout, looking at first and last chapters or first and last lines of paragraphs, and the headings used, examining any diagrams, charts or pictures, familiarising yourself with the reading. (This is similar to the stage of previewing outlined above.)
2. Question yourself about the structure of the text, thinking about the questions you will need to keep in mind while reading. Ask yourself how current the material is and how relevant it is to your own purposes.
3. Read actively, and quickly, looking to identify the main points of the text.
4. Recall the main points of the text, writing them down, together with any important facts and opinions that help support them. (Remember to note necessary reference information.)
5. Review, repeating stages 1–3, making sure that you have not overlooked anything, amending your notes, if necessary. Read through your notes once more to check them, and identify where the information fits into your assessment.

Activity

Use the SQ3R technique to read the following section on reflective practice and journal writing.

1. **Survey** – ***leafing through the pages; noting the layout; looking at the headings and sub-headings used; reading the first and last sentences of main paragraphs; and examining any diagrams, familiarising yourself with the material.***
2. **Question** ***yourself about the structure. What questions should you keep in mind while reading?***
3. **Read** ***actively and quickly, looking to identify the main points.***
4. **Recall** ***and write down the main points, together with any important facts and opinions. How would you reference a direct quotation from this text.***
5. **Review,** ***repeat stages 1–3, amending your notes if necessary. Where in your assessments can you use this information?***

Reflective practice and journal writing

While working towards your PTLLS Award you are required to think about how you can put theory into practice, and to record this in a reflective learning journal (RLJ). Your RLJ is personal to you, and will reflect your personality and learning experiences through a written collection of observations, thoughts and ideas put together, on a regular basis, throughout the programme. As its name suggests, your RLJ should not be a straightforward description of events and feelings, but an opportunity to evidence both your reflective thinking processes and the outcomes in terms of enhanced learning. Reflection is an important skill to develop, with many benefits.

Reflective learners tend to:

- be motivated, knowing what they are trying to achieve and why;
- use existing knowledge and experience to help understand new concepts;
- build current learning on a critical evaluation of previous experiences;
- be self-directed and self-aware, identifying and addressing their own strengths and areas for development.

Reflective learning is an active process that takes time and practice to perfect. It involves thinking through issues, asking questions and seeking out new information and perspectives to help understanding. It works best when you think about your actions and experiences both during and after the event, and then look back at the past with a view to the future. The 7D reflective cycle (Williams, 2010) provides a helpful structure to reflective practice beginning with 'Describe' (see Figure 3.1). Once you have completed the 'decide' phase of a reflective cycle, you are ready to start the cycle afresh, equipped with new insights.

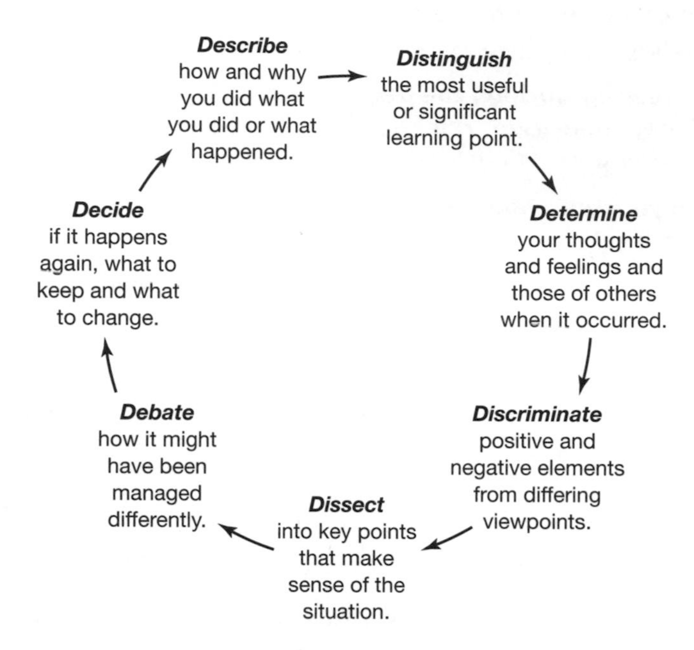

Figure 3.1 7D reflective cycle (Williams, 2010)

Activity

Use this cycle, or a similar one you have located in a relevant textbook, to focus upon your personal responses, reactions and reflections to new ideas and concepts that you have met recently through one of the following:

- ***a lecture, seminar or workshop;***
- ***research and reading;***
- ***a discussion with your peers;***
- ***a critical teaching or learning incident.***

It is important that you make time for writing your RLJ. Try to regularly set aside some time for reflection, writing down your thoughts as soon after each PTLLS teaching session as possible. Try to use the RLJ to help you to:

- identify the main points you have learned from the session;
- step back, exploring and analysing your own role, thoughts and feelings;
- consider potentially different perspectives of others involved;
- determine advantages and disadvantages, strengths and areas for development:
- make connections, where appropriate, with educational theories and research that supports your ideas;
- consider potential wider implications; for example, for your organisation, local communities, local and national government;
- show awareness of social and political influences;
- identify anything you find puzzling, difficult or contradictory, and how you might go about understanding it better;
- record any 'lightbulb' moments, where something that was puzzling you suddenly becomes clear;
- identify points you need to explore further, and ways to organise this;
- identify practical skills for development and potential opportunities;
- evaluate resources that have been particularly useful and/or interesting;
- recognise new knowledge, skills or understanding you have gained.

Genuinely reflective writing might involve disclosing anxieties, failures, and areas for development, as well as successes and strengths. Remember to consider the possible causes and ways to address these.

Example

Andrew attends a PTLLS session in which the group is studying learning styles. He had not known of the existence of learning styles theories before this session. The entry in his RLJ looks like this:

Today I found out that we all have preferred ways of learning, and that these can all be very different. I learned a lot about my own personal learning styles which are predominantly visual (Fleming, 2005) and reflector (Honey and Mumford, 1992).

Thinking about this has helped me to realise why sometimes I find it difficult to learn if the teacher doesn't use the whiteboard or PowerPoint to reinforce things like difficult spellings and new terminology. I also understand better why some people have a tendency to jump in and answer questions straight away, while I often take much longer before I am prepared to say anything. What struck me most, however, were the ways that I can adapt material that is given to me to make it easier to learn – by using spider diagrams and concept maps.

Example

To make my use of spider diagrams and concept maps more effective, I am going to look on the internet for some of the free software that our teacher talked about. I think I would really enjoy using something like that, and it would mean that I could have fun and be creative reviewing my notes.

I'm also going to go over my notes again, and carry out some more research to make sure I really understand the meanings of all the learning styles we covered so that I am confident when I introduce the learning styles questionnaires to my own learners. I'm also going to make a note in my bring forward box to investigate more different learning styles when I have time – after I have finished the PTLLS Award.

Writing an RLJ also gives you the opportunity to consider your long-term development.

- Have you changed your beliefs, values or opinions during the experience?
- How can you improve your learning, thinking and working in the future?
- Have you identified the next step(s) for your further development?

As well as the benefits derived from reflective practice itself, the very process of keeping a RLJ has its own advantages.

- It provides a record of your growing understanding of the teaching process, and developing thoughts and ideas. You can look back on your RLJ over time to see the distance you have travelled.
- It should help you to identify your strengths and areas for development, and also your preferred learning (and teaching) styles.

Remember to complete your RLJ regularly as you work through your programme. In this way it will act as a tool to help your learning and progression. If you can't make notes straight away, for example, you are on your journey home from a taught session, you could mentally run through a few points. Consider what you learned and how you could put theory into practice. You could always record your thoughts digitally or discuss them with others to help you write a truly reflective learning journal. If you leave it until the end of your programme to put together some hastily reconstructed notes, the experience will be frustrating and unrewarding.

Summary

In this chapter you have learned about:

- **researching using different media;**
- **choosing and evaluating texts and other resources;**
- **reading texts actively and critically;**
- **reflective practice and journal writing.**

Theory focus

Books

Denby, N., Butroyd, R., Swift, H., Price, J. and Glazzard, J. (2008) *Master's level study in education: A guide to success for PGCE students*. Maidenhead: OUP.

Fleming, N. (2005), *Teaching and learning styles: VARK strategies*. Honolulu: Honolulu Community College.

Honey, P. and Mumford, A. (1992) *The Manual of Learning Styles*, 3rd edn. Maidenhead: Peter Honey Associates.

Rowntree, D. (1998) *Learn how to study: A realistic approach*. London: Time Warner Books.

Williams, J. (2010) *Study Skills for PTLLS*. Exeter: Learning Matters.

Websites

2collab (research-focused online social bookmarking tool) **www.2collab.com**

Alta Visa (search engine) **http://uk.altavista.com**

Ask Jeeves (search engine) **http://uk.ask.com**

BeCal (information gateway) **www.becal.net**

BUBL Information Service (information gateway) **www.bubl.ac.uk**

Citeulike (academic-focused online social bookmarking tool) **www.citeulike.org**

Connotea (academic-focused online social bookmarking tool) **www.connotea.org**

Delicious (online social bookmarking tool) **http://delicious.com**

Diigo (online social bookmarking tool) **www.diigo.com**

Eurydice at NFER **www.nfer.ac.uk/eurydice**

Excellence Gateway (LSIS) (information gateway) **www.excellencegateway.org.uk**

Google (search engine) **www.google.co.uk**

H20 Playlist (academic online social bookmarking tool) **http://h2obeta.law.harvard.edu**

IngentaConnect (online journal abstracts and articles)	**www.ingentaconnect.com**
Intute (information gateway)	**www.intute.ac.uk**
LibraryThing (books-focused online social bookmarking tool)	**www.librarything.com**
Online Computer Library Center (Dewey) (OCLC)	**www.oclc.org/dewey/about/default.htm**
Questia	**www.questia.com**
Scholar (academic-focused online social bookmarking tool)	**www.scholar.com**
Wikipedia	**www.wikipedia.org**
Yahoo! (search engine)	**http://uk.yahoo.com**

CHAPTER 4
PRESENTING YOUR WORK

Introduction

In this chapter you will learn about:

- Presenting your work in writing:
  - deciding on a structure;
  - getting your ideas onto paper;
  - using pictures, charts, etc., to support your writing;
  - formal writing.
- Presenting your work in practice:
  - preparing for your micro-teach;
  - effective presentations;
  - information communication technology.

There are activities and examples to help you reflect on the above which will assist your understanding of how to present your work in writing and in practice.

Presenting your work in writing

Deciding on a structure

Before you start writing any text for formal assessment, you should produce a general outline and plan a timeline for completion. You should be given a deadline for submission; try to be ahead of this so that you are not rushing your work. You will need to read the question carefully, two or three times, to establish:

- the submission date;
- if there is a word count, and if not, roughly how many words will be needed to meet the criteria;
- exactly what the question requires; for example, a reflective account with examples from your own practice, a hypothetical case study or a written response to a question;

- the mode of final presentation; for example, academic writing, a summary or a table;
- whether you will need to include pictures and/or charts;
- whether you must word-process your work;
- the meaning of the question – a range of different verbs is used in the assessment questions, each requiring a specific approach; for example, *describe* or *analyse*.

Activity

How many of these words can you find in the word search, which includes some of the verbs commonly used in assessment questions? As you find each word, think about its meaning, and the type of information you might be required to include in your response.

(The answers to the word search are in Appendix 3.)

i t r n e d n r c x y x y t a e s

p i r d s t e o o i f f e c r e i

l a e n i u a l l u i y l l e e t

i n l i i s m t i t t y e i v y i

a s i a e a c m s v n l n m i e t

a s i e v a l u a t e n i f e d r

n e s c t a j p s r d r m n w i n

r a e e i e n a x s i e a a e e i

e r n x s e r a a e l s x p a a c

i e n p e t m p l i l e e r m i n

i m t l n y u i r y u n l c r o t

e c r o t m s e d e s c r i b e c

n l c r i t i q u e t e l p m o c

c x o e c u d o r p r n y i e y r

e s y l a n a y l l a c i t i r c

t e s e r u c e t v t e i c r e e

w i t i d t r c r s e e t i a t t

analyse	compare	complete	contrast
critically analyse	critique	define	deliver
describe	discuss	evaluate	examine
explain	explore	identity	illustrate
interpret	justify	list	outline
produce	review	state	summarise

(puzzle created using **www.armoredpenguin.com**)

Hopefully you are now familiar with the assessment terminology, and have given some thought to the type of information you might need to include to address the assessment questions. Table 4.1 gives a summary of the verbs you are likely to come across.

Verb	**Action required**
Analyse	Separate (a topic) into its main parts or important features, including their relationship to each other, and present these clearly in your answer.
Compare	Examine and emphasise similarities (between two or more topics), showing that you are aware of minor points of difference within areas of general similarity.
Complete	Bring (a topic) to a full conclusion, closing any gaps.
Contrast	Examine and emphasise the differences (between two or more topics).
Critically analyse or critique	Analyse the different aspects (of a topic), giving your opinion about merits and shortcomings. You should support your opinions with reasoned arguments and evidence.
Define	State or describe exactly the nature, extent, or meaning (of the topic).
Deliver	Actively present and engage your audience (with a concept or topic). This involves far more than simply reading from notes.
Describe	Give a detailed written account (of a topic).
Discuss	Examine (the topic), analyse carefully, and then present detailed considerations of advantages and disadvantages.
Evaluate	Give a reasoned judgement about the value or significance (of the topic). Give a personal appraisal, carefully identifying strengths and areas for development, advantages and limitations.
Examine	Study thoroughly to determine the nature or condition (of the topic).
Explain	Give an account of how or why (something happened), with reasons.
Explore	Investigate or discuss (the topic) in detail.
Identify	State or describe exactly the origin, extent, or defining characteristics (of the topic). This is similar to 'Define' above.
Illustrate	Make (the topic) clear by using examples, graphics, charts, etc.
Interpret	Decide what the intended meaning (of the topic) is.
Justify	Describe (what you have done/think), and give logical reasoning to support your decisions/conclusions.
List	Write a concise itemised list, using bullet points or numbering.
Outline	Give the main points, leaving out minor details.
Produce	Create or construct (an item, or plan, or argument).
Review	Critically assess (the topic), giving a well considered evaluation.
State	Present (your topic) in a clear, brief, format.
Summarise	Give an account of the main facts in a condensed form.

Table 4.1 Verbs used in assessment questions

Activity

Read through the assessment tasks or assessment criteria that you must evidence as part of your PTLLS Award. Identify and highlight the verbs. Now compare these with the verbs in Table 4.1 to ensure you can respond correctly.

Once you are certain of the meaning of the question and have established exactly what it requires, together with the mode of presentation and an overall word count, you can start to map the layout. For example:

- an academic essay will need to have an introduction, main content which may be separated into several sub-sections, a conclusion and a references list and/or bibliography;
- a written summary may need to be divided into different sections; for example, reviewing teaching roles, responsibilities and boundaries.

Having mapped your assessment task into appropriate sections, allocate word counts and mini-deadlines to each.

At this stage you can start to consider relevant theories, recent developments and potential research sources such as textbooks from the recommended reading list given to you by your teacher.

Evaluation

If you are aiming to achieve at level 4, you will need to include an element of evaluation in your written work, even though this may not be obvious from the assessment question. You may need to evaluate:

- two or more methods or approaches; for example, the different approaches regarding the setting of ground rules with a group;
- two or more theories; for example, contrasting the learning styles of Fleming (2005) with Honey and Mumford (1992);
- which of several items or methods is best for a purpose, stating why; for example, which assessment methods are best suited to initial, formative and summative assessment in your specialist subject area.

Nearly all evaluative writing involves the processes of comparing, contrasting, critically analysing and making judgements. Your writing must always be supported by research evidence, remembering to reference your work.

Getting your ideas onto paper

Now you can start the process of putting your ideas onto paper. To help make sure that your content is relevant and focused, start by writing the full question to be answered at the top of the page. Read the question often as you work, continually refocusing to ensure that each point is met. Break down the question into smaller parts as it might consist of several questions which must all be addressed. You might like to highlight different stages or points of the question in bright colours, deleting or crossing out the highlights as you tackle each point.

When answering questions, make sure, if you are already teaching (in-service), that your responses are specific to the subject you are teaching, your learners, the context (e.g. offender learning) and environment (e.g. workshop) within which you work. Refer to the records you use, along with relevant policies and codes of practice that you follow. If you are not yet teaching (pre-service), think about the teaching role you hope to undertake, and reflect this in your answers.

Drafting

You are now ready to start compiling your first draft. (Your final version will probably be the result of two or three subsequent drafts.) When you begin writing, start with the main body of the text. Do not attempt to write the introduction until you have completed the rest of your response. At this final stage, when you have worked right through the content, you will be in a much better position to outline and explain the way in which you have structured your response.

Write down sub-headings for each of the component parts of the question, together with any relevant examples and reference sources. The investment in developing a detailed outline at this stage will more than repay the time spent redrafting later. You can do this using hand-crafted linear notes or concept maps (see Chapter 2), or you might choose to brainstorm straight onto a computer using it to reorganise and build up your writing, stage-by-stage, into a final draft. Whichever approach you choose, restrict the first draft to recording ideas, categorising them into loose headings and identifying any links. Prioritising ideas and making corrections comes later.

Redrafting

At this second drafting stage you need to make any final adjustments to the headings in your written assessment, and write up the information you have gathered in full sentences under each of your headings. Now is also the time to check word counts against the word limits you initially allocated for each of your headings. If you are over, you will need to filter out the most important points, saving the rest for a future project. If you are under, you will need to carry out some additional work. You will need to find out if you can go over or under the word count by a certain percentage – this is usually 10 per cent.

Once you have a draft that looks sensible, you will need to read through it several times to check for sense and flow, possibly moving sections around so that the argument flows naturally between paragraphs. When you have done this, put your writing to one side, for at least a day, preferably longer: this will give you time to reflect.

Proofreading

Having left a little time between yourself and your writing, proofreading should be easier and much more effective. At this stage, it is a good idea to ask another person to look over your work for mistakes and clarity of meaning. When proofreading yourself, you should look for a smooth, logical flow between paragraphs, and examine your layout to ensure that it is consistent in terms of line spacing, use of headings, settings for right and left margins, bullet points, headers and footers, etc. References should be checked for accuracy, completeness and consistency, and you should also check your spelling, grammar and punctuation. Spelling and grammar checks built into your word-processing software can be very useful at this stage, but do not rely on them as they cannot fully account for context.

A brief outline of some key spelling, grammar and punctuation points, together with common areas of confusion follows here. For a more thorough investigation, you may wish to refer to specialist references, including the books detailed at the end of this chapter.

Spelling

If you find it hard to spell words that you have to use frequently, make an alphabetical list and keep it at hand. Try making up mnemonics (artificial aids to help memory including rhymes and acronyms).

Example

Susan has always found it difficult to spell the word 'because'. One of her peers suggested she use the mnemonic Big Elephants Can Always Understand Small Elephants (BECAUSE). She was dubious at first, but now she has found it works for her, she has started to research mnemonics for other words she finds difficult – and to create some of her own.

As well as using memory aids like mnemonics, you could identify the hard-to-spell words you use most frequently and apply a multi-sensory routine to learn them one at a time: looking at the word, saying it, covering it, writing it, saying it again and checking it. Carry out this routine two or three times a week for two or three weeks. Ongoing review is very important. You might be very pleased with the final result.

Many of the difficulties around spelling and grammar centre on nouns, verbs, adjectives, and the use of some suffixes. These are defined as follows.

noun	refers to people, animals, objects, substances, states, events and feelings; for example, *teacher, book*;
verb	refers to an action (*to study, to write*, etc.) or a state (*to be, to like*, etc.); for example, to *review* your role as a teacher;
adjective (modifies a noun)	describes the quality, state or action that the noun refers to; for example, the *big blue dictionary*;
suffix	a letter or letters added to the end of a word; for example, help*ful*.

Spellings which are a frequent cause of confusion in PTLLS assessments include the following.

- *advice* and *advise, licence* and *license, practice* and *practise* – especially when referring to the licence to practise. The rule here is that *c* is the *noun* and *s* is the verb – it may be easier to remember that *ice* is a *noun*.
- *dependant* or *dependent*. Passing the PTLLS Award is *dependent* (*adjective*) upon submitting a satisfactory portfolio. *Dependant* is the noun.
- *effect* and *affect* – the changes in timing of the session had an *effect* (*noun*) on learners' attendance, but the changes *affected (verb)* the learners.
- *principal* or *principle*. The *principal* (*noun*) of the college is committed to the *principle* (*noun*: belief or rule) of sustainable development and insists this should continue to be a *principal* (*adjective*: main) focus.
- Use of *suffix ise* or *ize* is also problematic. Some *verbs* are never spelt with *ize*, including *advertise*, *advise*, *arise*, *comprise*, *devise*, *exercise* and *revise*. Other words including *organise/organize* can use either, but always be consistent.
- Another set of words that need careful checking are *homophones*: words with different meanings and spellings, but the same pronunciation. Without care, the use of *there* (it's over *there*), *they're* (they are) and *their* (belonging to them) can become muddled, and this is something that the computerised spelling checker cannot help with.
- Do be careful that you are using the British English rather than the American English spellchecker.

Grammar

Grammar is the study of the structure of language. A few useful grammar points are listed here.

- Names of the days of the week and the months of the year are capitalised, but names of the seasons are not.
- Names of languages always start with a capital letter, but the names of subjects (other than languages) do not.

- Words with a direct connection to a place are capitalised (*Italian* architecture), and also those referring to nationalities (*Italian*) or ethnic groups, but their incidental use (*italian* salad dressing) is not.
- Titles of books, plays, etc., are usually in *title case*, where the first and every significant word is capitalised. However, when creating your references list, you may use title case or capitalise only the first word of the title. Whichever you choose, be consistent.
- The first word of a sentence should also always start with a capital letter.

Sentences in formal writing must always be grammatically complete, i.e. make sense on their own and use at least a verb and a subject, although usually sentences in English also contain an object.

Subject	Verb	Object
The teacher	prepares	the scheme of work

Be careful to ensure that your sentences are not too long by reading your work out aloud when proofreading. If you need to take a breath in the middle of a sentence, it probably needs to be divided into two (or more) shorter ones. Asking a friend or your mentor to read your work will gain another perspective.

Paragraphs, which are groups of at least three sentences of roughly similar length, should add information, explanation and clarification to a single idea until it is fully developed. Each paragraph should start with a topic sentence giving the main idea, continue with supporting sentences including description, discussion and analysis, to develop the idea, and end with a concluding sentence.

Syntax, another grammatical term, is concerned with word order in sentences and agreement in the relationship between words; for example, between subjects and verbs. Make sure that where you have a singular subject, you use a singular verb; for example, 'The teacher *models* good practice'. Similarly, a plural subject needs a plural verb, as do two singular subjects together: 'The teacher and the learner *work* together'.

Tense

Assessments should normally be written in the present tense, and you should also use this tense when discussing an author's work, even if it was carried out in the past.

Example

Knowles (1990) proposes that adult learners need to understand and accept the reasons for their learning.

However, biographical information about an author should be in the past tense.

Example

Knowles, who was born in 1913, was a leading academic in principles of adult education.

When talking about your own practice, ideas and opinions, you should write in the first person singular; otherwise you should use the third person, but never the second. Writing in the first person demonstrates your understanding and shows how you would put theory into practice. For example, 'I would establish ground rules with my learners by...' is correct; you would not write 'you would establish ground rules with your learners by...' or 'he would establish ground rules with his learners by...' as you are not talking about someone else. You need to claim ownership of your actions and writing in the first person does this.

	Singular	**Plural**
First person	I	we
Second person	you	you
Third person	he/she/it	they

You also need to distinguish between the active and the passive voice, always using the active voice in the first person. A sentence is said to be in the active voice if the subject performs an action (the subject being the person).

Example

***First person active:* I completed an excellent assignment.**

***Third person active:* The learner completed an excellent assignment.**

***Third person passive:* An excellent assignment was completed by the learner.**

Some awarding organisations require aspects of written assessments to be written in the third person passive. For example, *the scheme of work was prepared by the teacher* (third person passive) rather than *the teacher prepared the scheme of work* (third person active).

Punctuation

Punctuation is a system of using marks or characters within writing, to separate aspects of it, to make the meaning of a sentence clear.

The first four punctuation marks discussed can be thought of as units of pause, where a comma is one unit, a semi-colon two units, a colon two-and-a-half or three units, and a full stop is four (West, 2008).

Commas are used to mark off parts of a sentence to make meaning clearer, and they have four basic uses.

- Linking two sentences with a conjunction; for example, *or*, *but*, *while* and *yet*.
- Adding extra information. Information added at the start or end of a sentence requires only one comma. Information added in the middle needs to be bracketed by a comma at either end.
- Separating items in a list.
- Segmenting large numbers.

Semi-colons are used to:

- link together two sentences which are closely related or reflect each other; for example, *Abbas was pleased; he had completed his PTLLS Award*;
- separate listed items which are particularly long or have commas within them; for example, ... *the blurb, a short promotional description usually on the back page; the abstract, if there is one; ... references list; and bibliography*.

Colons are used to:

- separate a title and a subtitle; the year of publication from the page number in a reference in the body of the text; and the place of publication from the publishers in a reference list;
- introduce a word, list, summary or quotation; whatever comes after the colon should explain, show or resolve whatever comes before: *Only one thing is likely to result from an unplanned micro-teach: referral.*

A full stop should mark the end of a sentence. Using a comma instead will create an unacceptable run-on sentence or comma splice. Exclamation marks should also be avoided in formal writing. Question marks should always be used at the end of a direct question; for example, 'Is your assessment ready to hand in?' but not for reported questions; for example, *She asked him if his assessment was ready to hand in.*

Apostrophes have the following uses.

- To show missing letters.

I'm – I am	*You're* – You are	*It's* – it is
I haven't – I have not	*You can't* – You cannot	*Don't* – Do not

As the contracted form should not be used in formal writing, you will be concerned primarily with its second use.

- (a) To show that something belongs to, or is a part of, someone or something else.

Radcliffe's laptop	*The teacher's pens*	*This week's Times Ed.*
Ravi's sister	*The learner's portfolio*	*Yesterday's paper*

(The apostrophe goes after the word or name and before the s.)

(b) To show that something belongs to, or is a part of, more than one person or thing.

The teachers' files	*The learners' desks*	*Three days' work*

(Where the plural is created by adding an s, the apostrophe follows the s.)

The children's toys	*The people's decision*	*Everyone's safety*

(Where the word is already a plural, return to the first rule and put the apostrophe after the word, and before the s.)

- There is a different rule for *it's* and *its*.

To mean *it is* or *it has*:	*it's*
To show something belongs to *it*:	*its* (no apostrophe); for example, *its fur is soft*. This is also true of other pronouns: *ours, hers, yours*.

Apostrophes are not used when indicating more than one of something (plurals), or for decades; for example, 1900s, not 1900's.

Activity

Have a go at correcting the following.

Its important to ensure that all teachers are aware of their roles and responsibilities, especially with regard to Health and Safety. In the same way, its important for learners to recognise the need for them to ensure each others and other peoples safety. Its no longer enough, since moving beyond the 1900s, simply to put a sign above equipment warning of the dangers of its misuse.

The corrected version appears below. Well done if you were able to complete the activity successfully. If not, work through the explanations again.

> *It's important to ensure that all teachers are aware of their roles and responsibilities, especially with regard to Health and Safety. In the same way, it's important for all learners to recognise the need for them to ensure each other's and other people's safety. It's no longer enough, since moving beyond the 1900s, simply to put a sign above equipment warning of the dangers of its misuse.*

Brackets (parentheses) are of two different types.

- Round brackets are used to encase information that is relevant, but not essential, to a sentence, as well as to enclose the year of publication in the Harvard referencing system (see Chapter 1).
- Square brackets are used to enter extra information into quotations to aid clarity, and, in Harvard referencing, to signify an electronic source; for example, [online] or the date an internet site was accessed.

Quotation marks should always be used to denote direct speech, or short extracts taken directly from others' writing. Single quotation marks are generally used, but for quotations inside quotations, you should use double quotation marks; for example, ... a recent report concerning accessibility of venues stated that 'over 90% of respondents were "very happy" with provision'.

Quotation marks can also be used to denote a definition or name, but increasingly italics are being used for this purpose.

An ellipsis, three evenly spaced dots (...), with one space between the ellipsis and its surrounding letters or other marks, indicates that words have been purposely left out of a quotation, generally in the interests of brevity or to highlight key points.

Hyphens are often used for clarity when connecting two words; for example, *re-word, re-focus, twenty-one*. The hyphen is a shorter mark than the dash and has no spaces on either side.

The dash – which can be used for explanation, emphasis, or in the place of brackets or commas – is longer than the hyphen and has spaces on both sides.

Top tip: with any of these points above, if you are unsure, reword your text to avoid the problem.

Using pictures, charts, etc., to support your writing

Information can be communicated in a variety of ways. Pictures, charts, graphs, diagrams and symbols can all be used to add clarification and interest to your written assessments. Whenever you use such an illustration, however, you should take care to ensure that it is clearly labelled and supports or explains the text, or that text is included to describe the illustration.

Charts and graphs must always be carefully and accurately constructed, using a chart type and scale or scales that enable the most effective display of the data. Generally, you should place the dependent variable on the *y* axis and the independent variable on the *x* axis.

For example, as monthly college attendance figures (dependent variable) depend upon the months of the academic year (independent variable), the attendance figures would be shown on the *y* axis in a two-dimensional (2D) representation (with an additional z axis the graph is a 3D representation), and the months of the year on the *x* axis. See Figure 4.1.

			In the example (Figure 4.1) below
y axis (*z* axis 3D)	vertical axis	dependent variable	Number of learners
x axis	horizontal axis	independent variable	Months

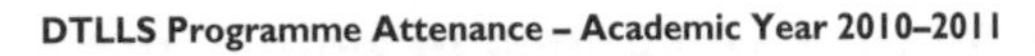

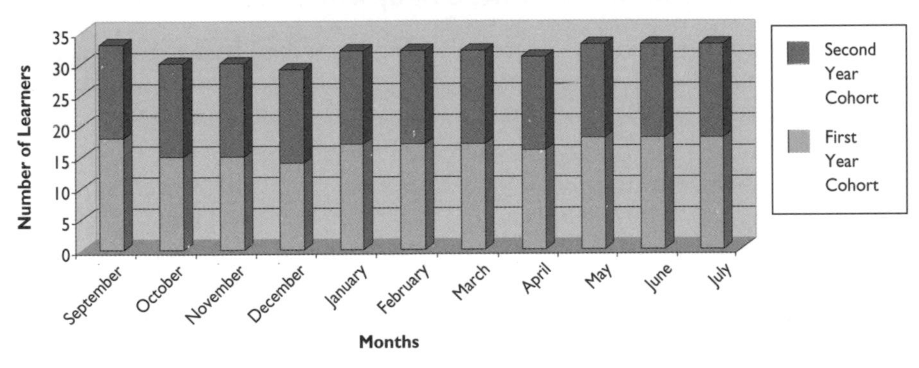

Figure 4.1 Column chart

You will need to give a title to the chart or graph and to the axes, as in Figure 4.1, and always include the units of measurement. The title appears above the chart or graph, whereas with figures it always appears below. If you have more than one set of data, show each series using a different colour or symbol and include clear labels. Effective graphs, charts and diagrams can be constructed using word processing or spreadsheet software and either cut and pasted or linked into your assessment tasks.

When using any illustrations or figures created by others, always check any copyright limitations and accurately acknowledge your sources when referencing.

Formal writing

Your written assessment tasks will need to be presented in a formal written style, following set procedures for structure and presentation.

General guidance for the structure of work

As you start to write more, particularly if you progress from the PTLLS Award to a higher-level teaching qualification, you will start to develop your own style. Perusing books and newspapers that you enjoy can help you to develop your knowledge of paragraphing, sentence construction and punctuation. Reading widely can also help your spelling and grammar. If you see words that don't look correct, it could be that you have always spelt them wrong but were not aware of it.

It is important that your written assessments are soundly structured with a logical flow. The introduction (which should normally be written last after you have addressed the requirements) should explain your interpretation of the question and how you have structured your answer in response, outlining the key content. The main content should then build on the introduction, and lead into a conclusion which should summarise the main points of your writing, picking up on the theme of the introduction. If you are aiming for level 4, you should extend your conclusion to suggest wider implications and maybe predict future trends or issues.

General guidance for the presentation of written assessments

Written assessments should be presented using a standard layout, giving consistency throughout all work submitted for your portfolio. You should always check with your teacher/assessor for any specific presentation requirements of the PTLLS Award.

Title

The title, usually in the form of the question to be answered, should be set out in full at the top of the first page.

Layout

As far as possible, all work should be word-processed in double- or one-and-a-half-line spacing. Use a standard font, which is easy to read (Arial or Verdana are good choices), usually in size 12 point. Allow a left-hand margin of at least 30mm to accommodate hole-punching or other binding.

Referencing

Harvard referencing should normally be used (see Chapter 1). Referencing your work is essential if you are aiming for level 4. If you are aiming for level 3, it is good practice to include a bibliography, although you must include a references list if you cite or quote other authors in your writing.

Word counts

Where you are given a word count, it is important to keep within this, and to state the number of words at the beginning or end of your writing. If you are given a word range; for example, 350–500 words, your assessment should be inside the range. Where you are given a simple count; for example, 500 words, you are generally allowed 10 per cent either side; for example, 450–550 words.

Identity

All your work should be identifiable. Make sure that you put your name and enrolment number on every page, and, as far as is practicable, on every piece of accompanying material, such as resources used for your micro-teach. It is most effective to include this in a header or footer, so that it will automatically appear at the same place on every page of a document, no matter how many times you add or remove content. The date of submission could also be added within the header or footer.

Page numbering

Your pages should always be consecutively numbered, preferably using the automatic page numbering facility; for example, 'page *x* of *y*'. This facility will automatically count the pages in each document and display the current page number relative to the total number of pages.

General guidance for compiling your PTLLS portfolio

Declaration of authenticity

You will be asked to sign a document confirming that the evidence you submit is authentic and a true representation of your own work. This is to help guard against plagiarism (the use of someone else's work without proper acknowledgement).

Anonymity of learners

If you are currently teaching and using examples from your teaching practice to contextualise your assessment tasks, be careful to keep learners' personal data confidential. If you do need to name learners, either use an identification system such as *Learner A*, *Learner B*, etc., or give your learners pseudonyms (or aliases). Where you choose the latter, make this clear by including a statement such as 'In the interests of confidentiality, all learner names used are pseudonyms'.

Safe-keeping

Any work submitted should always be securely fastened and you should always keep copies. It is rare for work to go astray, but if something goes missing, you will need to resubmit it. If you have to post assessments, sending them by Special Delivery Next Day or Recorded Signed For will enable you to track their delivery. All work produced on a computer should be backed up to an alternative storage device.

Extenuating circumstances

Note the deadlines for all assessment tasks and keep them to hand, checking your progress regularly. You will be expected to plan your study so that you can meet assessment deadlines around work, family and other commitments. If you do find that you need an extension owing to extenuating circumstances, discuss this with your teacher/assessor as soon as possible.

General guidance for the final presentation of your PTLLS portfolio

It is a good idea to ask about presentation of your portfolio early on in the PTLLS Award programme, so that you can compile it as you go. You will need to make sure your portfolio binder or folder is clearly labelled, on the front cover and the spine, with your name, programme title and level. Every page submitted should be immediately visible, which means that if you use plastic pockets, you will need one for every two sides of content. All evidence should be clearly cross-referenced to the assessment tasks, and having a contents list would be useful. Besides being assessed, your portfolio may be sampled by an internal and/or external verifier on behalf of the awarding organisation. They will not want to waste time searching through an unorganised file to find what they need.

Presenting your work in practice

Preparing for your micro-teach

Part of your practical assessment for your PTLLS Award will be to deliver a short micro-teach session either to your peers, or if you are already teaching, to learners at your normal place of work. The micro-teach will be for a minimum of 15 or 30 minutes, and will be observed by your teacher/assessor. Micro-teaching is a scaled-down teaching and learning experience designed to help develop new teaching skills and provide opportunities to polish and perfect existing ones. You will have an opportunity to put theory into practice, obtain feedback from your teacher and possibly your peers, as well as to undertake a reflective self-evaluation.

There are many benefits of an observed micro-teach; for example, you will be able to:

- build self-confidence;
- experiment in a safe environment;
- identify the positive qualities of others;
- develop processes of self-evaluation;
- give and receive feedback;
- have your good practice recognised and supported;
- start to develop a personal teaching style.

When preparing for your micro-teach, 30 or even 15 minutes may seem like an eternity. In reality, it is very little time, and you will need to plan your timings extremely carefully to make sure that you deliver a meaningful session to your peers or learners. Your delivery should consist of an introduction, development and summary. The latter should include revisiting your aim and objectives (or learning outcomes) and time for learner questions.

When delivering your micro-teach you should plan to:

- enable the group to learn a basic concept;
- demonstrate how to write clear and effective objectives or learning outcomes;
- select suitable teaching and learning approaches, and use resources effectively;
- carry out appropriate assessment.

Make sure that you obtain a copy of your assessor's observation checklist well in advance of your micro-teach session, so that you know exactly what they will be looking for.

You will need to write your session plan and prepare resources, including presentation slides and printed learning materials, in advance. It is important to make these as accessible as possible. For example, with handouts you should restrict the amount of text on the page, leaving spaces between columns and including wide margins and spaces between paragraphs. Headings and new sections should come at the top of pages wherever possible, and sentences and paragraphs should be kept within columns or pages. Use a clear font; for example, Arial, Comic Sans or Verdana, with a minimum font size of 12 point, and a maximum of 14 point. Number your pages clearly. If you have learners with any special requirements it's advisable to ask them if they would prefer learning materials with a different coloured background, or a particular font and size.

Readability

Readability is an attempt to match the reading level of written material to the reading with understanding level of the reader. For maximum readability, use short sentences, including only one main point, and ending with a full stop. Use the active voice, and where possible, simple, straightforward words. If you have to use technical terms, explain them first. There are several readability tests to assess density of writing. The quickest and easiest to use manually is the SMOG (Simplified Measure of Gobbledygook) readability formula, which calculates readability using sentence and word length.

Activity

Obtain a textbook or a newspaper and carry out a SMOG test using the SMOG calculator in Appendix 4. You might like to use a textbook in your subject area to see how relevant it would be for your own learners.

If you want a text to be readily understood by the majority of people, it should be at a readability level of 10 or below.

The following should apply to all printed learning materials, writing on white-boards, and presentation slides that you wish to use.

- Use a combination of upper and lower case letters as the shapes of the words helps word recognition. If you use only capital letters it appears as though you are shouting.
- Embolden text or surround it with a box for emphasis, and avoid positioning text at unusual angles.
- Use a ragged right margin. Justifying the right-hand margin distorts letter spacing and can give the appearance of rivers of white space running down the page.
- Wherever you use illustrations, make sure that these are in context and support the text, or they are likely to confuse.
- Proofread all your work carefully to eliminate errors.
- Reference any text from sources.

When it comes to the day of the micro-teach, do not worry if you feel tense: it is okay to feel nervous. You could try using some relaxation techniques.

Example

Today is the day of Simon's micro-teach. He listens to his favourite music on his journey to the venue, and finds that he arrives in a reasonably relaxed state.
As the time for him to start draws near, he shrugs his shoulders and tenses and releases his body gently while sitting in his chair. Immediately before starting, he leaves the room for two minutes, and standing outside, breathes deeply from his diaphragm. As he enters the room to start his session, he takes one deep breath, stands tall, and remembers to speak a little more slowly than usual. These preparations enable him to start his micro-teach in a reasonably relaxed state, and he is soon at ease as he falls into the rhythm of his presentation.

On the day, you will probably find that the time will simply fly past. Remember to position a clock where you can check it discreetly, and to note down your start and finishing time somewhere equally accessible.

For more detailed information about aspects of micro-teaching, please see Chapter 6 of *Passing PTLLS Assessments* by Ann Gravells.

Effective presentations

Being able to present information in an interesting and accessible manner is a key teaching skill that has to be learned and practised.

Delivering an effective presentation

One of the best ways to establish what something looks like when it works well is to isolate what happens when it does not.

Activity

Spend ten minutes identifying what you consider are the ten major mistakes made by presenters. Reflect on presentations that you have attended, or that you might have delivered yourself. Think about what happened from the start of the presentation, through to the finish. Make a note of your thoughts on a separate sheet of paper.

How many did you manage to come up with? The ten major mistakes made by presenters identified by Malouf (1997) are:

1. failing to speak to time;
2. using material unsuited to the audience;
3. information overload;
4. material that is too technical;
5. poor preparation;
6. failure to practise speech;
7. distracting visuals/verbals/vocals;
8. inappropriate pace;
9. lack of eye contact;
10. lack of enthusiasm.

These same mistakes also often occur in micro-teaches; after all, a substantial part of your micro-teach involves presenting to your audience of learners. You can adopt some of the following strategies to help make sure that these things do not happen to you.

Rehearse, rehearse, rehearse

Perfect preparation prevents poor performance. There is no substitute for planning and practising your micro-teach thoroughly, timing it as you do so. It is important to note, however, that your perfected rehearsal with a small, or even no, audience is likely to proceed much more quickly than the real thing. Always have an exercise that can be left out without detriment, or included to add value, depending upon how the time goes.

Prepare for set-up issues

Arrive at least 15–20 minutes early to set everything up, and carry out a check for any health and safety issues. Make sure you have a contingency plan available in case of last-minute equipment failures, etc.

Enthusiasm is contagious

It is difficult for your audience not to enjoy and engage with your presentation if you are delivering it with passion and enthusiasm. Furthermore, any nerves will abate when you are excited about your subject matter.

Speak to your learners

Reading from a script can cause you to lose eye contact with your group. Your voice projection will also be reduced as you look downwards into your paper. If you do want to use notes for support, write out key words or phrases onto a set of plain postcards (which should be numbered and treasury-tagged together so that they stay in order if you should drop them), or use an electronic slide presentation as a prompt.

Involve your learners

Be careful to engage with your audience. Find out about any prior knowledge that anyone might have, so that you can build on this throughout your session. Use your learners' names, and be careful to involve and ask questions to everyone. Observe your learners' reactions and try to keep up an appropriate pace.

Choose your material carefully

Remember your audience when designing your material. Make sure it is pitched at the right level and not excessively technical. Avoid the use of jargon, and explain technical words where they are necessary. Keep your content simple. You do not have a great deal of time.

Maximise eye contact and visibility

Be careful not to block your presentation material by walking or standing in front of your screen, whiteboard or flipchart. If you have an electronic presentation, using a remote mouse will allow you to advance slides without always being close to the computer. If you use the whiteboard, remember not to talk while writing with your back to your learners, to enable everyone to see and hear you.

Minimise distraction

When you decide on your outfit, avoid loose clothing, pockets or jewellery that might encourage you to fidget, and make sure you feel comfortable. Try not to overuse words or fillers such as *you know* or *erm*. Turn off, or put away from view, equipment such as digital projectors or props when you are not using them. If you are using Microsoft PowerPoint, pressing the *b* key on the keyboard will blank out the screen, and pressing it a second time will bring it back.

Designing an effective slide presentation

There are many advantages to using presentation software to support your micro-teach. Well-prepared slides including images can offer invaluable support to visual learners. The slides can also act as a focus for you, with your key information logically and sequentially ordered. The use of ICT will also help to demonstrate your application of this part of the minimum core. When using presentation software, the following will help to ensure an effective and trouble-free presentation.

Choose an appropriate slide design

Choose a simple slide background that offers good visibility. A dark blue background with yellow text is generally accessible to the greatest number of people. Some of the animation features can be used to good effect, such as bringing in bullet points one at a time, but use them sparingly.

Use clear text supported by appropriate pictures and charts

Titles should be in a font size between 32 and 50 point, with all other text between 24 and 32 point. A font such as Arial or Verdana is easy to read. Each slide should have no more than six to eight bullet points, showing key phrases. You should talk through your slides, explaining each item in complete sentences and giving examples. Use the slides purely for confirmation and emphasis. Use pictures and charts where they can help to clarify the text.

Test your presentation beforehand

It is always a good idea to test your presentation on the equipment you will be using prior to the teaching session itself. Issues of compatibility can arise with different hardware and different makes and versions of software.

Information communication technology

Being able to work effectively with ICT, whatever your subject specialism, is an important teaching skill, and ICT, together with literacy, language and numeracy, is now part of the required minimum core of teachers' knowledge, understanding and personal skills. As well as being able to use presentation software, you will usually be required to word-process your PTLLS assessments, and to use the internet and other electronic media such as e-books, CDs and DVDs for research. If you are undertaking a blended or online learning programme, you will also need to find your way around the VLE (virtual learning environment).

If you do not have access to a commercial word processing and presentation package, you could download OpenOffice (**http://download.openoffice.org**), which is a free package of programs compatible with many Microsoft documents.

Activity

Follow the link to the Open Office templates page at http://templates.services.openoffice.org/en/node/3247 and look through the lists of templates that can be downloaded. Examine in more detail any you think could be useful.

Specific information communication skills you will need

In order to produce assessments for your PTLLS Award, as a minimum you should be able to:

- create a new document;
- save a document to your computer hard drive and to a USB flash drive;
- open an existing document;
- input text;
- use the cut, copy and paste facilities;
- change margins;
- change font size and style;
- alter line-spacing – there is a simple automatic function to change line spacing anywhere in a document;
- create and use headers and footers;
- use automatic page numbering;
- use automatic bullets and numbering;

- create tables and sort the contents alphabetically;
- use the search and replace facility;
- use the automatic word count facility.

Due to the different software suppliers and different software versions, it is not possible to give information on how to perform these functions. You may, however, find some online resources helpful such as My Guide, **www.myguide.gov.uk**. This is a government website designed to help people take their first steps with computers and the internet. Registered users get access to an easy-to-use email system and a wide range of online courses.

Summary

In this chapter you have learned about:

- Presenting your work in writing
  - deciding on a structure;
  - getting your ideas onto paper;
  - using pictures, charts, etc., to support your writing;
  - formal writing.
- Presenting your work in practice
  - preparing for your micro-teach;
  - effective presentations;
  - information communication technology.

Theory focus

Books

Crystal, D. (2004) *Rediscover grammar*, 3rd edn. Harlow: Pearson Education.

Fleming, N. (2005) *Teaching and learning styles: VARK strategies*. Honolulu: Honolulu Community College.

Gravells, A. (2008) *Preparing to teach in the lifelong learning sector*, 3rd edn. Exeter: Learning Matters.

Gravells, A. (2010) *Passing PTLLS assessments*. Exeter: Learning Matters.

Honey, P. and Mumford, A. (1992) *The manual of learning styles*, 3rd edn. Maidenhead: Peter Honey Associates.

Knowles, M. (1990) *The adult learner: a neglected species*, 4th edn. Houston: Gulf Publishing.

Malouf, D. (1997) *How to create and deliver a dynamic presentation*. USA: ASTD Press.

Rogers, C. (1980) *Freedom to learn for the 80s*. New York: Free Press.
Truss, L. (2003) *Eats, shoots and leaves*. London: Profile Books Limited.
Watson, J. (1924) *Behaviourism*. New York: Norton.
West, C. (2008) *Perfect written English*. London: Random House Books.

Websites

ArmoredPenguin (word puzzles)	**www.armoredpenguin.com**
Microsoft Digital Literacy Curriculum	**www.microsoft.com/uk/education/schools/curriculum-resources/digital-literacy-curriculum.aspx**
My Guide	**www.myguide.gov.uk**
Open Office	**http://download.openoffice.org**
	http://templates.services.openoffice.org/en/node/3247
Royal Mail Group Limited – postage	**www.royalmail.com**
SMOG	**www.literacytrust.org.uk/campaign/SMOG.html**

CHAPTER 5
MOVING FORWARD

Introduction

In this chapter you will learn about:

- transferable skills;
- teaching in the Lifelong Learning Sector;
- lifelong learning.

There are activities and examples to help you reflect on the above which will assist your understanding of how to move forward after achieving your PTLLS Award.

Transferable skills

Transferable skills are skills and attributes developed in one context, in this case studying for your PTLLS Award, which can be transferred to other areas of your work and life. Examples of transferable skills include:

- decision-making;
- information communication technology (ICT) skills;
- numeracy;
- organisation and planning;
- presentation skills;
- problem-solving;
- self-direction and motivation;
- spoken and written communication skills;
- team-working;
- time management.

Activity

Spend 15 minutes reviewing and listing the skills you have developed while studying for the PTLLS Award. Refer back to the activities on learning styles and expert learner characteristics in Chapter 1, and the study skills and learning goals activities in Chapter 2. Revisit your reflective learning journal and your portfolio of evidence to remind you of work completed and distance travelled. Consider how you can apply these skills in different areas of your life; for example, other employment, hobbies and interests, or in the home.

It is useful to carry out a personal SWOT analysis (**S**trengths, **W**eaknesses, **O**pportunities, **T**hreats) at regular intervals to identify internal and external factors impacting on you and your continuing professional development (CPD). As well as providing a focus for specific professional development planning (PDP), this will help to highlight additional transferable skills that would enable you to perform more effectively in all areas of your life.

Example

Having successfully completed his PTLLS Award, Tariq starts work on a SWOT analysis as a focus for his future PDP. He uses the term areas for development, rather than weaknesses. Here are his initial entries.

Strengths	**Areas for development**
PTLLS Award at level 3 Fluent French and Arabic speaker Excellent ICT skills – ITQ3 Confident in, and good at, maths Self-motivated and enthusiastic	Achieve CTLLS Improve English spelling and grammar Work on inter-personal and team-working skills Pass driving test
Opportunities	**Threats**
CTLLS course starting in two months' time Volunteer teaching role at community centre Free English grammar course at local centre	College restructuring – redundancies Too few teaching practice hours Dependent on public transport

Once you have completed a SWOT analysis, you can use it to identify short-, medium- and long-term SMART (**S**pecific, **M**easurable, **A**chievable, **R**ealistic, **T**ime-bound) development goals. You should monitor these regularly, updating them when:

- your personal or professional circumstances change;
- new technology emerges that affects your subject specialism and/or teaching skills;
- organisational and wider developments impact on your job role.

Teaching in the lifelong learning sector

From the date of your appointment in a teaching role in the Lifelong Learning Sector, you have five years to gain your Licence to Practise. This is through achievement of the relevant qualification, a process of professional formation and an ongoing commitment to CPD.

Following achievement of your PTLLS Award, the next steps towards gaining your Licensed Practitioner Status are to:

- ensure you are registered with the Institute for Leaning (IfL);
- work out the date by which you need to achieve Licensed Practitioner Status (since August 2007 you have five years from when you started teaching);
- take steps to ensure your subject specialist knowledge is, and continues to be, current and sufficient;
- make the necessary arrangements to obtain the teaching practice needed;
- enrol on an appropriate teaching qualification course; for example, CTLLS for Associate Teachers (ATLS), or DTLLS/Certificate in Education/PGCE for Qualified Teachers (QTLS);
- consider how you will meet the requirements for the minimum core in literacy and numeracy, if you do not already have the evidence needed.

Activity

Follow the link,* www.move-on.org.uk/practicetests.asp, *to access the Move-on website where you can find a selection of literacy and numeracy National Test practice papers and resources. The National Tests at level 2 could be used to evidence literacy and numeracy skills for professional formation. Register on the site and explore some of the practice papers or hot topics.

You can obtain details regarding the minimum core at **http://www.lluk.org/3043.htm** which also includes ICT. Improving your own skills in these areas will also help your learners' skills.

Professional status

To gain professional status of ATLS or QTLS, following achievement of CTLLS or DTLLS, you will need to complete a period of professional formation. This is when you show, over a period of time, that you can apply your skills and knowledge effectively and meet the LLUK overarching professional teaching standards. These standards, which identify what teachers should know and be able to do, are divided into six domains.

A Professional values and practice.

B Learning and teaching.

C Specialist learning and teaching.

D Planning for learning.

E Assessment for learning.

F Access and progression. (LLUK, 2006)

Timetable

From the date of appointment, all new teachers must:

- register with the IfL within 6 months;
- complete the PTLLS Award within 12 months;
- complete CTLLS or DTLLS/Certificate in Education/PGCE and achieve ATLS or QTLS status within five years;
- demonstrate ongoing commitment to CPD.

Professional formation

Professional formation is the process undertaken after achieving CTLLS, DTLLS or the equivalent qualifications. It enables you to gain ATLS or QTLS status by demonstrating through professional practice:

- the ability to make effective use of the skills and knowledge gained during training;
- the capacity to meet the national occupational teaching standards.

The full process entails completing and submitting an expression of intent through the members' area of the IfL website, before providing evidence of:

- achievement of an approved teaching qualification at level 5 or above for QTLS, and level 3 or 4 for ATLS;
- achievement of numeracy and literacy skills at level 2 or above;
- current teaching and learning;
- subject specialist knowledge and currency;
- self-evaluation;
- developmental planning;

- reflective practice:
- a supporting testimony.

The evidence you provide will include scanned copies of qualifications, written statements and a declaration of suitability, made against IfL criteria. All your evidence should be submitted via the IfLs REfLECT webpage.

Continuing professional development (CPD)

Full-time teachers in the further education sector are required to undertake, document and reflect on at least 30 hours of CPD per year, reduced pro-rata for part-time staff (subject to a minimum of six hours). CPD includes any activity undertaken for the purposes of updating specialist subject knowledge or developing teaching skills (OPSI, 2007).

Opportunities for continuing professional development include:

- attending events and courses;
- improving own skills such as ICT;
- shadowing colleagues;
- researching developments or changes to your subject and/or relevant legislation;
- self-reflecting;
- study for relevant qualifications;
- reading relevant journals;
- relevant voluntary work.

Any method can be used to plan and document CPD, but as part of the services they offer, the IfL provide REfLECT, a dedicated and secure online personal learning space where members are able to plan, record and assess the impact of CPD on their practice (**www.ifl.ac.uk/cpd/reflect**). You can then self-declare completion of your CPD by completing a form on the IfL website. If you do not want to use their website, you can maintain your records manually or electronically in another form. If your CPD record is selected as part of the IfL sampling process, you will be asked to provide all your details. Results from this sample will form part of the IfL annual report.

Code of Professional Practice

All members of the IfL agree to be bound by their Code of Professional Practice, which came into effect on 1 April 2008. Based on six core principles, it defines the professional practice which, in the public interest, the IfL expects of its members throughout their membership and professional career. The six core principles are:

- professional integrity;
- professional practice;

- reasonable care;
- respect;
- responsibility;
- criminal offence disclosure.

The code will be subject to regular review to ensure that it remains relevant and reflects advances in professional practice. Full details can be accessed through **www.ifl.ac.uk/professional-standards/code-of-professional-practice**

Lifelong learning

Lifelong Learning UK (LLUK) is one of 25 UK sector skills councils and is responsible for the professional development of staff working in the Lifelong Learning Sector in the UK. As part of this role, it is responsible for developing the qualifications and setting standards for the delivery and support of learning. LLUK (2009: 15) views lifelong learning as '*a catalyst for a better society*' defining it as learning that happens outside a school environment. They suggest it can include:

> ...learning new work skills or updating existing skills as job requirements change. Or it might be the inspiration people find at a youth group, or the opportunity for learning at a local library.
> (LLUK, 2009: 17).

Lifelong learning therefore can be any learning undertaken at any age and at any time.

According to Microsoft (2008):

- many learners starting a three-year degree in 2010 are likely to find half of their first year's learning obsolete by the end of their studies;
- there are about five times as many words in the English language now as during Shakespeare's time;
- one week's issues of *The Times* probably contain more information than an average person saw in an eighteenth-century lifetime.

Together these insights provide the cornerstone of a clear rationale for lifelong learning, demonstrating its essential nature for both individuals and society, not only for advancement, but simply to maintain the status quo.

Organisations involved in the teaching reforms

Lifelong Learning UK (LLUK) represents the interests of over one million individuals in the learning and skills sector and is responsible for developing the qualifications and setting standards for the delivery and support of learning (LLUK, 2008). Together with the Qualifications and Curriculum Development Agency (QCDA), it is also responsible for granting awarding organisation status.

Standards Verification UK (SVUK), a subsidiary of LLUK, quality assures and endorses the qualifications put forward by LLUK. An Awarding Organisation, for example City & Guilds, will then produce a syllabus based upon the national occupational standards.

The Institute for Learning (IfL) is the professional body for teachers, trainers and assessors in the learning and skills sector. It is led by members for members, and embraces adult and community learning, emergency and public services, FE colleges, the armed services, the voluntary sector and work-based learning (IfL, 2009). It is responsible for learner registration and provision of the award of licensed practitioner status: Qualified Teacher Learning and Skills (QTLS) for full teaching roles, or Associate Teacher Learning and Skills (ATLS) for associate teaching roles.

Summary

In this chapter you have learned about:

- transferable skills;
- teaching in the Lifelong Learning Sector;
- lifelong learning.

Theory focus

Books

Gravells, A. (2008) *Preparing to teach in the lifelong learning sector*, 3rd edn. Exeter: Learning Matters.

Gravells, A. (2010) *Passing PTLLS assessments*. Exeter: Learning Matters.

IfL (2009) *Code of Professional Practice: Raising concerns about IfL members* (V2). London: Institute for Learning.

LLUK (2006) *New overarching professional standards for teachers, tutors and trainers in the Lifelong Learning Sector*. London: Skills for Business.

Websites

IfL – Code of Professional Practice **www.ifl.ac.uk/professional-standards/code-of-professional-practice**
IfL – Professional formation annexe **www.ifl.ac.uk/__data/assets/pdf_file/0015/4641/Professional-Formation-Annexe-A.pdf**
IfL – REfLECT **www.ifl.ac.uk/cpd/reflect**
Lifelong Learning UK (LLUK) **www.lluk.org/**
LLUK (2009) – The Big Picture **www.slideshare.net/LifelongLearningUK/the-big-picture-1747598**
QCDA **www.qcda.gov.uk/**
Microsoft UK Schools Shift happens **http://blogs.msdn.com/ukschoolsarchive/2008/09/11/shift-happens-uk-download.aspx**
Minimum core **www.lluk.org/3043.htm**
Move-on – Skills for Life practice tests **www.move-on.org.uk/practicetests.asp**
OPSI **www.opsi.gov.uk/si/si2007/uksi_20072116_en_1**
Standards Verification UK **www.standardsverificationuk.org/**

APPENDIX 1
PTLLS WRITTEN ASSESSMENTS: GUIDANCE

(Relates to the activity in Chapter 1)

PTLLS Level 3 written assessments	
Should have/do:	Should not have/do:
Question set out in full as the title unless otherwise instructed.	Spelling errors.
Double- or one-and-a-half-line spacing.	Mistakes in grammar.
Introduction, main body and conclusion well linked.	Mistakes in punctuation.
Acronyms and abbreviations expanded.	Ampersands (use the word *and* in full).
Clear font in 12 pt.	Contractions (such as *it's*, *isn't*): write words in full, i.e. *it is*, *is not*.
A clear focus.	Plagiarism – all responses should be in your own words (if any quotations are used, these must be Harvard referenced).
Word count at the end.	Jargon or informal language.
Headers and footers including your name, the date, page number, assessment number, task number and level.	
Note: It is good practice to include a Bibliography set out in the Harvard format showing wider reading.	
PTLLS level 4 written assessments	
as level 3, plus:	as level 3, plus:
Use of complete sentences with only minor use of bullets and tables.	Use of inappropriate references which have no provenance. (Provenance refers to origin and authenticity, see Chapter 3).
Be written in the third person passive, unless you are referring to your own practice, or presenting your own opinions (see Chapter 5 for clarification).	
Evidence of independent reading and research.	
Harvard referencing.	
Analysis and evaluation.	
Demonstrate understanding of the relationship between theory/principles and practice.	
Note: You should check with your PTLLS Award assessor to make sure you are aware of any particular awarding organisation requirements.	

APPENDIX 2
ANSWERS TO HARVARD REFERENCING ACTIVITY

(Relates to the activity in Chapter 1)

Question 1. This is the reference for Gravells' book in John's bibliography. Tick or cross the correct number for each part of this reference in the table below.

Extract from John's assessment

Gravells (2008: 23) states that 'using the senses – sight, hearing, touch, smell and taste – will enable you to learn and remember'.

1	2	3	4	5	6
Gravells,	A.	(2008)	*Preparing to teach in the life-long learning sector*, 3rd edn.	Exeter:	Learning Matters.

	1	2	3	4	5	6
Surname of the writer of the book	☒	☐	☐	☐	☐	☐
Publisher's name	☐	☐	☐	☐	☐	☒
Name of the book	☐	☐	☐	☒	☐	☐
Place of publication................................	☐	☐	☐	☐	☒	☐
Year of publication	☐	☐	☒	☐	☐	☐
The writer's initial(s)	☐	☒	☐	☐	☐	☐

Question 2. Emma has used the internet to research her assessment. Tick or cross the correct number for each part of the reference in the table below.

1	2	3	4	5	6
Petty,	G.	(2004)	*Active learning* [online]	available at www.geoffpetty.com/activelearning.html	(accessed 2 June 2010)

	1	2	3	4	5	6
Year of publication on the internet	☐	☐	☒	☐	☐	☐
Author's initials	☐	☒	☐	☐	☐	☐
Website address (URL)	☐	☐	☐	☐	☒	☐
Surname of author	☒	☐	☐	☐	☐	☐

Name of the article	☐	☐	☐	☒	☐	☐
Date that Emma accessed the internet site	☐	☐	☐	☐	☐	☒

Question 3. What does '(ed)' mean in this entry in Hasina's References section?

Desforges, C. (ed) (1995) *An introduction to teaching.* Oxford: Blackwell Publishers.

Edition .... ☐
Education .... ☐
Editor .... ☒

Question 4. What does '(edn)' mean in this entry of Ilona's References section?

Gravells, A. (2008) *Preparing to teach in the lifelong learning sector*, (3rd edn.). Exeter: Learning Matters.

Edition .... ☒
Education ..... ☐
Editor .... ☐

Question 5. What is the difference between a References section and a Bibliography?

References include only those books, journals, articles, etc., that you have used for quotations and citations .... ☒

References will be shorter than a Bibliography .... ☐

A Bibliography includes everything you have read and looked at for the assessment, even if you have not used it for quotations and citations.. ☒

A Bibliography will be a longer list than a Reference list .... ☐

Question 6. A direct quotation of two lines or fewer is encased in quotation marks and remains within the body of the text. How should a direct quotation that is longer than two lines be presented?

In exactly the same format as a shorter one .... ☐

Inset into the text, single-line spaced, without any quotation marks, but preceded by a colon .... ☒

Inset into the text, in the same line spacing as the rest of the text, without quotation marks.. ☐

Encased in quotation marks, inset into the text, in single line spacing .... ☐

APPENDIX 3 ANSWERS TO TERMINOLOGY WORD SEARCH

(Relates to the activity in Chapter 4)

i	t	r	n	e	d	n	r	c	x	y	x	y	t	a	e	s
p	i	r	d	s	t	e	o	o	i	f	f	e	c	r	e	i
l	a	e	n	i	u	a	l	l	u	i	y	l	l	e	e	t
i	n	l	i	i	s	m	t	i	t	t	y	e	i	v	y	i
a	s	i	a	e	a	c	m	s	v	n	l	n	m	i	e	t
a	s	i	e	v	a	l	u	a	t	e	n	i	f	e	d	i
n	e	s	c	t	a	j	p	s	r	d	r	m	n	w	i	n
r	a	e	e	i	e	n	a	x	s	i	e	a	a	e	e	i
e	r	n	x	s	e	r	a	a	e	l	s	x	p	a	a	c
i	e	n	p	e	t	m	p	l	i	l	e	e	r	m	i	n
i	m	t	l	n	y	u	i	r	y	u	n	l	c	r	o	t
e	c	r	o	t	m	s	e	d	e	s	c	r	i	b	e	c
n	l	c	r	i	t	i	q	u	e	t	e	l	p	m	o	c
c	x	o	e	c	u	d	o	r	p	r	n	y	i	e	y	r
e	s	y	l	a	n	a	y	l	l	a	c	i	t	i	r	c
t	e	s	e	r	u	c	e	t	v	t	e	i	c	r	e	e
w	i	t	i	d	t	r	c	r	s	e	e	t	i	a	t	t

analyse
critically analyse
describe
explain
interpret
produce

compare
critique
discuss
explore
justify
review

complete
define
evaluate
identity
list
state

contrast
deliver
examine
illustrate
outline
summarise

APPENDIX 4
SMOG READABILITY CALCULATOR

(Relates to the activity in Chapter 4)

To use SMOG

1. Select a text.
2. Count ten sentences.
3. Count the number of words which have three or more syllables.
4. Multiply this by 3.
5. Circle the number closest to your answer.

1	4	9	16	25	36	49	64	81	100	121	144	169

6. Find the square root of the number you circled in the table below:

1	**4**	**9**	**16**	**25**	**36**	**49**	**64**	**81**	**100**	**121**	**144**	**169**
1	2	3	4	5	6	7	8	9	10	11	12	13

7. Add 8 to this total and this will give you the readability level.

A readability level of 10 or below will be understood by most people.

QCF level	Readability level
Entry 3	8-10
Level 1 (broadly equivalent to GCSE grades D–G)	11–15
Level 2 (broadly equivalent to GCSE grades A*–C)	16–20

APPENDIX 5 USEFUL BOOKS AND WEBSITES

Books

Buzan, T. (1989) *Use your head*, 2nd edn. London: BBC Books.

Cottrell, S. (2008) *The Study Skills Handbook*, 3rd edn. Basingstoke: Palgrave Macmillan.

Crystal, D. (2004) *Rediscover grammar*, 3rd edn. Harlow: Pearson Education.

Gravells, A. (2008) *Preparing to teach in the lifelong learning sector*, 3rd edn. Exeter: Learning Matters.

Gravells, A. (2010) *Passing PTLLS assessments*. Exeter: Learning Matters.

Truss, L. (2003) *Eats, shoots and leaves*. London: Profile Books Limited.

West, C. (2008) *Perfect written English*. London: Random House Books.

Websites

2collab (research-focused online social bookmarking tool)	**www.2collab.com**
AdultStudent.com (tips for survival and success)	**www.adultstudent.com**
Alta Vista (search engine)	**http://uk.altavista.com**
ArmoredPenguin (word puzzles)	**www.armoredpenguin.com**
Ask Jeeves (search engine)	**http://uk.ask.com**
BBC/with the Open University (learning styles)	**www.open2.net/survey/learningstyles**
BeCal (information gateway)	**www.becal.net**
Brainboxx (John Fewings)	**www.brainboxx.co.uk**
BUBL Information Service (information gateway)	**www.bubl.ac.uk**
Citeulike (academic-focused online social bookmarking tool)	**www.citeulike.org**
Connotea (academic-focused online social bookmarking tool)	**www.connotea.org**
Department for Children, Schools and Families	**www.dcsf.gov.uk**
Delicious (online social bookmarking tool)	**http://delicious.com**
Department for Business, Innovation and Skills	**www.dius.gov.uk**
Diigo (online social bookmarking tool)	**www.diigo.com**
ESCalate (resources for post-16 education)	**http://escalate.ac.uk**
Eurydice, NFER (information gateway)	**www.nfer.ac.uk/eurydice**

Excellence Gateway (LSIS) (information gateway)	**www.excellencegateway.org.uk**
Find Articles (articles in magazines, journals, trade publications and newspapers)	**http://findarticles.com**
Further Education Teachers' Qualifications (England) Regulations 2007	**www.opsi.gov.uk/si/si2007/uksi_20072264_en_1**
Google (search engine)	**www.google.co.uk**
Gravells, Ann (resources and information about teaching)	**www.anngravells.co.uk**
H20 Playlist (academic-focused online social bookmarking tool)	**http://h2obeta.law.harvard.edu**
Institute for Learning	**www.ifl.ac.uk**
IngentaConnect (online journal abstracts and articles)	**www.ingentaconnect.com**
Intute (information gateway)	**www.intute.ac.uk**
LibraryThing (books-focused online social bookmarking tool)	**www.librarything.com**
Lifelong Learning UK	**www.lluk.org.uk**
Learning and Skills Network	**www.lsneducation.org.uk**
Maslow, Abraham	**http://maslow.com**
Microsoft Digital Literacy Curriculum	**www.microsoft.com/uk/education/schools/curriculum-resources/digital-literacy-curriculum.aspx**
Move on Skills for Life practice tests	**www.move-on.org.uk/practicetests.asp**
My Guide	**www.myguide.gov.uk**
NIACE	**www.niace.org.uk**
Open Office (free software)	**http://download.openoffice.org** **http://templates.services.openoffice.org/en/node/3247**
Open University Learning Space (free online resources)	**http://openlearn.open.ac.uk**
Palgrave Study Skills (Skills4Study)	**www.skills4study.com**
PCET	**www.pcet.net**
Pinakes (links to major information gateways)	**www.hw.ac.uk/libwww/irn/pinakes/pinakes.html**
QCDA	**www.qcda.gov.uk**
Questia (online library: search free, but subscription to access)	**www.questia.com**
Scholar (academic-focused online social bookmarking tool)	**www.scholar.com**
TEC (learning styles)	**http://tecweb.org**
TES Online	**www.tes.co.uk**
VARK (Neil Fleming)	**www.vark-learn.com**
Wikipedia	**www.wikipedia.org**
Williams, Jacklyn (resources and information about teaching)	**www.ProSolTeaching.co.uk**
Wordle	**www.wordle.net**
Yahoo! (search engine)	**http://uk.yahoo.com**

INDEX

Added to a page number 'f' denotes a figure.

Blue Slipper Bay

Wendy K Harris

W F HOWES LTD

This large print edition published in 2007 by
W F Howes Ltd
Unit 4, Rearsby Business Park, Gaddesby Lane,
Rearsby, Leicester LE7 4YH

1 3 5 7 9 10 8 6 4 2

First published in the United Kingdom in 2007
by Transita

A CIP catalogue record for this book is available from the British Library

ISBN 978 1 40741 004 3

Typeset by Palimpsest Book Production Limited,
Grangemouth, Stirlingshire
Printed and bound in Great Britain
by Antony Rowe Ltd, Chippenham, Wilts.

A NOTE TO THE READER

If you should visit the Isle of Wight, you can find many of the places mentioned in this story. But some of them belong in the realms of the imagination, or may have been washed away by the sea.

WKH Isle of Wight 2007

For Michael, Debbie, Samuel and Lachlan.
On the other side of the world, but here
in my heart.

CHAPTER 1

There was something troubling Ash. Jill watched him from the balcony of Cormorants, their imposing Victorian house overlooking Ventnor beach. His pale sweatshirt picked up the glimmer of dawn. Spying, she thought, I'm spying on him and he wouldn't like that. Ash never did anything underhand. Jill shivered and huddled deeper into her black velvet dressing gown. It wasn't unusual for Ash to be up early, exercising. 'Good for the bones,' he informed everybody. 'Got to keep my own in working order if I'm to fix other people's.' And whatever the weather he would be out at daybreak jogging along the curve of orange beach – or the esplanade if the tide was in – pausing to stretch ligaments and flex joints, a living example of how a set of two hundred and six middle-aged bones could be kept fully functional. Jill told him the locals referred to him as Bone Man. Ash lifted his chin as if honoured by this title. She imagined that one day he might slough off his thin layer of muscle and skin and revel in the full glory of his skeleton.

But this morning, Ash wasn't running or bending.

He wasn't doing anything at all, except staring out to sea. His shoulders seemed hunched, his neck drawn down between them like a turtle. The sharp salty air stung Jill's nostrils; she shuddered and clutched at her collar. Maybe he's overextended himself, she thought, letting herself back into the warm, yeasty kitchen. Or perhaps he's missing Rose. Yesterday, Ash had driven their eldest daughter back to her student digs near the Royal Academy of Music after a short visit. He'd been bereft for days the first time she went away. 'London's such a dangerous place compared to the Isle of Wight,' he'd said, moping around the house, irritating Jill.

'Rose will cope, she was born there – it's in her blood,' she'd retorted, wishing Ash would get back into his bones.

Jill switched on the kettle and heaved herself onto the hefty iron radiator, poking her frozen toes between its ribs. How nice it was to feel cold for a change and enjoy the comfort of warming up. The house was always overheated. Ash stoked the wood-burner as if his loved ones were tropical plants in danger of frost bite. Jill sometimes felt she might spontaneously combust, like one of Dickens's characters. Relishing the heat beginning to seep through to her, she surveyed the large room with its cheery clutter of bright crockery, the tray of rising croissants, the photo-camouflaged fridge and the kids' blobby artwork tacked on the walls. One of Fleur's insect paintings caught her attention – dozens of tiny red ladybirds crawled over the paper. In her mind she began sorting the dotty creatures into pairs, feeling the addictive anticipation of whether or not it would work out evenly. Damn, one left over, perhaps she'd miscounted. She shook her head, dismissing the temptation to begin the ritual again.

Flooded with heat, she shuffled her bottom off the radiator and undid her dressing gown. She noticed her big leather bag on a chair, flopped open. Rummaging inside, she unzipped an inner compartment and felt for the small sealed plastic envelope. Anxiety niggled – it wasn't enough – she'd have to get more. She fastened her bag – shouldn't leave it lying around like this. The kids might decide to have a nose. Propping herself against the table, she put on her reading glasses, yanked a few hairs from her head and studied them, wondering if any natural auburn – titian, she liked to call it – still survived beneath the henna. Either way the roots were grey.

She sighed. If she were efficient she could shower and prepare breakfast before Tom and Fleur woke. Sometimes she felt too old to be the mother of two small children, aged seven and eight. If she'd stopped after having Rose she would be in the almost-child-free-zone by now. Should have moved to the island sooner, had them younger. But that wasn't how it had worked. And she wouldn't be without them, even though they were perpetually locked in mortal combat.

She yawned, made a mug of coffee, slung her bag over her shoulder and crept back upstairs.

It was Saturday, no school run, kids unconscious, no obsessive clients to deal with – only herself. She took off her dressing gown and clambered naked into the big bed which still held pockets of warmth and smelled of Ash's embrocation. She wished he would come indoors, share his worries and revert to his normal predictable self. She needed the strength of those long, sound bones of his. They were the scaffold on which she supported her own unreliable body.

Rose, she thought again. Was that all that was troubling Ash? She couldn't think of anything else it might be. Cormorants Health Centre – his life's ambition – was up and running, well attended. Their relationship trundled along in its comfortable rut – except their busy schedules didn't allow much time together these days. It had to be Rose. Ash had overheard her talking with a friend about busking in London. He was convinced that she would never do such a thing, but it had alarmed him. Jill finished her coffee and slumped against the pillows, her limbs feeling heavy. She felt less fired up when Rose was away. Something inside her seemed to cool and slacken, like hot air leaving a taut balloon. She closed her eyes, hearing the drone of the sea and the creak of the old house as if it were a boat straining at anchor. She wasn't missing her eldest daughter at all.

Nick woke suffused with desire. He'd been dreaming of Keri again. He could feel the texture of her soft skin under his hands, making his palms tingle. He longed to drift back to her, to let his whole being immerse itself in the creation his mind had reproduced so flawlessly.

The dreams were becoming more frequent – overwhelming images imprisoned behind his iron curtain were seeping through. I have to stop this, he thought, my mind is a trickster. He threw off his sleeping bag, hoping the chill of the night air might cool his lust. He rolled off his bed and walked naked to the window. The newborn pink of dawn was brushing the horizon. He switched on the light to act as a guiding beacon, ran down the wooden stairs and opened the door onto the strip of concrete path that separated his cottage from the drop to the beach. He stood listening to the hiss and slide of the waves, feeling his passion subsiding as the little sorcerer residing in his brain lost its hallucinatory power. He jumped down onto the wet sand. It sucked at his feet as he walked to meet the sea.

He gasped as the freezing water welled against his legs, but he ploughed on. When the first wave slapped at his retreating genitals the shock momentarily seized his breath and he plunged in and started to swim. He should have worn his wetsuit; his muscles already felt leaden with the cold; he mustn't stay in for long or go out too far. He stopped and turned over to look back at the shore. He could see the light in his window, burning bright against the dark void of the cliff. He hadn't swum as far as he'd thought. Above him the heavens were softening, pearly, with a tinge of green.

Suddenly, he was reminded of Lake Tekapo in New Zealand – Keri's favourite place on earth, she told him, as they wandered waist high in pastel lupins at the edge of the turquoise water, the air sweet as honey. He remembered hoping it might become his favourite place too – their favourite place. A place they could return to for celebrations. A vision had rolled out before him of anniversaries and birthdays – maybe a child – Keri and he still clasping hands.

Nick shook his head. The sorcerer was sneaking back. He ducked below the surface, listening for the muffled thrum, the strange pulsing pressure of the undersea world. He opened his eyes and saw his arms floating like dead fish, the black tattoos stark against his pale flesh. He felt for the cord of plaited silk that Keri had woven. She'd made two, which they'd tied around each other's wrists the day they were married in the tiny Church of the Good Shepherd on the lake shore. 'Never thought I'd get hitched to a Pom,' she'd joked.

He wondered if her ashes might have found their way from the light water of Lake Tekapo, along underground streams, sensing their passage like migrating birds, merging with the drift of oceans, warm and cold, finding him in the dark waves of the English Channel that lapped Blue Slipper Bay.

* * *

Sophie stood in the bay window nibbling a slice of burnt toast, sipping orange juice, watching the mist shrouding the black branches of the trees above the wall of the cemetery across the road. She liked the fact there were no houses opposite – unusual for London – and the proximity of the dead didn't faze her. Her childhood home above the old theatre had backed onto a neglected graveyard through which she dawdled on the way home from school, patting the crumbling tombstones and wriggling between rusting railings of forgotten mausoleums.

Recalling those days triggered a vision of Tiggy in his spiky fur hat sitting on a bench, and she remembered her miracle box in the attic. She hadn't thought about it for ages. She felt an urge to rush up and retrieve it. She glanced at her watch. *Your life is now* – that's what Tiggy would say. But she didn't have time. She had to walk to Mum's and make sure she was decently dressed and fed before catching the bus to the clinic to supervise the Saturday morning bereavement group. A thick blanket of fatigue draped itself over her and she felt her body sag, her eyelids droop. She rocked her narrow shoulders as if casting it off. At least she had next weekend free. Audrey, her sister, was going to look after Mum, and Jill was driving up from the Isle of Wight. They often spent a few days together when Peter, Sophie's husband, was away. Rarely, Jill brought the children – but never Ash. Jill said the men were inhibiting, she and Sophie could indulge themselves better without Bone Man and Peter Pan around.

Sophie smiled, buoyed by her thoughts. Jill was always full of ideas, planning an itinerary of exhibitions to visit, new places to explore. But inevitably they would eat a great deal, drink too much and spend hours sifting through the jumble of their lives.

Sophie pushed up the sash window, swept the crumbs from her plate onto the sill for the robin, and took a chilly gulp of exhausted air before lowering it. She shivered. It wasn't much warmer inside the house. Or was it just her? She sometimes found it difficult to warm up these days, as if her internal thermostat had been turned down. Defiantly, she left her plate and glass on Peter's precious white oak table, wondering whether he would sense this imposition in America.

She went to the bathroom to clean her teeth and tame her hair and then pulled on her brown winter coat, glad of the warmth. Standing in the hallway, ready to tackle her day, she imagined she could hear her mother's plaintiff voice wailing for a cup of tea.

'I'm on my way, Mum,' she called, her voice echoing around her cold empty house.

'Could you pop in to see Rose next weekend, while you're at Sophie's?' Ash asked. Jill was snuggled in an armchair with Fleur, listening to her read from her homework book. Jill looked up at him. He appeared quite frightening sometimes for such a mild man. His eyebrows needed a trim, they were sticking up – two stiff tufts above his beaky nose – making him look hawkish.

'Oh, Ash! I won't be there long—'

'You could go on Thursday, instead of Friday. It would give you more time.'

'No! She's only just been home. She'll think we're checking up on her.'

'Okay, just wondered.' He opened the door of the woodburner and forced another log into the blaze, releasing a puff of sparky smoke.

Jill watched him, her eyes watering, only half-listening to Fleur. He picked up his new book on Egyptian mythology, flicked through it, put it down, paced around the room, then stood by the door holding onto the brass knob as if he couldn't decide where to go. He slowly bent his knees and straightened up again like a ballet dancer at the barre. Why couldn't he just sit down or go into the music room and play his cello? He hadn't practised for ages. It used to get on Jill's nerves – him grinding away, all bow and elbows – but right now she wished he would.

'I'll go and pick up Tom from his flute lesson,' he said.

'Bit early.'

'Well, I need to call at Wraith Cottage on the way – to see Marguerite about a patient we saw today.'

'Couldn't you phone her?'

'She's deaf, remember?'

Jill remembered but wasn't so sure about that. In fact she wasn't at all sure about Marguerite, a middle-aged child with flowing silver hair. 'I understood that Jane interprets for her.'

Ash went out to the hall and came back putting on his leather jacket. 'Too complicated,' he muttered. 'Anyway, it's hardly satisfactory having her sister listening in to our private conversations.'

'Private?'

'Case histories and stuff—'

'Can I come, Daddy?' Fleur struggled to get out of the armchair, but Jill held onto her.

'Not tonight, sweetheart. Business.' Ash picked up a heap of files and blew a kiss as he went out. 'And you haven't done your piano practice, young lady,' he called back.

Jill sat twiddling a lock of Fleur's glossy brown hair, resisting the temptation to divide it into an even number of strands. Ash was still not himself; a bit of him was absent. He said it was preoccupation with the health centre. But whatever was really causing his distraction, he wasn't saying. And she'd given up asking.

Fleur rubbed her eyes and looked up as if sensing that Jill wasn't listening to the word she was stumbling over. 'Can I come to London to see Aunty Sophie with you, Mummy?'

'Not this weekend, pet. Perhaps next time. Or, maybe I'll persuade her to come here.' If I can lever her away from all her bloody dependants, she thought.

Fleur toyed with Jill's chunky gold bracelet. 'Has Sophie got a daddy?'

'A daddy?'

'Like you and Daddy.'

'Oh, a husband you mean.' Fleur nodded, sleepily. 'Yes. He's called Peter, you've never met him.' And I wish to God I never had to meet the bastard again, Jill thought. Since she and Ash had swapped their Dulwich house with Ash's parents for Cormorants, she'd only seen Peter if she absolutely had to. He and Ash weren't close friends and it was easy for Jill to visit Sophie when Peter was away. Occasionally she took the kids; she wanted them to know Sophie, and Sophie could never organise enough time to come over to the island. Funny how that little stretch of water was such a barrier. Solent Syndrome it was known as locally. But the main obstacle was Sophie's mother – demanding old cow – pretending to be helpless. And Peter – still going through his adolescence in his forties. Sophie – beautiful wild-haired Sophie – could have had her pick of men, and a couple of gorgeous kids, if it wasn't for Peter. And the worst thing was, Jill had encouraged her to marry him. She remembered young Sophie's bewilderment, her soulful Italian eyes heavy with doubt. Jill had laughed. 'Good-looking men are incorrigible flirts – doesn't mean anything. And he's chosen you – lucky girl – don't let him go!' A hot flush of guilt radiated through her. She pushed her glasses to the top of her head and fanned herself with Fleur's book. Sophie's biological clock was ticking away – it was time to get things sorted.

'Why hasn't Sophie got any little girls?' Fleur murmured. 'Or boys?' she added as if they were a mere afterthought.

Jill hugged her tight. 'Poor Sophie hasn't been as lucky as me.' She felt Fleur squirm and released her. Next weekend she would bully Sophie – challenge her to change her life. And a glorious vision of a final confrontation with Peter rose in Jill's mind.

Nick walked. He should be at work. But only furious walking could release the knots of tension that seemed lodged in his brain, his guts, his muscles. He'd woken drenched with sweat – not aching with desire this time – but after a violent nightmare, his head ringing with bitter words, heavy with grief and remorse. Fighting hard not to remember the details, he'd tried to sit and watch his mind, like the monks had taught him. But the turmoil was too great; he had to walk. He set off early from the shelter of Blue Slipper Bay, through the Botanic Gardens where the palms were lashing, along the cliff path to Ventnor, deserted by all but the hardy. Rachel's café wasn't yet open for business. Too early in the year for tourists, although Rachel always told him to pop upstairs to her flat for a cup of something if passing. It was tempting, he was sorely in need of a soft heart, but he knew he couldn't speak without breaking down. So he pressed on, pulling his woollen hat down over his shaven head as the east wind scoured his flesh.

When he reached Bonchurch, his clothes damp from sea spray, he bought apple juice and biscuits in the village store and sat on a sharp stone wall watching ducks rippling the glassy surface of the pond. He was calmer now, hadn't felt that bad for a while – even found himself wanting a drink – imagining what it would be like to go into a pub and sink a few beers. He hadn't touched alcohol for many years – no drugs of any description. The strange thing was he seemed capable of destroying lives whether he was on drugs or working against them. Perhaps that was his dilemma, he couldn't trust himself; he had no confidence that his best motives would cause no harm. Harmlessness, that's what the monks had lived by. And Nick had tried, was trying.

He rubbed his cold hands together. The knuckles were scarred – they'd thrown a few punches in their time. Not at people – he'd never hit anyone as far as he could remember – just a few walls and doors.

The ducks had gathered, watching him expectantly. Nick looked at his packet of chocolate digestives and back at the ducks. Maybe he should have chosen a healthier option.

CHAPTER 2

'February is such a sodden month,' Sophie commented, clacking shut the silver blinds, mourning the damson velvet curtains that used to blot out the grey street.

'Sodden or sodding?' Jill asked.

'Both.'

They sat watching the gas flames leap unconvincingly in Sophie's new granite and pebble fire. Peter's really. He was going through a minimalist phase.

'Do you like that thing?' Jill slurped her wine.

'Hate it.' Sophie thought with a pang of her old quarry tiled fireplace.

'Then why did you . . . ?' Jill raised questioning eyes, sighed and shook her head. 'Honestly, Sophie.'

Sophie shrugged, screwed up a chocolate wrapper and flicked it at Jill. 'Don't say *Honestly, Sophie*, like that. It reminds me of my sister.'

Jill smirked. 'Audrey would have said *Rrreally, Sophiaah*.'

Sophie giggled – Jill's impersonation was spot on. She could portray people's characters in a couple of words and a fleeting face change. She should have been on the stage.

Jill sighed again. 'You shouldn't let him have his own way all the time.'

'He always convinces me I'll like what he chooses, and I can't raise the energy to argue these days.'

Jill frowned. 'I'm worried about you, Sophie. You look worn out . . . even your hair looks less springy. Do you think you're going through your mid-life crisis?'

'At thirty-seven?' Sophie tugged at a couple of her corkscrew curls and then spread her hands on her knees. They did look tired, thin and veined. 'I was expecting it more around your age – mid-forties.'

Jill looked surprised, as if it hadn't occurred to her that she might be about to change. She sat, glass poised, obviously thinking this through. 'Maybe you're right. Perhaps we could have a crisis together.'

'Might as well – we've done most things together. Except having children.'

'They're highly over-rated.' Jill grinned and yanked the cork out of their second bottle of wine. 'They just create war-zones.'

'That reminds me, I saw Rose the other day, busking near Marylebone station. I didn't know she could do all that wonderful Irish fiddling stuff. She was with a group of young folk playing tin whistles and bodhrans. They had a crowd enthralled. I managed to say hello to her between jigs.'

Jill became alert. 'How did she look? What did she say?'

'She looked stunning and happy and she said, 'Don't tell Dad.' I thought it was probably all right to tell you.'

Jill relaxed. 'Ash wouldn't like it one bit . . . his precious girl. He wants her playing at the Albert Hall not in the street.'

'Is that what she wants?'

'God knows.' She pulled a face. 'Anyway, enough about my little darlings. I want to forget about them for the weekend. Where did you say Peter had gone?'

'New York – on an I.T. conference with his latest P.A. who looks like Arwen Evenstar—'

'Who the hell's Arwen Evenstar?' Jill spluttered.

'Elf queen – *Lord of the Rings* – you know how he's always loved fantasy.'

'Twat!' Jill said, filling their glasses. 'I hope you're not playing victim, Sophie – forsaken little wifey.'

'Don't psycho-babble me. I'm your friend, not a client.' Sophie broke a chunk of chocolate from the giant-size bar, hoping Jill wasn't going to lecture her.

'I'm being a friend – trying to help.' Jill pulled off her black boots then removed her jangly gold earrings and oversized rings and piled them in a heap on the coffee table. Shaking her strong auburn hair free of its clasp she spread herself over the sofa, legs apart, breasts free-ranging.

Sophie suspected she was settling in for a long night of soul searching. 'So,' Jill said, 'we've got the whole weekend to talk. What are you going to do about your life?'

'I don't know.' Sophie thought how pathetic her voice sounded. 'I suppose I should confront Peter and ask him straight out if he's having an affair with Arwen Evenstar. But he'll accuse me of paranoia like he always does, and maybe he's—'

Jill held up a finger. 'Okay, item one on the list. What else?'

'I have to make a decision about getting Mum into full-time care. She's getting dangerously vague and I can't take any more time off work.' Jill held up a second finger. 'I'm overstretched at the clinic and I've been asked to write a series of mental health lectures for—'

'Stop, right there.' Jill held up her whole hand as if she were halting traffic. 'Forget about all that for a moment. What do *you* want – for yourself – your life?'

'I don't know.' Sophie felt lately as if her mind were slowing down, unable to consider anything beyond getting through her demanding day.

'That's because you've lost yourself in other people's lives.' Jill waved her arm, sloshing red wine over her black linen skirt. 'You're enmeshed with the branches instead of identifying with the trunk.'

'What trunk?' Sophie wondered if she'd missed something.

'Your trunk – the strong centred core of yourself. You need to reroute your energy back where it belongs, and aspire to fulfil your own potential.'

'Heavens! I think you've missed your vocation.' Sophie could just see her, tongue-lashing the masses from her pulpit. Her eyes were blazing with fervour, her face almost the same colour as the pink silk scarf around her throat.

'It's time for a change, Sophie. Make a new life plan – set some goals. Ditch Peter Pan before he ditches you. Let's face it, he'll never grow up. That's why he's always fantasising over those drippy fairy types. Your sister can take over your mother – she relishes all things domestic. You could do anything, go anywhere. You're still young and attractive and it's not as if you have any kids to tie you down.'

'But, my job, my home, my family . . .' Sophie heard her voice tightening into a frightened whine, 'I'd be all alone. It's much too late, Jill. I'm thirty-seven. I should have left Peter years ago and tried to find someone who wanted babies.'

Jill leaned forward, her eyes gleaming. 'So, have a baby.'

'How?'

'The usual method – in and out. You're basically healthy – just a bit knackered at the moment. I bet you could produce at least one enthusiastic egg before your ovaries retire.'

Sophie felt laughter welling up inside which she knew could easily erupt as tears. 'Any sperm rushing to meet one of my eggs would probably screech to a halt and turn tail!' she wailed.

'Nonsense!' Jill swung her legs off the sofa, her voice husky with excitement. 'You can choose your own sperm. Don't even think about begging for a begrudging dribble from Peter. Get yourself a decent bloke – if you have to have one at all. They're not essential to the process these days.' She gulped her wine and reached for the bottle. 'You need a break, a good rest. When did you last have a proper holiday? Why don't you come and stay with us? You've never been over to the island – I'm sure you'll like it – Ash and the kids would love you to come. And Cormorants is a fantastic old house.'

Sophie sat with her mouth ajar, trying to take all this in. Jill had never sounded quite so vehement about all this before, even though she and Peter had grown to dislike each other over the years.

'Look,' Jill continued, 'I know I've sunk a lot of wine, and I've been fooling around. But I'm concerned about you. If you don't step back and take your life in hand you're going to burn out.' Her broad face with its dramatic expressions grew still with concern. 'You're not indispensable, Sophie, are you?' she said softly.

Sophie felt as if the frozen ground she'd been standing on for months was starting to crack. Branches snowed down around her, exposing her naked trunk to the world. Jill always did this, challenging her when she felt stuck, implanting possibilities for change. But what she was proposing this time was far too drastic – utterly impossible.

'Leave Peter? Leave Mum?' Sophie stammered. 'But . . . I couldn't do that to them. How would they cope?'

The Solent was choppy, the ferry lounge almost empty. Jill bought coffee and biscuits and sat by the window watching the darkening sky, dramatic with banked crimson-edged clouds. As the lights of the mainland receded, she turned her back on it, relieved. Ahead, the small island twinkled, beckoning – safe and contained. She felt it set limits for her – like a good parent. She couldn't wait to be back at Cormorants with Ash and Tom and Fleur.

She finished her coffee and ate a shortbread biscuit, feeling slightly queasy with the motion of the boat. She screwed up the cellophane wrapper and watched it unfurl itself again. Poor Sophie, every aspect of her life seemed fraught, her dilemmas insoluble. Jill didn't envy her one bit. 'Liar,' she muttered. The fact was she had always envied Sophie, ever since the day Peter introduced her to Ash and herself as his new girlfriend. 'Won't last,' Ash had said, used to the never ending parade of Peter's vapid girls. 'Course it won't,' Jill agreed, determined that this one should last – she didn't want Sophie to evaporate like the others. Jill had done everything she could to encourage them to stay together because *she* couldn't let Sophie go.

Jill put on her reading glasses, gathered the biscuit crumbs into a tiny heap and sorted them into pairs. She had been manipulative and dishonest. Even now she was trying to manoeuvre Sophie for her own advantage. A conspiracy had grown up between them over the years – largely unconscious on Sophie's part, Jill knew. They related as if downtrodden Sophie needed fixing, and Jill – decisive and clear – was the rescuer. But Sophie possessed a sound foundation of wisdom and compassion beneath the problems in her life that Jill had never been able to lay down. Sophie had studied transpersonal psychology because she wanted to understand her natural abilities in order to be more effective in her work. Jill had been desperate for explanations but knew she used her own behavioural qualifications to mask her own baffling psyche. Sophie was simply a good person. She was just overloaded, that was all, couldn't say no, always saw the reasons underlying everyone else's bad behaviour – including Jill's.

Jill sighed, brushed the crumbs away and took off her glasses. Nearly there – time to go down to the car deck. Somebody got up from another table and walked past her to the stairs. A big guy with a shaven head. Jill recognised him as the man who was renting a cottage at Blue Slipper Bay from Kyp and Evie. A recluse, they said. Jill wondered what he was hiding from; he looked a bit thuggish to her. She hoped they'd asked for references – Kyp and Evie had two little kids who ran wild on the beach down there.

It was the first time Nick had been over to the mainland – North Island as Evie jokingly called it – for almost a year. He wondered how he would feel boarding the ferry, crossing the sea. Would it awaken his desire to travel, to take off without a plan? But it hadn't. He'd simply felt lonely at the conference, in the midst of people who all seemed to know each other and never stopped talking. A couple of men had tried to chat to him between lectures but had soon tired of Nick's unresponsiveness. It wasn't that he didn't want to talk to them. The trouble was he had nothing to say. He couldn't raise much enthusiasm about the so-called guru that he'd come to see either. He seemed more like a life-skills coach than a spiritual master. It was his own fault – he obviously hadn't read the information properly.

He'd left the conference early and cycled around Portsmouth and the docks for a few hours, watching the ships and the construction of the Spinnaker Tower. Late afternoon, he bought fish and chips and ate them watching a group of lads hurling themselves over benches and along concrete walls on their skateboards. They were noisy and obviously uncaring about the destruction of the public area – but relatively harmless. As dusk fell, the skateboarders gave way to groups of youngsters who huddled together with a more sinister agenda, faces invisible under floppy hoods. Nick wondered how many of them were destroying lives rather than concrete. He wished he still had the bottle to saunter over and shock them into thinking about what they were doing, before it was too late.

Nick felt that in some ways he'd been lucky. He'd ended up with Iris – a tough-love foster mother who literally threw him out of her house if she found a fiver missing from her purse.

'I don't wanna hear no more of your crap,' she'd shout in her gravelly voice if he tried to deny it. 'And don't bother coming back till you decide to come clean 'cos the door will be locked.' Nick pretended he didn't care. Hands in pockets, he'd saunter off and doss down with the dregs until it was so unbearable he'd go back to Iris and apologise. And maybe he would have ended up as a dreg himself if he hadn't gone for that joy-ride, high on crack, and watched a mate lose his legs in the tangle of metal that was once somebody's expensive car. That was when Iris called in Marley – her nephew – who had eyes like lasers and cut through Nick's façade in a few minutes.

'You gonna live or die, man? It's your choice.' Nick had shrugged and looked at the ground. Marley had whacked him so hard that Nick's shoulder blades ached for a week. 'You understand what I'm sayin' here? It's no-one's choice but yours. And no-one gives a shit.' He pointed to Iris who was watching *Coronation Street*. 'Except her.' Marley grabbed Nick by the front of his tee-shirt and pulled him close. 'And I care about her. So yer gonna have to choose or fuck off out of her life.'

Marley seemed to have access to the worst of London's hell-holes and relentlessly dragged Nick into them. Nick thought he'd experienced some rough places before but they seemed like nursery school compared to the sewers that Marley took him. He was offered every conceivable concoction of mind-altering substances and bizarre physical gratification, in stinking dens where he couldn't always tell if the occupants were alive or dead. But Marley was thorough and unflinching – forcing him to make choices – driving him on until Nick was exhausted and physically sick with disgust. He didn't know whether it took days or weeks.

'Like cures like,' Marley commented eventually, when he had done with Nick and dumped him, weak and chastened, back on Iris's doorstep. And it had worked. Why Iris and Marley had bothered with him he would never know. But it changed his life – and it had given him a purpose.

'Hey, slap-head! You a perv or what?'

Nick looked up from his reverie. Several pale faces were turned towards him. Cans were being kicked around. What was he doing here amongst these kids, these buildings? He couldn't help them, not now. Nick got on his bike and headed for the ferry, thinking about Blue Slipper Bay.

Nick noticed the woman from Cormorants Health Centre sitting in the lounge on the boat. Her pile of dark red hair, fastened with a big clip, caught his attention. She was the osteopath's wife, some sort of psychologist, he thought. He'd seen them having supper at Kyp and Evie's fish restaurant last summer. The woman had stood out, an extrovert, laughing loudly, running on the sand with the children, her curvaceous body bouncing in its black bikini. There was something about her exuberance that reminded him of Keri – that ability to enjoy herself. But she didn't seem very lively at the moment. She sat hunched over, obsessed by something on the table in front of her. Nick recognised that concentrated posture – almost as if she were preparing a line of coke to snort. Of course she wouldn't be – not in public. But he couldn't help noticing that she seemed to be muttering to herself.

Nick got up and zipped his jacket, preparing to go downstairs to collect his bike. She glanced towards him without recognition, her expression inward, preoccupied. She looked so different; he wondered if he'd mistaken her for someone else.

CHAPTER 3

Peter left Sophie on the morning that her mother died. It was April the first. Dazed and exhausted, she concluded she was being fooled. She clutched her mum's new dentures in one hand and Peter's scribbled note in the other and squinted through the slats of the blind in the bay window. Peter was bound to show up soon, remorseful that he'd played such a cold-blooded joke. At midday Sophie stood shivering on the wet pavement, peering up and down the street. But there wasn't a soul about, dead or alive. She felt as if something inside her that had been slowly cooling down for years had finally frozen solid.

She went back inside the house and looked in the hall mirror. A ghostly woman with brambly-hedge hair and crater eyes stared back. Sophie couldn't think who it was. Her hands reached up and scraped back the brambles into a rubber band. Her arms tunnelled themselves into her coat sleeves and she picked up her bag to go to work, automatically locking the front door behind her. Halfway down the road the cardboard cut-out of herself checked to make sure it wasn't still wearing the rosebud pyjamas and matching slippers that Audrey had given her for Christmas. She'd spent several nights at the hospital counting Mum's stertorous breaths and her internal clock was confused.

The world was like a film set. Birds hung about in pairs; a couple of crows scuffled in the road, trying to unpick a flat rat from the tarmac; two blackbirds tutted at a cat whose only intention, tail aquiver, was to crap in someone's wallflowers. Dismembered plane trees aimed cold drips at her head as she passed. She could feel them tracking down through her wilderness of hair, watering the roots, chilling the forest floor. Sophie observed her body like a defeated parent surrendering to an autonomous child. It seemed decisive, untroubled by *what-ifs*.

At the mental health clinic, her colleagues glanced up from behind stacked case notes and murmured their usual greetings. Sophie wondered why they were being normal, but then it occurred to her that they didn't know her life had emptied out. She kept her coat on, knocked on her supervisor's door and announced she was leaving without notice. Her words whizzed round the office network faster than the worldwide web. The staff seemed upset and suggested she take time off to recover. As she walked out, the buzz of their concern hovered around her head like a swarm of gnats. How would they cope? Who was going to take over the twilight-zone patients that were Sophie's speciality? Had she become one?

Her body went into the first estate agent on the high street and put their house on the market. By the time she'd walked home, the first viewer was tapping her stiletto heels impatiently on the doorstep, beside Sophie's terracotta pot of dead daffodils. She was a thirty-something professional with no surplus time or flesh. She strode through the house, stabbed at her mobile, and the house was under offer.

'I can't believe she's actually done it.' Jill sat at the kitchen table still holding the phone. 'After all these years.'

'Sounds like she's had it done to her,' Ash remarked, taking the phone out of her hand and setting it back on its base.

'But she's walked out of her job and sold the house.' Jill stared at Ash as if he might explain it.

'Shock,' Ash stated. 'Her mother dying, Peter leaving—'

'Bastard. How could he at such a time?' She pulled the large gold hoops out of her ears and clanked them on the table.

'I thought you'd be glad. It's what you've always wanted for her.'

'But not at this moment when she needs support. But then he always was a real swine.'

'Was he, always?'

Jill jumped up and began clattering saucepans into the dishwasher. 'Yes, always—'

'Then why has Sophie stayed with him all these years?'

'She's too soft, too forgiving—'

'Perhaps she loves him.'

'He's a lecher, a womaniser—'

'You know that for certain, do you?' Ash picked up one of her earrings with his long fingers and began polishing it on a napkin. 'I still don't know why you feel you have to protect Sophie. She's a grown-up and can make her own decisions.'

'She can't!'

'Then why are you so adamant that Rose can look after herself? Aren't most men lechers given the chance?'

Jill, uncertain, leaned against him, feeling his bony frame. 'You're not.'

Ash held her by her upper arms and moved her away from him. He scanned her face with eyes that seemed sorrowful to Jill. She felt a prickle of anxiety in her solar plexus.

'You women,' he murmured, 'you don't realise . . .'

'What? What don't we realise?'

Ash dropped his hands from her arms and turned away. 'You think what men feel is simplistic compared—'

'Dad, come on. We're late!' Tom burst through the door, elbowing Fleur roughly in the chest in order to get in first. She yelled and hit out at him. Ash caught her arm.

'Now now, you two. We won't go to the cinema at all unless you behave kindly.' He smiled ruefully at Jill. 'See you later,' he said.

* * *

Nick noticed that spring had arrived in The Undercliff. Last year it must have passed him by – he didn't remember all this lush vegetation spiking out of the earth, fat sticky buds unfurling on the trees, carpets of camellia and magnolia petals littering the paths – pink and red and white. And there was so much yellow – daffodils, primroses, forsythia, cowslips, gorse. Cheerful, he thought. He stood by the lighthouse at St Catherine's Point and watched the swallows arriving. Such tiny birds – how could anything so frail survive that journey? And they didn't rest even when they reached land – they swooped low over the lush meadows catching flies. Survival – all living creatures seemed to have that inbuilt impulse. He supposed he must have it too. Why else would he have continued to live?

'You shouldn't have made those decisions while you were shocked and exhausted, Sophia,' her sister lectured, again. Audrey was the only person left to call her Sophia, now that both their parents were dead; everyone else called her Sophie. They were walking along the neat crematorium path to the garden of remembrance. Sophie preferred overgrown graveyards – she hoped Audrey wouldn't notice that she'd forgotten exactly where their father's rose was planted. She kept a step behind so she could stop when Audrey did. They stood looking down at his brass plaque for the statutory minute that implied reverence. Audrey sniffled and lifted the plastic urn out of her Liberty print shopping bag. She unscrewed the lid and, awkwardly, they both tipped out the contents. Sophie imagined that Mum's anxious ashes wafted around the base of Dad's rose checking it was him, before settling with a sigh, as if she'd damped down his ardour at last.

Sophie went back to Audrey's for tea. Audrey stood, tapping her nails on her anti-bacterial worktop while she waited for the kettle to boil. Her kitchen set Sophie's teeth on edge. Everything skidded and screeched. No buffering layer of grime anywhere. Did Audrey pumice her kids' fingertips so they wouldn't leave any prints?

'Did you really believe you could make sensible decisions while you were exhausted and shocked?' Audrey repeated. 'And depressed,' she added, in case Sophie had missed her point. Sophie sat, twiddling tendrils of her errant hair, watching Audrey brew Darjeeling tea leaves in a white china pot. Not a trace of a tannin stain. Did she douse everything with bleach before she went to bed?

'I *was* exhausted, and shocked,' she said, 'but not depressed.'

'How can you say that when our mother just died? And what about splitting up with Peter?'

'I didn't split up with Peter. He left me – the morning Mum died. Remember?'

'That's what I'm saying,' Audrey said, looking confused. 'Honestly, Sophia! I've not seen you cry once.'

'I cried for years when I was with him. I've done with crying.'

'If only you and he would talk.' She lowered her voice. 'I'm sure he'd change his mind about not wanting children. Women have babies much later these days. You could still have one – if you were quick.'

'Audrey, I wouldn't want a baby with him now. Not even if he possessed the last pair of fertile testicles on the planet.' Sophie could see by her sister's tightened mouth that she'd gone too far.

'Really, Sophia!' She glanced towards the sitting room where William and Joanna drooped silently over their homework. Audrey was five years Sophie's junior, but having achieved her desired status of wife and mother she lumped Sophie in with her children. 'I still can't understand why you have to give up your lovely home and your job – everything you've worked for.' She sat down at the kitchen table and poured the tea. She was never going to understand.

'It's because I don't want to be responsible for anything, or to look after anybody, for a while.' Sophie's words seemed to skitter across the polished table and drop off the edge. Audrey shook her elfin head, her dark eyes big with disbelief. She actually managed to look like Audrey Hepburn, which must have been a relief to their film-buff father, after Sophie had inconsiderately turned out to be as unlike Sophia Loren as was humanly possible.

'But, you don't *have* anybody to look after, now.' Audrey bit her lip, looking unsure about this conversation.

'Audrey, we've always been carers, you and I. We took care of Mum while she pined over Dad's philandering. I've spent my working life nursing the sick and counselling the tormented. And I lived with a husband who would wonder what he was going to eat if he found my head in the oven instead of his dinner.' Audrey's eyes began to water. Sophie reached for her soft hands, which got protected from the bleach with heavy-duty rubber gloves. 'And what about you, Audrey? You're trying to look after me now, as well as John and the kids.'

'It's what I want to do. That's what life's all about, isn't it? Caring for others.'

'But sometimes it's all one-way traffic.' Sophie felt as if she were lecturing Audrey like Jill lectured her. Audrey's eyes started to go blank as if she were focusing on an internal sermon about give and take. Sophie squeezed her hands. 'I need to change something.'

'But not everything, surely.'

'It's sort of symbolic. I had to sell the house anyway. It's half Peter's.'

'You could buy a flat. Keep your job, or go back to proper nursing. We're your family. The children will miss you if you go away.' Her tears were beginning to brim. Sophie, still detached, wondered about the critical amount of fluid the eyes could contain before the first drop spilled over.

'I don't know what I'm doing yet. I'm going to Jill's for a holiday before I decide.'

Audrey pulled her hands away. 'Jill! She'll only encourage you to do more impetuous things.'

'You make us sound like adolescents.'

'If it wasn't for her, you'd still be a ward sister instead of involved with all this mental stuff.'

'Jill's a qualified psychologist. Anyway, I wanted to get out of nursing. I was spending more and more time in my office filling out reports. I hardly ever got to see a patient.'

Audrey patted her little nose with a tissue. 'Sophia, promise me you won't do anything rash.' Her voice trembled with pathos. Sophie could just see her with a diamante cigarette holder, beguiling Cary Grant.

Rash, Sophie thought. Was there anything else rash she could do? Her old life was irretrievable. She didn't think she was clinically burned out or broken down, although that was the official verdict of those who knew her and felt the need to parcel her up and apply a label. Frozen – that was a more suitable description. And she just wanted to stop, find a warm place, and thaw out.

CHAPTER 4

'It's what students do, Ash. Don't you remember?' Jill was in her consulting room, filing away case histories, glad to be done with her day of listening to people's problems. Now here was Ash, his face falling into worry-lines over Rose.

'But she promised she was coming home for the bank holiday.'

Jill shoved the drawer of the filing cabinet closed, wobbling the jar of dandelions that Fleur had picked for her. 'When you were that age and you had the choice of a long weekend with your parents or hanging out with your mates, was there much of a decision to be made?'

'She didn't even say where they were going.' Ash shrugged his white coat off his shoulders, then pulled it back on again. 'Got someone else to see,' he muttered, turning away.

Jill caught hold of his arm. 'You've got to let Rose go. She'll only resent you if you question her life too much.'

Ash nodded thoughtfully. He put his hands on Jill's shoulders and squeezed them. 'I know you're right. But I feel I'm losing her and I fear for her safety. Rose is such a beautiful young woman. Sensual – like her mother.'

'Me? I'm an old trout!'

'You certainly are not. Do you think I don't notice the way men still look at you? Perhaps that's the trouble – I've seen it all before and Rose is a carbon copy.'

'I'm not sure what you're saying. Seen all what before?' Jill was beginning to feel unnerved by this conversation, guilty even.

Ash grinned suddenly, looking more like his old self. He ran his fingers through his short, greying hair, making it stick up on end. 'Oh, take no notice. I'm going through a cynical stage.'

Jill smiled, relieved. She locked her cabinet and they walked out into the reception area where Elgar's violin concerto was playing softly and a couple of Ash's students were still hanging about. She gave Ash a quick kiss on the cheek. 'Don't work too late,' she whispered. 'I like your hair like that, by the way. Trendy.'

Sophie stood on the balcony of Cormorants. It ran the entire length of the front of the house and seemed to beckon her from every room. The sea sparkled and glittered in the warm May sunshine, dazzling her eyes. People sat on the beach in clumps, absorbed in paperbacks, digital cameras or each other's bodies. A few hardy souls ran in and out of the foamy waves sweeping the crescent of sand.

Sophie couldn't remember spending more than a few hours at the seaside, mainly Brighton, when Audrey and she were kids. Family holidays were always endured in cities so their father could indulge his passion for stage and screen. Other children came back to school after the summer looking tanned and healthy. Audrey and Sophie acquired a pallor to their olive skin, and panda eyes from sitting in the dark. They lived over a small curlicued theatre in south London, which their dad managed as if it were the Coliseum. Strangely, he never encouraged his daughters to take up acting. He was probably aware there were too many predators like him in the business.

'I sometimes find it hard to believe I'm living here,' Jill said, manoeuvring a tray of drinks through the French windows. 'I was so determined to live the rest of my life in London after my rural childhood.' She placed the tray on a round mosaic-topped table and flopped into a canvas chair. 'I said I'd give it a year – that was nearly nine years ago.'

'But you don't regret it,' Sophie said, clattering ice cubes and fruit juice from the jug into glasses.

Jill gave her hoarse chuckle, acquired in her smoking days. 'Not one bit.' She leaned forward to peer through the ornate iron balustrade. 'Just look at them.' Ash, Fleur and Tom were playing cricket down on the beach, running barefoot, shrieking with fervour. 'I've realised kids and marriages need space to survive.'

'That's just what I was thinking before you came out – about the space. Just this little beach, and piled up houses,' Sophie stretched, inhaling a lungful of tangy air, 'and masses of sea and sky. I hadn't noticed space before. London seems so closed in.' She sat down and sipped her drink. 'You're settled for life then, you and Ash?'

'Looks like it. No reason not to. I wouldn't mind seeing a bit more of him – he's completely obsessed with the health centre. But I guess it's still early days, and it is his dream realised.' She pulled her black tee-shirt over her head, knocking her sunglasses crooked and her hair tumbling, then moved her chair so that a patch of sunlight settled on her freckled naked breasts. Sophie used to worry about that vulnerable pale skin but Jill was constantly casting off items of clothing, undoing buckles and buttons, as if freeing herself. They joked that she should join the naturists. 'Anyway, the kids are happy,' she continued, 'and we all love this decrepit old house.' She thumped a large foot on the floor. 'Dear old Cormorants. I understand now why Ash persuaded his parents not to sell, even though it still needs a fortune spent on it.'

Sophie smiled. 'I remember when you used to come here for holidays to your in-laws. You were always complaining about going to the Isle of Wight when you'd rather go to France.'

'Well, I felt resentful that Ash expected me to like it as much as he did. It's home to him, he was born here. You know how bloody-minded I can be if someone presumes something on my behalf.'

Sophie nodded, grinning. 'The first time I met you at that restaurant, you were intimidating a waiter because he asked Ash, or Peter, to sample the wine and ignored us.'

Jill let out a yelp of laughter. 'I don't remember that. But I do recall the first time I saw you, a dark-eyed dreamy girl, gazing at Peter like Juliet pining for Romeo. I sat and stared at you, struck by your colouring and that mass of curly hair.'

'My sallow skin and frizz you mean.'

'No. You looked calm and exotic. I was never calm.'

'I was probably petrified of you,' Sophie laughed. But she knew what Jill meant. Her young self was able to sit and observe – not in the detached way that she'd experienced lately, but from a tangible place of warm comfort. When she was a child she remembered asking her mum what that bit of her was called, needing a name for it, like tummy or heart. Later she'd heard her parents talking. 'Do you think Sophia's right in the head? Perhaps we should take her to one of those psychiatric doctors,' her mum had said. Her dad had laughed. But Sophie could see her mother's point, looking back. She had been a strange little girl, often silent and withdrawn. No wonder her mother regarded her with suspicion. These days she would probably be labelled borderline autistic. Audrey must have been such a relief – sweet and sensible. Sophie felt more at home in her inside world. In the absence of an anatomical name for that luminous part of herself, she called it her glow-worm, but kept it secret until she met Tiggy – and he knew exactly what she meant. He'd called it, *the place where miracles are born* – which sounded nice to her. Where had that feeling gone? When did it leave? Maybe it was an inevitable part of growing up. She reached out and squeezed Jill's hot arm.

'And now, here we are,' Sophie said, moved by the reminiscence of their first meeting.

'Here we are,' Jill repeated.

'Except, you ended up with a husband, children, home and profession. I, on the other hand, have nothing to show for all those years.'

'Think of it as a transition phase in your life – a pause between two stages.'

'I'm worried I might pause for ever.' Sophie imagined stopping a film in mid-scene, waiting for some reason to re-start the action.

'You've only been here a few days; don't think about going back yet.'

'I've nothing much to go back to. Just a few possessions in boxes at Audrey's. I told Peter to take whatever he wanted from the house, so he took nearly everything.'

'Then don't go. Stay until something inspires you.'

'I feel guilty about Audrey. She's missing Mum – and Peter and me.'

'She'll be fine. She's got her own family.'

'There's the question of money. I can't eat too far into my capital. I may never get back into the housing market.'

'You could work in the health centre. We'd welcome your expertise. You must come and meet the staff.' Jill grinned. 'We've got a part-time volunteer called Solveig. I'm terrified of her. I call her The Valkyrie. She's qualified to do remedial massage but she had a car accident and can't work. Ash has been giving her free treatment and she helps us in return.'

'Doing what?'

'Reception and supervising the students that come here to do their clinical experience. She also boards some of them in her house.'

'That's useful. Who else do you have?'

'An acupuncturist, a homoeopath, a herbalist, and a masseuse who uses aromatherapy.'

'Sounds pretty comprehensive. I'm sure you don't need me.'

'Oh yes we do. You know how hopeless I am in the twilight zone. This island is groaning with folklore and ghost stories. Even Ash is becoming bewitched.' She giggled. 'I'd have all the weirdoes sectioned.'

Sophie laughed with her. 'You have other skills.'

'I just bully my clients into changing their behaviour.' Jill shifted her chair to keep the sun on her breasts. 'And we seem to have acquired a healer on our team – Marguerite – extraordinarily beautiful.'

She frowned. 'Ash and the others think she's a gift but I can't fathom her. She doesn't appear to be deaf – unless she's an exceptional lip-reader, but she doesn't speak. Ash says she has x-ray vision, which is most unlike him and of course is complete nonsense. But she does seem able to make a deep connection with patients, straight to the unconscious – a bit like you.'

Sophie thought about people she'd worked with in their dark, confused states, helping them construct imaginative boundaries between realities, enabling them to cope with everyday life. She did this naturally, intuitively. But if she overstretched herself with the never-ending demand, she could become depleted, as if she were parting with her own life-force. She shuddered. Jill was watching her.

'I'm not ready,' she said.

Jill put her hand on Sophie's. 'Take all the time you need, otherwise you'll burn out again. You've made massive decisions in the last few weeks.'

'Most of them were made for me – Mum dying, Peter leaving—'

'You gave up your job and sold the house and let it all go. You never give yourself credit, Sophie.'

'No, I don't, do I?' she smiled. 'I'll never be Sophia Loren.'

Jill lifted her large breasts and let them flop. 'Big tits aren't everything. Anyway, Ms Loren has had her day. You've only just begun.'

* * *

Nick gazed at the obstructive rock on the path that once led to the hotel. He willed himself to lift it. Its flinty surface winked in the sun, as if challenging him. He braced himself, planting his legs firmly apart, bending at the knees, back straight as a weight lifter. He hooked his arms under its bulk, and taking a deep breath, hefted the stone onto the pile waiting to be reclaimed by the tumbled wall. His breath left him with a grunt and he wiped his hand across his face, feeling satisfied. He wouldn't have attempted that a few years ago, not before he met Keri and she initiated him into the joys of physical activity and the great outdoors.

He sat down on the grass and gulped half a bottle of water. The pungent smell of the ecosystem he'd disturbed filled his nostrils. He watched frantic woodlice and grubs dispersing and hoped he hadn't killed too many of the tiny creatures. Perhaps he should become a Jain monk and walk around sweeping the ground in front of him and wearing a mask, so as not to harm any living thing. Ahimsa – that was the word – the practice of non-violence.

The sun felt hot on his head. He must remember to get some sun-block. Keri was always on at him about that. He'd told her it was her antipodean dread of melanoma, and she didn't need to worry in the northern hemisphere. But she insisted on plastering them both with her slippery cream before they set off on their mountain treks, or canoeing, or cycling through disused railway cuttings. And he enjoyed massaging the lotion into her sturdy shoulders while she lifted her blonde hair off her neck.

He rubbed his eyes, got up and stretched, feeling the ache in his muscles. Walking to the top of the slope he surveyed the foundations of the old Wraith Cove Hotel, mapping out steps and terraces, lounges and dining rooms, long since carted away by demolition crews.

Nick was glad that Jane Newcombe had inherited this place. She told him she hadn't been aware of its existence before it became hers last year. She almost sold the land and the cottage and could have lost all the history that went with it. But then she discovered she'd inherited Marguerite too, and the old fisherman, Neptune, and the place had become priceless to her. Evie had introduced Nick to Jane as a gardener, which wasn't strictly true. He'd worked for Marley on landscaping projects for a few years before becoming heavily involved with youth work and the drug programme. He'd enjoyed it and learned a lot. Jane said he was just what she was looking for.

He'd pored over archive photos and plans with Jane and her husband Chas, and assisted by Marguerite and Neptune's memories, they pictured the past. Jane's dream was to retrieve the lost garden and rebuild the hotel to look as much like the original as possible. Her blueprint was beginning to emerge from the undergrowth. Nick turned to look at the grounds before him which extended to where the cliff dropped into the glittering sea.

There was Jane now, in the long red caftan that she wore when she was writing. She was wandering through the garden of Wraith Cottage at the cliff's edge, which she liked to do when she finished her morning's work. Neptune's yellow fishing boat was heading for shore, churning a white wake, bringing Marguerite home for lunch. Jane shaded her eyes, watching them approach and then turned as if searching for Nick. He picked up his shirt, waved it, and began to walk down to the cottage where a place at the table would be laid for him.

Jill lay awake thinking about what Ash had said. He was right; men did still look at her in that way. She had a sensual quality to her that attracted them; she'd known that since she was a young girl – far too young. Her cheeks flamed at the memory and she turned on to her side away from Ash. Her hands smelled of lavender oil. She and Ash had given each other a late night massage before making love, as Ash called it. She thought of it as having sex. Or rather, Ash having sex. She usually just lay there while he jabbed away, his hip bones digging into her flesh. It wasn't that she didn't want him. She just never felt really sexual towards him. But she loved him immeasurably, without question. He was her rock, the responsible family man, always so much older in outlook even though they were the same age. She wanted him never to change; hated the fact that Rose had the power to disturb his equilibrium. Psychologically speaking, she supposed he was the father she'd never had. And maybe one just didn't – or shouldn't – feel sexual passion for a father figure. She sighed, remembering the passion she had felt with so many men, without loving them at all.

Jill knew it was convenient to blame parents and go on blaming them for ever. She had no patience with that in others. But she also knew that she had never forgiven her mother for taking her to live in the commune where she'd grown up witnessing permissiveness that would be X-rated on film, even with today's standards. She hadn't realised, until she left to go to university, exactly what mixed messages she'd grown up with. Bits of her that she couldn't control had to go underground to find an outlet. It had been a struggle to try to untangle her crossed wires and construct some code of conduct for herself that would prevent her from alienating people with her destructive need to compete for men. She would have given anything to have been brought up in the much derided nuclear family.

She turned onto her back. The bedroom window was open slightly, the curtains moving in the breeze. She could hear the waves shifting the fine shingle on the beach. Ash was breathing deeply; the rest of the house silent. It seemed strange to have Sophie sleeping in the attic room above her. Jill smiled to herself. It was appropriate – Sophie had always been above her. She wondered how she was going to persuade her to stay. It was hard to believe that Sophie had accepted her marriage was over. She rarely mentioned Peter and appeared to be recovering well. It seemed such a massive step in the direction Jill had longed for.

She felt herself begin to drift. Maybe it really would work out.

CHAPTER 5

Ash showed Sophie around the refurbished health centre on the ground floor of Cormorants. She'd resisted being back in an environment where people came with expectations of healing. But he was eager for her to see it. She could feel his enthusiasm impressing itself on her.

'It's my dream come true, Sophie,' he was saying, throwing doors open, revealing ivory paint and pale leather couches. 'The house is plenty big enough and, living upstairs, we get the best sea view.'

'Does it pay?' Sophie asked, trying to show interest. 'I mean, Ventnor's a small place.'

'It's beginning to.' He swished open a blind in his own consulting room and unrolled a length of paper towel along his treatment couch. 'I'm fully booked – but then osteopaths usually are. And the other practitioners are getting busier by the week.' He took a crisp white coat out of a cupboard and flipped open his appointment book. 'You must meet them.'

'Jill told me about Solveig – The Valkyrie. And Marguerite – the healer with the x-ray eyes.'

Ash glanced sharply up, unsmiling, and Sophie wondered if she'd sounded flippant.

'They are both exceptional. Solveig's extraordinarily wise and Marguerite's a gifted healer.' He sounded edgy. 'Her sister brought her in for treatment, and Marguerite astonished us with her abilities.'

'What does she do?'

'It's difficult to know. She's silent, mute. She uses a sign language of her own and draws patients' hot spots for us to work with. Intuitive diagnosis, you might say. She goes in and out of the treatment rooms.'

'Isn't that disruptive?' Sophie couldn't imagine a strange woman walking in on one of her sessions and waving her hands about. Could send a disturbed patient right over the top.

'Wait until you meet her – I really can't explain.'

'Will she be here today?'

'Maybe. She comes when she feels called. Sometimes Jane – her sister – drives her over.' He smiled. 'Sometimes she comes by boat – an old fisherman called Neptune brings her.'

'She sounds quite a character.'

Ash looked thoughtful. He appeared healthier, more energetic than when she'd last seen him at Christmas visiting his parents in Dulwich. His skin looked lightly tanned and his hair was a bit spiky at the front.

'They've opened a new dimension for me – Solveig and Marguerite. You know how conventional I've always been. I'd appreciate a talk with you sometime about the cranial stuff I've been experimenting with – it's truly amazing. Some people experience repressed trauma from their childhood, or even past lives.'

'I've heard that can happen,' Sophie said. Ash's eyes looked slightly glazed as if he were recalling something compelling. Sophie hoped he was having proper instruction. 'You need to take care—'

'Jill scoffs at it,' he interrupted. 'She's as scathing about some of the complementary therapies as some doctors are about psychology.'

Sophie laughed. 'That's our Jill. She will only go so far.'

Ash came over and touched her lightly on the shoulder. 'I'm glad you're here. I know you understand these things.'

Sophie felt herself wanting to withdraw. She didn't want to talk about *these things* – not with Ash, not with miraculous Marguerite, not to anyone.

The door opened and a tall, broad-shouldered woman came in. Sophie guessed she was Solveig. She had white hair, swept back in a tight pleat. She glared at Sophie accusingly as if she were a patient arrived too early. Ash introduced them and she shot out a stiff hand to shake Sophie's. She could see why Jill found her intimidating.

'I'd better go and let you get to work,' Sophie said, glad to escape. Outside, a gardening crew was landscaping the terraces, manoeuvring railway sleepers and fully-grown palm trees. Jill was doing the school run and then had clients booked in. Sophie walked down the steep side street which emerged onto the esplanade. There were few people about; the holiday season as yet in low gear, beach shops open according to the weather.

She descended sandy steps to the beach. The sun felt warm against the sea wall. She took off her fleece and sat on it. The waves lapped and smoothed the sand and gulls paddled and bobbed. Men in yellow rubber dungarees hauled crates of crabs and lobsters in the small harbour, releasing the whiff of fish. She felt relieved to be alone. Jill and Ash's lives were hectic and they'd crammed in excursions to Osborne House, Carisbrooke Castle and The Needles. Sophie had viewed the Isle of Wight from the best and highest points and could see why they loved it here.

She'd had fun with Fleur and Tom too. Jill and Ash's children were a different species to Audrey's. When she read bedtime stories to Joanna and William they sat either side of her, smelling of shampoo and toothpaste. She'd ask them if they were enjoying the story and they'd nod, even if their eyes had glazed over. Fleur and Tom would yank a book from her grasp, hurl it away and fight over another choice. She could see Jill and Ash's point about encouraging free expression. On the other hand, there was something heart-warming about tucking up two sweet innocents, knowing they weren't plotting to kill each other when she went downstairs.

She sat, sifting sand through her fingers, wondering, yet again, what she was going to do. Jill and Ash both wanted her to work in the health centre, and stay with them. And Audrey had written to say she could live with her and John until she sorted herself out – when she returned to London.

Sophie remembered what Jill had said about being the trunk, not the branches. What did *she* want? She imagined sitting in her therapist's chair and still felt strong resistance. And living with her sister? She would have to be squeaky clean. She thought of the cacophony of London, the clogged air, and the under funded NHS clinic which barely scratched the surface of suffering. She didn't want to go back, but she still couldn't picture her next step forward.

She got up, brushed herself down and dawdled back up to the esplanade. A woman was rolling up the shutters outside *Rachel's Café*. She smiled at Sophie.

'I might as well open up,' she said, 'even if I only sell a few cups of tea. Better than sitting on my backside upstairs.'

'Well, I'll have one,' Sophie said.

'Good. Urn's rumbling. Come and join me. I'm Rachel, by the way.'

Sophie sat by the window in the empty café. It was painted in shades of blue and green that swirled around the walls, bringing the feel of the sea inside. The ceiling was draped with fishing net. Everything looked fresh and clean, but not sterile like Audrey's. She breathed in the bitter tang of coffee and the sweetness of freesias which stood in tiny cut-glass vases on each table. Lively Irish music was playing and Rachel sang along while she made tea and sliced bakewell tart. She wore her coppery hair pinned back at the sides with emerald butterfly clips. She had a sweet smile and her greenish eyes widened when she spoke. Sophie wondered if she felt as happy as she looked.

'I've seen you with Jill and Ash; are you staying with them?' Rachel asked, pouring tea into china cups, decorated with rosebuds.

'Mm,' Sophie said, biting into the delicious pastry. 'Do you know them?'

'A little. I know Rose best. She comes in with her pals to see my boys and borrow my CDs – loves Irish folk music like me. Isn't she a great musician? She's much in demand for local concerts.' She smiled. 'Also ceilidhs – her daddy doesn't like that so much. But I expect you know all that.'

Sophie nodded. 'Jill and I – I'm Sophie – have been friends for about nineteen years. Ash, and Peter – my ex – introduced us. I was a shy student nurse. Jill was great, so flamboyant, always encouraging me to try new things, wouldn't let me say no.'

'Yes, she strikes me as being quite, er—'

'Forceful?' Sophie laughed. 'It was what I needed.'

'Well then, that's lovely to have such a friendship. And will you be here long?'

'I don't know,' Sophie said, and found herself talking about her indecision. She rarely spoke to strangers about her private life, but all Rachel did was give her a few prompts and she was away. Rachel seemed all-accepting, without barriers. Sophie felt as if she'd known her for ever. Rachel listened until she'd talked herself dry and then refilled their cups and sat looking at her, thoughtfully. Then she reached across the table and gently tapped Sophie's arm with her fingertips.

'My advice is to gather together every shred of self-worth that you can summon, plus all your memories that make you feel good. Hold onto them like mad and fashion a new life for yourself doing what you want.' She tapped Sophie's arm again. 'Ditch the rest; it's not worth the headspace. And don't try to see too far into the future either. Do what's right for you now.'

'That sounds like the voice of experience,' Sophie said.

'It is. My husband left me with our two boys to bring up.'

'He did? I'm amazed, Rachel. You seem so, I don't know, confident and happy.'

'I wasn't at the time. It was the end of my world. I felt rejected and helpless.'

'So, how did you cope?'

'I woke up one morning and realised I was actually happier without Connor and his catholic hypocrisy so I decided to stop bitching and re-assess my own resources. I loved my boys; we had a roof but no income; I was a good cook. So I got jobs in restaurants, learned the trade and ended up here as manager. Right on the sea front – just what I wanted. And eventually I bought it.'

'And you achieved all that on your own?'

'I've had a few fellows. I like a bit of – you know. Wouldn't want a live-in one though. They're all right as long as they don't reside under the same roof. Then they start to have the same old expectations about food, socks and sex.'

Sophie found herself laughing. Rachel tapped her hand.

'You're free and resourceful – you could do anything, go anywhere.'

'That's what Jill says.'

'So where would you choose to be right now?'

'Actually, I'd like to stay here. I'm getting fond of this place. But I don't want my old job back. At least, not yet.'

'That's wise.' Rachel topped up their cups. 'Would you fancy working here?'

'Here?'

'I need someone to help me run the place for the summer. I can't pay big wages, but people leave tips and you can eat unlimited cream teas and apple pie. I expect all your grief has made you lose weight.'

Sophie glanced down at her body, which she hadn't given much thought to recently. 'I've always been a bit scraggy.'

'Scraggy! And who told you that?'

'Oh, my father, my husband, myself.'

'Rubbish! Most women would kill to look like you.'

'Oh, Rachel,' Sophie wiped her eyes on a napkin. 'I don't know whether I'm laughing or crying.'

Rachel got up as the door opened. 'Think about the job,' she said.

A large man came into the café and made his way to the table in the far corner. His head was shaven and he wore round, dark glasses. He was dressed in loose linen trousers, a shirt of the same stone colour, and leather sandals. A worn canvas bag hung from his shoulder. Sophie thought – noticing how quick her mind was to judge – that if he'd been wearing something black and hooded, she might have found him intimidating. Rachel took him a mug of coffee and stood, chatting quietly to him. He removed his sunglasses, gazed up at her, and then smiled, softening his serious face. As Rachel moved away, he took a notebook from his bag and started writing.

Sophie sat and looked out at the esplanade. More people were wandering about now, licking ice cream, dipping into bags of crisps. A family came into the café and sat at the next table, parents bantering, kids giggling. She felt a sudden flood of warmth wash through her, as if the frozen nub deep inside her was beginning to thaw. Here she was, sitting in a welcoming place with ordinary people, no-one expecting anything of her. She couldn't remember having felt this soothed for a long time. She recalled the feeling she had as a child of observing from her glow-worm place within, where everything was okay. Perhaps it wasn't dead after all – just trapped under the ice.

She got up and went to the counter to pay her bill. 'When can I start?' she asked Rachel.

Rachel beamed and pushed the money back. 'Now's a good time.' She indicated the shaven-headed man still writing at the table. 'Would you go and ask Nick if he'd like another coffee? And then I'll show you the ropes.'

Nick enjoyed sitting in Rachel's café. He liked Rachel, felt eased by her presence. She'd invited him to sleep with her once. He was attracted to her warmth and comfort but realised he must not mistake that for love. He knew what love felt like and he didn't want to hurt her, or himself. And he'd been honest, explaining the monk-like existence he'd been leading and his need for celibacy. She'd told him she didn't want a partner, just someone to have a cuddle with, if he should change his mind.

He wondered if he should stay away, but she said she liked him being there; the things he talked about interested her. She would come over to him and chat when there were no customers to serve. Or, if he was writing, she would just let him be. He told her he dabbled at poetry, but actually he just doodled and scribbled down some of his thoughts. He threw away his musings later. It was a method of clearing his mind when he felt overwhelmed by the past. A Vietnamese Buddhist monk whom he'd studied with in France had taught him to do this. 'And afterwards,' the monk had said, bowing his head with reverence, 'it is wise to sit on the earth and breathe and smile.' Nick tried to do this as well.

He glanced up from his notebook, distracted by a flicker of colour. A woman sitting at a table by the window was wearing a tee-shirt, the shade of apricots, which gathered the glow of the sun. Her dark hair sprang around her head and shoulders in little curls and ringlets as if it were full of joy. She was looking at Rachel, an uncertain smile tilting the corners of her mouth. Nick's mind, emptied by his writing, suddenly filled with the warm evening smell of olive groves and ripe grapes. She got up, went to the counter and whispered to Rachel who grinned and leaned forward to answer her. The woman turned to look at him, her dark eyes as unsure as her smile. She came over to his table, clasping her hands in front of her thin body.

'Would you like another coffee?' she asked.

CHAPTER 6

Jill sat in her BMW at the traffic lights in Newport, flicking through the tissue paper pages of the long airmail letter from her mother. Why couldn't the woman learn to use email? she thought, ignoring the fact that Stephanie worked in a tin hut clinic in Niger with barely enough surgical instruments for her work, let alone a computer. She glanced through the pages of detailed stories of the girls Stephanie had helped by repairing their torn bladders and butchered genitals. 'Pity she didn't think to look after her own daughter's vagina,' Jill muttered, flinging the letter on the passenger seat as the lights changed.

'I've got a vagina,' Fleur announced from the back of the car, as if Jill had spoken through a microphone. 'And you've got a horrible willy,' she added for Tom's benefit.

'I haven't. I've got a penis,' Tom retorted.

'It's horrible,' Fleur said.

'Yours is horrible.'

'Stop it,' Jill yelled. 'They're both nice.' But troublesome, she thought.

'Is that letter from my grandma in Africa?' Tom asked.

'Yes, it is. She says she might be coming home this year to see you.'

'Oh, goody,' Tom said, as if he remembered her. Strangely, Jill had always spoken highly of Stephanie to them, telling them stories of how their grandmother helped desperate people like the ones they saw on television.

'Rachel's Café, are you serious?' Jill looked as though Sophie had announced she was going to work for Al Qaeda. She dumped bulging supermarket bags on the kitchen table.

'Does that mean I can have free ice cream?' Tom asked, hopping on one leg in anticipation.

'And me,' Fleur said, tugging at Sophie's hands. 'And cakes too, Sophie.'

'I asked first.' Tom pushed in front of her, as if staking his place in the queue. Fleur poked him in the back. Sophie held them apart by their shoulders.

'I haven't started properly yet. And they won't be my ice creams to give away.'

'Go and change out of your uniforms and wash your hands.' Jill sounded snappy. Fleur and Tom looked at her with surprised eyes. Sophie tousled their warm heads which held that ancient smell of school, then gave them a gentle shove towards the door. They slunk out of the room, unused to taking orders. Sophie unpacked the shopping, while Jill crammed it into the fridge.

'Well, you did insist I could do anything, go anywhere,' Sophie said.

'When I said that, I had in mind more exotic climes. You know,' Jill rippled her hands and swayed her hips, hula-style, 'Polynesia or the Seychelles. And a café – well, maybe a beach bar in Barbados.'

'Ventnor is about as exotic as I can cope with at the moment. And the job feels like a relief – something I don't have to lug home with me like a yoke.'

Jill kicked off her shoes and sat down at the table. 'You're over qualified and you'll be bored witless once you've learned the routine. Imagine wiping tables after sticky holiday crowds – and piles of greasy washing up.'

'It'll be interesting, meeting people in a different environment. And Rachel's lovely – she gave me a pep talk which left me feeling as if I'd been resurrected.'

'Yes, she's good at the agony aunt stuff. Not very deep though.'

'I think I've had enough of deep for a while. She's refreshing. And she's a dumped wife too.'

'If I'd known you wanted a domestic job, I'd have offered to pay you to skivvy for me.'

Sophie thought Jill sounded miffed, as if she'd belittled her profession. 'I didn't have any idea what I wanted. This just came up. It's only for the summer.'

Jill sighed. 'Well, at least we get to keep you

around for longer.' She grinned, jumped up from her chair and gave Sophie a rib-crushing hug. 'You can still stay with us and you can always chuck the job if you don't like it. There are plenty of students looking for seasonal work.'

'I'd love to stay on here. But we need to sort out my board and lodging. I'll feel happier knowing that I'm paying my way.' Guilt had started to nag like a dull toothache after Jill and Ash's unremitting generosity.

Tom and Fleur barged through the kitchen door, dressed in shorts and bright tee-shirts. Sophie felt a burst of energetic love for them. 'Fancy a run on the beach you two, while Mum puts her feet up for an hour?'

Rachel opened the café according to the weather. The end of May approached, settled and sunny, and a constant trickle of people came in for drinks and light lunches and afternoon teas. Rachel despised anything shop bought and baked those four-and-twenty-blackbird-type pies that looked as if they might burst open and start singing at any moment. The smell of her cooking wafted out of the door, wrapped itself around unsuspecting passers-by, aroused their taste buds and drew them inside. One mouthful and they had no choice but to carry on eating. Her younger son, Aidan, helped out at weekends and after school. He was like his mum, extrovert and funny, with the same sweet smile. His hair was gelled in wayward clumps and his jeans expensively slashed. Sophie noticed the girls watching him, dreamy-eyed. Rachel's other boy, Patrick, was just finishing his last year at university. She was so proud of them.

'So you should be,' Sophie told her. 'And you're a great mum.'

Sophie soon got to know some of the regulars, locals from the beach shops, retired couples, loners wanting to bask in Rachel's warmth for a while, nattering mums with babies in buggies blocking the floor space.

'We get a few celebrities hanging out,' Aidan told her. 'Like when the rock festival's on in the summer. And loads of sailing people, you know? Ellen MacArthur's cool.'

Rachel sliced hefty slabs of bread pudding for Aidan to serve. 'And the island's always had its share of writers and artists,' she said.

'Anyone famous?' Sophie asked, pouring creamy custard, resisting the temptation to run her finger around the lip of the jug.

'Well, in the past, Tennyson lived here – poet laureate to Queen Victoria. Swinburne, Dickens, Keats – so many I can't remember – all came here to write.'

'Are they names of fossils?' Aidan joked.

'Ignorant child. I see a dirty table.' Rachel flicked a tea towel at his neat behind as he went. 'Creative people do come here. I suspect that's the nature of islands. We have Anthony Minghella, the film director. And have you heard of Jane Newcombe?'

'The novelist?'

'Uh, huh. She lives just along the coast at Wraith Cove. I'll point her out to you when she comes in.' She giggled. 'You'll see a lot of people scribbling in notebooks or sucking pens. I think they're aspiring to be the next J K Rowling and make millions.'

'The first time I came in here, there was a bald-headed man doing just that. I can't remember his name. You seemed to know him.'

'Oh, that was Nick. He writes poetry. Bit of a loner, but nice. Haven't seen him lately. He lives in a place which attracts artists and poets.'

'Here, in Ventnor?'

'No, Blue Slipper Bay, a bit further on from the Botanic Gardens.'

'Blue Slipper Bay – how romantic is that? And you mentioned Wraith Cove.'

'Yes, and there's Puck's Bay, where Neptune lives.'

'Neptune? Ash said something about him.'

Rachel plonked a cloth in Sophie's hand. 'Can you clear those tables? Aidan's been waylaid by his fans and I need to cut cakes.'

Sophie found after a day's work at the café her legs and feet ached. She felt physically tired instead of mentally and emotionally exhausted. It was bliss to sink into bed in her attic room and let her body relax. And it was freeing to have so few possessions to care for. Just her clothes, a few personal items and photos. And she had decided to bring her miracle box. It sat on the chest of drawers unopened, but it was comforting just to have it there adding to the atmosphere. Her mind had room to listen to the rhythm of the sea, the wind buffeting, and the early morning birdsong. She felt as if the space around her had opened up a space within.

The only anxiety that niggled at her mind was an underlying tension she was picking up between Jill and Ash. It broke the surface this evening at dinner. Fleur and Tom were tired and tetchy, goading each other. Usually Jill and Ash let them sort it out for themselves, unless it became life-threatening.

'I hate you, you smell,' Tom muttered.

'And you're a stinky boy,' Fleur retorted. Tom nudged her arm as she was about to take a drink of water and her beaker tipped over. She screeched and hit out at him.

'Right, I've had enough!' Jill got up and yanked both of their chairs back. 'Go to your rooms and don't dare come out until I say.' She propelled them out of the kitchen door and slammed it. Both children could be heard wailing their way up the stairs.

'That was a bit harsh, wasn't it?' Ash said, his fork of spaghetti suspended in mid-air throughout the drama.

'If you thought you could handle it better, then why didn't you?' Jill snapped. She unclamped her hair, gathered it more securely and re-clamped it. Sophie noticed her hands were trembling.

'I didn't want to interfere.'

'Why not?'

'Well, parents united, that sort of thing.' He grinned uncertainly.

'That's just it, Ash. We're not united are we? You leave everything up to me.' Her voice was jumping octaves. She looked near to tears. Sophie was astonished; Jill was always so cool around her children.

Ash put his fork down. 'That's not fair. I do my share.' He glanced at Sophie. 'I'm New Man personified.'

But Sophie could see his joking attitude wasn't working. Jill plonked herself down in her chair with such force Sophie feared for its safety. Jill filled her glass to the brim with wine.

'You notice them when it suits you. You think about nothing but the health centre.'

'That's not true. What are you talking about?' His voice had toned down. This was getting serious.

Sophie got up from the table and filled the kettle, unsure whether to go or stay.

'You know what I'm talking about. Your preoccupation with this regression fad. You shouldn't be messing with it. It's a dangerous, fantasy world, full of disturbed borderline cases.' She pointed at Sophie. 'She'll tell you. Look at the state it got her in.'

'Hold on, Jill.' Sophie felt she had to speak up.

'That's not true. It didn't get me into a state – not on its own. It was an accumulation—'

'Sorry, I didn't mean it like it sounded.' She frowned at Sophie. 'It's just that Ash was never interested in this when he worked in London and he has no experience or proper training. It's risky to bring up repressed stuff with people. Once it's done, you have to know how to handle it.'

'Prejudice is your problem,' Ash growled. 'You want the health centre to be respectable with no *lunatic fringe*, as you so tactfully put it.'

'Well, I think that's reasonable. We agreed that we want to gain the confidence of the public and build up the business.'

'But you won't even consider hypnotherapy or reflexology. The homoeopath only scraped in because he cured Tom's hay fever.'

'I don't know what's got into you! This is a small community, an island. We said we'd stick with what we're sure about. People talk, word spreads. You're always telling me that. I don't want weird people wafting around spouting esoteric nonsense.' Her voice was getting hoarse.

Ash sat back and folded his arms. 'I see where this is going – you've been antagonistic ever since Marguerite came on the scene, haven't you?'

'All right. Yes, I have. I don't want her wandering about. She's like something out of a fantasy film.'

Sophie lined up the coffee cups, wondering if Marguerite knew Arwen Evenstar and if Ash had been bewitched by the elf queen spell like Peter.

'Have you any idea of the help she gives us?' Ash glared at Jill, her eyes blazed back at him. He got up and threw his napkin onto his congealing spaghetti bolognese. 'Then maybe you should bother to find out.'

Sophie felt shocked. Not so much at what was being said, but by Ash. She had never, in all the years she had known him, seen him furious like this. She dithered, shuffling the kettle and the coffee maker about on the wooden work top. Perhaps she should just go. But, before she made the decision, it was Ash who stalked out, slamming the door behind him.

Nick walked along the coastal path to work. In the winter he seldom saw another person, but these fine mornings of early summer enticed others from their beds as if to savour the exhilaration of the cliffs before the captivity of their working day. The meadows were bright with buttercups and daisies. Red clover sweetened the breeze and the hedgerows chattered and hummed with birds and insects. Piercing white gulls swooped through the blue, and pink sea thrift trembled on every ledge.

Nick was glad to be working on an open air project. Each day he set himself a task that demanded all his strength and concentration. It gave him a sense of achievement and completion with no clogging residue to worry over. Today it was a felled sycamore. He began by hacking down to expose the roots. A smell of damp and decay released itself from the dark earth, reminding him of places he'd visited when he worked in London. When he applied for the job in drug rehab, he'd had an idealistic vision of working in a purpose built unit, conducive to healing. But he'd spent most of his time closeted in dead-aired rooms with youngsters as sullen and obstinate as he'd been. It was their choice whether they stayed in the programme. If they chose to opt out that was that. But Nick took it upon himself to search in back-alleys stinking of urine and vomit, trying to find those vanished children. He believed in them, like Iris had believed in him. That's when he'd decided to adopt the same sort of tactics that Marley had used. He'd taken such risks, broken all the rules.

So much heartache. He wondered about the broken parents of those lost kids. What must it be like to raise a child only to have them disappear, or turn into a haggard, desperate stranger? He thought about his own child. Lara, he'd named her. The pathologist had asked him if he would like to know the sex of the foetus. Nick preferred to think of her as his unborn daughter. Lara – that was the name he and Keri had chosen if their baby should be a girl.

He shuddered, dispelling the little sorcerer from his mind and re-focused on the stump of the sycamore at his feet. He lifted his pickaxe high in the air and thumped it down into the stubborn roots. He felt the force of the blow reverberate throughout his body and tasted flecks of salty earth on his lips. He remembered punching his fist against the bleak wall of the mortuary after he'd been to formally identify Keri's body, vowing never again to build up the potential for such anguish.

CHAPTER 7

Jill hovered in the doorway of Ash's consulting room while he tidied up between patients. He glanced up.

'I'm running late,' he said.

'Two minutes.' Jill shut the door. They didn't usually interrupt each other at work. 'I was just wondering – perhaps it's a good thing Sophie's taken this job at Rachel's. It means she won't be rushing back to London too soon. What do you think?'

'Possibly.' Ash unrolled fresh paper over his couch. Jill was aware of a terseness in his voice since their row – even though they had both apologised.

'I'm, er, just a bit concerned for her – working in a café – that's all.' Concerned wasn't the right word – jealous was more accurate. Rachel was an attractive, well-liked woman – one of those big-hearted souls who had time for people. She even let a group of older teenagers use the café in winter, when it wasn't officially open, to keep them from hanging around Ventnor High Street. Rose used to spend a lot of time in there before she went to university. Jill hadn't minded that, but now it would be Sophie.

'I wouldn't have thought you need be concerned. Sophie seems to be recovering well.' Ash stretched his arms above his head.

'Yes, but—'

'Look, why don't you stop trying to run Sophie's life for her? You're her friend not her guardian.'

Jill bit her lip. She didn't want Ash to talk like this.

He let his arms fall and gazed at her, frowning. 'You're always accusing me of interfering in Rose's life. Maybe you should look at your relationship with Sophie.'

'That's different,' Jill felt affronted. 'You're a parent.'

Ash raised an eyebrow. 'You'll have to go now.'

'I love The Undercliff when it's misty,' Rachel said. 'It's magical. I swear it shifts its shape.' The day had begun with panache but a sea mist had sneaked in, blotting up the sunshine, driving people inland to seek sheltered amusements. Rachel was peering out of the café window. 'Shall we go for a walk?' she asked.

'Sounds good – if you're sure there's nothing for me to do here,' Sophie said.

Rachel glanced around. 'Everything's prepared. If the mist lifts we can scoot back and open up for snacks or afternoon tea.'

They walked along the esplanade and up onto

the coastal path. Sophie saw what she meant about the mystique. The sea and sky blended into one pale blur. A treacherous fringe of grass overhung the cliff so you couldn't be sure of the edge. Sudden slopes loomed ahead.

'Lots of foul deeds have occurred along here,' Rachel said cheerfully. 'Wars, smuggling, shipwrecks – take your pick. Not to mention the old TB hospital and suicides. I've been on the ghost walks – great fun. Do you believe in all that, Sophie?'

'I don't disbelieve. I've worked with people who've had strange experiences that defy science.'

'And you? Have you had any?'

'Well, I call it a *change of atmosphere*.'

Rachel put her arm through Sophie's and shivered. 'This misty, moisty morning is perfect for spooky stories. Have you seen *The Exorcist*?'

'Possession's a murky area,' Sophie replied, wondering whether she really wanted to get into this.

'Can it really happen though?'

'The psychological view is that a traumatised person could disown part of their personality and then sense it as something trying to take them over.'

'And the non-psychological view?'

'A so-called discarnate entity has actually taken over and needs to be exorcised – deliverance it's called these days.'

Rachel shuddered again. 'Have you ever done that?'

'I've experienced it with a specialised team of people.'

'Jesus! Nothing that exciting has ever happened in my café. What else have you done?'

Sophie realised she didn't mind talking to Rachel about her work in this light-hearted way. Maybe she had always taken it too seriously. 'Well, people can get obsessed with past life experiences. Mostly that's okay. But disturbed patients can get confused as to their real identity and need a bit of help.'

'A bit! You make it sound like giving someone a hand with the housework.' They stopped, panting, at the top of some steep steps and leaned on the rail looking out to sea. 'I take it you believe in reincarnation then.'

'Not in the conventional way.' Sophie smiled. 'You must think me awfully wishy-washy. But I've listened to so much stuff from people, that I'm open to anything, but absolutely certain about nothing. I suspect some stories are genuine and some are from minds lacking boundaries, picking up experiences that just float around – like radio waves.' She looked out at the blurry sea. The lighthouse beam swept round from St Catherine's Point, illuminating the swirling mist.

'You sound a bit like Nick, that bald-headed guy that comes into the café. He says that everything that has ever been or ever will be is present in this moment. I haven't got a clue what he means, but I like listening to him.' Rachel pointed up ahead.

'After we've walked through the Botanic Gardens, if the mist still isn't moving, we could go down to Blue Slipper Bay and I'll show you where he lives. You won't believe it.'

'Why won't I?'

'Wait and see.'

They set off again, Rachel pointing out different places along the cliff path where various hapless folk had ended it all.

'I've been coming here since I was small,' she said, when they reached the gardens. 'I can just about remember it being a pile of rubble after the old chest hospital was demolished. It's so haunted – all those poor tubercular souls who died here.'

'It's beautiful,' Sophie said, impressed by the profusion of plants and shrubs, spicing the moist air with their smells.

'Do you sense anything?' Rachel asked. 'The unquiet dead?'

'No,' Sophie laughed. 'I'm not really psychic. My mind easily connects with the unconscious mind of others – a sort of transpersonal thing – that's all.'

'That's all? I think I'll stick to cream teas.'

'Well, look how easily you identify with people, Rachel. They flock to tell you their troubles, just like I did.'

'Oh, I just enjoy a wee bit of gossip. Now, over there, that's where Jane's poor old dad fell off the cliff. Jane's the author from Wraith Cove, you haven't met her yet. He'd had a stroke and they think he lost his balance.' She looked up at the sky. 'I think we could just nip down to Blue Slipper Bay before we head back.'

They threaded their way through an overgrown narrow path close to the edge of the cliff until they came to a fork. Rachel kept up her chatter.

'Most people head inland at this point. But it's all right as long as you know where you're going. There are some lovely coves and bays along here in The Undercliff, if you don't mind a bit of a scramble.'

They followed the path down and through a rocky promontory. Sophie rounded the corner and there, to her surprise, was a tiny horseshoe bay. The tide was not at its highest. There was a yellow strip of sand, some piled rocks, a strip of concrete path, and built against the cliffs, three small buildings with wooden balconies on stilts. The right-hand one was painted white with faded blue shutters, the middle one was watery green with lavender shutters, and the one on the left, pale terracotta and turquoise. Beyond them, in the curve of the bay, a blue fishing boat stood on a concrete slip-way, a jumble of nets and floats beside it. At the head of the slip-way stood a long wooden cabin with a terrace sheltered by a canvas awning. The stable door was half-open and it had a blackboard fixed to it advertising fresh lobsters and crabs. Weather beaten pink geraniums trailed from pots and balconies, and amongst the buildings grew a profusion of palms and ferns and giant cacti.

And then there was a jagged timber breakwater and more tumbling cliffs.

'What a picturesque place,' Sophie said. 'It looks as if it should be on the shores of the Mediterranean.'

'When the sun shines it is like a little Spanish cove,' Rachel said. 'Let's see if Nick's home. He can make us a cuppa before we head back.' She walked up to the white cottage and tapped at the wooden door underneath the projecting balcony.

'Who is it?' a gruff voice called from above, and Nick's shaven head appeared over the rails, making Sophie think about trolls.

Rachel stood back and looked up at him. 'You've got visitors,' she said. 'Get the kettle on.'

'Come on up,' he said, and disappeared. They went through the door and up a wooden staircase, through a hatchway in the floor and emerged into a square room. It was almost empty, just four upright chairs and a table by the French doors to the balcony. A single bed – complete with ginger cat and a rolled up sleeping bag, stood against the inner wall. There was a woodburning stove in the stone fireplace, bare floorboards and a few shelves. Everything beyond the windows was misty sea. Sophie felt as if she were on a boat. Nick stood looking at them as if he didn't quite know what to do. 'Kettle's on,' he said, indicating a doorway through to a tiny kitchen.

'Great,' said Rachel. 'It's about time you made me one for a change. Do you remember Sophie?'

Nick held out his hand.

'We've met before,' Sophie said, shaking his rough hand, 'briefly – my first day at the café.'

'I remember.' His voice sounded hoarse. 'I haven't been in recently. I caught a cold, out fishing with Neptune. Neptune's seventy-six and never catches colds.'

'You do look a bit peaky,' Rachel said. 'We wondered where you'd got to. So we thought we'd better come and find you.'

Sophie wished Rachel hadn't included her in that statement, she hardly knew him, and he didn't look too friendly with his stark hairlessness. Sophie was aware of her own hair, which had frizzed up like a bush with the damp air. She had more than enough for both of them.

'Tea?' he said. 'I don't have any coffee. Make yourselves at home.' He went back to the kitchen. They took off their wet fleeces and sat at the table. Nick brought in mugs of tea.

'How do you like working for the Earth Mother of Ventnor?' he asked Sophie.

Rachel snorted and Sophie laughed. 'I'm enjoying it, very much.' She gazed around the room. 'Is this a holiday let?'

'No, I live here.'

'What, all the time?' she wondered if this sounded rude, but she was surprised. It looked so temporary.

Nick nodded. 'All the time.'

'Isn't it dangerous?'

Rachel tapped her arm. 'It is very dangerous. You should see it here in a storm. The shingle flies against the windows – it's terrifying.'

'I close the shutters, the glass is toughened and the structure is sound.' Nick said. 'These little houses are built of heavy stone underneath their rather charming exteriors.'

'But the waves come right up underneath it sometimes, Sophie. Can you imagine that at night?'

Sophie wondered if Rachel had experienced this. Was Nick one of her non-live-in men? 'And do other people live here – in Blue Slipper Bay?' she asked.

'Artists and writers rent the middle cottage from time to time. Kyp and Evie live in the end one most of the year and they own this place. They catch fish, run a little bar, sell sea-food suppers on their terrace and let out rooms in their cabin.' Nick broke off to clear his throat as if he wasn't used to talking so much. 'But it never gets too busy down here. It's a bit of a trek from the road and you can't drive down. The only other way is the way you came, over the cliffs.'

Sophie sipped her tea while Nick and Rachel chatted. He was telling her about his work for Jane Newcombe, re-discovering the lost garden at the old Wraith Cove Hotel. It sounded like hard work. But he was a big man; his body looked muscular under his grey track suit. His hands were work-scarred, the nails blunted. He seemed nervous, toying with a plaited cord tied around his wrist, twisting it constantly as he spoke. She wondered how he felt about them being there. His voice was pleasant, slow, with the rasp of his cold. She was only half listening to the conversation. She was imagining what it must be like living here alone in the winter with the sea and wind raging outside. She pictured Nick sitting with the fire roaring in the chimney, the cat at his feet. There was no television or stereo in sight. Perhaps he was a reader. Sophie glanced around; there were no books on the shelves. The only ornament was a flaky wooden Buddha on the mantelpiece that looked as if it might have been rescued from a junk shop. There was no clue to his interests, his personality. The place was spartan.

Was this what she meant when she told Audrey that she didn't want to look after anybody or own anything? Had it been an attempt to solve her own sense of being overwhelmed – get rid of everything and start again? Had she been too drastic? Perhaps she should have stayed and tried to take control of her life instead of slamming the door on it and chucking the key.

Was Nick obliterating his past too? It looked as if he'd erased everything, even his own hair. Or did possessions and people hold no interest for him? He seemed at ease with Rachel. He was gazing at her, his brown eyes steady, the whites slightly inflamed. She was tapping his hand as she spoke, like little transmissions of warmth.

Nick's eyes suddenly moved to Sophie's face. She felt as if she'd been caught out. Her face flushed but she couldn't look away. He blinked slowly without his gaze wavering. She had a sudden pang of intense longing, like homesickness. Not for her childhood home or her home with Peter – just home – her home. And she didn't know where that was.

A ray of sun lit up the room. Rachel put her mug down.

'The mist's lifting. If we hurry back, we'll just make it in time to open up for light lunches.'

Sophie got up. 'Thanks for the tea.'

Nick smiled, and Sophie remembered the transformation of his serious face that she'd witnessed in the café. 'Come again,' he said, as he followed them down the stairs. 'Come over one fine evening and we'll have a fish supper at Kyp and Evie's.' His voice sounded as if he meant what he was saying. Perhaps he hadn't minded their surprise visit after all.

Nick had been pleased by Rachel's unexpected visit but uncomfortable that she'd brought Sophie with her. He felt unprepared, not that he had anything to prepare if he'd known she was coming. It was more to do with his mind. He'd been alone for a few days, recovering from his cold. It was hard to speak when you hadn't spoken to anyone for such a long time.

But Rachel had diffused any awkwardness with

her easy talk. She entertained them with tales of the café clientele and the antics and achievements of her boys. And he answered her questions about the progress of the gardens at Wraith Cove. Rachel enjoyed knowing everybody's business but he knew she was no gossip. He thought how attractive she looked, pink-cheeked and healthy from her walk.

While they'd chatted he was aware that Sophie didn't say much unless asked directly. She sat still, her long ringless hands clamped around her mug. She wore a plain white shirt and black trousers, the same as Rachel's – it must be their uniform for the café. He noticed her gaze flickering from her tea to his face and then around the room. Her eyes were a heavy, rich brown, a deeper shade than his. Her hair was dark and dense, but not quite black; a few silver strands threaded through it. He'd wondered how old she was; it was difficult to tell with women these days. She could be about thirty, or maybe a bit older – around his age. Tiny sparkles of moisture were trapped inside her curls from the sea mist. She attempted from time to time to smooth it back, and he glimpsed the glow of amber earrings, like two plump teardrops. He pondered on the amount of time she must spend trying to tame so much unruly hair and wondered what she must think of his own bald scalp. He imagined she was thinking he lived a frugal life, devoid of any comfort or interest. He noticed her glance at his empty shelves and thought of the writing that he destroyed; the books he read and gave to Oxfam. He couldn't keep anything. She must think I'm a boring, dried up old sod, he thought, and realised that he cared about her opinion of him.

Only half listening to Rachel's banter, words had begun to form in his mind, fluttering inside his skull, distracting him, as if they longed to be set free. He wanted to tell the two women that he knew about waking up in the night and feeling awash with joy that someone you loved was breathing beside you. He wanted to say he'd experienced that moment of knowing that you are deeply loved simply for being who you are. He realised he was twisting the woven cord on his wrist around and around.

He'd glanced at Sophie. Her slender face was calm. She was watching Rachel, but it was as if she were present only on the surface, the rest of her focused inside herself. Rachel mentioned that Sophie had recently split up with her husband. Well, she would have a lot to consider – especially if, like Rachel, she had children to raise. Why should she care about his experiences? Suddenly their eyes met and he sensed he was seeing her self-protection, feeling her defences. He understood the need to withdraw from other people's emotions, to disengage from the possibility of pain.

Then Rachel had stood up, the mist was lifting. Nick, having broken his solitude, found he didn't want them to go. He followed them down the stairs, stumbling over his words, asking them to come over one evening for a fish supper at Kyp and Evie's. He thought he sounded too eager.

And now, a different atmosphere seemed present in his room, as if something feminine had been left behind. A mixture of warm dampness and a spicy fragrance softened and filled the familiar emptiness.

CHAPTER 8

'What's wrong, Jill?' Sophie had just got the kids to bed and was sitting on the sofa watching her putting toys away. Something had happened to Jill's energy. She seemed closed in on herself, less expressive. Earlier, her eyes had difficulty keeping focused while Sophie recounted her visit to Blue Slipper Bay. Perhaps she was exhausted after her busy day.

'Oh, nothing really.' Jill closed the doors of the pine cupboard with her foot as if she couldn't be bothered to bend down. 'Tired, that's all. And I've been thinking about this job at the doctors' surgery. The GPs are keen to acquire a behavioural psychologist on their team. It would only be one or two evenings a week.'

'Would you like to work there?'

'Yes, I think it would be good to strengthen relationships with the medical community. They send Ash a number of referrals.' She sighed and sat down in the armchair opposite Sophie. 'I was going to ask you if you could look after Tom and Fleur, if I decide to do it.'

'Well, I could. But why can't Ash?'

'I couldn't rely on him. He has emergencies and student tutorials some evenings.'

'Then, of course I will.' Even as Sophie spoke she noticed a sinking feeling, as if her head were agreeing to something that her heart didn't want to do. And she knew this wasn't what was really on Jill's mind. 'Is everything okay now – between you and Ash?' She hadn't seen them talking together since their flare up.

Jill shook her head. 'We apologised to each other but we're not communicating properly. I know he's avoiding me as much as possible. He doesn't want me to question him about what he's up to.' She raised troubled eyes. 'I'm so scared that he's going to ruin everything, bring the health centre into disrepute.'

'Is it really that serious?'

She shrugged, biting her lower lip.

'Why don't you call a practitioners' meeting to discuss how everyone thinks the centre is progressing?'

'We do that regularly. Nothing came up at the last session and I felt I couldn't raise the subject without seeming disloyal to Ash. They all seem happy with Marguerite's involvement.'

'And nobody is trained to give supervision?'

She frowned. 'That's the problem. Some of these other disciplines have little or no practitioner back-up. You know how dangerous that is, Sophie, from working in the NHS. Look at all the doctors and nurses who have break-downs.'

'So, what's the answer?'

'I wondered whether you'd talk to him. He trusts you.'

'Jill, I don't know whether I could handle it just yet—'

'Please, Sophie, just a chat.' She looked away. 'We've always been there for each other, haven't we?'

Sophie couldn't believe Jill was saying this. She must be feeling really desperate. She didn't want to talk to Ash, but Jill was right, she'd been there for her, every step of the way. 'Okay, I'll try.'

Jill's expression brightened. 'He's down there now, doing paperwork.'

'Now!'

'Please, just a tentative chat, that's all. He's such a good osteopath, I couldn't bear to see him mess it all up.'

Sophie looked at Jill's beseeching face and she couldn't say no.

She went downstairs and let herself into the health centre. She stood in the reception area. The light was dim; the smell of sandalwood oil hung in the air. At first she thought nobody was there and she'd missed him. Then she heard a sound and noticed that Ash's consulting room door was open a fraction. She moved towards it but then heard his voice. He must be seeing a client. What a good job she hadn't walked in. She felt relieved that she had an excuse now not to talk to him. But then she heard a strange sound; a woman's voice crying and mumbling. Sophie couldn't make out the words but it sounded as if she were pleading.

'We've got to stop this.' She heard Ash's voice, low and desperate. 'Do you understand? It's got to stop.'

Sophie felt stunned; her heart pounding. She didn't want to hear any more. She turned to creep away but Ash suddenly burst out of his room and saw her. He ran his hands through his hair. He was wearing a white coat over his trousers but it was undone and his chest was bare. He looked distraught. 'Sophie,' he murmured hoarsely, as if he were drunk. 'Sophie, I need help. I can't handle this.'

'What's going on, Ash?' she whispered.

He closed the door to his room. 'I've got myself involved . . . out of my depth . . . please, help me.' He caught hold of Sophie's arm and pulled her towards him. He was sweating and she could smell something – a musky perfume and . . . oh, God . . . he'd been having sex. She tried to back away. He held onto her arm. She could feel him shaking.

'Let go of me, Ash.'

'Please, Sophie, talk to her.' He gestured towards his room. She could hear a low moaning noise from within.

'I can't. Not me. You must get professional help – a supervisor. I'm not qualified in your field.'

'But, you're the only one that can understand.'

Sophie pulled away and ran outside, through the

garden, along the steep street, across the esplanade and down the steps to the beach. Not Ash; straight, dependable Ash. He was the last person she could imagine having an affair. He was always taking the moral high ground. How could he? There must be some explanation; she had to be mistaken. There were still some people loitering along the water's edge in the dusk. She strode as far as she could and then turned and ambled back in the opposite direction, trying to gather her thoughts. She could see the light on above Rachel's café and was tempted to call on her. But Aidan might be about and anyway, she couldn't betray Jill and Ash's confidence.

She sat on the sea wall dangling her legs, not knowing what to do. She was getting sucked back into other people's lives. She'd agreed to look after Fleur and Tom while Jill worked, and now Ash was dragging her into this inexplicable drama. What was she doing, falling back into the same old role? Was she going to end up as an agony aunt, confidante and safety net for other people's families? But Jill was her best friend, unstinting in her generosity. She jumped down off the wall. She had to talk to Jill, be open. But she couldn't tell Jill her suspicions about Ash. Jill was strong, but how could she tell her that her husband appeared to be having sex with a client? Sophie hoped to God she was wrong, but feared she wasn't.

She walked slowly back to the house. Jill was

lying on the sofa with a glass of wine in her hand. A novel was resting on her stomach, her reading glasses perched on the end of her nose. She was listening to one of her old Blues recordings. A woman's voice warbled desolately from the stereo . . . *a man is a two-face, a worrisome thing—*

Jill picked up the remote and stopped the music.

'Where's Ash?' Sophie asked.

'Shower, I think. Did you speak to him?'

Sophie shook her head. 'He was busy – seeing someone, so I went for a walk.'

Jill sat up and took off her glasses. 'Did you see who it was?'

'No.'

'Was it Marguerite?'

'I wouldn't know. But I heard voices. I thought you said she didn't speak.'

Jill shrugged and slumped back against the cushions. She seemed self-absorbed, gulping her wine.

'Jill, I need to talk to you. Move over.' Sophie shoved Jill's legs and sat down on the end of the sofa. 'I don't want to be a go-between for you and Ash. You and he have to sort this out.'

'Yes, I know, I'm sorry. I shouldn't have—'

'It's okay. I'd do anything to repay what you've done for me. But I have to be honest; you're always telling me that.' Jill blinked her eyes. Sophie could see she'd had a lot to drink. 'I think it might be better if I looked for somewhere else to live.'

'Move out?'

Sophie nodded. 'I need to experience living

alone – to see how I cope with my own company. After all, it might be the way I'm going to live the rest of my life.'

'But, aren't you happy here? I need you, Sophie. I've only got you to rely on to help with the kids and everything.'

'I know. That's part of the problem.'

Jill sat up, surprised. 'You don't want to help me?'

'Look, I love Tom and Fleur. But I don't want to look after them so much, and it's getting more and more.'

'But Fleur's your god-daughter.'

'I know she is and I adore her. I'm just trying to be honest here. I still want to look after them, but at more specified times, so I know where I am.'

'I'm sorry if I've been imposing on you.'

'Oh, Jill . . .'

'Sorry—'

'It's all right. I know you're worried—'

'But you can't help.'

'No, not with this, I don't think I can.'

Jill struggled to get up off the sofa. 'Then maybe you had better find somewhere else. Then we'll know where we stand.'

Sophie lay awake, tossing and turning. The night was muggy and it felt airless under the eaves. For the first time in her life she felt she'd put her needs before somebody else's. And she realised now why she'd always done things the other way round. This was far more painful, feeling she'd let down her best friend, after all Jill had done for her. A bit of her wanted to run to Jill right now and undo all the things she'd said and tell her she'd look after the kids and the house and make everything all right again. But the other part of her – the part that had walked away from her job and sold her house – felt good. To live alone . . . how would that be? Suddenly she thought of lonesome Nick. Into her mind came his brown eyes, his slow blink. Of course, it was Tiggy – his eyes reminded her of Tiggy, her graveyard friend that understood her fascination with the dead and listened when she told him about glow-worms.

She got up, went over to the chest of drawers and rubbed her hand over the worn lid of the old shoe box. The faded writing was still there in her childish print. *Miracles happen when droplets of truth seep through the membrane of the dream.* That's what Tiggy had told her and she'd tried to remember it accurately because it had seemed so important. She smiled. 'What an odd little girl I was,' she murmured. But that was how she'd started her miracle box and Tiggy had continued to tell her things to write down. Or had he actually told her anything? She seemed to remember him asking her all the questions. For the first time it occurred to her that he might have been an imaginary friend like many children have.

She opened the window and looked out at the moonlit sea. Down below, in the garden, she spotted something moving. Someone was walking out of the shadows of the veranda. At first she thought it was one of the children. But then she saw it was a woman; the moonlight shone on her extraordinarily long hair which glinted like silver. She stood motionless, staring up at the house and Sophie wondered if she was seeing her first island ghost. Then the woman walked out of the garden, down the street to the esplanade. A figure broke away from a red Mini parked under a street light and went to meet her. It was another, larger woman, with dark, bobbed hair. She put her arms around the silver-haired woman and helped her into the car. Sophie heard the engine start and it crept slowly away. She wondered if the woman who had been staring up at the house was the same one that had been in Ash's consulting room earlier. Oh, Ash, she thought, what on earth have you got yourself into?

It was the third anniversary of Keri's death and Nick was urging himself to phone his mother-in-law in Kaikoura. He'd never returned to see her like he'd promised as they watched the calm water of Lake Tekapo receive Keri's ashes.

'You have to stop blaming yourself, Nick,' Marina had said, weeping with him, holding his hands. 'You'll always be part of our family. Come back, one day.'

Nick remembered nodding and sobbing, gulping in the honey smell of a million lupins fringing the lake, engulfing the little Church of the Good

Shepherd. He tried to fix the scene in his mind like a living photograph. But it seemed to him that the colours of the petals were fragile and might melt into the water. And their fragrance and the toll of the bell could be carried away by the slightest breeze.

'There's more here than you realise, Nick.' He'd heard Keri's voice inside his head. And for a brief moment he felt the presence of an enduring strength that could be relied upon – if he only knew what it was. That was the beginning of his search.

But, now he needed to phone Marina. He didn't have a landline and it was impossible to get a signal on a mobile in Blue Slipper Bay. He had a choice of walking up to the main road and having a difficult payphone conversation with Marina, or asking Kyp and Evie if he could use theirs. He knew they wouldn't mind. He'd told them about Keri. Not the full story, just that she'd died. They'd been good friends to him. He'd met them on Milos, Kyp's family home, where they escaped each winter from the English chill. He'd been travelling non-stop after his trip to New Zealand to scatter Keri's ashes with Marina. From there he'd been all over India and Europe, staying in spiritual centres. He'd ended up island-hopping and working in Kyp's beach bar to earn some money for his next destination. He'd told himself he was searching for answers, but he'd been attempting to run away from his own mind, he could see that now.

It was Evie who had told him about Blue Slipper Bay and the terrace restaurant, the cottage to rent, and her vision of creating a retreat where artists could work – and eat Kyp's freshly caught fish. She had been born on the Isle of Wight, inheriting her father's business. So she and Kyp were both islanders in their ways.

'Come back with us, Nick,' she'd said. 'You have to go back sometime. And it's England – but not quite.'

CHAPTER 9

Jill walked into the café feeling apprehensive. She hadn't been in there since Sophie had started working for Rachel and she didn't quite know how to fit in. Sophie didn't notice her straight away; she was busy behind the counter. Rachel spoke to Sophie and she looked up and saw Jill hovering. She seemed delighted, and gestured towards a window table for Jill to sit down. Jill watched as Sophie served the coffee to the customers, smiling and chatting, smart in her black trousers and white blouse, as if she'd been doing it for years. But then Sophie could always adapt herself to other people – it was her gift. She came over to Jill's table, pad and pen poised.

'What can I get for Madam?' she asked, grinning.

'Coffee – got time to have one with me?'

'I'll ask the boss.' Sophie went to speak to Rachel, came back and sat down. 'Rachel's going to bring us a treat,' she said.

Munching their way through a pile of home-made scones, layered with jam and cream, Jill realised she was enjoying the holiday atmosphere and the cheerful Irish music playing in the background. 'Looks nice in here,' she conceded. 'Rachel does it well.' The café was emptying out after the mid-afternoon tea rush; the customers eager to get back to the sunny beach. Rachel came and sat with them.

'Must be our busiest day so far,' she said.

Sophie smiled. 'What will it be like when the schools break up for summer holidays?'

'Your feet will swell up and threaten to explode,' Rachel said, pouring herself some coffee.

'Nice. Presumably we will have more help?'

'Aidan will muck in. Not sure about Patrick – he's thinking of taking a job at Wraith Cove Hotel. Jane and Chas are looking for a foreman to supervise the workers on the site.'

'I thought that was Nick's job,' Sophie said.

'No, he's sorting out the gardens.'

'That creepy bald guy?' Jill exclaimed.

Rachel looked up sharply from plastering her scone. 'Creepy? Nick? I think you've got the wrong person.' She flourished her knife. 'Anyway, there are always plenty of students around looking for summer jobs. What about Rose?'

'What about her?'

'She said to me a while back that she wanted to earn some money—'

'Working here?' Jill felt alarmed, Rose hadn't said anything to her and Ash wouldn't like it.

'Uh, huh. Told me to let her know if I needed anyone. But I always take what the young ones say loosely – they change their minds like their hairstyles.'

Jill took a bite of scone, wondering how she would feel with her best friend and her daughter both working for Rachel – with herself confined to her consulting room listening to the woes of the world. Maybe she should ask for a job here too. But she planned to take some time off this summer. She wanted to relax for a while and enjoy the island – spend time on the beach with Tom and Fleur and Sophie. But Sophie would be working. She sighed. Perhaps it wasn't a bad thing. If Sophie was really enjoying this job and found a place of her own to live she would be more likely to stay. Maybe it would be best to let Sophie find her own feet, as Ash kept saying.

'Scones are delicious, Rachel,' she smiled. 'I must come in more often.'

Audrey phoned at nine, every Sunday evening. Sophie imagined that she'd pored over her timetable and sorted out the best slot. Joanna and William would be bathed and bedded, their school uniform on hangers, waiting to entrap them. John would be ploughing through *The Times* supplements in the lounge and Audrey, having just placed the last polished glass back in its cabinet, would sit down at the telephone table in the hall, check her watch, cross her legs, and ring Sophie's number.

'Peter came to lunch today,' she said, after giving Sophie a detailed account of her week.

'Did he?' This snapped Sophie's attention back to what Audrey was saying. She'd been gazing out of Jill's living room window at a fairytale cruise ship sailing to paradise along the shell pink horizon. 'Why?'

'He wanted to see William and Joanna. He misses them.'

'Since when?'

'Well, since you split up, of course.'

'I keep telling you, Audrey. We didn't split up. He left me for a woman who looks like Arwen Evenstar.'

'Who?'

'Elf queen. *Lord of the Rings*.'

'Nonsense, Sophia. She doesn't look a bit like her.'

'So, she came too?' Sophie felt betrayed. It had never occurred to her that Audrey would consider entertaining her ex-husband and his lover. What had happened to her high morals?

'Not this time. I mean, he wanted to talk about finances, privately.'

'Not this time! He's been before then – with Arwen?'

'Her name's Melissa.'

'I know what her name is.' Sophie just couldn't bring herself to say it.

'Anyway, Peter said to tell you that your share of the house money should be in your account by tomorrow.'

'Why couldn't he tell me himself?'

'Because you said you never wanted to speak to him again.'

That was true, she had said that. 'Bastard,' Sophie muttered, mainly to shock her sister. Audrey was always so good, Sophie felt compelled to be bad. She would never hurt her, but Audrey's parental attitude triggered a kind of tough-kid streak in Sophie that lay dormant the rest of the time. 'Sorry, Audrey,' she added.

'When are you coming back?' Audrey's words had clipped edges.

'Not just yet. I have a job for the summer at least.'

'You're still working in that café then?'

'I like it. Look, why don't you come for a holiday? The kids would love it here. The beach is just across the road and there are loads of things for them to do.'

'But where would we stay?'

'I could book you in somewhere.'

There was a pause. Sophie imagined her crossing and uncrossing her legs, frowning.

'It's a long drive. Joanna gets car sick.'

'It's only a couple of hours from London to Portsmouth. Or you could come by train.'

'Then there's the ferry.'

'Half an hour. It's fun. I'll meet you.'

'I'll think about it. I'll have to see what John says. Anyway, I'd better go. I must get ready for the morning.'

Sophie put the phone down and stood watching

the cruise ship. The lights were twinkling. She imagined the passengers in slinky evening dresses or white tailed suits, lusting after each other over little paper umbrellas bobbing in their cocktails. Or, maybe, leaning on the rail, looking toward this small island with its own string of lights winking back at them. Were they imagining the islanders were doing wondrous things too, or were they ordinary folk, like her, looking and fantasising? She could hear Tom and Fleur still running around upstairs, making demands on their frazzled parents. The altruistic part of her nagged that she should offer to read another chapter of Harry Potter. But her selfish-self won and she crept through the kitchen, out of the back door and ran down to the sea like a truant teenager.

She kicked off her sandals, rolled up her jeans and paddled. The water refreshed her as if it were drawing out the tension from her body. She didn't want to build up stress again after having shed so much. But, she was aware this weekend not only of the sniping, darting back and forth between Jill and Ash but also how much the atmosphere was winding up the children. She found herself playing the role of peace keeper. She felt sorry for Jill and Ash and wished they could get down to sorting this out. To give them the opportunity, she'd taken the children to Blackgang Chine for the day to burn off some energy. They'd rushed about happily like normal kids, then as soon as they got back home they started whinging again. But the thing that troubled her most was that Jill still seemed cut off. Although she said she understood Sophie's need to try living alone, she could tell that Jill felt hurt.

She wandered back up to the esplanade and glanced up at Rachel's. She was leaning out of her window, smiling.

'Look at you. You're just a big kid really.'

Sophie glanced down at her bare feet, plastered with sand. 'I should have brought a towel with me,' she said. 'But what the hell.'

'Have you got time to come up and have a drink with us?'

'I can't think of anything I'd rather do.' She rushed around to the back of the café and up the steps before Rachel could change her mind.

Rachel laughed at her eagerness and gave her a towel. 'You're worse than a dog. Come in. Nick's here.'

'Nick?' Sophie had expected Aidan to be with her.

'Aidan's in his room, studying for his A levels. We can't be too rowdy in case we get ticked off.'

Nick was sitting by the window, looking healthy in an opennecked white shirt. 'Hello, Sophie,' he said. 'Have some wine?' The hoarseness had gone from his voice and his eyes were bright and clear in his tanned face.

'I hope I'm not interrupting,' she said, feeling embarrassed. She could see the remains of supper things on the table, and Rachel was looking alluring in a cleavage-friendly, leafy-green sun dress. This was obviously an evening they had arranged.

'Not at all,' said Rachel. 'We're bored silly with each other. Come and tell us about your day.'

'Well, I took Tom and Fleur to Blackgang Chine and gave them all the things to eat that they're not allowed to have. By tomorrow their teeth will have rotted and they will be clinically obese. We also went on every ride and watery thing a dozen times and I've lost at least two stone.'

'A good day out then,' laughed Rachel.

'You must really like children,' Nick said. 'Do you have any of your own?'

Sophie leaned back in her chair and sipped her wine, thinking about this. 'No, I don't have any. But, yes, I do like them, I suppose.'

'You don't sound too sure,' he said.

'Oh, I do. But it would be nice to have a quiet day to myself. Whenever I'm not working, the kids are there. I shouldn't moan, they're great, and I don't have the responsibility for them that their parents have.'

'That makes it harder sometimes though,' Rachel said. 'You can't clip them round the ear or tell them to bugger off, can you? You have to be nice Aunty Sophie.'

'I tick them off occasionally. But, I have been thinking, now I'm working, it would be nice to get a place of my own.'

'You're going to stay here?' said Nick.

'For the summer, at least. I want to carry on

working at the café – if Rachel will have me.' Sophie glanced at her, suddenly worried that she might prefer to have her usual students.

'I think I can put up with you,' Rachel smiled. 'The punters seem to like you, can't think why.'

'Perhaps they imagine they're walking into an Italian restaurant,' said Nick.

Sophie laughed, relieved. 'I don't suppose either of you happen to know of somewhere I could rent for the rest of the summer?'

Rachel frowned. 'The trouble is, anyone who has property to let bumps up the price for the season. It would be very expensive – more than I pay you.'

'This is only an idea,' Nick said. 'But the middle cottage will be empty at Blue Slipper Bay for the summer. The owners are going abroad this year. They asked me a while back if I knew anyone reliable who might rent it and not wreck the place.' He shrugged, as if it was a silly idea. 'Just thought . . . maybe they've found someone . . . I could ask them . . . if you wanted . . .'

A tidal wave of excitement appeared to surge through Sophie's body. What an incredible place to live. She wanted to say yes, without thinking it through. 'But,' she stammered, eventually, 'how would I get to work and isn't it dangerous?'

'You can drive along the main road, park and walk down. Or the healthy option is to take the cliff path. The bay is only dangerous in a storm, then we nail up the shutters and pray.' He gave his rare smile. 'It's good for the soul – living with death at your door.'

Sophie looked at Rachel, not knowing whether he was serious. She was grinning. 'You've probably put her off already, Nick.' She patted Sophie's arm. 'I think it's a great idea. If the weather gets bad you can always kip on my sofa instead of going home.'

Sophie gulped her wine as if it were lemonade, she felt full of bubbles. 'How can I find out? Who do I contact?'

'The owners are there at the moment,' Nick said. 'They always come at the beginning of June for The Old Gaffers' Festival, and then they plan to sail away for the summer. I can speak to them when I get back if you like, to see if they still want someone.' He got up. 'I must go before it gets too dark and I fall off the cliff.'

'Thank you, Nick.'

'No problem.' He went out into the hallway and Sophie could hear him talking to Aidan, wishing him well for his exams.

Rachel and Sophie looked at each other.

'I think Nick likes you,' Rachel said, filling their glasses. 'He doesn't usually offer to do things like that.'

'Perhaps he'd had too much wine and will regret it tomorrow.'

Rachel pointed at a bottle of grape juice. 'He doesn't drink.'

'Oh. Maybe he meant it . . . Rachel, just so as I know the situation . . . are you and he—'

She shook her head. 'It's not for want of trying – on my part that is. I'm probably older than him, but I do find him very attractive. I stayed the night once at his place when a sudden storm blew up and I couldn't get back. I was petrified. Kyp and Evie had guests so I slept in Nick's bed and he had a sleeping bag on the floor. I did suggest we could both squeeze in together, but he was very polite and said he needed to be celibate at the moment.'

'Is he gay?'

'I don't think so. He's been on some sort of spiritual quest – lived in monasteries. Evie told me he'd once been married. He seems reluctant to talk about the past, so I don't question him. Nick's a bit of a mystery – but a very nice one.'

'Do you think I'm doing the right thing?' Sophie felt her more rational self re-surfacing.

'What, moving out of Jill's, or moving into a beach hut?'

'Both.'

She skewed her mouth to one side, thinking. 'I believe couples need their space. Once you've moved out you'll be able to resume your old friendship again. And the beach hut? Well, it'll keep you on your toes. Go for it. You can always move in here if one of the boys goes away for the summer.'

Nick felt surprised at himself after he'd so readily suggested that Sophie move to Blue Slipper Bay.

The idea had popped into his mind and out of his mouth before he could contain it. Just like the time he'd invited Sophie and Rachel to come over for supper. He hadn't followed that up yet, feeling shy about asking again. It was unlike him to act without thinking things through. Would he have to feel responsible for her if she came? Would she look to him for help with the inevitable teething troubles of moving? He waited for the regrets to start arising that he'd acted so impetuously. But none surfaced.

He sensed that she needed a refuge; that was why he'd done it. She'd seemed friendly and open after her paddle in the sea. And when she spoke of her discomfort at living with friends, he recognised her longing for solitude. But she seemed wary of expressing her needs in a serious way, in case she alienated people. He wondered if she'd had enough, and was running away from her compulsion to be what others expected. If so, she would need time alone, to feel what it was like to be un-needed.

Nick felt unnecessary to other people's lives. It was what he'd chosen. He could move on tomorrow if he wanted to, without causing harm. Jane and Chas would hire another gardener. Neptune and Marguerite would have more room in the fishing boat – he never caught anything anyway. Kyp and Evie would find another tenant for Fair Wind. And Rachel, well she had other friends, including Sophie.

Nick lifted his statue of the Buddha from the mantelpiece and stood looking at it. It was about a foot tall, carved from wood. The topknot and nose were missing, the body worn and grooved. But the face still looked serene. A square recess was cut into its back. An old Tibetan woman told him that the monks transcribed intricate prayers on thin manuscript to fold and place in there for blessing. The tiny door was missing. A spider had been living inside for some time. Nick could just see her watching him through a white veil of web. He carefully put the Buddha back on the mantelpiece. He felt comforted to know the spider was still there, living her solitary life alongside his own.

It might be nice to have someone more permanent living in Sea Spray, even for a few months. Holiday folk were always knocking on his door, asking where they could get this or that. And Sophie had looked exhilarated by the idea – her eyes wide, her hands fluttering, her body leaning forward, her mouth trying to form the questions he felt were rushing into her mind.

Nick realised he was smiling at the memory of her delight. He hoped she wouldn't be disappointed.

CHAPTER 10

'Blue Slipper Bay! You can't live there, it's practically in the sea,' Ash said, at breakfast, when Sophie told them. He poured himself more coffee, splashing it on the table. 'Tell her, Jill.'

Jill had her back to them, plaiting Fleur's hair for the second time. 'Sophie's old enough to decide for herself where she wants to live.'

Ash stared from one to the other of them. His eyes looked heavy, his jaunty hair lay flat. Fleur suddenly burst into tears.

'Don't go and live in the sea, Sophie,' she wailed.

Sophie got up and put her arms around Fleur. 'Don't worry, sweetheart, Daddy didn't mean—'

Fleur wrenched the bobbles off the ends of her plaits and threw them on the floor. Her silky hair started to unwind itself again. 'I don't want you to go,' she sobbed, resting her weight against Sophie. Her small body felt hot, encased in its complicated uniform. Jill gave up on the plaits, grasped Fleur firmly by the shoulders and pulled her away.

'Get in the car. Tom's waiting. We'll be late for school.'

Sophie was left alone with Ash. She'd been dreading this, trying to avoid it. He opened his mouth to speak but Sophie interrupted. 'You must talk to Jill. Tell her what's troubling you. You're both strong; you can get through this together.' She threw her arms out in an expansive gesture. 'You've got everything going for you here. Don't throw it all away.'

He nodded miserably. 'But, I need help, advice. Marguerite . . .' he shrugged, 'she's such an innocent, too unworldly. I can't—'

'Jill knows you're in trouble, Ash. Trust her, talk to her. She's feeling cut out by you.'

Jill marched back in and grabbed her bag, avoiding their gaze. 'I'm off, see you later,' she said.

Ash sat pushing toast crumbs around his plate. Sophie fiddled with the dishes, trying to work out how she could leave the room. He raked both hands through his hair and sighed deeply.

'She won't understand.'

'Try her. She's a psychologist for heaven's sake. She knows how the human psyche works, probably better than any of us.'

'Yes, but it's different when it's yourself, isn't it?' He sounded bitter. 'It's fine dealing with other people's problems. We can all do that when we're not emotionally involved. But it falls apart when our own animal nature rears its ugly head.'

Sophie continued clearing the breakfast debris. She just wanted to get out of here and take refuge with Rachel in the café doing simple things – brewing coffee, slicing cake. Ash was still running his hands over his face and hair.

'Sophie, I—'

'Please, don't tell me, Ash. I don't know whether I could keep it contained. Jill's my best friend. I can't withhold any more from her. It will ruin our relationship. You must tell her, whatever it is. She's already upset with me because I'm not supporting her enough and I'm moving out.'

'You don't have to move out because of me.'

Typical arrogant male, Sophie thought, assuming she was planning her life around him. 'I'm moving out because I want to live on my own. Blue Slipper Bay will be an adventure for me.'

Ash scraped his chair back and came towards her, suddenly seeming tall and gaunt. 'An adventure? You have no idea, no understanding of this island. You think it's all romantic, stuck somewhere back in the nineteen-fifties, don't you?'

Sophie was astonished by his vehemence. He had never spoken to her like this before. She stepped away from him, her back against the sink. 'I didn't mean—'

'There's been untold suffering along this coast. Drownings, piracy, shipwrecks, murders, disease, drug-running. People's property falls from the cliffs into the sea. Did you know that? Nature has her way in the end.'

'I'm sure—'

He caught her roughly by the arm. 'Do you know how Blue Slipper Bay got its name?'

She shook her head, feeling his fingers digging into her flesh, wondering what on earth all this was about. 'Its shape?' she said feebly. 'Colour?'

'Blue Slipper is the local name for the blue gault clay in the cliff. The upper layers of the land slide over it and drop off the edge into the sea, taking everything with it.' He let go of her arm. 'Sorry to burst your bubble,' he said and went out.

'Is it really dangerous, this slippery blue clay thing?' Sophie asked Rachel, while they dished up sizzling lasagne and frilly green salad. She was hoping there'd be some left over, her mouth was watering. She was tempted to cross it off the menu board.

'Well,' Rachel said, deftly sprinkling chopped parsley, 'here, take these and then I'll tell you.'

Sophie carried the plates to the hungry holiday-makers and got caught up in a little light chatter. She went outside to clear the two round tables Rachel managed to squeeze in on the pavement. The weather had cooled since the weekend heat-wave and the beach was emptier. When she went back inside, Rachel had wiped clean the lunchtime menu board and saved the last two slices of lasagne.

'I was hoping you might,' Sophie laughed.

'It had something to do with your slavering jaws,' Rachel giggled, pushing a plate towards her. 'Anyway, I think the lunchers are finished.'

They hid behind the coffee machine shovelling down lasagne as if they hadn't eaten for days. Rachel loved food and Sophie found that infectious. 'Blue clay?' she prompted.

'Well, there haven't been any massive landslides for decades, not since the Old Blackgang Road was cut off. But there are always small slips going on. Oh, and there was quite a big chunk of road that collapsed near Niton a couple of years ago.' She wiped her mouth on a napkin and poured two glasses of water. 'They say that the dry summers are making it worse. The land cracks and then fills up with water.' She bustled off to clear tables, while Sophie tidied up the small working area. 'But,' she continued, 'there's engineering work going on to drain the land and delay the inevitable. The whole area is closely monitored.' She grinned. 'You should talk to Jane. Her cottage is right on the edge of the cliff at Wraith Cove. She was petrified when she first went there but she loves it now. The locals are very blasé about it.'

'So what about Blue Slipper Bay?'

'I've never heard of any problems there. I think people are blown away by the beauty of it. And, because the cottages are so near the shore, there's a wee frisson of fear to add to the romance.'

The bell jingled as the door opened. Two women came in. Sophie was just about to put the afternoon tea menus on the tables and stopped abruptly. One of the women was slender with silver hair hanging right down her back to her thighs. The other was larger with a shoulder length brown bob. She was talking avidly to the silver haired woman who was smiling and moving her hands as if she were using sign-language.

Rachel appeared from behind the counter. 'Jane!' she said. 'We were just talking about you and Wraith Cottage.'

The dark-haired woman smiled across at them. 'Hello, Rachel.' Her eyes swept over Sophie. 'Are you Sophie?'

Hardly able to shift her gaze from the silver haired woman, Sophie nodded.

'I've got a message for you from Nick. He said to tell you that he's spoken to the owners and wondered if you wanted to go over to inspect the cottage after work.' She looked at the other woman and then back at Sophie. 'This is my sister, Marguerite.'

'Hello,' Sophie stammered. 'Thank you for the message.'

'That's okay,' Jane said. 'I'm being nosey – Nick's never very forthcoming – are you thinking of staying at Blue Slipper Bay?'

Sophie nodded, still dumbstruck, trying to piece things together. Marguerite – Jane's sister. What were they doing outside Jill and Ash's house the other night? 'I, er, yes. I'm thinking about it.'

'Wonderful,' said Jane. 'Don't let anyone put you off. We go there to eat at Kyp and Evie's sometimes, don't we, Marguerite?'

Marguerite looked at Sophie, her large pale blue eyes shining. She smiled and Sophie found herself smiling back. And then Marguerite held her hand out and grasped Sophie's. It felt warm and strangely comforting. She was much older than she looked at first glance. Her face had fine lines around the eyes and mouth. But she was strikingly beautiful. Sophie turned away as Rachel took their order. She retreated behind the counter so she could observe them without seeming rude. Jane was talking to Rachel, constantly turning to Marguerite as if to include her. Marguerite didn't speak, just smiled and moved her graceful hands constantly. Sophie presumed she was deaf. And there was a slight degree of lopsidedness about her shoulders as if she had a physical disability.

She put a teapot and cups on a tray, her hands working automatically. What was going on here? Surely Ash couldn't be having an affair with Marguerite – she didn't look the type. But now she was judging again. What was the type, for goodness sake? But why was she outside the house in the early hours gazing up at the windows? Why was Jill so against having her in the centre? Rachel came to collect the tea. She whispered in Sophie's ear.

'You'd never believe those two were twins, would you?'

Nick had ridden his bicycle to Wraith Cove, sawn his way through a tough rhododendron patch, and left early so that he could be back at Blue Slipper Bay when Sophie came to view Sea Spray. The owners had already sailed away to catch the tide. They'd been dubious about letting their cottage to someone they'd never met, but Nick assured them Sophie was a friend and promised to take full responsibility if anything should go wrong.

He was still feeling amazed at himself. Responsibility wasn't a quality that he'd given much thought to in the last few years. It was something to be avoided, inextricable from other factors, such as guilt and loss.

He let himself into Sea Spray and checked to make sure it was pristine. He couldn't find a speck of sand, even in the shower. On yet another impulse he went outside and gathered a bunch of wild roses and honeysuckle that grew on the cliff face. He found a vase in the kitchen, arranged the flowers, and placed them on the mantelpiece. He stood back and contemplated the effect. Did they look too contrived? He moved them to the hearth but they didn't catch the eye so much there. He put them in the middle of the table.

He decided to go for a swim, touch the earth, and calm himself, before Sophie arrived. And then he would give her the key and leave her to it, so she could have the space to explore and make up her mind without feeling any pressure from him.

Jill had persuaded Ash to block out some time in his diary so they could both meet the children from school for once and drive down to Binnel Bay at St Lawrence. They all loved this particular small stony beach in The Undercliff. For some unknown maritime reason the sea delivered up especially good driftwood here and the kids wanted some for sculptures they were making at school. The walk from the car park was fun, calling at the glassworks to buy luscious Minghella ice cream and brilliant marbles for Tom and Fleur. And then down through the little wood to the board walk.

The tide was going out, revealing the rock strewn sand and interesting pools. Ash had his trousers rolled up and was paddling with Fleur. Tom was skimming stones. Jill kicked off her sandals, unbuttoned her blouse, shook out her hair, and sat down on a boulder to watch. We should do more of this, she thought. It was part of the reason we came here. Ash turned and walked up the beach towards her. He smiled – not his usual relaxed easy grin. But at least it was a smile. Jill felt suddenly reassured. It wasn't just Ash – she needed to chill out too. And there was no reason why she shouldn't. Sophie was here, much happier now, and Rose would be coming home soon for the summer which would make life better for Ash. And then maybe they could start communicating properly again. She held out her hand to him as he approached. 'Hello, Bone Man,' she said.

He clasped her fingers and sat down beside her. 'We should do more of this,' he said.

'Just what I was thinking.' Jill leaned against him, resting her head on his shoulder. 'You smell nice.'

'It's those oils the aromatherapist uses,' he said, shifting away from her. 'They cling.'

CHAPTER 11

Sophie saw Nick before he saw her. He was sitting cross-legged on the sand, wearing white shorts and a towel draped over his shoulders. His hands were loose in his lap as he gazed out to sea. His posture reminded her of the statue of Buddha that she'd noticed on his mantelpiece. How nice it must be to obtain the degree of self-containment and peace that he appeared to possess. It seemed a shame to disturb him. She felt unsure what to do, but then her foot crunched on a patch of shingle and he turned his head towards her.

'Jane gave me your message,' she said.

Nick got up. 'The owners have gone, I'm afraid. They had to set sail because of the tides. But they left the keys for me to show you round. I'll go and fetch them.'

Sophie stood looking about her, trying to see Blue Slipper Bay through cautious eyes. She peered up at the treacherous, slippery cliffs and the three leggy, pastel cottages nestling against them for protection. She stared at the gentle waves lapping the sand and willed herself to imagine them thundering in, engulfing the blue fishing boat and the lobster pots, dragging everything out to sea. But all she could feel was safety. She felt as if she were enclosed in a small refuge that was complete in itself, needing nothing from her – only that she should be herself. In that moment she had no doubt that she was doing the right thing.

Nick was standing outside the middle cottage waiting for her. He'd put on sandals and a grey tee-shirt. As she walked up the slip-way towards him, two small children ran out of the terracotta cottage, called out a greeting to Nick, and scampered past her down to the sand. They had buckets and spades and started digging at the water's edge. Sophie looked around for a parent and spotted somebody moving about inside the cabin.

'They're Jack and Mila,' Nick said, indicating the children. 'Otherwise known as the Water Babies. Evie gave birth to them in the sea.'

'You're kidding. I hope it was summer.' She wouldn't be telling Jill this.

Nick smiled. 'In the shallows of a warm Grecian sea.' He handed her a key. 'This cottage is called Sea Spray. Mine is Fair Wind and Kyp and Evie's is called Sun Spot. Bit corny, but there we are.'

'No, I like those names. They're just right.' She put the key in the lock, wishing she could view Sea Spray by herself. She felt greedy with anticipation. She wanted to explore and concentrate on her feelings without talking.

'Why don't I leave you to it?' Nick said. 'I'll go

and put the kettle on and you can report back when you've seen it. Take your time.'

Perfect, she thought. The front door was painted lavender to match the shutters. She opened it. There was a flight of stairs leading up, the same as Nick's, but these were varnished wood with a tiny landing at the top and a proper door opening into the big room. She let herself in. The place was awash with sunshine and the scent of honeysuckle. The wooden floorboards were polished, mellow oak. An iron woodburner stood in the hearth with logs stacked either side of it. There were two large blue sofas slanted towards the French windows and the sea view. Once again she had the sensation that she could be on a boat. Shelves lined the walls opposite the fireplace and held a miniature television and stereo. There was a vase of flowers on the pale wooden table. How nice of the owners to think of that. She opened an oak door to a small, well designed stainless steel kitchen and another to a gleaming white-tiled shower room. A spiral staircase led up to a gallery, utilising the roof space. There was a thick mattress up there on a slatted base, under a sky-light.

She opened the French doors leading onto the balcony. The railings were painted lavender and there was a round table and two chairs squeezed in amidst terracotta pots of pink geraniums. She looked down onto the sand. The Water Babies were still busy digging. A woman was with them wearing a striped vest and shorts; her hair was sandy-gold, cropped close to her head. She must be Evie.

Sophie went back inside; her heart thudding with exhilaration and apprehension. How could the owners bear to leave it? Supposing they changed their minds and came hurrying back? She stood in the middle of the large room, held her arms out and slowly circled around. It was perfect. She wanted to move in immediately and live here for ever.

The door of the sitting room moved and Nick's ginger cat strolled in. He looked at Sophie, gave a mighty yawn and blinked his green eyes as if he'd just woken up. He sidled over to her and rubbed against her legs. His fur felt warm from lying in the sun. She picked him up and he started to purr like a little engine.

'What are you doing in here?' she asked him, and he pressed his hard head into her neck. She carried him downstairs, reluctant to leave, and tapped on Nick's door. He called out for her to come up. He was standing in the middle of his bare room, just like he'd been the last time she was here. How could he live like this?

Nick had done nothing but pace up and down while Sophie inspected Sea Spray. He couldn't understand why he felt so restless. He supposed it was because he had initiated the whole thing and might feel a bit foolish if she didn't like it. He suddenly remembered that Commie was on the loose and might well go to have a nose to see who was in there. He hoped Sophie wasn't allergic to cats. He should have thought of that. But she hadn't seemed to mind Commie that time she came with Rachel. The cat had been curled up on his bed then.

He'd peered out of the window. She was taking her time. That would be good, wouldn't it? She was obviously looking into every cupboard, wondering where her things might go. But perhaps the place was too big for her – or too small, if she had loads of stuff. She'd seemed very enthusiastic about it at Rachel's. He hoped the reality lived up to her expectations. Maybe now she was here she would be scared by the proximity of the sea. Perhaps Jill and Ash had talked to her about landslips. But she'd appeared eager to see the cottage when he'd looked up from his meditation and saw her standing on the beach. She was wearing the apricot tee-shirt that she wore the first time he'd seen her. Her hair was bunched up and tied with a dark gold scarf. As he'd walked with her to the door of Sea Spray he caught a whiff of the spicy smell she'd left behind before.

He'd heard her knock on his door, and called to her to come up. Restraining himself from immediately asking what she thought, he made the tea. But she'd been smiling when she came in, carrying Commie, and he could tell by her face, which had lifted its veil, that Sea Spray and Blue Slipper Bay were right for her.

'I found your cat,' she said.

'Oh, Commie. He's not mine. He's communal.

He makes himself at home in whatever cottage happens to have its door open. He never goes short of food here.'

Commie jumped out of her arms and onto Nick's bed, preparing to settle down for another doze. Nick brought in the tea and they sat at his table by the window.

'So, what did you think?' he asked, as if he didn't mind either way. Perhaps he liked not having neighbours to disturb his solitude.

'I love it. I want to move in as soon as possible.'

'I thought you might. They've done it up nicely, haven't they?'

'If anyone else comes to view it, please tell them it's about to fall into the sea. I'm going to write a warning notice and nail it to the front door before I leave. How do I let the owners know?'

Nick laughed. She thought it might be the first time she'd heard him laugh. 'They've left it up to me,' he said. 'I have an agreement for you to sign – for three months, and then a further three if you want it. They don't want a deposit, just the rent, which I can bank for them here.'

'So it's mine!' Sophie clapped her hands like a child. 'They're very trusting. They don't know me.'

'They said they trust my judgement.' He smiled. 'I promised to be accountable if you should prove to be unsuitable.'

'But, you hardly know me either. I might throw wild parties.' She put a hand to her mouth. 'I shouldn't have said that, should I?'

'Well, I trust my intuition. And I trust Rachel.'
'Thank you, Nick.' Sophie wanted to tap his hand, like Rachel did, but managed to restrain herself.

'So, you're moving on Friday?' Jill was sitting on the sofa; she glanced up from the novel Sophie knew she was only pretending to read.
'Mmm. Rachel's given me the day off to get organised. I won't have time at the weekend because Aidan will be at the rock festival.'
'I won't be able to help you until the evening. I've got clients and the kids are going horse-riding after school.'
'I know. Don't worry. Nick and Kyp and Evie are going to help me and I haven't got much stuff.'
'You can borrow some bedding and whatever else you need from here.'
'I bought some things today, in Ventnor. I had to get some basic provisions so I thought I might as well.'
Jill shrugged and turned another unread page. Her hand reached up and opened the clasp holding her thick hair. It bounced down on her shoulders and immediately she was transformed into the girl Sophie had met all those years ago in the restaurant. Sophie felt her eyes fill with tears. She had never known Jill so withdrawn. She sat down in the armchair opposite.
'Jill,' Sophie's voice felt strangled,' please don't be upset. I'll still be able to baby-sit for you. I'll only be a mile away.'

Jill let her book drop onto the sofa beside her and took off her glasses. 'I know, Sophie. I know. It isn't a problem. I'd been intending to employ someone to help me out ages before you came.'

'What is it then? We've never fallen out before – not like this. But then we've not really lived together, have we? Just holidays and things.'

'We haven't fallen out. I'm tired, that's all.'

Sophie wasn't going to let it rest there. 'So, I suppose it's because I won't talk to Ash. But you and he must talk, Jill. Why is it so important that I do it?'

'Because you stand in between our extremes. I'll lose it, and make things worse, I know I will.'

'Why will you?'

Jill sat up and put her face in her hands, rubbing her eyes. She let out a long sigh. 'I think all this stuff that Ash is getting interested in is unearthing my aversion to my mother's hippy lifestyle. I still cringe with embarrassment when I think about it. I hated bringing friends home in case there was some chanting and incense-wafting going on. You must remember all those weird people at Morgan's Hall with hair drifting down to their bums, floating about saying things like "far out" and quoting Indian gurus.'

'I never went there. You were happily married to Ash when I met you – remember? And very nearly pregnant with Rose. You vowed you'd never go back home to Morgan's Hall.'

'Home!' Jill grimaced. 'The Morg. That's what we used to call it.'

'But your mum – Stephanie – is lovely. She was so friendly and interesting to talk to whenever I met her in London. I always wished she was my mother.'

'Did you?'

'Yes, you were the envy of our group of friends who had ordinary parents.'

Jill frowned. 'They were always taking the piss.'

'Only because they were jealous.'

'I used to dread her coming to visit in case she sauntered in jangling bells and beads.'

Sophie smiled, feeling the tension between them easing. 'You should have had my parents to contend with. I was always scared my dad would pinch my friends' bottoms.'

Jill grinned. 'They might have enjoyed it. Your dad was fun. He always made everything into a special occasion. He was like a dashing actor out of the old movies with his dark flashing eyes and theatrical gestures.'

'Exactly. How embarrassing was that?'

'The women liked it.'

'Except my mother. She was always inspecting his collars for lipstick and sniffing his washing. She didn't realise that Audrey and I were watching.'

'You know, I don't believe your father had affairs at all. He worshipped your mum. I think it was a game they played ending up with hot sex when you girls were in bed.'

Sophie laughed. 'I can't imagine my mother having any kind of sex let alone the hot variety.'

They were both laughing now and it felt so good. Jill got up and fetched wine and unearthed a king size slab of chocolate from beneath a pile of professional publications. 'Well, anyway. That's why I'm so paranoid about all this stuff with Ash and Marguerite. I want to be straight, Sophie. I'm just about mainstream with what I do, and so is Ash. If he screws it all up for us, I'll kill him.' She wrenched the cork out of the bottle and poured the wine.

'You should have become a doctor like your mother and then you could have qualified as a psychiatrist.'

'Emulating her was the last thing I wanted to do. Anyway, psychiatry involves too much drug therapy.'

'There, you see? You are a bit alternative, after all.'

'But I have strict boundaries, beyond which I won't go. And I don't want Ash to either.' She broke off a hefty portion of chocolate and handed Sophie the bar.

Sophie felt frustrated. Why was Jill being so obstinate? 'Then tell him exactly how you feel.'

'I've tried. He's dismissive and I get angry.' She leaned forward. 'But he'll listen to you. You're good at dealing with fringe issues but you're NHS trained, straight, respectable.'

Sophie slumped back in her chair. Silence settled in the space between them.

'I met Jane and Marguerite in the café,' Sophie said, eventually.

'Oh. What did you think of them?'

'Jane seemed friendly, lively, as if she were taking everything in. I suppose writers need that, for their inspiration. And Marguerite is very unusual, striking, I would say. Rachel told me they are twins. I was amazed.'

Jill nodded thoughtfully. 'The gossip is that they never met until last year. They were separated at birth.'

'That sounds like soap-opera material.'

'Nobody knows the full version, but rumour has it that Marguerite was a recluse and Jane has been trying to introduce her to the world.'

'She appeared perfectly happy in the café. What sort of disability does she have?'

'I don't really know. Maybe some sort of birth trauma.'

'She struck me as being open, innocent . . . I was wondering . . . why don't you speak to Jane if you're worried about her being at the centre?'

'What could I say? I think she's a bad influence? The other therapists think she's God's gift – so do the patients by all accounts. She's becoming a bit of a celebrity. Even the GPs have asked me about her.'

'Then the problem is?'

'Ash – he's disturbed, restless. He's acting strangely and I'm worried. He's even been sleeping downstairs some nights, and he's not interested in sex.'

'You don't think, I mean, he's not having a fling?'

Jill's eyes widened, searching Sophie's face. 'This is Ash we're talking about,' she said. Her body went perfectly still. 'What makes you say that?'

Sophie shrugged. 'What you were just saying, I suppose . . .'

'But, Ash, he would be the last person on earth . . .' She laughed but the ease had gone from her face. Their good humour vanished.

Oh, God, Sophie thought. What an idiot. Why had she said that? Jill hadn't been suspicious at all, and now she'd put the idea into her head. She didn't know what to say. She put her glass down, carefully.

Jill blinked rapidly as if she had just woken up. 'I've been thinking that I might start going to church,' she said.

'Church! That doesn't sound like you.'

'I just feel the need for something, that's all.' She gave her wine glass a little push away from her. 'And I'm drinking far too much. I need to sort my head out.'

Sophie knelt in front of her and took her hands. They felt sweaty. 'Look, Jill. I'll try to have a chat with Ash. But if he tells me things in confidence that I can't tell you, how will you feel?'

Jill returned her clasp. 'Please, Sophie. I trust you. I'll be fine with that, if it helps Ash.'

CHAPTER 12

Jill tried to concentrate on what her client was saying but her mind kept removing itself, imagining Sophie upstairs packing her things.

'I walked right along the high street in Newport and back,' the woman was saying. 'I couldn't believe it was me.'

'That's wonderful,' Jill replied automatically. 'Did you give yourself a reward?'

'My daughter went into a travel agent and got me some brochures to look at.'

'Do you think you might be able to go into a shop – maybe the travel agent?' The woman looked doubtful, shook her head.

'Okay, that's fine. But the next time, I want you to stop outside a shop – any shop you choose – and just put your hand on the door. You don't have to think about going in.'

'I'd need someone with me.'

'That's all right. But don't be pushed.'

The woman started to talk about who she might ask to come with her. She was wearing a grey silk blouse with a row of tiny pearl buttons down the front. Jill started to count them in pairs . . . good, an even number. The woman was still deliberating.

'I'll come with you – if you can't find anybody. We'll need to book a double session.' Jill glanced at her watch and got up to show her out.

If her next client was punctual she might be able to catch Sophie before she finished packing and left. But Jill had already said she was tied up all day. And what could she say without appearing negative? But if she wasn't her usual bitchy self that she'd been lately, then she might cry instead. And what purpose would that serve? She really didn't want to spoil Sophie's big day.

Jill retrieved her bag from under her desk and unzipped the middle compartment, feeling for the plastic bag. A sudden burst of panic radiated inside her like a firework going off. She would have to go to London soon.

'Could Sophie use another pair of hands?' Jane offered, when Nick explained why he needed the afternoon off.

'Well, Kyp and Evie are helping and I don't think she's got much to move.'

Jane smiled. 'Another minimalist?'

'I think she has a few more worldly goods than me.'

Chas let out his deep rumbling laugh. 'Well, that wouldn't be difficult, Nick. Just one book would do it.'

Jane gestured around the crowded sitting room

of Wraith Cottage. 'If you ever feel like adopting a few books come and help yourself. There's at least fifty years worth here. Marguerite and I keep intending to sift through them but can never bring ourselves to get started.' She ran a finger along the spines of a row of gardening encyclopaedias. 'I think they're welded to the shelves.' She moved over to the table and picked up a new paperback from a pile. 'Does Sophie read novels?'

Nick shrugged. 'I hardly know her.'

Jane signed her name inside the cover. 'Well, give her this as a welcoming present – my latest – hot off the press. But tell her she doesn't have to read it.'

Chas laughed again. 'Yes she does. Jane will be over to question her on it in a few days.'

'Oh, go and do something accountanty – add up a column of figures,' Jane said.

Nick cycled back to Blue Slipper Bay. A welcoming present – why hadn't he thought of that? He could give Sophie a bottle of wine, leave it on the table for her to find. And he could buy one of Evie's hand-painted cards. Kyp and Evie had done that for him when he moved into Fair Wind. They'd taken a lot of convincing that he was happy with it the way it was. They were planning to refurbish it, like Sea Spray, before letting it out.

He stowed his bike under his balcony and went to see Evie. She already had a card prepared, waiting for his signature to add to theirs. 'Why is it that women always think of these things before men?' Nick asked.

'Well, you thought of it too. Kyp thinks of things – but usually at the last minute or the day after.' She laughed. 'Women can't afford to do that. Just imagine it. Schools full of kids with no clean pants or socks.'

'Pooh!' said Mila, holding her nose. 'Look Nick.' She pointed to her name scrawled on the card like a furry caterpillar. 'I wrote that, all by my own. And I'm only three.'

'You are a very clever girl,' Nick said, looking at her delighted face.

She put a sticky little hand on his arm. 'And Mummy's got flowers too, for the new lady.'

'I'm sure Sophie will be very pleased.'

Mila jumped up and down a few times, put her thumb in her mouth then leaned against his legs as if she were tired. He felt the weight and warmth of her small sturdy body. She was so like Kyp. He experienced a wave of tenderness. He would have liked to pick her up and hug her, but he brushed a bit of sand out of her hair instead. Three years old. It suddenly struck him that Lara would have been almost the same age as Mila, if she had lived. He imagined looking down on the head of his own daughter. Would she have been blonde like Keri, or plain mousey-brown like him? He felt tears fill his eyes. He gently moved Mila away from him. 'I must go,' he said softly. 'Sophie will be here soon.'

* * *

Sophie stood looking around the sitting room and something swelled up inside her, making her tingle. She couldn't quite put a name to the feeling. It was like a special-day-happiness – a child having a good birthday. She found herself wandering from room to room, just taking it in. Her few clothes were hanging on the rail upstairs in the gallery bedroom. Commie was already staking his claim to the new blue and white striped duvet cover. The tiny shower room and kitchen were stocked and she'd scattered the big room with cushions and rugs in brash holiday colours. As if there wasn't enough sea surrounding her, she'd bought a stunning aerial print of The Needles from the Wight Light Gallery in Ventnor. She unearthed her miracle box from a carrier bag and put it on a shelf. 'You here again?' she said, giving it a friendly pat.

The weather had been hot and sunny for her moving day. A bit too warm for trundling boxes and bags along the narrow lane that wound down to Blue Slipper Bay from the car park on the main road. But Nick came home from Wraith Cove at lunch time and then Kyp chugged up in the fishing boat and heaved boxes effortlessly onto his broad shoulders.

'He's used to it,' Nick panted. 'He hauls fishing nets for a living.'

'Don't give me that,' Kyp said. 'You dig up tree roots and shift rocks.'

'It must be a Greek thing then,' Nick replied.

'You're genetically engineered to work under blazing skies.'

Kyp was indeed a big muscular man, loud and funny. He made a joke of everything, accentuating his accent, and Evie chivvied him constantly. They appeared to be forever bickering but were always touching each other and exchanging warm, funny expressions. Jack and Mila helped carry a few things when Jack came home from school. They were adventurous kids, climbing and balancing, giggling and chasing each other, asking questions about Sophie's belongings and whether she had a little boy or girl coming to live with her. In no time it was all done. And now, here she was.

She took her mug of tea and sat outside on the balcony, thinking she might try out the shower then make a salad and maybe go for a wander. A light breeze was blowing from the sea. She could taste salt on her lips and smell the seaweed which glistened around the rocks, disturbed by the incoming tide. There were a few yachts zipping along and half a dozen holidaymakers still sitting in deck chairs on the sand, eating and laughing. Kyp and Evie rented out the chairs and sun shades and sold light refreshments and ice cream from the cabin. She could see them on the terrace; they were setting up a barbecue and putting a blue cloth on the long trestle table, obviously expecting people for a fish supper tonight.

Sophie went back inside and pulled off her sweaty shorts and tee-shirt. The shower was powerful and she came out feeling scoured, her arms and face tingling from the sun. Wrapped in a towel, she poured herself a glass of red wine from the bottle that Nick, Kyp and Evie had left on the table along with a vase of white and yellow daisies and a welcome card. She lay down on one of the sofas, took a few sips and felt overcome by tiredness. She just about managed to lower her glass safely to the floor before dozing off.

She was woken by a loud bang. She sat up groggily, wondering where she was and if the cliff had decided to collapse on her first day. She tottered to the French window and out onto the balcony. Another loud bang made her jump and a firework rained brilliant showers of pink and silver stars over the beach. It wasn't dark but it still looked impressive. There were people below, Sophie's eyes were dazzled. They must be the holidaymakers. When her vision cleared she realised it was Nick and Kyp and Evie laughing and calling to her. And then she recognised Rachel and Jill and Ash and the kids.

'Put some clothes on, slut,' Jill called, 'and get down here.'

Sophie dashed up to her bedroom and threw on clean jeans and a coral silk shirt. Her hair was a mess. Having gone to sleep without brushing it, she could now hardly get a comb through it. 'Oh, what does it matter,' she said to Commie, who was watching her with slitty eyes.

Rachel had said she was busy this evening when

Sophie'd asked if she would like to come over and celebrate her first night at Blue Slipper Bay. Sophie had felt briefly disappointed but consoled herself there would be plenty of other times. So Rachel had obviously been cooking this up with the others.

She ran downstairs; the cabin was decked with balloons and fairylights, just beginning to glitter in the fading sunset. It was still very warm. Fleur and Tom were racing about the beach with Jack and Mila and a small yappy dog. The tide was in and they splashed each other, screaming with delight.

'Thought we'd have a little celebration,' Kyp said, 'to welcome you.' He gave Sophie a hot squeeze and a garlicky kiss. 'Come and get a drink.'

Sophie hugged Rachel, Jill and Ash, and they sat at the table, chatting while Evie brought out dishes of olives and pistachios, pitta bread and humous. Sophie was relieved to see Jill and Ash relaxing together and wondered if they'd had a chance to talk yet.

'Here comes the rest of the rabble,' Kyp called.

Jane, Marguerite and two men were making their way across the sand. Marguerite was holding the older man's arm. She was wearing an ankle length silvery-blue dress. Jane was wearing a magenta salwar kameez. Sophie was starting to feel under-dressed. Marguerite let go of the man's arm, kicked off her sandals and went down to the water's edge. The children called out to her and the dog barked, its tail wagging madly. She hitched up her dress and waded into the sea.

Jane introduced Sophie to the men – everyone else seemed to know each other. The larger, middle-aged man was Chas, Jane's husband, and the other elderly one was Neptune. He was a real person after all. The name suited him. He looked craggy, like the cliff-face, as if he'd spent most of his life facing the sea. He didn't say much. His gaze kept going towards Marguerite and the children. Sophie wondered if he was Jane and Marguerite's father, but then remembered Rachel saying Jane's old dad had fallen from the cliff. She shuddered involuntarily.

'Cold, Sophie?' Rachel asked.

'No, just excited. I never guessed you were planning this.'

'It was Kyp's idea,' she laughed. 'But we never miss an opportunity to come down here and have one of Kyp and Evie's suppers.'

'Indeed,' said Chas. 'I've driven all the way from Herefordshire for this.'

'I thought you lived here,' Sophie said, 'at Wraith Cove.'

'My business is based at our other house, near Ledbury,' Chas said. 'But we get down here as often as we can, don't we, Janey?' He put his arm round Jane's shoulders and she lent against him.

Another apparently happy couple, Sophie thought. Maybe marriage does work for some people after all. Kyp was singing loudly while doing amazing things with lobsters and crabs and Evie was bringing out huge bowls of pasta and salad.

'Could you assemble the kids, Jill?' she asked. 'I've barbecued some sausages – no good trying to force good food down their resistant little throats tonight.'

'I'll go,' Ash said. 'You give Evie a hand dishing up.' Jill glanced towards the sea, her smile fading as Ash got up and walked away. He bent his angular body to speak to the children then turned to Marguerite. She put her hand on his arm and leaned forward to brush sand off her legs, her long hair swung over her shoulder, sweeping the rocks. They walked slowly up the beach, Ash talking and smiling, her hand remaining on his arm.

Sophie heaped her plate with delicious food and listened to the banter of Kyp, Evie and Rachel and the chatter of the children. She couldn't believe that all this had been arranged in her honour. The wine flowed and Kyp kept toasting her. He played Greek music on the stereo and danced with the kids on the sand. Sophie thanked Jane for the book she'd given her as a welcome gift.

'Are you writing anything at the moment, Jane?' Jill asked.

'I'm about half-way through a novel. This one is taking me a lot longer than usual. It's a bit different to my usual stuff.'

'More mature,' said Chas, laughing, a slow deep chuckle.

Jane laughed too. 'About time, isn't it?'

'I like your books,' said Rachel. 'Don't change them too much.'

'Well, I hope you'll like this one. You must all come over to supper with us one evening.' She turned to Sophie. 'If you think this is a risky place to live you'll think it's a safe haven after you've seen Wraith Cottage.'

Evie came to sit with them. She was smoking a thin cigar. Her short hair was damp from the heat of the kitchen and clung to her head like a cap. She was a slight woman with a delicate face and high cheekbones, but she gave off an aura of strength. She blew smoke out of the side of her mouth.

'How long before your hotel's up and running, Jane? I'm itching to start expanding my artists' holidays.'

'It'll be ages. But the good news is that we're rebuilding the stable block first and that will be available. Chas has got a whole army of nephews and nieces and students arriving for the summer to work on it.'

Sophie became aware that they'd split into two groups. The women congregated around the table, chatting about their lives and families. The men and the children were kicking a ball around on the sand. She noticed a solitary figure at the water's edge. It was Neptune, looking out to sea. The small terrier was running around near him giving an occasional sharp yap at the waves.

She got up and wandered down there. For a moment she felt awkward, he didn't acknowledge her, and she didn't know what to say. She sniffed the air. The breeze was warm and smelled sweet, as if it carried the perfume of flowers.

'That's elderflower – grows up on the cliffs,' Neptune said, as if he were reading her thoughts.

'What's it like where you live, Neptune?'

'A bit like this, only Puck's Bay is smaller, with just my old fisherman's cottage. I'm on my own there, apart from Loot.' He indicated the dog who crouched on the sand looking up at him expectantly. 'I'll row you round there sometime to see it if you like. Nick often comes out with me.'

'Thanks, I'd like that.'

'Do you work at that Cormorants centre?'

'No. I work in Rachel's café.'

'But you are some sort of psychiatrist, aren't you?'

'No, a nurse, but I'm having a break from it.'

'I'm not keen on all that therapy stuff,' he said. 'I don't like Marguerite going there.'

Sophie was beginning to wish she hadn't come down here. Why was it she seemed to constantly be drawn back to this? 'Is Marguerite a relative of yours?' she asked.

'I've known her all her life. Saw her born. Been a father to her.' He turned to look at her then, his deep-set eyes looked salt-rimmed. 'She needs watching over. Doesn't understand the world like we do.'

'But Jane looks after her, doesn't she?'

'Yes, thinks the world of her. But Jane reckons it's good for her to meet people and try new things.'

'And you don't?'

'Some, yes. But she's too trusting. She'll get hurt.'

'She's not a child. She's a middle-aged woman.'

'But she is a child, you see. That's what Jane doesn't understand. She's known her less than a year.'

'Jill mentioned that.'

'Didn't know Marguerite existed until her mother died and left her Wraith Cottage.'

'How incredible.' Sophie wondered what effect that must have had on them both.

'Marguerite is incredible.' Neptune turned to face her. 'Would you keep an eye on her for me?'

'I don't really see her. Especially now, I'm not living with Jill and Ash.'

'The Bone Man. He's the one that worries me.'

Sophie didn't want to hear this. She turned to walk back to the others. Neptune caught her arm.

'You don't need to be scared, about living here. The cliffs are right enough. Learn to respect the sea, that's all. It means you no harm.'

She returned to the table. Marguerite sat at one end drawing pictures with the children. Jack and Tom were scribbling away with their pencils. Fleur and Mila were playing with Marguerite's long silver hair, winding it around their fingers, looking sleepy. Sophie could see what Neptune meant about Marguerite. She was childlike, absorbed in what she was doing without self-consciousness. Kyp lolled back in his chair, satiated, his arm around Evie. Chas and Jane chatted with Nick and Rachel. Ash was leaning against one of the posts that supported the canvas awning, watching Marguerite draw. Sophie looked at Jill, unusually quiet, standing in the cabin doorway, sipping her drink, wearing a tight black dress which revealed a large amount of golden bosom. Her hair was loose around her face. Raising a hand to push it back, she swayed; her eyes were on Ash. Sophie felt a pang of guilt that she still hadn't been able to help her. And now that she'd moved out, she didn't know when or how she was going to get an opportunity to speak to Ash. Jill lurched out of the doorway.

'I think it's time to go, kids,' she said. 'Get your shoes on.'

'Do we have to?' Tom moaned. 'I haven't finished my picture.'

'You can finish it at home. Busy day tomorrow. Come along.'

Ash moved reluctantly and started to gather up their belongings. It meant Rachel had to go too; they were giving her a lift back to Ventnor. Sophie thought she looked disappointed. Kyp had just put on one of her Irish CDs and asked her if she fancied a dance.

'You can stay with me,' Sophie whispered.

Rachel squeezed her arm. 'Better go. Early start in the morning.'

Jill gave Sophie a hug and started off towards the path, dragging a reluctant Tom. Marguerite got up and gave Ash a light kiss on his cheek. He put his arms around her for a moment and then lifted Fleur on his shoulders and set off after Jill.

The rest of them started carrying things inside. The cabin was far bigger than it looked. Half of it was a small holiday apartment, nicely furnished, the walls hung with Evie's watercolours. Sophie thought you might have to appreciate the smell of fish to stay in it. They sat at the table watching the moon, drinking a lemon liqueur that Chas had produced from somewhere. It was sweet and strong. Evie and Kyp sat with a sleepy child on each of their laps.

Chas gave a mighty yawn. 'I suppose we'd better head off, too, before we have to carry someone.' He indicated Marguerite, asleep with her head on Neptune's shoulder. His eyes were closed.

Jane and Chas kissed Sophie, repeating their supper invitation. To her surprise, Neptune didn't go with them. He rolled up his trousers and pushed a small blue and white dinghy out into the sea and hopped nimbly in. Loot jumped in after him.

'Will he be safe?' Sophie asked.

'Hopefully,' said Jane. 'You don't argue with Neptune!'

Sophie thanked Kyp and Evie for the evening and walked back with Nick to their cottages.

'What a wonderful welcome,' she said. 'They are such warm, kind people. Imagine doing all that when they hardly know me.'

'I guess they feel easy with you,' Nick said. 'You flow with them, accommodate their viewpoint. Human beings respond to that.'

Sophie lay on her big, deep mattress, smelling the new linen, and the sweet salty air wafting through the open window. Commie had gone, probably to hunt mice on the cliffs. She stretched out her arms and legs, unable to feel the edges of the bed. This was the first time she'd slept in a double bed since leaving the home she'd shared with Peter. In the first few weeks of his absence she'd wake, finding her hand searching for him, his name on her lips – out of habit she supposed. She imagined him curled up with Melissa. She pictured Kyp and Evie, Jane and Chas, Jill and Ash, Audrey and John. And then she thought about Rachel, choosing to live alone, and Nick. But they were on their own through choice. Had she chosen this? *Everything I experience is the result of all I have thought*. She smiled – that was her miracle box talking. And she couldn't think of anyone that she would want to be snuggled up with right now. But neither could she imagine being on her own for the rest of her life either. Never to make love again . . . to grow old alone . . .

She lay thinking about the new people in her life and how relaxed they all seemed compared to her frantic London friends. Except Jill and Ash. She needed a little more time to adjust and then she would think about what she could do to help them. She didn't want to believe that something could be happening between Ash and Marguerite that might be considered unethical on his part. But she had become involved now, whether she liked it or not. She tried to clear her mind, not wanting to go to sleep anxious. She listened to the rhythmic sound of the waves and started to drift. Nick said that she was a flowing person, accommodating – she'd felt surprised by his perception. Is that how others saw her? She wasn't accommodating Ash and Jill's problems at the moment. Sophie didn't know if she wanted to flow freely. Into her mind came an image of a beaver building a dam across a stream. Maybe that's what she needed to do.

Nick lay in his narrow bed, on top of his sleeping bag, thinking about the evening. It hadn't been his idea to have a welcoming party for Sophie. He thought she might have preferred to be left alone to settle in and rest. But it was Kyp's way. He loved celebrations and the chance to go full out with his cooking skills. He'd laughed off Nick's protests, shrugged his hairy shoulders, and got on the phone to Jane and Rachel and Jill.

Nick wondered why he felt the need to protect Sophie. He knew protection could be a misguided notion. She was a grown woman, perfectly capable of making her own decisions. She could have stayed for just an hour if she'd wanted to. But she seemed to have enjoyed herself, getting to know everyone and exclaiming over the food. The first experience of sampling Kyp and Evie's cuisine could be bliss. She'd spent a lot of time listening to the others talking, her dark eyes flickering over their faces as if searching for the things they couldn't say. Sometimes he noticed she went missing, as if she retreated behind her eyes into that place of her own. Nick realised he was recognising in her his own familiar way of being in the world.

He'd been aware of the tension between Jill and Ash and how Jill seemed to be drinking much and talking little. Maybe they were both exhausted by launching the health centre and raising their family. Neptune was quiet, observing. But that was just him; he liked to sit back in the shadows and ponder. Nick knew he didn't approve of the way Jane encouraged Marguerite to try new things. But Nick thought Jane was right. Marguerite had been closeted away in Wraith Cove all her life, until Jane had discovered her. And she had so much to offer with her healing gifts. People were drawn to her, awed by her otherworldliness and her beguiling innocence. And she seemed fulfilled by her work, as long as she knew where Jane and Neptune were.

He had enjoyed the evening, thankful for the friends he'd made along this crumbling little stretch of wild coast. He'd watched Sophie being kissed and wished well by everyone. How quickly people warmed to her – almost as if she possessed something they wanted – yet she seemed unaware of the effect she had on others. She'd given him a hug too. He remembered the feel of her silky shirt sliding against his arms.

He turned on his front. Good, she was here, settled in. She could get on with her own life now. He wouldn't have to worry about her any more.

CHAPTER 13

Jill clenched her teeth and her fists as she watched the traffic crawling along Piccadilly from the window of the familiar room above Peter's club. It was ages since she'd been here and the only time Peter had needed persuading. Loyalty to Melissa indeed! What had Sophie called her? The elf queen – poor cow.

She turned back to the room. 'That was absolutely the last time.' She glared at Peter who was lying on the bed, smoking. 'Give me one of those.' She snatched the packet of cigarettes, fumbling to get one out. She lit it and inhaled deeply, trying not to cough, her eyes watering.

'Thought you vowed you'd never touch another,' Peter grinned, propping himself up on one elbow to stub his out. 'But then your resolutions never did amount to much.'

Jill was tempted to grind out her cigarette on his bare chest. She didn't want the damned thing but she would have to smoke it now. Everything was a contest between them. Maybe she could just let it burn away in her fingers without him noticing. The ash dropped onto the thick crimson carpet. Ash, she thought, a cold shiver running through her hot body. She usually managed to block him out of her mind in this situation but it wasn't working today. She was out of practice.

'Cold?' Peter asked. 'Come and get warmed up.'

'I said that was the last time!' Jill balanced the cigarette on the ashtray and started to put on her clothes. Peter watched as she dressed and then suddenly sprang up and grabbed her arm.

'If this is the last time, we'd better make it a double.'

Jill tried to pull her arm free. Peter twisted it painfully. Rage welled up inside her and she grabbed at his hair – that forelock of his that always hung over his forehead so boyishly. How she hated it – hated him. Peter yelped and let go of her. Jill scooped up the rest of her things and burst out of the door, still feeling strands of his hair tangled around her fingers.

Sophie's life seemed to space out after she moved to Blue Slipper Bay, almost as if there were a conspiracy to avoid her. She wondered if Rachel had told Nick that she wanted time alone and he'd informed Kyp and Evie.

She'd started off driving to work but soon found that by the time she'd walked up to the car park, driven into Ventnor and sought a parking space, it was easier to walk. The weather was quiet and sunny, the coastal path a constant delight. She'd never been one for walking, or observing nature other than that which came with the graveyard. People were her focus – usually desperate ones. Yet she was discovering she could be halted by the sight of little green lizards darting across her path or a big black bird stretching umbrella wings on a beacon out at sea. She didn't know what species they were and she didn't need to. She wanted to see everything just as it was without having to use her intellect. *Words are but symbols of symbols* – Tiggy had said that, or had she made it up? Those moments of wonder felt almost sacred, and she held them in her mind's eye, like Wordsworth's daffodils. She felt fitter, enjoying the sensation of her striding legs and the sea breeze on her skin. She bought a backpack so she could wear shorts to work and change when she got there.

Sometimes she glimpsed Nick as he went off to work at Wraith Cove, in the opposite direction. They waved to each other but didn't stop to speak. Sophie thought he probably wasn't the type to stand and chat. At other times she saw him swimming in the sea or running around with Jack, Mila and Evie. Kyp seemed to prefer lazing in a deckchair with his cap over his eyes and a beer in his hand, when he wasn't working. She wondered if the others thought she was being unfriendly, but she didn't quite know how to go down to the beach and join in. They seemed so established. Would she be an intruder? Maybe she should just wander down casually and sit on the sand. She didn't like swimming, felt unsure of all that surging sea. But she could paddle, or play with the kids. It's just a bit too soon, she concluded, giving herself a break. She recognised her tendency to want to be seen as friendly, welcoming. Before she knew it she would be offering to babysit or help Kyp and Evie in the kitchen.

She'd called in at Cormorants a couple of times during breaks, but Jill hadn't been in the house. Rachel was busy too. The café was doing good trade with all the sunshine. She spent evenings baking, and making sure Aidan revised for his exams. She promised when he'd finished they'd all have a big night out.

Sophie whiled away the evenings lounging on the sofa in front of the open French windows. She had no desire to watch television or hear the news or listen to music. She'd never done much of that anyway. Her favourite thing had always been browsing – old buildings – places with atmosphere. She liked to stand and stare – if she ever got the time. She tried to read Jane's novel, but invariably found herself dropping the book into her lap and being entertained by the changing formations and colours of the sky and sea. Her body relaxed like an inanimate object whilst her mind felt free, as if she were travelling with the clouds. She imagined herself still going through the process of defrosting, and soon she might end up as a puddle of water on the floor. Sometimes Commie wandered in but even he kept his distance, stretching out at her feet, purring from time to time but never trying to jump on her lap. She didn't think she could recall a time in her life when she had spent so much time alone, with nothing to do. She realised that she'd stopped dwelling on Peter and Melissa. Even Audrey couldn't ring here with no available signal. She wondered how long this would go on – this desire to be solitary.

Today, on her way to work she'd decided it was time to put more effort into seeking Jill out. Plucking up her courage she'd ventured into the health centre but Solveig told her Jill had gone to London for the day and Ash was very busy. Sophie caught a glimpse of Marguerite as a door opened and closed.

Suddenly, a blast of wind gusted in the café door, spraying sand over the floor. The menu board outside tipped over with a clatter.

'They did forecast a storm,' Rachel said as the sky blackened and the café emptied after afternoon tea. 'I think I'll close up. And you'd better get home before it really breaks.' She went outside to close the awning and Sophie followed to rescue the tables and chairs before they blew away along the esplanade. 'Actually,' Rachel added as she came back in, 'I think I'd better run you home, the coastal path will be blustery.'

'Don't worry; it won't take me long now that I'm so fit and healthy.' Sophie held up her arms and flexed her biceps. 'Anyway, it's quite sheltered through the Botanic Gardens.'

Rachel frowned. 'Well, go now, before the wind gets any stronger, and stay well away from the edge.'

'Yes, Mum.'

Rachel laughed and handed her a plastic bowl of pasta salad. 'Put that in your backpack and don't be so cheeky.'

Sophie enjoyed the walk home. The salty wind whipped at her hair and stung her eyes. The sea was surging and moaning as if a restless monster was stirring beneath the surface. The palms and tree ferns were whipping their fronds in the Botanic Gardens and as she reached the path down to Blue Slipper Bay the first heavy drops of rain started to smack the ground, releasing such a pungent smell from the vegetation that it was hard to inhale. Her senses seemed heightened by the energy of the weather; as if something pent up was about to break loose. She wanted to strip off her clothes and run on the beach, yelling. For the first time, she wished she had someone to share this with.

She made tea and stood at the French windows, watching. The sea was full of dark streaks and the white edged waves surged sideways driven by the squally, whining wind. She could feel a vibration beneath the floorboards as the cottage was buffeted. But she didn't feel scared. Why hadn't she enjoyed the drama of weather before? It had been a nuisance in her life up until now, making patients complain of stifling wards or draughts, disrupting transport and precipitating accidents.

The sky grew darker, clouds banked, mauve and broody. White flecks of foam started to fly past the windows like snow. A light flashed on in the cabin. Had Nick made it home from Wraith Cove? And where was Commie? She hoped he'd taken refuge somewhere. She ate pasta salad, watching an oil tanker rising and falling, imagining complacent sailors playing cards below deck without feeling queasy.

The evening darkened, the sea turned grey-brown and the rain started to lash at the windows. Leaves and small branches were blown onto the balcony. She wondered if she should bring in the outdoor furniture but it seemed tightly wedged and it would be difficult opening the doors. She consulted the tide table that Kyp had given her. It was on its way out but waves were still roaring up the beach, pounding the rocks, sending spray over the top, which hit the cottage with an alarming rattle as if it contained sand and small stones. Spume was building up in a cliff hollow like a giant's laundry tub. She remembered what Rachel had said about the danger here, and Nick laughing it off.

She couldn't come to any harm, could she? The others would have warned her by now. They would be preparing to evacuate. She told herself not to be so silly, cleared up her dishes and picked up her book. And then the lights went out. Now she did feel nervous. It wasn't a deep dark, just past the summer solstice. She could see quite well when her eyes adjusted. But her heart was thumping. She didn't have any candles or even a torch. She must remember to buy these things tomorrow. She wondered whether she had an excuse to pop along to Nick's or Evie's to borrow a candle, but didn't want to be seen as a wimp with the first little storm. Maybe she should just go to bed. But what if the weather should get worse and she did have to leave in a hurry? She kept her clothes on and sat down. And then there came a knock on her sitting room door. Somebody must have let themselves in downstairs without her hearing them.

'Who is it?' she called, tentatively, her ear pressed to the wood.

'Kyp.' His voice sounded loud. She jumped back and opened the door, pleased to see him. 'So sorry,' he said. 'You didn't hear me knock downstairs.' He was wearing his yellow waterproofs which wafted the smell of fish into the room and from which he produced a bunch of candles. 'Evie thought that you might need these. We forgot to say that the power goes off here when we have a strong westerly.' He smiled, showing his big white teeth. 'The good news is that it comes on again quite quickly.' He thrust the candles at her. 'Now, do you want to come over to us or are you all right?'

'I'm fine, I think. Just tell me I'm safe and I'll believe you.'

'You are perfectly safe. But you are also welcome to join us if you'd like to. The weather can be frightening if you aren't used to it. But the tide is going out. The real danger is when the wind comes straight in from the south, and we have a spring tide. The water can surge right under the cottages then. It's quite spectacular.'

'That makes me feel a whole lot better,' Sophie laughed. 'Do you know what, Kyp? I think I'll stay here and prove to myself that I can survive. And thank you for the candles.'

'No problem. I'm afraid I've dripped on your stairs,' he called back.

She lit a couple of Kyp's fishy candles and settled back on the sofa, listening. At one stage there was a thump on the roof and she wondered if it was a branch or a bit of slippery blue cliff. She persuaded herself to undress and go to bed. She lay awake, aware of thuds and crashes and the fact that her mind kept wishing it had been Nick that knocked on her door.

Nick wondered if Sophie would be frightened by the storm. But he couldn't decide what to do. He didn't want to patronise her by knocking on her door and asking her if she was all right, but he didn't want her to think he was uncaring either. So here he was, sitting with uncertainty, yet again. He never used to be like this. He'd always been quite definite in his actions. But look where that had got him. Now he thought long and hard before making decisions. Except when he'd suggested Sea Spray to Sophie. He sighed. Maybe that had been a mistake after all. He did feel responsible, even though she'd asked him for nothing. In fact, she looked extremely self-sufficient, striding off to work in the mornings with her backpack on, giving him a cheery wave. He half hoped she'd come down to the beach when he'd been swimming with the kids. If she'd been the first to join in, he wouldn't feel so intrusive now.

Keri would have told him, 'Do it or don't do it, but stop wavering.' She would have had no hesitation in knocking on Sophie's door and asking her round for a drink. But then, that was different; woman to woman.

And then the lights went out. Come on, he told himself, you only want to be friendly to a new neighbour.

He got up and found a spare candle. He put on his waterproof jacket and went down the stairs. As he prised open the front door against the wind, he saw Kyp approaching, head down, obviously going to check on her. Nick went back inside, and took off his coat. That was all right then. He didn't have to be concerned now. Kyp would reassure her. Maybe she would go back with him to their place. He noticed he felt a twinge of disappointment.

Jill arrived at Cowes feeling dirty. Usually she would have had a shower before leaving London.

She walked to Terminus Road where Ash was parked waiting for her. She was late; the Red Jet service disrupted by a bad storm the crew told her. There was an unearthly hush over Cowes. No wind rattling ropes against masts, no seagulls crying, no traffic creeping along the dim, narrow high street. Or maybe it was just her – the lull after her own storm. She could see Ash under a street lamp, leaning against the car. He hadn't seen her; he was gazing into the distance. Usually he would be craning his neck, watching for her. She was almost beside him before he seemed to notice her.

He smiled. 'Seminar worthwhile?'

Jill got into the car quickly before he could kiss her. 'It was okay, mainly cognitive stuff. I hear there's been a storm.'

'Big one. Stopped suddenly – eerie.'

A silence fell between them as they drove out of Cowes and down into Newport. Jill gave an exaggerated yawn as if tiredness were the reason for her lack of chatter. She was usually the one who did most of the talking. The town gave way to the countryside, the car sending up walls of water from the puddles and Jill felt as if she were cooling off as they headed south through Rookley. The moon was shining; wild roses were luminous in the glistening hedgerows. A slender fox crossed in front of them, turning its head to look at them, its eyes blazing briefly in the headlights. Jill looked at Ash; his face was stern, concentrated. She knew how he dreaded hitting a wild animal. The car slid through Godshill – quiet as midwinter. No late night holiday makers. It must have been one hell of a storm.

'Was Solveig happy to babysit?' she asked to break the silence.

Ash nodded.

'And the kids were okay with her?'

He nodded again. Jill sighed, don't part with too much information, she thought.

'Sorry,' he commented, obviously registering her sigh. 'Rose phoned tonight. She's not coming home next week. She wants to go travelling for a while with some of her friends.'

'Oh. Did she say how long for?'

Ash took a hand off the steering wheel and ran it through his hair. 'No. I tried to pin her down but she said a group of them were going back-packing, they didn't know where yet – probably France – maybe doing some casual work.' He put his hand back on the wheel with a thump. 'She was so evasive.'

'Maybe she genuinely doesn't know.'

'She must have some idea. She said one of her friends had it all in hand.'

'Which friend?'

'Didn't say.'

'No details at all?'

'Well, she just said she'd keep in touch – by phone – and email from internet cafés.'

Jill knew it would be pointless trying to tell him

that Rose would be okay, she was an adult now – all that stuff that she said so often. He was concerned for her – overly-concerned in Jill's opinion – and she couldn't comfort him. She had an urge to reach out to him, to give his thigh a reassuring squeeze. But she didn't have the right to touch him, even though she'd scrubbed her hands in the ladies' room at Waterloo.

I won't ever do this again to you, Ash, she thought. It's over and done with. She put a hand on her bag. She'd got what she wanted.

CHAPTER 14

The day before Sophie's thirty-eighth birthday, Jill called into the café. Sophie was so pleased to see her she almost begged her to sit down and have a coffee. But Jill wouldn't stay. She invited Sophie to dinner with her and Ash the following evening. This was difficult. Aidan had finished his exams and Rachel and Nick had arranged a joint celebration for tomorrow night. Sophie could tell Jill was disappointed. She saw her eyes flicker away and fasten on Rachel's back as if she'd like to sink a knife into it. But then she lifted her chin in the stance of the old defiant Jill she'd always known.

'Well, why don't you come out with us tonight instead? Ash and I are taking the kids up to Cowes to see the Queen Mary sail. We could have a bite to eat there.'

'I'd love to, Jill, thanks.' But Sophie still felt the need to reassure her. She lowered her voice. 'I'm really sorry about tomorrow. I would put it off, but it's Aidan's treat too.' She hoped she didn't sound insincere. But the thought of a light-hearted evening with Rachel and Co. seemed infinitely preferable to a few hours caught between Ash and Jill's cross-fire.

Sophie walked up to Cormorants after work and showered and changed there. It seemed strange to be back in a noisy family. She thought about Sea Spray, imagining it waiting for her, peaceful and undemanding. She held the image in her mind, an inner retreat, as she sat in the back of the BMW, between Fleur and Tom, diffusing their bickering with I-Spy.

It was the eve of the annual Round the Island Yacht Race and Cowes was crowded with sailing enthusiasts. They parked at Egypt Point and walked along the sea front towards the town centre. Ash seemed in a good mood, striding along the pebbled beach, stopping to lob stones in the water and generally fool around with his kids. Sophie felt relieved to see them acting like a family again, although Fleur seemed a bit clingy. She kept looking towards Jill, occasionally returning to hold her hand. Sophie could see that Jill wanted to talk, but didn't want to push Fleur away.

'Go and see if you can beat them at stone-throwing,' Jill encouraged her. 'You mustn't let the men win, Fleur.'

Fleur reluctantly let go of her hand. Her bottom lip pouted. Poor Fleur, Sophie thought, remembering how her own mother used to banish her in just the same fashion when she was little. It was usually when Mum wanted to have a private talk with Dad. Sophie knew that – even when she was very young. And Fleur knew now, she was sure.

Jill put her arm through Sophie's. 'I wanted to tell you that I'm sorry for being so bitchy,' she said. 'I realise now what a predicament I put you in with Ash. I should never have tried to involve you when you are only just recovering from your own traumas.'

'It's all right, Jill, honestly.' Sophie pressed her arm. 'I did call in at the centre a couple of times but Ash was busy, guarded by The Valkyrie.'

She laughed. 'Well, you don't need to worry any more. I think we've sorted things out.'

'You have?' Sophie felt her stomach plummet with relief as if it had been dropped down a lift-shaft. 'How? I mean, did you manage to confront him?'

She nodded. 'In fact, he seemed quite keen to talk about it. I think he'd had enough of whatever it was he was up to. I still don't know the details and I don't think I want to.'

'I'm so glad.' Sophie wondered if she should ask more questions but decided to let it rest. Ash and the kids were deeply involved now in a stone skimming contest. Jill and Sophie sat down on a bench to wait. Sophie felt Jill had more to say; the air between them seemed full of unsaid things that wanted to be heard.

'It was Solveig, you know,' Jill said, suddenly.

'What was?'

'It was she who taught him about regression.

You know he treats her in return for helping out in reception. She's recovering from her car accident and she's been giving him head and shoulder massage. She taught him techniques to release deeply imbedded trauma which sometimes taps into past lives. Or so she says. Ash says he had some amazing experiences with her. He wanted to tell me about it but I said I would rather not know. He was tempted – and tried it – with some of his clients. The type who never improve for no apparent reason.'

'Did Solveig supervise him?'

'No. He says she knew nothing about it. But he got frightened when he realised what a powerful tool it was and felt unsure how to handle it. He told Solveig and she was furious. She said he shouldn't meddle with such things and that he must have a student or Marguerite or even herself, in the room with him, especially with females, until he gets stable.'

'Good heavens. Did he take all that from her?'

'Apparently, yes. He certainly seems more grounded. He set up a practitioners' meeting and we discussed the whole problem of students. When they're not sitting-in with the therapists they clog up reception and make mistakes with the bookings. And then there's Marguerite floating around.'

'And what was the outcome?'

'Solveig is now working full time for a proper salary. She makes the appointments, takes the fees and supervises the students – she knows them, some of them lodge with her. She talks to the clients when they arrive to get their permission for a student, or Marguerite, to be in the room during their consultation. Most of them are co-operative – it makes them feel important. And I think Ash feels safer, that he's less likely to venture off his chosen path, so to speak.'

'Has he given up his interest in things esoteric?'

'Not altogether. But he has promised that he won't experiment without further study and doing some proper training.'

Ash was walking towards them from the beach. He had an arm around each of the children and they were having a friendly squabble.

'Shall we find somewhere to eat?' he said.

They wandered along to Cowes Yacht Haven to see the boats packed in ready for the big race. People were hopping over rails from deck to deck to get ashore. Sophie wondered if there might be a few inadvertent cold dips later, after the drinks flowed. The crews were crammed into the restaurants and pubs and marquees, many of them overflowing onto the pavements. Music spilled out of windows and a live band was rocking. Young men milled about everywhere, looking like a tanned and healthy army of Williams and Harrys. The delicious smell of cooking wafted about but it didn't look as though there were any free tables to be had.

Jill leaned on the wall, watching the ferries and the harbour taxis zooming around the packed vessels.

'As a special treat, seeing as it's Sophie's birthday tomorrow, why don't we have fish and chips and eat it out of the paper? Then we can watch the boats,' she said.

'Grab that bench,' Ash said, as some people got up. 'And Sophie and I will go and get it.'

That would mean Ash had something to say to her, she thought. The fish and chips didn't need two people to carry them. Once out of sight of Jill, he slowed down, as she knew he would.

'I expect Jill told you that we've made some changes at the centre.'

'Yes, it sounds much better, more organised.'

'I hadn't realised that we would get so busy so soon. I thought we could get by with making our own appointments with the students helping out. But they don't want to do that, they want to be sitting in, learning.'

'Of course they do. A good receptionist is essential.' Just listen, she thought, joining the end of the queue. Don't ask anything.

'Sophie, I . . . er. Please don't take this the wrong way. But, could I ask you not to mention, to Jill, what you saw that night? I was overwrought at the time.'

His eyes were searching her face. He put his hand on her arm, gently. She just wanted this to be over. 'Don't worry, Ash. But please don't ask me to keep anything from Jill ever again.'

'I won't, and I'm sorry.'

The fish and chips were hot and crisp, liberally

sprinkled with salt and vinegar. The kids blew on the food, and licked their fingers. They squeezed onto the bench together and it felt to Sophie like old times. The air was still and warm, the sky streaked with pink and lilac.

'Look!' said Ash. And they saw the lights of the Queen Mary as she sailed out of Southampton Water into The Solent. A hush seemed to fall on the revellers; the music quietened as she majestically headed straight for them, then gracefully turned. Lights twinkled along her tiered decks like an apartment block. They could see passengers waving and Tom and Fleur dumped their chips on Jill's lap so they could jump up and wave back. As she passed through the narrow stretch of water she gave some low blasts on her horn and a chorus of hoots went up from the small vessels in response.

It was breath-taking. That hackneyed word, awesome, sprang to Sophie's mind. She glanced at the other faces around her. They all seemed mesmerised by the sight. She looked at Jill and Ash; he put his arm around Jill and drew her to him. Tom and Fleur were leaning against their parents. Sophie heard herself sigh.

Nick felt someone was watching him. He backed out from the thicket of blackthorn that he was cutting back and looked round. Jane was standing on the newly cleared path, waiting for him to emerge.

'I thought if I stood here long enough, wafting this, you would take notice.' She held out a plate with a large slice of ginger cake on it. 'Marguerite's been baking.' She sat down on a wall and balanced the plate on it.

Nick put down his saw. His arms were smarting with scratches. He reached for the cake. 'Share it?' he asked.

Jane shook her head. 'I've just had some. It's very good, thought you could do with a break. It's getting late and you've been battling in that undergrowth for hours.'

'I enjoy it.' He took a bite, thinking how thoughtful Jane was to have walked all the way up here. She and Chas were good to work for.

'I wanted to ask you if you had any plans to go away this summer,' she said.

'No. I am going back to New Zealand some time. But I think that will be next year.'

'Chas and I were wondering if you'd keep an eye on Wraith Cottage for us, if we go away next month. Neptune will be around but the builders are coming in to put in the new bathroom, and I don't want them knocking the old place about too much. I had planned to spend the summer here but I want to take Marguerite away for a while – show her a bit more of the world.'

Nick noticed that Jane had a slight frown on her usually clear face. He wondered if something was wrong.

'Does she want to do that?' he asked.

'She likes new experiences, as long as I'm close by. But so far I've only taken her back and forth to Herefordshire. I might be a little more adventurous next time. Perhaps, London – or Paris.' She smiled. 'Don't tell Neptune, he already thinks I'm polluting her mind.'

'I can't imagine Marguerite being polluted.'

'No, she's quite strong about what she wants to accept.' She turned her face away to look at the sea. 'It's the health centre that troubles Neptune.'

'Cormorants? But isn't that the ideal place for Marguerite? She seems to fit in there.'

'She does, and it wasn't my idea that she should get involved. It was hers, and I respect that.'

'I'm picking up that you have some reservations.'

She nodded. 'Marguerite gets very preoccupied with it. I can tell she's anxious. Sometimes I've had to drive her over there during the night because she can't rest until she's stood outside for a while and done some of her tuning in.'

'Tuning in to what?'

'Well, there are no patients there at that time. I can only think it's Ash.'

'Ash?'

Jane nodded. 'He's helped her so much – she gets painful spasms in her weak side. She's grown fond of him. I don't know what that means for her, or whether he's even aware of it. She has no experience of that sort of relationship and I'm unsure whether she can handle it. I can't decide whether to say something to her, or just trust that she's a grown woman and respect her privacy.' As she turned to face him, Nick could see that she was full of self-doubt. 'And now I feel I'm betraying confidences – hers and possibly Ash's. Then there's Jill and the children. I know Jill isn't too happy about Marguerite working there.'

'Has she said anything?'

'She asked me if I had any concerns. She said Marguerite seemed very vulnerable. I told her Marguerite could decide for herself. But that was before she became so distracted.'

'Jane.' Nick sat down on the wall beside her and knew that he wasn't going to hold back. 'If you're worried about Marguerite you must tell her your fears. I'm glad you felt you could talk to me. Don't worry about confidentiality or breach of trust. You love her and she needs you. It's as simple as that. It might all blow over, but if some sort of crisis is brewing and you keep quiet when you could have spoken out, you'll never forgive yourself.'

Jane sat looking at him. 'You sound as if you're speaking from personal experience, Nick,' she said, gently.

Nick looked down at his earthy hands. 'I learned the hard way,' he said.

Jill had thought she might feel better after she and Ash had talked. He'd initiated it, waking her during the night that she'd got back from London, pouring out all that stuff about feeling taken over by new ideas and all the uncertainty around what he was getting into. 'I feel like a man possessed,' he'd said. He'd talked and talked until the birds started to chirrup and then he'd fallen into a sound sleep, leaving her exhausted and wondering what it had all really been about, whether she should pursue it further, or whether to close the door on it and hope for the best.

He certainly seemed more normal now, especially after putting all his safeguards into practice. He polished his cello and put more vigour into his morning jog and games with the kids. He even appeared accepting that Rose was going travelling and transferred some money into her account. 'Emergency fund,' Jill heard him telling Rose on the phone. Jill raised her eyebrows, knowing what students spent their funds on.

It had felt good to be able to tell Sophie that things were better and apologise for her belligerent behaviour.

'Well,' Sophie said, her dark eyes sparkling. 'We said we'd arrange to have our mid-life crises together, didn't we?'

'Have we had them then?' Jill said.

'Done and dusted,' Sophie replied.

But Jill didn't feel better deep down. Whatever had precipitated this change was forcing her to take her next step. She'd avoided confronting herself for too long. She was going to have to do it alone. But do it she must, if she was ever going to be able to like herself.

CHAPTER 15

'You're very chirpy today,' Rachel said to Sophie as they cleared up the café for the evening. They'd been busy with people crowding in out of the rain, wanting to see the yachts go by.

'Chirpy?' Sophie said. 'I haven't had time to speak.'

'I've seen you, chatting up all those lovely yachty men – just because it's your birthday.'

'I was simply taking their orders.'

'What, no phone numbers?'

Sophie threw a tea towel at her. 'Honestly, Rachel, we're not all sex-mad like you.'

'Are you sex-mad, Mother?' Aidan appeared in the doorway from upstairs.

'Wish I had some sex to get mad about,' Rachel replied, unperturbed.

Sophie smiled at Aidan, thinking how accepting he was that his mum might possibly still be a sexual being. She couldn't imagine saying anything like that to her mother when she was a kid. Mum would have taken to her bed with smelling salts.

Rachel tied up the rubbish bag and handed it to him. 'Dustbin,' she said. Sophie put her hands on her hips and looked around the tidy kitchen. She had an eye for it now. Things out of place, needing attention, were soon pounced on by one of them. They worked well together and both got satisfaction out of knowing they'd provided people with good food and drink and a warm welcome, even if they did mess up the place continuously.

'Right,' Rachel said. 'Let's go upstairs and put our feet up for half an hour before we throw on our glad rags and Nick arrives.'

Sophie dropped onto Rachel's sofa. Her feet felt as if she were back in her student nurse days. Aidan made coffee and sat on the floor telling them about the rock festival and how David Bowie could still hit the spot even though he was a crusty.

'He's ours,' Rachel said. 'You stick to Eminem.'

'The best ones last for ever, Mum. Come on, like, you still rate The Beatles and The Stones, yeah?'

'Yeah,' Rachel agreed.

Sophie looked around the small sitting room. There were many photographs of Aidan and Patrick when they were babies, school photos, sports days. She wondered how the boys felt that their father wasn't in any of them. They still saw Connor from time to time. She supposed when you had children there would always be that link. Peter and she would probably never see or hear from each other again. She would receive the divorce papers eventually, sign them, and that would be it. She would never know how his life would turn out, whether he would stay with Melissa or have children with someone eventually. And Peter would never know about her, unless he kept in touch with Audrey. But why would he? She stretched her arms out above her head and yawned. It felt so good to be free of the anxiety of him, to be unselfconscious of how she looked and behaved when she was at home by herself. And now the worry about Jill and Ash seemed to have evaporated too. Lying there at that moment, relaxed, listening to Aidan goading Rachel, and the anticipation of enjoying a good meal with them and Nick later, she felt she wouldn't trade places with anyone.

The doorbell rang downstairs.

'Nick's early,' Rachel said. 'Oh, well, he'll just have to wait while we get ready. I'll go and have a shower.'

Aidan got up. 'I'll let him in then, seeing as you two old birds are clapped out.' The doorbell rang again. 'Okay, okay,' he grumbled, going downstairs. Sophie could hear him unlocking the door of the café and briefly wondered why Nick hadn't come round the back. Aidan reappeared. 'Sophie,' he said, 'there's a guy outside asking for you.'

'Me?' She sat up. 'Promise me, Aidan, it's not a kissagram or anything like that is it? A male stripper?'

'He doesn't look the type. But you might be lucky.'

'Did he say what he wanted?'

'Like, er, you.'

She got up. It was most likely a customer who had lost something, asking if they'd left it here. She went downstairs and into the café. A man was standing looking out of the window at the rain. He was wearing a grey suit, dark with damp on the shoulders. His light hair glistened with raindrops. She felt as if her heart was going to leap out of her chest. Her hand automatically went to her hair, smoothing it down. He turned round.

'Peter! What are you doing here?'

He looked her up and down, just as he'd always done. She felt under scrutiny; some things never changed.

He smiled, his face tight and tanned. 'I was working in the area and remembered it was your birthday, so I thought I'd call in.'

'Working where? How did you know where to find me?'

'I've been attending a conference at a hotel in Sandown. I called in at Jill's. She wasn't there,' he grinned, 'but Ash told me where to find you.'

Thank you, Ash, she thought. She knew Jill wouldn't have informed him.

'What do you want?'

'I don't want anything.' He pulled a chair out from one of the tables. Sophie didn't want him to do that, upsetting the neat café, all set up for the morning. He sat down. She noticed he'd left wet footprints on the clean floor. 'I just called to wish you happy birthday, that's all.' He waited for some response from her but she stood paralysed, needing him to go away, not to enter into her territory.

'Is Melissa with you?' The words seemed to come out of her mouth of their own accord. Why, oh why, had she said that?

He smiled; she noticed he'd had his teeth whitened. 'No, this is a work trip.'

'It didn't stop you before.' Oh, God. It was as if someone else was speaking through her. She didn't want to be saying these things. He would think she cared.

'Look, Sophie. I would like to put the past behind us. We've both moved on.' He glanced around the café as if assessing what she'd moved on to. 'I just wondered if you were all right, how you were faring. We were together a long time. I can't just forget about you as if you never existed.'

Sophie almost bit through her tongue in her effort to stop herself sniping. 'I'm fine,' she managed to say.

'Do you live here, upstairs?'

'No.'

He held out a hand. 'Sophie, why don't you sit down? I'm not meaning to upset you. I genuinely wanted to see you, to catch up with you, that's all. Please, can't we try to be friends? I've kept in touch with Audrey and John, I expect you know that. I want to keep on seeing William and Joanna. They are my nephew and niece. They're great kids. And you know I've always been fond of Audrey, she's kind, a good listener.'

'I suppose you've been telling her what a rotten wife I was.'

'No. I wouldn't do that. But she does understand that marriages don't just fall apart for no reason. It's not all on one side, you must know that, all those people you counselled.'

'I never had affairs, Peter.'

'No, but sometimes it felt like it.'

'What do you mean by that?'

'You were always absent—'

'Sorry? *Me* absent?'

'Yes. Always concerned with other people and their troubles, never there for us.'

'So it was my fault, is that what you're saying?'

'No. But I am saying that I'm not entirely to blame.'

'I immersed myself in my work because you were never home—'

'So, you see, it was the same for both of us. We both felt neglected. Didn't we?'

Sophie sank down on a chair opposite him, suddenly feeling exhausted. He always did this to her. He was so good with words. He would twist everything around until she was left wrung out and feeling that, yes, after all she was the guilty one. She could feel him staring, willing her to agree. She raised her eyes to look at him. 'You left me the day my mother died—'

'But I—'

She heard a light tap at the café window. Nick was outside; he must have seen the light on, otherwise he would have gone up the back stairs. She got up to let him in. He pulled the hood back from his raincoat.

'Happy birthday,' he said. And then paused as he scrutinised her face, aware that something was wrong. He caught sight of Peter, sitting at the table. 'Oh, sorry,' he said. 'Am I interrupting?'

At that moment Rachel appeared in her dressing gown with a towel around her head. She looked questioningly at Peter. He got up and held out his hand, giving her his most charming smile.

'I'm Peter,' he said. 'Sophie's husband.'

She hesitated, but shook hands. 'Rachel,' she said.

'He was in the area,' Sophie stammered, as if she had to explain. 'On a conference. He's just leaving.'

Peter turned to Nick. 'And you are?'

'Nick. Sophie's neighbour and friend.' He didn't smile.

Peter put a hand on Sophie's shoulder as if he were laying claim to her. 'Well, I'm glad you've made some new friends.' He looked around the café, his smile fixed as if he were doing the smiling for all of them. 'Ash told me you were working as a waitress now. I hope you don't feel too deskilled.'

She felt her face flush with embarrassment. As usual, all her words seemed to retreat inside her as if escaping from the fate of being unheard. Later, she knew, they would reassemble and taunt her with all the things they could have voiced. She opened the café door; a gust of damp wind blew in. 'Goodbye, Peter,' she said.

'Goodbye, Sophie. Think about what I said.' As he passed her, he whispered in her ear. 'Don't tell Jill I called in. Ash said he wouldn't. You know what she's like.' He planted a kiss on her cheek, which she was too slow to avoid.

Nick pedalled hard along Undercliff Drive, feeling the burn in his muscles. It was early morning and he couldn't sleep. He hadn't seen another soul, only a pheasant squawking across in front of him. The road was closed to traffic, littered with diggers and drilling rigs, endeavouring to delay the slip of land towards sea. He swerved down towards the Old Blackgang Road, determined not to slow until he came to a halt where the road disappeared under the landslip at Windy Corner. He leant his bike against the National Trust notice and climbed to the highest point and sat looking out to sea. The morning light was clear. The Needles jutted, white against the blue. He could see the Dorset coastline, the Purbeck Hills and a glimmer of the Old Harry Rocks, reaching out towards The Needles to which they were once joined. Nick wondered if they pined for each other and if several fathoms deep they were still at one.

Nick thought about the interconnectedness of everything. He thought about the smiling walnut face of Geshe Donchen who had told him the cause of his suffering was his delusion of being separate and impermanent. 'Life is eternal,' he said. 'The opposite of death is birth not life.' Nick observed the peace of the monks and the nuns going about their daily tasks and could sense that some lived from this place of inner peace. He sat with them, watching the rise and fall of his breath, listening to their intonations, intoxicated by the flowers and incense. He had imbibed tracts of Sanskrit texts, could quote Hindu and Christian mystics. But still his thoughts washed in and submerged him in his dead sea.

Why was it so difficult to move on and stop dwelling on the past? 'The past is over, the future yet to come, this moment is all there is,' he could hear Geshe saying. But it seemed to him that his past always intruded into this moment. Even at times when he felt happy at work or relaxing with his friends, out of the blue like a falcon stooping, wham, there it was.

He thought about Sophie and how her past had appeared to hit her with some force last night. She had seemed to diminish under the critical scrutiny of Peter. After he'd left she'd tried to make light of it. They'd had dinner at The Spyglass as planned, laughing at Aidan's adolescent wit. But Sophie was dragging her past along like an albatross; he could sense the weight of it and wished he could hoist a wing onto his own shoulders. Even sunny Rachel had to make an effort, as if memories of old encounters with her ex-husband had been prodded and stirred.

He looked up at the mighty cliffs. The young peregrines should be leaving the nest soon. Their parents would teach them survival skills and let them go without grieving.

Jill took her mail into her consulting room and opened the large brown envelope. It was a brochure on retreat centres that she'd sent away for. She flicked through the pages of beautiful houses in idyllic surroundings. She started to read – but they all seemed so religious. Would she have to join in rituals and get up early to pray to some unknown God? That didn't sound quite what she had in mind. She read a little more. In fairness the blurb did stress that you wouldn't have to join in any form of worship. But even so, she might find herself surrounded by the pious.

She closed the brochure and shoved it in a drawer. Maybe a health spa – but what could a bit of pampering and self-indulgence possibly do for her? A hermit's hut on the side of a bare mountain would probably do her more good.

CHAPTER 16

'I was going to give you a pay rise,' Rachel said, scraping the icing from the mixing bowl and handing Sophie the spoon to lick. 'But seeing as you're eating me out of a profit, I've changed my mind.'

'Sorry,' Sophie mumbled, enjoying the sticky vanilla. 'It's your own fault for being such a tremendous cook.'

Rachel paused, hands on hips, surveying her. 'It can't be right to eat so much and stay so slim. Ever thought you might have worms?'

'Rachel!' Sophie choked. 'I think I would have noticed.'

'Mm, well, it's just not fair.' Rachel wrestled the spoon from her and threw it in the sink. 'I had been thinking about a rise though. You work very hard for your pittance. But I wondered if you would like to have more time off instead. If you're only planning to be here for the summer you're not going to have much time to explore the island, are you?'

'But you won't be able to manage on your own. Look how busy the café is, now it's July.'

Rachel dried her hands and sat down. 'Aidan is looking for a summer job. He's decided not to go camping. He's fallen in love with a lass from St Lawrence. I haven't said anything to him yet, about working here; I wanted to run it past you first. If you fancied a bit more freedom, you and he could do shifts.'

Sophie lent against the counter, thinking. More free time sounded tempting and she could manage on her small wage. In the last few days she had found herself gazing out at the holidaymakers wishing she were outside on the beach or walking the cliffs. 'If you're sure it's all right, then yes, I would like that.'

Rachel patted her hand. 'I'll have a word with Aidan then.'

How perceptive of Rachel, Sophie thought. She really loved working in the café but needed time to think. Peter's visit had disturbed her, made her realise how inadequate she felt in his presence and how her new sense of freedom and confidence hadn't yet grown as strong as she'd imagined. Why hadn't she just told him it was nice to see him, and of course they could be civilised about the past? Instead, she'd made snide remarks about Melissa and let herself down.

When she arrived home, Nick was splashing around with the Water Babies. Usually Sophie just waved and went inside to have a shower. But today, she felt herself hesitating and before her mind had time to censure her, she was unhitching her backpack and kicking off her sandals. The cool waves washed over her aching feet. Jack and Mila rushed up, grabbing her hands, urging her to go in further. Sophie laughed and gasped as the waves hit her thighs.

'Slow down kids, I'm getting my clothes wet.'

'They're only shorts, Sophie,' Mila giggled. Her dark hair was wet, sticking to her brown back.

Jack splashed Sophie and she yelped as the cold water trickled down her front.

'Hey, Jack. That's enough,' Nick called. Sophie retreated to the water's edge and Nick came to stand beside her. 'They think everybody should like the water as much as they do.'

'It's okay. I enjoyed it.' They stood for a while in silence. She wondered if she'd interrupted his game with the children. 'Please,' she indicated the water, 'don't let me stop you—'

'No, really. I was looking for an excuse to escape. I can't keep up with their energy.' He pointed to the little beach. 'Do you want to sit down for a while to dry off?'

They sat on the trunk of a tree that had been washed up by the storm. It was worn silvery smooth, warm against Sophie's legs. She wondered where it had come from. She watched the kids tumbling in the waves with a rubber tyre.

'Busy day?' Nick asked.

'Very. But Aidan and I are going to start working shifts so I will have more time to myself.'

‘That’s good. It will give you a chance to enjoy the holiday season.’

‘I thought I’d like to go walking. I’ve really enjoyed my walks back and forth from work. I want to go further afield.’

‘The island’s a wonderful place for walking. There are more than five hundred miles of footpaths.’ Nick smiled. ‘I sounded just like someone from the Tourist Board then, didn’t I?’

‘Rachel said the same thing – about the walks, I mean. I hardly used to walk anywhere in London, apart from up and downwards.’

‘You never really see a place until you’ve walked it. If you sometimes want a companion, let me know.’

‘Thanks, Nick. That would be nice.’ She hadn’t expected him to say that and wondered if he would regret it. How would he be able to say no, now that he’d offered? And did she want someone with her? She’d seen it as a chance to be alone. But perhaps it would be nice to have company occasionally. They probably wouldn’t talk much anyway.

Nick shaded his eyes and looked out to sea.’ There go Neptune and Marguerite,’ he said.

Sophie could see a yellow fishing boat. ‘Are they checking the pots?’

‘Probably. Or maybe he’s collected her from Ventnor, from the health centre.’

‘He’s very protective of her, isn’t her?’ Sophie felt she was picking her words carefully.

'She's extremely precious to him. He worries about her.'

'Yes, he mentioned that to me – at my welcome party. He asked me to keep an eye on her. But I said I wasn't often at Cormorants these days.' She glanced at Nick; his dark eyes were focused on her face as if he wanted to ask her something.

'Jane is a bit concerned about her too,' he said.

'Why?'

'She thinks she's infatuated with Ash.' He toyed with the woven cord around his wrist. 'Sophie, please don't think that I'm a gossip or trying to spread rumours. It's just that if anything is going on that we all feel uneasy about, I think we should share it. What if something happens to Marguerite that we could have prevented? I know she's an adult, but she has an entirely different take on the world.'

Sophie nodded, wondering why she felt relieved to be talking like this with Nick and then realised it was because he wasn't asking for her help. He simply cared about Marguerite.

'Okay,' she said. 'I suspect that something has been going on. But both Jill and Ash have spoken to me, separately, and it seems that whatever it was is over. Ash got hooked on some sort of regressive therapy that Solveig taught him, and he started experimenting with it. I don't know how deeply Marguerite was involved. But Jill's not keen on her being at the health centre.' She felt unsure whether she should tell him any more, but found she couldn't stop. She read nothing but concern on his face. She found herself telling him about the evening she'd gone down to look for Ash, her suspicions that he'd been having sex, the strange noises. And then, the same night, seeing Marguerite looking up at the house. 'But,' she added. 'I thought that Marguerite was aphasic – silent.'

Nick shook his head. 'She does laugh – and cry. And occasionally I've heard her make a sort of singing noise.' He was frowning. 'Do you think I should confront Ash?'

'Well, as I say, both he and Jill have told me that he's come to his senses and Solveig has organised the whole place it seems.'

'That's good to hear. And Jane plans to take Marguerite away soon.'

They looked at each other as if they were searching for a mutual solution.

'Then maybe we should wait,' he said. 'I know we can trust each other not to let this go any further. We'll see what happens when Marguerite comes back. But if you, or I, have any further suspicions, shall we tell each other? And then we can decide what's best to do.'

Sophie nodded, feeling glad that she wasn't alone with this any more but also wondering why Nick felt so involved. He was still looking at her. He took a deep breath as if making a difficult decision.

'Something happened to me once that I'll always

regret. I didn't speak up when I could have done. It cost a life – two lives.'

He turned away to watch the children, who had been joined by Evie. The yellow fishing boat had chugged out of the bay. Sophie didn't know what to say to Nick. The children called to him and he got up and walked down to the sea.

Nick walked to the top of St Catherine's Hill and realised he was hardly out of breath. This was the second highest point on the island, topped only by St Boniface Down behind Ventnor. He circled the Pepper Pot – the tiny medieval lighthouse – as if it were a Buddhist stupa. He could imagine a solitary Christian monk sitting here, tending the fire, intoning a mass for the drowned. The evening air held patchy mist and the smell of rain. On a crystal clear day you could see practically the whole island from here, even the coast of France, so Kyp said.

He stretched his body, feeling pleased with his fitness. He remembered the first time Keri had invited him on a hike – a tramp, they called it in New Zealand. He asked her if it would be strenuous, worried about his town-boy flab and lack of stamina – he was so much older than her. She'd looked at him in amazement. 'It's just a stroll, Nick. I could do it in high heels.' They'd taken the ferry along the coast and been dropped on a beach in the Abel Tasman National Park. They had to walk thirteen kilometres back, negotiating two landslips. The scenery was stunning, azure sea beckoning through the native bush. But the path was rocky and narrow and steep. Nick thought he was going to die every time they rounded a bend and he realised how far there was still to go. He hadn't brought enough water and he was bitten by sand flies. Keri strode along on her strong brown legs, pointing out this and that splendour. When at last they arrived at the ferry pick-up point, Nick had fallen onto the boat and collapsed in a stupor.

He realised he was smiling at the memory and how they'd laughed about it afterwards. He looked out on the English Channel, a colder, smaller sea than the Pacific. A Brittany ferry was making its way across to France. Maybe he should go away again. Perhaps he had stayed too long in Blue Slipper Bay. He was getting involved with people, feeling the sensation of roots stealthily insinuating themselves into the ground. After Keri's death he'd vowed to himself never again to withhold information that might affect others. The trouble was that being honest seemed to bring with it a degree of intimacy, arising from trust. He hadn't suspected that would happen.

He sat down on the rough grass, watching the ferry. A part of him yearned to be aboard, sailing away alone, unfettered from the possibility of affecting other people's lives.

'How would you like to stay with Grandma for a while during the holidays?' Jill asked Tom and Fleur, as she drove them home from school.

'In Africa?' Tom asked. 'Brill. We might get attacked by a lion or something.'

'Or, or a giraffe,' Fleur added.

'Giraffes don't attack, silly.'

'Hush!' Jill said. 'I meant your other grandma. The one who lives in London – and Grandpa, of course.'

'With the dogs! We can play with the dogs!' Fleur said.

'Cool,' said Tom, sounding disappointed about marauding lions.

'Okay,' Jill said. 'How about on your own – without me and Daddy?'

'Why?' asked Tom.

'Well, Daddy is working very hard at the moment and I want to go somewhere else.'

'I want to come with you, Mummy,' Fleur's voice had turned whiny.

'I'll stay for a little while at Grandma's, and then go away and come back – and maybe Daddy will come and join us then. What do you think? It will be a real adventure.'

'But where are you going?' Tom's voice had an anxious edge now.

'Not far – just, er, to visit some old friends. You'd be bored. They haven't got any dogs or children to play with.'

'Grandma and Grandpa haven't got any children either,' Tom said.

'What about the children next door? You had great fun last time in their swimming pool – remember?'

Jill sighed with relief as she listened to them beginning to get excited about the trip. She had to free up some time. She'd set some goals for herself and needed to get started. The first step was to retrace her footsteps and lay some old ghosts to rest. She smiled to herself – what a load of old clichés! But she knew she needed to go backwards before she could go forwards with a clearer head than the one she was carrying on her neck at the moment.

CHAPTER 17

Nick was right. There were so many walks; Sophie didn't know where to begin. The tourist shops were full of books on pub walks, nature walks, beach walks, historic walks; there was even an annual walking festival. She went into Newport and bought herself a pair of hiking boots, an Ordnance Survey map and a small pair of binoculars. She also bought lightweight waterproofs – not wanting to be a fair-weather walker. A flexible schedule had been amicably worked out with Aidan and she was looking forward to going off on her adventures.

She started with the local area, striding along the sea wall to Bonchurch on a blustery day, waves lashing, leaving her with a salty coating and hair like a scouring pad. She explored the tiny Saxon church and discovered Swinburne's grave and the house where Charles Dickens wrote six chapters of David Copperfield. She had intended to walk from there up to the top of St Boniface Down but realised that was over ambitious. By the time she'd arrived back at Blue Slipper Bay she was exhausted and limping with a blister rubbed by her new boots.

Evie, Kyp and the kids were outside the cabin, looking at the overcast sky. They waved to Sophie and instead of waving back and going indoors, she hobbled over to them.

'You look as if you've overdone it,' Kyp said, grinning. 'Park your behind and have some tea.'

She sank gratefully onto a chair and removed her boots while Evie and Kyp argued about whether to serve supper inside or outside.

'The weather forecast definitely said rain,' Evie said, pouring tea.

Kyp held up his hands and stuck out his bottom lip. 'Okay, okay. But you can never tell in The Undercliff.'

'I know. I know all about the special micro-climate. But we don't want to have to rush everything inside if it pours, do we?'

Kyp put his big arms around her waist from behind and squeezed her, winking at the children. 'Don't be cross with poor Kyppie,' he whined.

'Oh, get off, you big clown,' she said, laughing with the kids. 'Where've you been then, Sophie?'

She told them about her exploration of Bonchurch, and Evie was telling her some local history, when Nick arrived. He glanced at Sophie's discarded boots and winced.

'I know how that feels,' he said. 'But they'll soon toughen up – your feet, I mean, not the boots.'

Evie poured him some tea and he told them about some challenging walks that he'd done in the Himalayas.

‘Can we go? Will you take us there on Saturday?’ Jack said. He and Mila had been listening, enthralled.

‘It’s a long way, far across the sea,’ Nick said.

‘We’ve been across the sea lots of times. I was born in the sea,’ Jack said, clapping his hands, eager for more stories.

‘So was me,’ said Mila, leaning against Nick’s knees. ‘Your fingers are all dirty, Nick.’

‘That’s because I’ve been digging,’ he said. ‘I’m going to go home now and get cleaned up.’

Sophie got up and picked up her boots. ‘Me too.’

She walked gingerly across the path to Sea Spray, Nick carrying her backpack. He handed it to Sophie at her door.

‘I was going to ask you if you wanted to go out for a drink tonight,’ he said. ‘But I expect you just want to rest your feet.’

‘Well, I’m working in the morning, but—’

‘Oh, well, another time, perhaps,’ Nick said, backing away as if he’d changed his mind.

Sophie went inside, Commie slipping past her legs to run up the stairs ahead of her. She had a hot shower and dabbed calendula on her heels. They weren’t as bad as she thought; her leg muscles ached more. She cooked herself some beans on toast and sat at the table watching the heaving sea and billowing clouds as she ate. It was still quite early. She could hear laughter as Kyp and Evie's evening guests arrived. For the first time since she'd moved into Sea Spray, she felt restless, wishing she had the company of a friend. Rachel perhaps, or Jill. She hadn't meant to turn down Nick's invitation; it was as if he'd expected her to, before she had a chance to think.

She went up to the bedroom and took off her dressing gown and put on jeans and a shirt. What the hell, she would ask Nick if he wanted to share a bottle of wine – or something non-alcoholic. Why did she find it so difficult to just be friendly? She supposed it was the sex thing that always got in the way. But surely they were both old enough for that not to be an issue. Rachel had said he didn't want a relationship, and neither did she. So he could only say no, couldn't he? And that was okay between friends. With bare feet she padded down the stairs feeling as if she were taking a risk but also letting down a barrier.

Nick scrubbed at his nails, wondering whatever had induced him to ask Sophie out for a drink and then retract it before she'd even had a chance to think about it properly. He recalled the look of bewilderment on her face as he'd turned away. No wonder she was confused, he confused himself all the time these days. It was as if one part of him acted independently, and the other cautious part took its time to catch up and step in.

Caution. Stop, caution, go. Perhaps he was stuck at caution and would never go again.

Suddenly he recalled standing on the very edge of a tiny platform, poised over the Kawerau Gorge, the green river winding far below. His arms were raised, his ankles tied together. He felt paralysed with fear.

'In yer own time, Mate,' the man said, behind him.

'Go for it, Nick,' he heard Keri call.

His body tipped forward and he felt himself plummeting through space, the river hurling itself up at him. There was no way he was going to be able to stop. He was going to die. His head and shoulders broke the water in an emerald shoal of bubbles, then he was catapulted back into dazzling air, gasping as if he'd just been born. He felt exhilarated. He wanted to leap straight up to the bridge and do it again.

Nick dried his hands and looked at himself in the bathroom mirror. His eyes were sparkling, his heart drumming with the memory. He went into his tiny kitchen and took a bottle of elderflower from the fridge, deciding to take the plunge before his mind could rationalise him out of it.

Just as he was about to knock on Sophie's door, it opened, and there she stood clutching a bottle. They both started to speak at once and then began to laugh.

'We're obviously not the world's greatest drinkers,' Sophie said, watching Nick sip at his elderflower. She toyed with her wineglass. 'One or two glasses are my limit; I fall asleep after that.' She felt they were dancing around each other, wary of encroaching on each other's privacy. They tentatively made hints about prospective walks, as if hoping the other one might make a decision, backing off if there was any hesitation.

'Do you like swimming?' he asked, as if trying to move on.

They were sitting on Sophie's balcony. Both their heads turned instinctively towards the sea. She'd seen him swim out a long way, arms rising and falling as if he were pitting his strength against the waves. She'd watched him with anxious fascination.

'Only in the children's pool with my feet on the bottom and my niece's inflatable armbands on.'

Nick tipped back his head and laughed. 'I take that as a *no* then. Don't you like the sea?'

'Oh, yes. I love it. I enjoy watching it and the sound of it. I quite like paddling too.'

'But?'

'It scares me, I suppose. It seems so ruthless . . . greedy almost. It drags and pulls as if it wants to draw everything into itself.'

Nick looked at her thoughtfully. 'Yes, that is in its nature. It's good to respect it.'

Sophie looked back out to sea, feeling as if her words had been received, acknowledged. Peter would have told her not to be so childish – endowing the sea with motives. She felt a tension slipping away from her, similar to the feeling she had sitting in Rachel's café the day she accepted the job. She turned back to Nick. He seemed lost in his thoughts. She wondered if he was bored. Peter would have been by now. He didn't like to sit and talk. She took a slow breath.

'Nick, I don't want you to think I'm intending to invade your territory. I sense you prefer to be alone. I would like to go walking with you, but only if I know you will be truthful with me and say no when you'd rather not. And I need to be able to do that too.'

Nick sighed. 'I was plucking up the courage to say the same thing to you. Yes, Sophie. Let's start our friendship with a pledge to being honest with each other. It's good that we both want the same thing.'

Perhaps being honest isn't so difficult after all, she thought. She raised her glass. 'Let's drink to that.'

Nick clinked his glass against hers. His face seemed softened in the evening light and she felt something radiating from him. Something genuine, as if he too yearned for a safe place that he could trust. He closed his eyes for a few moments, reminding her again of Tiggy. When he opened them they seemed enlivened.

'Would you like to see a dinosaur's footprint?' he asked.

They set off before work the next morning. It was too far to walk. Nick suggested that Sophie borrow a bike from Evie.

'I'll have blisters on my bottom as well as my feet,' she protested. They compromised and went in Sophie's car which started with a surprised splutter. The beach at Compton Bay was deserted and they left Man Friday footprints behind in the sand as they walked.

'There,' said Nick, pointing at some rocks.

Sophie couldn't see anything except boulders, stones and seaweed. 'Can you give me a little more information?' she ventured.

Nick bent down to indicate a large stone with three distinct projections. 'That's a nice one.' He stood up and indicated the multi-layered crumbling cliffs. 'The cliffs disintegrate and the footprints fall out of them. They're casts really. The imprints filled up with sand and hardened over the millennia.'

Sophie looked again at the huge footprint. 'Are you pulling my leg?'

'Honestly.' He put his hands over his heart. 'If you don't believe me there's a National Trust sign up above which warns people against stealing them.' Nick placed one of his feet on the stone.

'Don't do that!' Sophie cried. 'Someone might see you.'

Nick laughed. 'People walk all over them. They disappear under the tide every day. I don't think my boot will do them any harm.'

She put her foot beside his on the footprint. 'It's incredible,' she said. 'So old, just lying here.'

'Let's see if we can spot some more. There are all sorts of things lying about – sharks' teeth and fossils.'

They pottered about as the sun warmed up, divesting themselves of boots and socks, rolling up jeans, paddling in the shallows. Sophie felt like a little kid, forgetting all about the time, she became so absorbed.

'Breakfast!' Nick called. He was sitting on a rock, pouring tea from a flask. They sat contentedly munching egg sandwiches, watching other people arrive to forage along the shoreline and scratch and poke at the cliffs.

'Have you always been the outdoor type?' Sophie asked.

'Reasonably – but not really fit. I was quite flabby – with flowing hair – usually to be found parked in front of the television in my spare time.'

Sophie stopped eating and turned to look at him. He didn't have an ounce of surplus flesh on him, as far as she could see. Let alone hair. 'I can't imagine that,' she said. 'What changed?'

Nick carefully put down his half-eaten sandwich as if giving himself time. 'I met Keri,' he said. 'She was from New Zealand.' He laughed, a different laugh from his usual one. 'You know how fanatical the Kiwis and Aussies can be about sport and the great outdoors?'

Sophie nodded slowly, watching his eyes defocus, aware that she wanted to hear more but if she spoke he would stop. He heaved a great sigh that seemed to empty his body.

'She was a lot younger than me. She persuaded me to go to the gym with her and encouraged me to work out.' He grimaced. 'Even when I pleaded that I was at the point of death.' He stopped abruptly, picked up his sandwich and resumed eating. Sophie wondered if that was that. She waited until he'd finished his sandwich and offered him an apple. He tossed it up and down in the air a few times before biting into it. 'That was a few years ago but I got hooked on the outdoor thing – not sport particularly – walking and being in touch with nature.'

'And Keri?' Sophie ventured.

'We were married,' he said, simply. 'We were expecting a baby. And then she died.'

Something as huge as a dinosaur footprint seemed to rise in Sophie's throat at the sound of his voice. She spontaneously reached for his hand and he grasped hers tightly. They sat in silence for what seemed like ages.

'Time for work,' Sophie murmured. They gathered up their things and walked back to the car. She dropped him off at the gate of the Wraith Cove Hotel. He bent to look in the car window.

'Have you seen a red squirrel yet?' he asked.

Jill woke with a start. Damn, she'd overslept. She got out of bed quickly, feeling the contents of her skull trying to catch up with the rest of her body. She'd drunk too much wine again last night despite her new resolution. Why hadn't Ash called her? She could hear the children bickering downstairs – she hated being late, there was a lot to fit into her day before she could even think about her job. And then she remembered, Ash *had* woken her – there was a cold cup of tea on her bedside table. She'd had a restless night dipping in and out of her thoughts, half-dreaming about all sorts of junk.

Her mouth tasted foul, she gulped down the cold tea and opened the bedroom window to get some fresh air. There were already a number of people on the beach enjoying the beautiful morning. The sky was clear blue, lightening the sea to almost turquoise, yachts scattered the bay like little white flags. She had a sudden urge to rush downstairs and tell Tom and Fleur they could have the day off school, pack a picnic and drive to one of the small beaches where she could strip off her clothes and lie down with an empty mind, listening to her children laughing. And Ash – he could come too if he wanted.

She took some deep breaths and stood watching the people. She spotted Rachel standing by the railings on the esplanade, wearing her black and white striped apron, talking to someone. Rachel was always talking. She'd probably been up for hours serving breakfasts and baking cakes. Jill recognised the young man Rachel was chatting to – he was her eldest son, Patrick. He had been to Cormorants occasionally with the group of youngsters that Rose was friendly with. But usually Rose went off with them to wherever they hung out. He was a nice lad – polite and good looking. So he was probably home for the summer from university. Hadn't Rachel mentioned it was his last year? Maybe he was back for good – if he could get work here. Rachel would be pleased – she adored those sons of hers.

Ash would be feeling glum again when he realised the students were arriving. But maybe Rose would come home soon – hopefully not too soon.

Nick thumped his spade into the hard earth, trying to get underneath the root of a tough elder. He wondered whether he'd already messed up his friendship with Sophie. He hadn't meant to start telling her about his troubled past. It was far too soon and he knew she was still in a recovery process herself. Hadn't Rachel told him that she needed a break from all that? And they'd been having such a carefree time, exploring the beach like a couple of children.

He discarded the spade in favour of a pickaxe. The heavy spike soon got beneath the root and he heaved until he thought his biceps might burst. The root suddenly gave way and he nearly fell backwards. He sat down to drink water, sweat running down his face. He remembered flopping down like this when Keri was encouraging him to get fit. She would pat his paunch. 'Look at this puku,' she'd laugh, using the Maori word. And he'd laugh too, pulling her to him. He squinted down at his firm six-pack, thinking she would approve. He sighed. She had always been so straightforward, so honest with him. And look how he had treated her.

He got up and retrieved the pickaxe. Never again, he thought, thudding the point into the ground. Never again will I be dishonest with anyone. He was glad that he'd been open with Sophie. That's what they'd both agreed to have as the basis for their friendship. He realised then that he wished he'd told her everything before his iron curtain had clanged down.

CHAPTER 18

'Look, there!' Nick whispered, close to Sophie's ear. Her eyes scanned the branches frantically and then saw the flick of a tail. 'Oh, yes, I see it.' The little red squirrel suddenly scampered the whole length of the branch. The sun shone, firing up his tufty ears and dainty arched body. They'd been sitting in the hide in Parkhurst Forest all morning, trying to catch a glimpse of the shy animals. Nick handed her his powerful binoculars.

'Get a close-up,' he said.

She rested her elbows on the ledge, trying to focus, but the squirrel had gone.

'Never mind,' Nick said. 'We'll try again later.'

They tramped down the cool forest path until they found a bench. It had been raining and the smell of the pine trees hung in the air which appeared tinged with green.

'Keri and I spent a few weeks in Australia once,' Nick said, between mouthfuls of cheese sandwich. 'We went to the Blue Mountains and the air there is genuinely blue with the vapour given off by the eucalyptus trees. Good for colds.'

'Must be,' Sophie agreed. 'Whoever heard of a koala with a cold?'

'Exactly,' Nick smiled.

Sophie noticed that he could mention Keri more easily now, and even laugh as he let out little snippets of their life together. It occurred to her then that she never talked about Peter. They'd spent all those years together; surely it would be natural for his name to crop up occasionally. She tried to think of something to say that might include him but nothing sprang to mind.

'What did you use to do – as a job, Nick?'

'Landscape gardening – nothing skilled – a friend's business. And I got involved in youth work – spent a few years working with drug abusers in London.'

'Really? And I had you pegged as the next David Attenborough.'

'I probably would have been more successful at that, looking back.'

'Drugs – that's a difficult one.'

Nick shuddered. 'If only I'd known . . .'

'Is that how you met Keri?'

'Yes and no. I mean, she wasn't in that line of work. I was lurking undercover in a bar when we met.'

'Undercover? As in police?'

'No. But I acted as if I was. I was trying to trace a kid who'd disappeared from the rehab centre. I used to take it upon myself to play God – thought I could go it alone and disregard all the rules.

It's a long story.' He took a Kit-Kat out of his pocket and broke it in half. 'Fancy something naughty?'

'I'm all for it. I'm ravenous after all this walking and wildlife hunting.'

'Anyway,' Nick continued. 'Enough about me and my murky past. Tell me something about your life – if you want to, that is.'

Sophie made him laugh telling him about her father's aspirations for his daughters to resemble Sophia Loren and Audrey Hepburn.

'You might meet Audrey,' she said. 'I've persuaded her to come over to the island for a holiday soon.'

'She doesn't sound a bit like you.'

'No, she's neat and clean.'

Nick grinned. 'And you're not?'

'Well,' Sophie stuck out her legs, surveying mud-caked boots. 'She wouldn't be seen dead in these.'

'Do you get on, as sisters?'

'For a few minutes at a time. She disapproves of me. She thinks I should have stayed with Peter and worked things out. For better, for worse – that type of thing. And she reckons I ought to have pursued my career in orthodox nursing and not strayed into mental health and other wastelands.'

'Mental health – another tough area.' He took the chocolate wrapper from her and tucked it in his pocket. 'No wonder you're enjoying being a waitress.'

'And you a gardener.'

They looked at each other. She felt understood and sensed that he did too.

'And Peter?' he asked, his voice gentle.

'Silly mistake. I married my father – carbon-copy. Took me a long time to realise it. I hung on, thinking it would come right when we had children.'

'But it didn't happen?'

Now Sophie was the one to look away. She felt her eyes slide from his gaze and her insides constrict. At times like this it was as if a cold mist rolled into her mind and she wanted to go to sleep.

'He never wanted any. But I did get pregnant – once, by mistake. I had a miscarriage,' she said heavily. 'Peter could hardly conceal his relief – he went out on the town with his friends.'

This time it was Nick's hand that reached for hers. And she clung on.

'What is it that has kept you here, Neptune?' Nick asked, watching the old fisherman picking over his nets and pots. Jane had told him that Neptune had never left the island. Indeed, there were parts of this tiny island that he hadn't been to. Nick found this hard to imagine. He had spent so much time travelling across vast countries.

Neptune continued his net inspection as if he hadn't heard. But Nick knew that the answer would come, when he'd had enough time to think it through. In the meantime Nick picked up another fish to gut, mentally thanking it for its life, as a shaman friend had taught him in South America. Eventually, Neptune cleared his throat.

'This,' he swept an arm around to indicate his ramshackle cottage under the cliff. 'And this,' he nodded towards the expanse of sea. 'Her,' he gestured vaguely towards Wraith Cove, further along the coast. Nick assumed he was meaning Marguerite whom he looked upon as his daughter. 'Love, I suppose you'd call it.'

Nick looked at Neptune's weather-beaten face. His eyes were so deep-set that they seemed like two deep creases under the shadow of his cap.

'Did you never feel the need for a partner? Did you ever fall in love?'

The old man's face quivered for a moment and Nick wondered if he'd gone too far. But Neptune smiled and lobbed a stick across the beach for Loot to retrieve.

'Oh aye. I knew love all right. I was born in this cottage. And I lived here with the one I loved until death paid us a visit.' He rubbed a knobbly hand over his face. 'And there were others – at Wraith Cove – we were like a family. It's those memories that keep me here. Why would I go away from my place of love?'

Nick stared unseeing at the fish in his hand and wondered about love. He'd known love too, and it had felt as strong and stable as an anchor. But it had come adrift and he had floated around the world. He looked up at the cliffs and the never-ending blueness of the sky and the sea, wondering if he should leave soon. But he realised that he wasn't ready to go away again. Not yet.

Sophie found she could make Nick laugh. He said she had a zany sense of humour.

'It comes from dealing with things too awful to contemplate,' she told him. 'A lot of nurses and doctors develop it in order to survive.'

'It was the same in my world,' he agreed. 'If we couldn't laugh at some of life's agonies, we would go insane. I think you have to be on the inside to understand that, otherwise it can appear callous.'

Sophie enjoyed his laughter. It was spontaneous and natural and it seemed to surprise him as if it was something he'd forgotten he possessed. His laughter triggered hers and sometimes they would just laugh until tears came, as if something wordless were gushing out. But, she thought, they both knew they weren't saying all there was to say. She could see the veil come down, the slight lowering of his lids dulling the shine of his eyes, his fingers reaching for the thread around his wrist. She was amazed to have Nick as a friend. It was the first time in her life that she'd had a relationship with a male without underlying expectations. She felt they were good for each other. They didn't offer advice but let the intensity of their listening and empathy move them forward. And he was helping her develop a passion that she never knew she possessed – a sense of wonder for the natural world. Keri had given him that gift and he was offering it to her.

Sophie hired one of Kyp and Evie's mountain bikes that they kept for their holiday folk. It was hard to find a helmet to fit over her springy hair but Evie said she wouldn't let Sophie have the bike unless she wore one.

'You'd better do as she says,' Kyp said. 'She means it.'

'I think I need stabilisers as well,' Sophie grumbled, wobbling along the path outside the cottages while Mila and Jack giggled. But she soon found her balance. Her legs had strengthened with walking to and from work. Their first excursion was along Undercliff Drive. The road was narrow, green and shady. It was closed to through traffic because of drainage work to prevent the land sliding. But still Sophie's heart was in her mouth when the occasional car sped by, threatening to pitch her over the ivy-clad wall. She had to stop frequently to work out how to shift gears. 'Why can't it just do it automatically?' she whinged.

'It's a bike, Sophie, not a computer,' Nick laughed.

'Can we have a rest yet?'

'We've only done a mile.' She saw Nick searching her face, picking up that she was nervous. 'Of course we can. Let's stop at Wraith Cove Hotel and I'll show you the grounds.'

'Oh good. Then can we go home? I've done biking.'

* * *

There was a lot of activity going on at the hotel. The gates had been removed, the original driveway cleared, and access made to an adjoining field.

'That's where the caravans are going,' Nick said.

'Caravans? It's not going to be a caravan park is it?'

'No, just some temporary accommodation. The stable block is being renovated and Jane and Chas's nephews and nieces and assorted students are arriving for the summer as a labour force to help me and the builders.'

They walked through the overgrown, neglected garden. Nick described how it had once been and the work that he had already done.

'I like overgrown and neglected,' Sophie said.

'You do? As in wild gardens?'

'As in graveyards.'

'Graveyards!'

Sophie stopped and sat down on a pile of rocks. 'I used to spend a lot of time creeping about the graveyard backing on to my childhood home – looking for glow-worms. Not the usual sort of glow-worms – it's hard to explain. Anyway, I had a friend I used to meet there – a little old man called Tiggy.'

'And nobody called the police?'

Sophie smiled and shook her head. 'Nobody knew. I used to mess around there on my way home from school and one day I noticed him sitting perfectly still on a bench.' She felt something warm inside her expand with the memory.

'I crept up to him to see if he was real. It had been raining and he was wearing a brown fur hat that was all spiky. In fact he was all brown – his coat, his skin, his eyes. He reminded me of Mrs Tiggy-Winkle.'

Nick was sitting on the grass looking up at her. 'Don't tell me his name was really Tiggy?'

Sophie shook her head. 'No, but he said I could call him that.'

'You weren't scared of him then? This small brown man – and you a little girl?'

'Not at all. We were great friends – for years – I, er, really loved him.' Sophie looked down at her hands. 'He understood what I felt . . . about the dead.' She glanced at Nick, expecting a reaction, but he continued to gaze at her. 'My four grandparents died all in the space of one year. My family grieved all around me and I couldn't work it out because I knew they were all right.'

'How did you know?' Nick whispered.

Sophie clasped her hands together. This felt risky, as if she were revealing something far too precious too soon. But he seemed almost to be drawing it out of her. 'Because . . . I could still feel their glow.'

Nick didn't look away as she feared he might. 'And Tiggy . . . he understood this?'

'Yes, he asked me questions and told me things to write down.'

'What sort of things?'

'I'll show you sometime.' Sophie smiled. 'He also used to nod and smile a lot and blink slowly.'

'He wasn't Tibetan, was he?' Nick asked.

'I have no idea. He was one of those people whose nationality was hard to place.'

'And what happened to Tiggy?'

Sophie got up and brushed the back of her shorts. 'One day he wasn't there.' She stretched out her arms and looked around. 'Does all this land really belong to Jane?'

'Jane and Marguerite. It goes back a few generations I believe. They intend to resurrect it from the ruins.'

'What a task. It must be costing a fortune.'

'It's something they believe in.'

Sophie wondered what it must be like to look far into the future like that. She couldn't seem to think much further than the day ahead, her shifts at the café and her exploration of the island. Nick was still sprawled on the grass; she flopped down beside him. He was tracing the complex pattern of one of the tattoos on his forearms with a finger.

'Are they Celtic?' she asked.

'Maori. A friend of Keri's did them for me.'

'What do they mean?'

'They mean that I was a very silly boy who got nasty things tattooed on his arms which he lived to regret until a skilful artist disguised them.'

Sophie smiled. 'A cover up?'

Nick nodded. 'I had no vision as an adolescent.'

Sophie gently touched his arm, reminding herself of Rachel. 'Never mind. That mistake formed a base for something very beautiful.' She listened to the faint sigh of the sea and a skylark joyously ascending into the blue. 'Do you think about the future, Nick?'

'Not really, not any more. There was a time when I thought I had my life mapped out.' He picked at the grass. 'Then I found out that life isn't something you can control.'

Sophie nodded, recognising that pattern in herself. 'Yes, I had a plan too – work, love, marriage, kids. Very conventional. I never thought that at my age I might have to re-think it all.'

'What do you want now?'

'I don't know. I feel too old to start the whole process again.' In fact she felt exhausted just contemplating it. 'And yet I can't see an alternative, nothing seems to shape my future.'

'And children?' he said quietly. 'How old were you when you had your miscarriage?'

Something jarred inside her; his question seemed too abrupt. But she needed to answer him, needed to get it over with.

'I was twenty-nine,' she said, looking down at her brown legs stretched out on the grass. A tiny insect was crawling over her knee. She watched it carefully. 'I was twenty weeks pregnant . . . half-way.'

'Long enough to form a relationship, isn't it?' he said gently.

Sophie nodded. 'When I was a nurse I was used to seeing terminations, miscarriages, and the reactions of the women – some relieved, some devastated. But I never truly knew what it was all about until I went through it myself. That's what experience does for you, I suppose.' She looked at him. 'Maybe it's just as well that men are still more or less in charge. If it were women the whole world might be paralysed by the pain of it all.'

'Perhaps that would be a good thing. We might get somewhere then.'

'Perhaps.' They sat in silence for a while. Sophie found herself threading a daisy-chain. Nick turned on his side, propped on his elbow, watching. He began handing her daisies.

'Keri was five months pregnant when she died,' he said. 'Our baby was a girl.'

Sophie felt her chest heave and her eyes fill with tears. 'Mine too.'

'Did you name her?' he asked, softly.

Sophie shook her head. 'Did you?'

'Lara,' he whispered.

'That's such a beautiful name.'

Nick handed her another daisy. She completed the chain and looped it over his head.

'That's what they do in India. Except they use marigolds.' He touched the garland. 'I think I prefer daisies.'

'Nick . . . what happened to Keri? I mean, how did she die?'

They were looking straight at each other now. She could sense his struggle, knew part of him wanted to run.

'She was killed.' The words came out slowly, mechanically.

'In an accident?'

He shook his head. 'She was murdered.'

Sophie felt the air turn cold and a prickle of shock run through her body.

'Oh my God, Nick.'

He caught hold of her hands quite roughly. 'Please, promise me you won't tell anybody. The only way I can live here is if nobody knows.'

Uncxpected anger rose up in her. 'As if I would! How could you think that?'

He let go of her hands, looking stunned. 'I . . . I don't know. I'm not used to . . .' His arms waved in the air, looking for expression.

'Trusting?' she ventured.

He nodded, biting his lip. She could see a pulse beating in his throat.

'Oh, Nick.' She wanted to put her arms around him but he looked too raw to be touched.

'Hello there!' They both jumped. Chas was coming towards them across the garden. 'I wondered who those bicycles belonged to – thought we had trespassers.'

Nick clambered to his feet. 'Hi, Chas. Just thought I'd look in to see how the work was progressing. You've met Sophie, haven't you?'

'Indeed, yes. At Kyp and Evie's.' He held out a big hand to shake hers. 'Do come down to the cottage and have a drink. Jane and Marguerite would love to see you.'

'I thought they'd gone away,' Nick said.

'They had plans, but it didn't quite work out.

Anyway, they wanted to see the building progress too, so we popped back from Ledbury. It isn't far. Coming on, isn't it? Those scallywags of mine will be arriving soon. Hope they behave themselves. Jane tells me you used to work with youngsters. Nick. Perhaps you could keep an eye on them.'

Nick held up his hands. 'Sorry, Chas. The only thing I will keep an eye on is the gardens. My youth-sitting days are over.'

'Fair enough, old chap. Rachel's eldest boy, Patrick, is just home from university looking for summer work. Thinking of employing him to act as foreman – strapping lad.'

Sophie sat at the long wooden table in Wraith Cottage, sipping tea, looking around at the driftwood and shells and dried bunches of herbs and flowers that hung from every beam. Everything was old, the armchairs and the piles of books heaped on shelves. She hadn't expected it to be like this. She'd imagined a smart re-furbished cottage full of polished antiques and an expensive kitchen. A black cat was curled against an ancient range among a heap of walking boots and wellingtons. The only modern piece of equipment she spied was Jane's laptop on a little desk under a window facing the sea.

There was an old sense of comfort about everything, as if you could simply sit down here and feel at home. Even the garden she'd walked through, perilously close to the cliff-edge, had seemed as if it had been there for ever, unperturbed by the proximity of the English Channel.

Nick was looking at the architect's plans which Jane had spread out on the table. She was pointing out things to him while Chas stood, smiling at her enthusiasm. Marguerite came from the kitchen carrying a delicious looking lemon cake which could have rivalled Rachel's. She smiled – Sophie felt unsure how to communicate with her.

'Are you still working at the health centre?' she asked.

Marguerite stopped cutting the cake and looked up at Sophie with her extraordinary pale blue eyes.

'I haven't been there much lately,' Sophie added. 'It always seems terribly busy when I've called in to see Jill and Ash.' She realised then how neglectful she'd been of Jill and the kids. She'd been so caught up in her new life at Blue Slipper Bay. She resolved to call in tomorrow after work.

Marguerite moved her head from side to side and lifted a hand in the air in what seemed like an expression of vagueness. Sophie sensed Jane's attention.

'We've been up to Herefordshire,' she said. 'We've just come back for a couple of days.' She laughed. 'Can't keep away can we, Marguerite?'

Marguerite smiled back at her sister, her eyes shining. She shook her head.

'Do you like Herefordshire?' Sophie asked.

Marguerite nodded and moved her hands like flowing water.

'A river?' Sophie asked.

Marguerite smiled and handed Sophie a slice of lemon cake.

'Have you known Jill and Ash long?' Jane asked, sitting down at the table.

'Ages. Our respective men were friends – studying computers together. Ash wanted to use one in his practice.'

'And would you recommend him, as an osteopath?'

The room seemed to grow still suddenly. Marguerite put her hand on Jane's arm.

'He's an excellent osteopath,' Sophie said, looking from one to the other of them. 'Haven't you had some treatment from him?'

Marguerite nodded stretching her neck.

'Yes, we found him very good,' Jane said, and put her hand over Marguerite's.

Sophie wondered why she'd asked. She began to feel a little uncomfortable, as she always did these days when forced to think about Ash. 'That was wonderful cake,' she said to Marguerite. 'I won't tell Rachel that I've met a cook to rival her. She might get nasty!'

Nick got up. 'We'd better go, Sophie. I've promised the Water Babies a game of cricket this evening. I expect you'll get dragged in too.'

'I'll be too stiff after my bike ride,' she laughed.

'What? That's not a bike ride, that's a little jaunt.'

'Well, I'll plead blisters then – on my backside.'

'They'll want to see them.'

At the door, Marguerite took hold of Sophie's arm. She handed her a large envelope. It had a card stuck on the front. It was one of Ash's business cards.

'You want me to give this to Ash?' Sophie asked.

Marguerite nodded, her face serious. Anxiety seemed to drain her vitality; her eyes were transparent, watery. Fine lines showed around the corners of her mouth. Her long silver hair gleamed in the sunlight. Sophie had forgotten that she was a middle-aged woman. She hoped she hadn't sounded condescending when speaking to her.

Jane stepped forward as if she was going to take the letter. But she looked searchingly at her sister and Sophie saw her face soften. In that moment she could see the resemblance between them. Jane ignored the letter and reached for Sophie's hand, smiling.

'I haven't forgotten the supper invitation,' she said. 'I'll make sure Nick knows when we're here next time.'

Sophie looked at Nick and realised he was still wearing her daisy-chain.

CHAPTER 19

Murder! Nick couldn't believe that he'd said the word. Chas had interrupted at the worst moment. But maybe it had been the best. After all, what might he have said next to Sophie? He recalled her shocked face, her astonished eyes. What was she thinking now? They'd had to put everything on hold, swallow it all back down in order to seem normal to the others. Even after they'd left Wraith Cottage and walked back to the bikes they hadn't been able to return to that word – as if it were petrified between them. They'd cycled home, played cricket on the sand with the kids, laughed with Kyp and Evie, and all the time it hung, suspended.

Sophie had promised she wouldn't tell anyone. He'd been surprised at her reaction to his insistence. She must be wondering about him now. He'd told her he was involved in the dangerous world of drugs, now murder had crept into the picture she must be forming of his background. Maybe she'd think he was a fugitive, hiding down at Blue Slipper Bay.

He paced restlessly up and down his room.

Perhaps he should knock on her door and talk to her. He glanced at his watch. It was two o'clock in the morning. Sophie was sure to be asleep. He stopped pacing. Why should he even be considering that she cared? She'd probably hardly given it a thought. He suspected that few things would shock her after the years she'd spent working in mental health. He grimaced. He just needed to sort his own mind out – he was being self-important again. He realised it was because Sophie's friendship was becoming meaningful to him and he didn't want to alienate her.

He opened the door to his balcony and stood leaning on the rail, looking at the sea. The moon was dark. The flash of the lighthouse beam picked out the edges of the waves as it swept the sea. He could hear the rustle and snuffle of an animal foraging in the vegetation – a fox maybe, or a badger. He took some deep sighing breaths, trying to focus on the night sounds and the sensations of his body. But the tight knot in the centre of him refused to let go. He tried to imagine Keri's hands on his shoulders, massaging, soothing. But when he allowed her face to enter his mind it was white, her lips tinged with blue, her eyes vacant.

He went back inside and lay face down on his bed.

'So, what's going on with you and Nick?' Jill asked. Sophie sensed this was coming. Jill was pouring coffee after they'd managed to arrange a lunch break together and Jill had been scrutinising her while they'd eaten Waldorf salad and crusty bread. Jill's face still looked strained, but her hair was freshly coloured a deep red with black streaks, and her eyes were carefully made up. Her gold jewellery jangled as she poured.

'What do you mean by "going on" exactly?'

Jill pushed a mug towards her. 'Oh, every time I call in to the café, Rachel informs me you're out walking with Nick, cycling with Nick, bird-watching with Nick, squirrel-hunting with Nick.' She leaned back in her chair, a grin spreading across her face. 'What else are you doing with Nick, I wonder?'

Sophie laughed. 'Sorry to disappoint you but we're just good friends.'

'Really? As in *When Harry Met Sally* – just good friends – talking orgasms instead of having one?'

'It is possible to have a platonic male friend you know.'

'No, I don't know. Never had one, don't know any woman who has.'

'Come off it, Jill. What about all your male colleagues?'

She looked thoughtful. 'Yes, but isn't there always that question hanging in the air? Are they shaggable or not? If not you just get on with working together. But, Nick is, isn't he?'

'What? Shaggable?'

Jill raised sculptured eyebrows. 'You tell me.'

This came as a bit of a surprise to Sophie. She

seemed to remember Jill talking about him in a derogatory way. He hadn't seemed the sort of man that women go for. Not with his shaven head, serious face and uncool clothes. But then Rachel had said she fancied him.

'I honestly don't see him like that. We get on well – we're similar in some ways. And . . .' Sophie waggled a warning finger, 'neither of us is looking for a partner. So don't you start meddling.'

Jill threw up her hands in mock surprise. 'Me? As if I would.' She sipped her coffee, still looking at Sophie, quizzically. 'You are looking good though, Sophie. I can't believe he hasn't tried it on. Are you sure he isn't gay?'

'Sometimes I find it hard to believe that you're a psychologist,' Sophie laughed. 'You have no subtle understanding of the complexity of human relationships at all. You're stereotyping him – and me.'

Jill laughed too and reached out to grab her hand. 'And you know I'm just fooling. I wish life was that simple.'

Sophie thought it was about time to change the subject. She was feeling concerned that Nick was avoiding her. Ever since the day they talked at Wraith Cove he seemed to be working late. She hoped he wasn't regretting what he'd revealed about his wife's death. But he was busy supervising the caravans and workforce with Patrick. And she had been in the café full-time again to let Aidan have a break before she took a week off to be with Audrey and the kids when they arrived. Maybe she should call in to see him, ask him out for an evening walk.

'Audrey's coming next week,' Sophie said. 'I don't know what I'm going to do with her.' She wondered whether she'd done the right thing, demolishing Audrey's excuses not to come.

'Well, whatever you do, don't bring her here. She'll be turning out my cupboards and looking in the kids' ears.'

'I thought I might take her to Osborne House and Mottistone Manor, and, if the weather's good we can spend time on the beach – the kids will enjoy that. Can I borrow Tom and Fleur for them to play with?'

Jill glanced at her crammed kitchen calendar. 'Actually, we won't be here. I'm taking them to visit the grandparents in Dulwich. I'm going to leave them there and go off on my own for a while.'

'On your own?' Jill wasn't a loner. She was gregarious, seeking company and activity.

'I just feel the need. Ash and I have been through a tough time and I want a break from people. I might go on some sort of alcohol-free retreat. I rather fancy the Western Isles – Iona, or something.'

'Ah, the hippy in you is emerging at last. I knew it must be in your genes somewhere.'

'Perhaps it is.'

'But, you and Ash are all right now?'

'Better. He seems to have regained his senses.

But he's so involved with the centre, I hardly ever see him. I'm not worried about his esoteric shenanigans anymore. Solveig seems to have everything under control. She organises the students and Marguerite is away.'

Sophie thought about the letter Marguerite had given her for Ash. She'd called into the centre and left it on the reception desk.

'And your work?' Sophie asked.

'Good. I'm enjoying working at the surgery. The home help that Solveig found for me is conscientious and the kids like her. I just need a holiday I think, to get myself back on track.' She gave a half-smile. 'I'm okay.'

'Couldn't you and Ash go somewhere together?'

'He won't hear of it. He wants to make sure the centre is firmly established before he has a break.'

Sophie glanced at her watch. 'I must go. You will call in at the café to say goodbye before you set off, won't you? Bring Tom and Fleur. I'll give them the ice-cream treat of their lives.'

'As long as I get one too.'

They got up and hugged each other. Sophie felt Jill cling on a little longer than usual, as if she needed something that she couldn't express in words.

Ash had been surprised but agreeable – rather too agreeable, Jill thought – when she'd told him about her plans to leave Tom and Fleur with his parents and go off alone.

'Okay. I'll use the time – with Rose away as well

– to do a bit of intensive work with the students so they can complete their clinical hours. I could have a break then – maybe come and join you.'

Jill went upstairs to start packing. She sat on her bed and thought about Sophie. She was looking better than she'd seen her for years. Jill wondered what was really going on between her and Nick. Jill had been perturbed when she realised how much time Sophie and Nick were spending together. She still didn't like the look of him even though Rachel obviously fancied him. Jill didn't want Sophie entangled in yet another unsatisfactory relationship – maybe on the rebound. Nick wasn't at all what Jill had in mind. But Sophie genuinely seemed surprised at Jill's insinuations and she hadn't asked for Jill's advice like she usually did. Jill felt a bit hurt – was Sophie trying to keep her at arm's length now?

She got up, opened her wardrobe and stared at the rack of clothes. Just concentrate on going away, she said to herself. How can you expect to sort out other people's lives when you haven't sorted your own?

CHAPTER 20

Audrey, Joanna and William arrived soon after school broke up, as if having decided to visit she was determined to get it over with as quickly as possible. Sophie wished John had come with her so they could have had their own car. They might have gone off for a few days then, exploring on their own. Sophie picked them up at Cowes. She watched Audrey walk cautiously into the terminal carrying a smart suitcase. William and Joanna each carried a smaller version. Sure enough one of the crew followed behind carrying her second case. Audrey seemed able to awaken an old-fashioned gentlemanliness in even the most Neanderthal of men. Sophie half-expected him to doff his cap or kiss her hand. Audrey pecked her cheek, holding her body away from contact.

'Hi kids!' Sophie said, avoiding William's outstretched hand and giving them both a resounding hug and kiss. Audrey had a fixed smile on her face as if attempting to appear to be enjoying herself.

'Well,' Sophie said. 'Where shall we go first? There are loads of things to see.' She'd sent them some brochures to wet their appetite.

'Blackgang!' Joanna cried enthusiastically.

'Dinosaur Isle,' William yelled.

'I think we should go to the hotel first, to have a wash and brush-up after the journey,' Audrey said, looking at her hands.

'Yes, I did mean after that,' Sophie said. Surely Audrey didn't seriously think she'd drag her around the island without her inspecting the hotel's plumbing, kitchen equipment, laundry facilities and fire escape first.

'Can we go to see your house too, Sophie?' Joanna asked.

'Of course we can. There are two children who live next door to me who want to meet you.'

'You'll have to be careful,' Audrey said to them. 'It's very near the sea.'

'Yes,' Sophie teased. 'I can dive out of my bedroom window straight into the water.'

'Brilliant!' said William.

'Don't be silly, Sophia,' Audrey said.

Sophie left Audrey to fuss and titivate in the hotel at Shanklin and took the kids down to the beach. They didn't immediately run around madly like Tom and Fleur. Joanna held her hand and William stood and watched the other children playing.

'First one to get their feet wet can choose where to go first,' Sophie said, sitting down, undoing her sandals. That's all it took. In no time, they were running barefoot along the edge of the waves, splashing and screeching. Out of breath, Sophie sat down on the sand to watch them.

'You could have waited until they changed into their beach clothes,' Audrey said, creeping up behind her.

Sophie looked up at her and laughed. Audrey smiled back and shook her head.

'Really, Sophia!' Sophie said, before Audrey could.

Audrey grumbled a bit about the hotel but Sophie could tell by the tone of her voice that it passed her quality control specifications. Sophie forgot about taking her to historic houses and decided to cram in as much as possible for the kids' enjoyment. They went to all the theme parks, up and down countless slides and chutes. They visited the zoo and wildlife sanctuaries and the dinosaur exhibitions. They took a boat trip to The Needles, rode the chairlift down to Alum Bay to see the coloured sands and filled up dolphin-shaped containers with it in the shop. But the best fun for the kids was playing on the beach at Blue Slipper Bay with Jack and Mila. Audrey seemed to relax as the week sped by. She shed her tights and her timetable and sat in a deckchair, her legs uncrossed. She bought one of Evie's paintings and squealed with delight when Kyp picked her up and ran into the sea with her without getting her wet. She also seemed to conquer her fear of drowning, falling rocks and jellyfish stings.

'How long do you intend staying here?' she asked Sophie on her last evening. They were sitting on the balcony watching Evie playing ball with the children down on the beach.

'I don't know. I find it difficult to plan ahead these days. I want to stay for as long as there is work at Rachel's, maybe longer.'

'But what will you do? You can't live here in the winter. And you'll need to earn money. Is there a hospital nearby where you could work?'

Sophie suppressed a shudder. 'I really don't know, Audrey. I'll see what happens when the time comes.'

Audrey picked up her glass and took a tiny sip. Sophie could feel the tension building as her sister totted up an internal list of questions that needed to be asked in order to satisfy her feeling of responsibility.

'Have you thought about coming back to London?'

'What for? I mean, apart from you of course. There's nothing else I want to go back for.'

'Peter?'

'Peter!' Sophie stared at her. 'You are joking, Audrey.'

'Listen, Sophia. I've been seeing quite a lot of him. He told me he'd called in to see you on your birthday. That was thoughtful of him, wasn't it?'

Sophie let out a snort of laughter. Audrey looked startled.

'He was so looking forward to seeing you, surprising you. He was intending to take you out to dinner but he said you were already going out with your waitress friend.' She twirled her glass. 'He was very disappointed.'

Sophie was so astonished at what Audrey was saying that she couldn't speak.

'He's changed, you know,' Audrey continued, not reading Sophie's expression. 'He really regrets that you split up the way you did. He says you never would talk it through properly.'

'How often do you have these little heart to hearts – you and Peter?'

'Oh, he pops in quite often. About once a week on average.'

'Does he now? And does the elf queen know about this?'

'Don't be petty, Sophia. Her name's Melissa—'

'I know what her name is. Does she come too?'

Audrey pushed her glass around in little circles. 'To tell you the truth, I don't think they're together any more. But don't tell him I told you that.' She put her hand to her mouth as if she'd given away a state secret.

'Don't worry. I have no contact with him.'

Well, Sophie thought, the elf queen's charms didn't endure. But he'd soon find another unearthly creature to get his teeth into.

'I shouldn't really say this,' Audrey said quietly, as if someone might be listening in, avid for gossip about Peter. 'But I think he's regretting not having a family. You ought to see how affectionate he is towards William and Joanna. And, perhaps

I shouldn't say this either, but he mentioned your er, miscarriage once. He seemed quite upset.'

Sophie jumped up out of her chair, anger seething through her like hot lightning. 'I don't want to hear another word about Peter; do you hear me, Audrey?' Her voice shook.

Audrey put her face in her hands. 'I knew I shouldn't have said anything,' she bleated. 'I was only trying to help you both. He told me—'

'Not another word,' Sophie hissed at her, and flew down the stairs to join the kids. She ran headlong into Nick on the path. He grunted with the impact.

'Sophie! What on earth is the matter?' He held onto her.

She put her arms around him and hugged him tightly. 'I'm an angry, bitter woman, Nick. That's what the matter is.' She held onto him for a few more moments and then let him go. 'Come for a walk with me soon?'

He unclasped his hands from her arms and gently pushed her hair back from her hot face. His eyes seemed luminous in the fading light. 'Let's do that,' he whispered.

'Sophia,' Audrey touched her arm. The kids were in bed and Sophie was just about to leave the hotel. 'I didn't mean—'

'I know you didn't, Audrey.' Sophie looked at her sister's stricken face. The relaxation she'd achieved during the week seemed to have vanished. Sophie felt sorry that she'd reacted to her the way she had, especially on her last evening. She sat down on her bed. 'It's okay, really.'

Audrey sat down beside her and took her hands. 'I just want you to be happy, that's all.'

'I am happy. I'm enjoying life here.'

Audrey looked doubtful. A little crease formed above her eyes. 'That bald man – Nick – you're not in love with him, are you?'

She must have seen Sophie fall into his arms earlier. Sophie was beginning to feel like a celebrity, with all this inquiry into her love life. 'Why do you ask that?'

Audrey folded her arms across her chest. 'You look different – sort of casual. You don't put your hair up anymore. And the clothes you wear . . .'

'Go on . . .'

'I'm not saying you don't look nice – just not so smart.'

Sophie laughed. Audrey crossed her legs.

'Peter wondered—'

'Audrey . . .' Sophie said, a deep note of warning in her voice.

'Sorry, sorry,' she said.

Sophie got up. 'I'll pick you up in the morning in plenty of time for the ferry.'

Nick looked at Sophie's shawl draped over the back of one of his chairs. She'd left it behind some time ago and he hung it there so Commie wouldn't curl up on it. He kept meaning to return it, but every time he saw her he forgot. She must be thinking she'd lost it. The shawl was made from a fine iridescent material with a silky fringe. It was swirled with different shades of burnished orange, gold and sand. It created a patch of warmth in his stark room, a focus of brilliance that reminded him of sunsets and deserts. When the sun warmed it, spicy molecules of her perfume were released which seemed to dance around the room and find their way into his kitchen and bathroom.

He realised he was reluctant to part with it. It seemed to him that his room would be poorer without it. He sat down on his bed. When had he lost the colour from his life? After Keri's death, he'd felt a strong need to live simply, to not become attached to anything or anyone. He thought about the detachment of the Buddhist monks that he'd known, and their belief that suffering was caused by desire. He thought of the Tibetans and their ornate temples and mandalas, their offering bowls laden with marigolds, saffron rice and exotic fruit, the intoxicating smell of the incense and the rich drone of their chanting and horns. They didn't preach abstinence or indulgence. They trod a middle path towards understanding the truth that everything physical is impermanent, which made it easier to let things come and go. Their peace of mind came from directly experiencing that which lay beyond material form. Because of this they enjoyed the physical world but could let it pass without regret. Even grief was impermanent, they said.

But this philosophy seemed now to be just words

to Nick. At the time he thought it would be his salvation. He couldn't let go, that was his problem. What would he let go into? He could never get past the guilt and grief that he carried inside him.

The sun came out and lit up Sophie's shawl – a small oasis in his parched environment. Keri had loved bright colours too. She wouldn't approve of this room, his lifestyle. He smiled. 'Get a life, Nick, why don't you?' he could hear her say. He got up and picked up the shawl. He must give it back to Sophie and look out for something vibrant of his own. He needed to call on her anyway, to arrange a walk and to find out what had disturbed her so much when her sister was visiting.

'Audrey lives in a sanitised bubble of niceness,' Sophie complained to Nick. 'She has no idea what other people's lives are like and no desire to find out. She thinks that if everybody lived like her the world would be put to rights.'

'How does she manage to keep it at bay in this media driven age?' Nick said.

'Bleach,' Sophie retorted.

Nick grinned. 'Do you want to walk all the way to The Needles?'

'Absolutely. I want to burn off all my frustration.' She jumped up from the bench they were sitting on under the Celtic cross, memorial to Alfred, Lord Tennyson, high on the downs. The coastline curved and twisted below, white cliffs and blue scalloped sea narrowed to the western point of the island.

Nick stayed sitting, looking up at her quizzically. 'Do you think it's possible, to burn off feelings?'

Sophie sat down again. 'Sometimes. But I suppose it's a bit like taking a painkiller. It won't remove the chronic cause – if there is one.'

'Is that what you did when you were working with people, help them remove the chronic cause?'

'Or maybe just accept it.'

'Did it work?'

'Not always.'

Nick gave a rueful smile. 'Did you try bleach?'

'Should have done, obviously,' Sophie laughed. 'I really saw myself just nudging people to remember something they'd suppressed. Of course if they didn't really want to then they wouldn't.'

'Don't we all carry painful memories though?'

'Yes, but I'm talking about pain that prevents us getting on with our lives. Sometimes it comes up in symbols – dark caves, monsters – something tangible to focus on. Better than confronting nothing.'

'Like an iron curtain?'

'Well, that isn't nothing. It's very common and great to work with.'

'Is it? How would you work with it? Would you envisage tearing it down or blowing it up?'

'That's up to the individual. But I always feel it's better to befriend it. After all, its purpose is protection from pain.' He was looking at her intently. She decided to press on. 'I spend time relaxing and attuning with a client first. Eventually I see colours, patterns swirling. I lock onto one that appears consistent and prompt the person towards their own insights.'

'Amazing. And iron curtains – do people ever dissolve them?'

'We are talking about you, Nick, aren't we?'

He looked away but then nodded. 'When I lost Keri and Lara it was as if something clanged shut inside me. I've travelled the world and tried all kinds of spiritual practices. They give me a degree of peace and containment but I know the core of me is shut down.'

Sophie took one of his hands in both of hers and studied it. It was brown and strong. Traces of soil from the garden were embedded in his knuckles and nails. She wanted so much to help, but she was personally involved with him now, had become his friend. She could support him, but wasn't the one he needed to guide him through this.

'I think the spiritual path is great,' she said, cautiously. 'It's something we all need to explore. But if there's a big block – like a dam in a stream – it needs to be addressed. I'm sure none of your spiritual teachers told you to ignore it, did they?'

'No. And I do acknowledge that it's there.'

'But you have to encourage it to shift – be compassionate towards it – ask it what's stopping it from moving.'

'I know that too. It's fear.'

'Fear of what's behind it?' He nodded. 'But you know what's behind it, don't you?'

He sighed deeply. 'I just can't bear to let it out. I'm scared that if I start to release the pain then I won't be able to deal with it. I'll crack up, Sophie, I know I will.'

'Nick, listen to me. You're more likely to crack up if you don't let it out. And my experience is that when someone is ready to do it, it's because subconsciously they know they can handle it.' Oh, God, that sounded straight from the text book. 'How about if I ask Jill if she can recommend a good therapist for you to talk to? Someone who can listen without emotional involvement.'

Nick got up. He was shaking his head. 'I've been uninvolved for the last three years, Sophie. I've had it with detachment.'

'That's not what I meant. I'm sorry – I was using counsellors' jargon.'

But he was already walking away. She sat and watched him go, feeling helpless and totally misunderstood. Just like Peter, she thought, remembering all the times he'd walked away when they were getting down to the important bit. She could feel anger rising up inside her again. She was usually good at keeping that well stomped down. 'Well, good for you, Sophie,' she could hear Jill say, 'go and smash a few plates, or better still, Peter Pan's head.'

She jumped up and started to run after Nick. Breathless, she caught up with him. 'Friends don't walk away from each other just because something hurts,' she yelled, her voice whipped by the wind.

Nick turned abruptly. He was wearing his round black sunglasses. The ones he had on the first time she'd seen him in Rachel's café when she thought him intimidating. Sophie stopped short, suddenly fearful about what she was doing. Who was Nick? What was so terrible in his past? Drugs, murder, what was this all about? She took a step backwards. They stood facing each other. Nick removed his glasses and tucked them in the pocket of his shirt. His eyes looked red but that could have been the wind. He held out a hand to her.

'I'm sorry, Sophie. I don't know how you put up with me. I'm a screwed up old bugger.'

She took his hand. 'Me too. Show me a human being who isn't.' She grinned. 'Let's give The Needles a miss today. Why don't we go to the pub and have a ploughman's and a pint of bleach?'

They went to Freshwater and treated themselves to lunch at Farringford, the lovely old mansion where Tennyson used to live and write. Nick told her that the poet had a secret spiral staircase built as an escape route from his study. If his wife spotted one of his admirers making their way towards the house, she would blow a whistle so that he could run down the stairs and out onto the downs.

'Sounds a bit of a miserable old git,' Sophie commented.

'Mm, a bit like me,' Nick muttered.

CHAPTER 21

Nick sat in Neptune's boat listening to the flip of the water, pondering on Sophie's words. He suspected she was right. He had to let his grief out, or end up as a sorry old man, keeping himself barricaded, for fear of feeling pain. Maybe, if it was time to do it he would be able to handle it. He had hoped to talk to Sophie about Keri's death. He didn't want to talk to a stranger, a blank superior being. He craved – like a stricken child – to be enfolded by warm unquestioning compassion. He didn't want to be fixed; he needed a soft but unyielding buffer to absorb the force he was frightened to unleash. He'd spent several evenings sitting in his room, eyes closed, invoking an image of an iron curtain, waiting for a symbol of supernormal power to manifest in his mind and instruct him – in the language of the wise – how to dissolve his impasse. He imagined wielding a laser beam like Luke Skywalker. He envisioned the first pickaxe landing on the Berlin Wall. But nothing melted or cracked inside him. He needed help. *When the pupil is ready, the teacher appears.* That was a saying that had been tossed at him a few times on his travels. Did that apply to the psyche as well as the soul?

His fishing line twanged taut.

'Got summat?' Neptune asked.

Nick reeled in his line, unsurprised to have caught his usual clog of seaweed. He watched Marguerite haul in her catch. Three fat mackerel goggled and flapped on the hooks. Fish seemed to give themselves willingly to her. 'Have we got enough for lunch?' he asked. She nodded, deftly extracting the hooks and stroking each fish before placing them in the bucket. She seemed to possess her own set of rituals; he'd noticed it before – a bit like a shaman. Neptune started to row towards shore; they were in his blue and white dinghy that bore his name. He'd saved for this boat and renovated it when he was young. He'd been nicknamed after it and the name had stuck. Nick wondered what Neptune's original name had been. He was always surprised by the old man's strength. Nick used to offer to row but Neptune always refused, as if conceding might allow the onset of old-age.

Nick and Marguerite began gutting the fish while Neptune got the fire crackling on the little beach at Puck's Bay. Nick enjoyed this ritual that the three of them enacted. It was something primitive and complete.

'You didn't stay away for long, Marguerite,' Nick said. 'Did Wraith Cove call you back?'

Marguerite nodded and put a hand to her chest.

'That's the call of the heart,' Neptune said. 'You

can't ignore it for too long. It'll get you down if you do.'

Nick thought about this, a fish hanging limp in his hands. He wondered if he had a heart any more. Nothing seemed to call him. He glanced up and saw Marguerite staring at him, her blue eyes intent, as if she were trying to transmit something. Sudden clarity hit him like a revelation and he dropped the fish onto the sand. Of course, that was the problem. His heart was imprisoned behind his iron curtain and he was never going to feel love again. Friendship, yes, and the awe of nature, the satisfaction of hard work, the fun of running on the sand with other people's kids. But not deep, passionate love, the kind that sears through your body, melts your insides and fells you to your knees. Not the wash of astonishing light, creating brilliance where before you saw dross.

Neptune picked up the dropped fish, rinsed it and put it in the sizzling pan. 'Did I ever tell you about Woody?' he murmured. 'He used to live here with me.'

Nick shook his head, feeling as if he'd just returned from somewhere else. He felt dizzy and sick.

'Woody was my partner – that's what they say these days, isn't it? Homosexual we were. Had a hard time of it back then, I can tell you.' He speared a fish with his fork and turned it over. 'But whatever anybody thought of us, or called us, we loved each other.' He spoke matter-of-factly, as if he'd spent all his passion. 'I wouldn't have been able to carry on without him if it hadn't been for Marguerite and her mother and my friend, Emmeline. They kept me going, kept my love alive with their love. That's what I reckon anyway.'

Nick had no idea who Neptune was talking about but it didn't matter. What mattered was that someone was talking to him about loss and the survival of love. 'What . . . happened . . . to Woody?' he stammered.

'What happened? He was murdered. That's what happened.' Neptune, unhurried, scorched another fish. 'He tried to help a young girl in trouble and there were those who didn't like it.' He gestured towards the cliffs behind them. 'Followed him, pushed him over. Fifty years ago now, isn't it, Marguerite?' She nodded and put a hand on his arm without taking her eyes from Nick's. 'It was her mother Woody was helping. Other people's suffering hit him hard you see. A loving man was Woody.' He leaned forward to inspect the fish, sniffing the steam. 'Blamed myself for a long time. Thought I should have seen it coming. But I tell you something, guilt is crippling and it does no-one any good in the end.'

Nick could feel Neptune's simple words burrowing into his head and chest with such ferocity that he felt he might burst open with anguish.

'My . . .' he began. Marguerite and Neptune were both gazing at him now. The pressure of their concern was too much. He felt something inside him cave in. 'My wife and child were murdered,' he cried.

Neptune slid the mackerel onto a wooden board and covered them with newspaper.

'Fish can wait,' he said.

Nick was trembling from head to toe. His teeth clattered when he tried to open his mouth. Marguerite moved closer to him. She took both his hands in hers. He looked into her face and felt as if he were going to fall forward. But her eyes held him with a calm that seemed to support him. He licked his dry lips, trying to focus his thoughts. The fire crackled and flared suddenly in a small gust of wind and he had a flashback of dark alleyways, and fires under archways at night. The rotten stench of squalor and desperation hit him in the face. Nick found himself lapsing into the street language he'd used when he was searching for lost youngsters.

'I used to be an arrogant bastard, broke all the rules, you know? I was looking for a kid, involved with drug-pushers. He was nearly clean but they got at him. I got obsessed with finding him. I crawled into some shit-holes, night after night. Ignored all the warnings – thought I was invincible.' Nick took a deep breath; a feeling of desolation was turning his limbs to lead. 'Keri, my wife, knew I was up to something but I wouldn't tell her. I was macho-man – protecting her – shutting her out. One night . . . I got home in the early hours . . . thought she was asleep and . . . oh, God!' Nick's heart was thudding, he could feel the reverberation in his throat. He wondered if he might have a heart attack. He was aware that Marguerite and Neptune were soundlessly urging him on. Nick stared unseeing at their faces. His throat tightened and he felt as if he would choke. His voice squeezed out, high pitched and eerie. 'It was all my fault – I killed them!'

He couldn't breathe. He closed his eyes and Keri's drained face and blue lips appeared before him. He wanted her to accuse him, to sentence him. But her eyes were empty. He felt his body move. It got up slowly as if it were being controlled by something other than him. He started to run. He ran round in mad circles on the sand trying to escape from himself. He heard a strange noise, a howling, like a wolf. He plunged into the sea, not feeling the cold. He swam and swam, gasping in air and letting it out with a yell. And then his body stopped and he felt himself sinking down, down, the heavy water gurgled and slapped over his head, blocking out the sky. The next breath would stop the pain, his airway would clamp shut, his lungs would close down and that would be the end.

He'd known he wouldn't be able to survive this. Hadn't he told Sophie that? He saw his own hand float in front of his face. The plaited strands of silk still clung there. He'd told Keri he would wear it until it fell off. Would Keri be waiting for him? She would be angry with him, he knew. She had no patience with people who gave up on life. 'It's too short to waste, Nick,' she would say. 'Get over it and get on with it.' He watched her smiling face hovering above him, felt her fingers touch his lips. 'You weren't to blame. I made my own decision,' she said, her words bubbling in his ears. 'Everything is as it is. You'll understand eventually.'

Nick found himself floating up to the surface. His face broke through the water and he took an involuntary gasp. Sunlight blinded his eyes with glitter. He wondered where he was. Had he been dreaming? His chest and throat were burning. He blinked hard and looked around. He was in the sea, far from shore. A boat was coming towards him, the oars clonked against the wooden hull. Hands reached down to haul him in, nearly capsizing it. He fell into the bottom of the boat, coughing up water, his vision turning black. And then he was lying on the sand and Neptune was rubbing him hard with a towel. He felt warm fluid trickling through his lips and his head being cradled. He looked up to see Marguerite's wide eyes looking down at him and he felt engulfed by love. His own eyes started to run as if he had the whole ocean inside him wanting to pour out. He began to weep. His sobs rose up and dispersed themselves as if they knew what to do and he could just let them. He felt as if he cried for hours as Marguerite held him and Neptune sat tending the fire. And then he slept.

* * *

Jill had driven all the way from Scotland to the Welsh border, stopping only for petrol and a pee, so she wouldn't have a chance to change her mind. She sat in her car outside the entrance to the drive of Morgan's Hall, scared to turn off the engine. Suppose it wouldn't start again and she was stuck? The Morg, she thought, can't believe I'm here after all these years. She hadn't been back to the place since she'd left to go to university. And she couldn't understand why her mother insisted on keeping her share in the commune, even though she was hardly ever in this country. It was raining – that sort of fine misty rain that she remembered whenever she crossed the Welsh border. She looked at the big stone gate posts with their leering gargoyles, the rusty iron gate, propped back amongst the rhododendrons, the pot-holed drive – it looked just the same. Had no-one bothered to fill in the craters in all that time? She started to edge the car forward into the drive. She had planned to walk up, but felt safer in the car – she could shoot into reverse if she changed her mind.

The house came into view. It looked smaller, but then bigger – she seemed to remember a burnt out end of one wing – perhaps it had been rebuilt. Jill stopped the car where the drive opened out into a large parking area at the front of the house. It wasn't as ugly as she remembered. In fact it looked quite interesting with all its different coloured stone and brick and tiles and various rambling roses, ivy and wisteria climbing right up to the gables. There were two cars parked but nobody about; no dogs barking out a warning. Her heart was beating fast and she was sweating. She didn't really know what to do next. She hadn't made a plan – just thought she would get here and take a peep. Nobody would recognise her – she could say she was lost if anyone asked.

She got out of the car and walked towards the flaky stone-pillared entrance porch. There was a small ornate balcony above it covered with virginia creeper – she remembered the flaming red it turned each autumn, forming a dense curtain. She had a sudden flashback of sitting up there hidden behind the leaves, smoking her first joint with her friend Tammy and that Indian woman – Shakti. Shakti had let her orange sari fall from her shoulders; she wore nothing underneath and sat there with bared breasts. She'd encouraged Jill and Tammy to do the same. Jill remembered giggling – she was only thirteen – maybe just fourteen, but well developed and it felt okay to do what Shakti said. After all she was a grown-up and Jill had seen loads of naked bodies at The Morg – but none as beautiful as Shakti's.

Jill shuddered and walked up the stone steps. The massive oak front door stood slightly ajar – just as it always had. She pushed it and stepped into the big flagged hall. A familiar smell of cooking vegetables hung there. It was like a time warp, as if nothing had changed. She stood listening – a faint sound of music came from somewhere deep inside the house. The doors to the kitchen and sitting rooms leading off the hall were closed. She looked up at the wide stone staircase and the branching landings. Jill had lived on the ground floor with Stephanie in two large rooms which opened onto the wilderness at the back of the house. Jill stood biting her lip – should she dare to wander down the passage that led to them? But maybe her mother had a different room now. And suppose someone came out of one of the doors and saw her? Perhaps she would have to come clean and tell them she was Stephanie's daughter. She took a deep breath and crept slowly down the corridor. There were more rooms than she remembered, but her body suddenly stopped outside one of the doors as if it knew instinctively. Her hand reached for the china doorknob and turned it. It had to be right – it even smelled like Stephanie – that mixture of herbal soap and incense. She slipped into the large room. No doubt about the owner – the walls were adorned with pinned up articles, old snapshots of Jill, Ash and the kids and enlargements of stunning photos that Stephanie had taken in Africa and various other locations that had lured her away. The shelves were stacked with medical books and journals and files labelled with the various projects that she was involved with. Jill glanced up at the platform where Stephanie's bed was covered with a hand-stitched quilt of rainbow colours. She wondered how long it was since her mother had slept there. It must be at least two years since she was in this country but the room was alive with her presence.

Jill stood in the centre of the room, hardly breathing, it was all so vivid. Her eyes scanned every picture, every object as if she were looking for something. She wasn't sure what it was she wanted, why she had felt so compelled to come here. How was this going to help her resolve anything? All it was doing was making her heart thud. A door led from this room into the adjoining room which had been hers. When she was little she wanted to keep it ajar to feel the presence of her mother. But as the teenage years approached she had kept it locked from her side, keeping Stephanie out of her territory. She walked to the door and turned the knob. It was locked. She wondered who was occupying the room now – maybe a friend of Stephanie's, another altruistic person dedicated to helping the needy in distant lands. Jill sighed and let herself out into the corridor. Would Stephanie sense that her daughter had stood in her room? Would she pick up some kind of vibration when she returned – a disturbance of the atmosphere?

Jill closed the door and stood listening. Still that distant sound of music, and birdsong filtering through the dirty windows along with some watery sunbeams. She stared at the closed door, her gaze wandering to the adjacent one – her old room. Surely she wouldn't dare – how would she explain if someone saw her? But she couldn't resist. Her hand reached for the knob and she turned it. Not locked – no-one used to lock their rooms, she remembered. She pushed the door open – just a crack. The room was dim as if the curtains were closed. She could see the old round light switch and the dusty pink Laura Ashley wallpaper with the tiny white flowers that she had chosen. My God, hadn't anyone decorated it? She stepped inside, the light glowed through the curtains – yes, even the curtains were the same ones, matching the wallpaper. She peered around – the room was smaller than Stephanie's, without a platform. Boxes were stacked against the walls – perhaps it was used as a storeroom. There was a bed heaped with duvets and a pine chest of drawers with a mirror on top. Jill walked over to it and touched the wood, hardly believing that it could be her old one. She wondered if there was anything in it – perhaps her mother had kept her old school reports and stuff. She pulled at one of the drawers – it stuck and the mirror wobbled dangerously. She put up a hand to steady it, seeing her own white face reflected. What on earth was she doing here? There was nothing to be gained in resurrecting her past. She should get out before somebody spotted her and she would have to explain herself.

She turned to go but then froze. The heap of duvets was moving. Someone was in the bed, turning over. Jill held her breath, her heart threatening to burst out of her chest. The duvets settled and grew still. Perhaps it was a cat or a draught of air, or perhaps she'd imagined the whole thing. Her mind was burning up. Step by step she crept towards the door. Suddenly the duvet was thrown back and a bare arm flopped out. Jill could see the head and shoulders of someone lying there. Dark hair was spread across the pillow, sleepy eyes in a pale face, flickering open. It was a young woman. Jill watched mesmerised as the girl licked her lips and raised her head. She felt as if someone was playing a bizarre trick – it was her own young self lying there. The girl's eyes seemed to snap into focus and she sat up abruptly.

'Mum! What the fuck are you doing here?'

Sophie couldn't find Nick. She'd knocked on his door at various times the last few days and there had been no answer, no lights on, even quite late in the evening. He hadn't mentioned that he was going away. But then, why should he? He was a free soul wasn't he? But she did feel a bit disappointed that he hadn't let her know.

She wandered over to speak to Evie who had her easel set up outside the cabin, scrutinising the sea. Sophie wondered if she should interrupt an artist considering composition. But Evie spotted her coming and put her brush down.

'Hi, Sophie, fancy a coffee? I was just going to have a break.'

'I've only got ten minutes. I'm off to work.'

'Long enough,' she said. 'The pot's simmering.'

'Have you seen Nick?' Sophie asked, sipping her strong brew.

Evie lit one of her thin cigars and blew the smoke out the corner of her mouth. 'He's at Puck's Bay doing bloke stuff with Neptune.'

'Bloke stuff!'

'Oh yes. Kyp's seen them. They're out fishing at odd hours and,' she leaned forward conspiratorially, 'they have fires on the beach and have been spotted smoking pipes and dancing in the nude.'

Sophie lent back in her chair and giggled with delight. 'No, I don't believe that for one minute.'

'Well, neither do I. It's one of Kyp's attempts at humour. But the fishing part is true. I think Nick's just having a holiday with Neptune and enjoying a bit of self-sufficiency.' She spat a fleck of tobacco from her lip. 'It might be good for Nick. He's such a loner and Neptune is a dark, deep old sod. If he wants to spend some time with Nick it could be quite profound I should think. They've known a lot of grief, those two.'

A sudden surge of irrational jealously swept through Sophie. She thought Nick was her friend. But then she had intimated that she wasn't the one he should splurge his grief on. This was crazy. What were friends for, for goodness sake? This was the trouble with being a therapist. The boundaries became fuzzy between just being a friend and suddenly finding yourself counselling. She'd let Nick down. And what about Jill and Ash? Why couldn't she be like Rachel and talk and listen and share feelings without being precious about it? After all, she wasn't a therapist now. And then she realised in that moment that she didn't want to be one any more. She wished she could put the clock back and start again with Nick.

She finished her coffee and got up. 'So you don't know when he's coming home?'

Evie shook her head. 'I'm hoping he'll be back by Saturday. The kids tell me it's his thirty-ninth birthday. I've never been able to get it out of him before. But apparently they asked him and he told them. Mind you, he might have been joking with them.' She stubbed out her cigar and picked up her paintbrush. 'Kyp wants to do a surprise supper, but I'm not sure he'll like it. What do you think? We could invite Rachel, and Jane and her lot – except they might not be here. They come and go like the tides these days.' She frowned. 'And I should hate to embarrass Nick.'

'We could do something just for us – here in Blue Slipper Bay – keep it small. After all, he may not turn up.'

'And then we could just have supper together anyway, couldn't we?'

'Yes, and drink to absent friends.'

'Good thinking, girl.'

'I must fly. See you later.'

Sophie raced along the cliff path to work. The café was usually packed out now that the summer holidays were at their peak. Patrick had promised to help out during August before starting work at Wraith Cove, but had suddenly decided to have a holiday. Rachel was straining pasta when she arrived, her face pink in the cloud of steam. 'I think we're going to be stretched,' she called. 'I've asked Aidan to stay on for a while.'

And stretched they were. Aidan stayed until the lunches were over and they managed to get cleared up and organised for afternoon teas. In this weather there wasn't much of a lull. Rachel kept up her sunny chatter, diffusing any stress that threatened to build up.

'You're a marvel, Rachel, do you know that?' Sophie gasped, as she bolted down a slice of lemon meringue pie to keep her strength up. 'How do you keep going?'

'I think about my bank balance and fantasise that my knight in shining Bermuda shorts could walk in the door any moment and make off with me.'

They both looked expectantly towards the door and Sophie froze, mid-bite, lemon meringue poised. There stood Peter, gazing round the café.

'Help!' she said, flattening herself against the cake cabinet. He walked up to the counter; sickeningly cool in a lilac polo shirt and white jeans. Rachel folded her arms.

'Rachel, isn't it?' he dazzled at her.

'And you are?' she said, as if she'd never seen him before.

Spot on, Rachel, Sophie thought, knowing that

would injure him more than anything she could have come up with.

'Peter, Sophie's husband.' He was trying hard not to look deflated. 'We met once before.'

'Did we?' Rachel appeared puzzled.

Sophie carefully placed her pie on a plate for later. It was much too good to forsake for him. 'What are you doing here, Peter?' she asked.

'There you are, Sophie,' he said. 'You do look hot.'

She immediately became self-conscious. She must look a fright with her hair screwed back in a frizzy bunch and her red perspiring face. 'We're very busy, as you can see.'

'Not too busy to make me a pot of tea and a cream scone, I hope.'

'Go and sit down,' Rachel said, 'and we'll bring it to you. There are some tables outside,' she added, as if she didn't want him in her café.

Peter ignored her and found a table in the far corner. He kept glancing in Sophie's direction; she could feel his critical gaze. She decided to take his tea to him. She knew he wanted to say something and thought she might as well get it over with. He put his hand on hers as she put the tray down.

'Sorry to turn up like this, but I can never contact you. I can't phone, I don't know your address.'

'Why do you need to contact me?' She unloaded his tea and scone.

'There are things we need to discuss.'

'Such as?'

'Divorce. How we are going to split some of our finances.' He glanced around. 'We can't talk about it here.'

'Our solicitors can sort all that.'

'Have you any idea how much they charge just to write a two line letter? If we can tell them what we want it will be to our advantage.' He sat back and looked at her. 'We can be adult about this, can't we, Sophie?'

She sighed. He was right. She was behaving childishly. 'What do you want to do then?'

'Can we meet when you've finished here? We could go for a drink and get it sorted, once and for all.'

'I work until seven.'

'I'll be outside.'

Sophie just had time for a quick wash after work. She had the choice of wearing the sweaty white blouse and black trousers that she'd worked in all day or the creased tee-shirt and shorts that she'd rushed over the cliffs in that morning. In the end Rachel lent her a jade-green shirt and she made do with the trousers.

'Can we just go to a pub?' she asked Peter. He'd arrived early and looked fresh and calm.

'But I've booked at table at The Rex,' he said. He had obviously showered and shaved and selected his pale linen suit with care.

'I'm not hungry. Rachel stuffs me full of food all day.'

'You can just have something light. You look as if you could do with a good meal.' He lightly touched her shirt collar. 'Green was never your colour.'

She ignored this, having decided she wasn't going to rise to any of his remarks tonight.

They sat in The Rex, watching the sea through the tall windows, while Peter dissected the menu. The restaurant was cool and spotless. A piano trilled in the background.

'Why are you back on the island?' Sophie asked.

'Oh, another conference. The company liked it so much last time they decided to use the same venue.'

'Audrey and the kids came for a holiday.'

'Yes. She said she had an enjoyable time.'

Sophie wondered what she'd really said. She couldn't think of anything else to say and didn't want to make small talk. Peter deliberated with the waitress over the wine. Sophie ordered a salad. He filled their glasses and sat back, looking around.

'Nice place.' He raised his glass. 'Here's to an amicable evening.'

'I can't stay long, Peter. I'm tired. Let's just get on with it, shall we?'

His face fell. 'I just wanted to make it pleasant, that's all.'

Sophie felt contrite. 'Well, that's nice of you. But I want to get this over and done with, so we can both move on, don't you?'

'Of course I do. That's the point.' He held his wine glass up to the light, and squinted at it for a while. 'How are you going to move on? Do you have any plans?'

'A few,' she lied. 'What about you? Are you going to re-marry?' Why did she ask him that? 'I mean, er, do you need to hurry the divorce through?'

'Re-marry! Good Lord, no. Whatever gave you that idea?'

'Well, there's Melissa.'

'Didn't Audrey tell you? We split up.'

'She thought you might have done. But she didn't really know.' Sophie felt stupid now, as if she'd been fishing for information. 'But, you bought a house together.'

'No, just rented – I'm still living in it. She went back to her husband.'

Sophie could tell this was difficult for him. He wouldn't want to admit he made a mistake. 'I'm sorry.'

'I'm not.' He looked at her sharply. 'She was a strange woman. All she wanted was to be admired. She was like a cardboard cut-out.'

Sophie found herself laughing. She could have told him that, countless times, with so many of the women he fell for. To her surprise he started to laugh too.

'Oh, Sophie,' he said. 'I've missed your laugh, your face transforms when you're happy.'

This wiped the smile off her face immediately. 'Right,' she said, 'back to business.'

'Okay, well there are our joint investments and stocks and shares. Do we leave them or cash in and divide? We could lose out on interest, you see.'

'But surely, we'll have to split everything. That's what happens isn't it?'

'Unless we delay the divorce until it's a better time to sell.'

'Let's just do it, clean break.'

'If that's what you want.'

'Don't you, then?'

He sighed. 'It's the big one isn't it – divorce? So final. I didn't realise until I started reading through the papers. To tell you the truth, Sophie, It's shaken me up. Made me realise what I'm letting go.'

'You're not letting me go, Peter. I'm choosing this too.'

'I asked for that. Sorry.'

He looked down at his plate, pushed his food around. 'Would you like me to get the relevant forms – to do the cashing in?'

She nodded. 'And I'll make an appointment with a solicitor here.'

'Wait until we've sorted the finances. It'll make everything easier.'

'Okay, will you send me the papers to sign?'

'Where to? Audrey didn't give me your address – just mentioned some bay or other.'

'Send them to Rachel's Café – it's easier.'

He nodded slowly; his face looked slack. Sophie

got up. 'Peter, I'm going now. I want to get home before it gets dark. Thanks for the meal.'

'I can give you a lift.'

She shook her head.

He stood up and took both her hands in his. 'I miss you, Sophie,' he whispered as he kissed her cheek. 'I've been such a fool.'

CHAPTER 22

Nick had no idea what day it was. He slept for eternities and from time to time found himself lying on a narrow bed. He thought he could hear Neptune's voice and Marguerite seemed to float in and out of his awareness. He felt hot and cold and his skin prickled. Occasionally one of his limbs would jerk, waking him out of his stupor. It reminded him of all the times he'd spent recovering from alcohol and a cocktail of drugs. But he hadn't taken any drugs – was he ill then? Or was it his body remembering . . .

Marley had taken Nick back to his foster mother's house after he'd made his choice to live. Iris was watching *Dallas* and told Marley she didn't want Nick back. Nick had knelt down beside her, tunnelled his head into her lap and sobbed until her programme was finished.

Iris sniffed loudly. 'Go and have a bath,' she said, pushing him away. 'You stink.'

When Nick had come downstairs wrapped in a towel because all his clothes had disappeared, she had cooked him baked beans on toast.

'Your stuff's in the shed,' she said. 'Better go get it before the mice chew it up.' She plonked a mug of tea on the table and stood staring down at him, her eyes watering. 'This is it, Nick,' she said gruffly. 'You get no more chances. Understood?'

Nick nodded, shovelling down the food. Beans had never tasted so good.

Marley had hauled him out of bed the next morning at seven o' clock. 'You gonna work with me, you get up early.' He threw Nick's jeans at him. 'Make Iris a cup of tea and get out to the van.'

Nick had worked hard, mainly digging and moving earth from one place to another. He was physically weak and so exhausted in the evenings he fell into bed. It took months for him to toughen up and fully realise just what Marley and Iris had done for him. And the better he felt the more he wanted to repay them. He dug up Iris's back yard, planted potatoes in it and never forgot her morning tea. Marley took him along to the youth club that he ran and set him the task of looking out for drugs on the premises. This put Nick in a different position – he felt responsible for the first time in his life – as if someone trusted him. He knew, as a result of his surveillance, that Marley singled kids out for the same kill or cure treatment that he'd put Nick through.

Over the years Marley had initiated Nick into his methods and Nick had learned how far he could push the youngsters. Marley introduced him to so many people involved in the drugs wars – on both sides. It was Mike – one of the officers from the drug squad – who recommended Nick for the job in rehab. They liked to have contacts who knew their stuff. But Nick had found himself too much confined to a building with too many rules restricting him. He'd worked by Marley's rules – risky and unconventional, but he'd experienced them for himself. That's when he took it upon himself to act as saviour, without any backup, searching for lost kids. Especially Robbie, whom he'd allowed himself to grow fond of . . .

Nick realised he'd been talking out loud. Neptune was handing him a mug of tea.

'Aye, drugs are a menace,' he said. 'With Woody it was alcohol. He tried to block out his war horrors with it.' He took a swig of his tea and began slicing a loaf. 'Nothing worse is there – seeing someone you love destroying themselves?'

Nick shook his head. 'And there are always predators waiting for the opportunity to strike.'

Neptune sighed, gave Nick a hunk of bread and cheese and went to stand in the open doorway. Loot, asleep by the range, opened one eye as if checking up on him. Nick nibbled the bread. He liked being here, in Neptune's cottage. It smelled of dog and fish and sooty log fires. It was cluttered with tools and bits of boats and fishing equipment. More like a large shed really. It was as if Neptune saw no difference between his work and his life.

'Did you ever find out what happened to the lad you went looking for?' Neptune asked.

'Robbie? No. There are many ways of disposing of a body without trace.'

'You think he died then?'

Nick nodded. 'Undoubtedly. He wouldn't have stood a chance. And I should have known that. All I did was add two more deaths to the toll.'

'Not purposely.'

'No. But irresponsibly. I should have let the drugs squad handle it. I knew the rules. Like I said, I was a cocky bastard.'

'Majority of young fellows are in my opinion. I know I was.'

'Yes, but most kick a few shins on the football pitch, they don't mess with the drugs low-life. Anyway, I wasn't young, Neptune. I should have known better.'

Neptune dragged his gaze from the sea and looked at Nick in silence. 'What you have to remember is that you were doing something out of love. Okay, it was foolish, looking back, and it led to a terrible tragedy. But your intention was to help someone you cared about.'

Nick bit his lip; he could feel the tears springing to his eyes again. 'I did care about him,' he said. 'He was just a little kid, behind all that street-wise stuff.' He put his plate on the floor and lay back on the bed.

'Then grieve for him too, as well as your wife and child. It's the only way through.'

Nick closed his eyes. He heard Neptune go out and Loot scuffling to his feet, following him. His thoughts drifted; he could picture skinny young Robbie as clearly as if he were standing beside him. His dark eyes glistening under his grubby white cap, his swagger, his baggy jeans and huge trainers, the bolshi way he stuck up for his mates. His torment had surfaced at night, erupting in violent nightmares. Nick had held him, like a father. He could see now that he'd been identifying with his own young self. And he knew he would have gone after him again, given the choice. But he should have been honest with Keri. What good was it to love someone and tell lies? Who had he been protecting? Would he have felt cheated if he'd simply handed information to the police? Neptune had talked about intentions – were his intentions really that honourable, or simply egocentric, wanting to play the hero?

He slept again and when he woke the sun was shining through the window. He'd dreamt that Marguerite was sitting on his bed, holding her hands to his head and chest. Was it the same day or had another night passed? He felt hot. He pushed back the blanket and sat sideways on the bed. He put his face in his hands and was amazed to feel the thick stubble on his chin. He ran his hands over his head. His hair hadn't been this long for ages either. How many days since he'd washed? He must stink. He stood up feeling shaky. He was wearing a pair of blue canvas shorts – they must be Neptune's. He staggered to the open door and went outside. The bright light made him screw his eyes up. Neptune wasn't around. The fishing boat was gone. Nick walked down to the sea and tentatively put his feet in. Perhaps he should wait until Neptune returned, he felt too weak to swim. But at least he could wash. He waded in up to his waist and sluiced the water over his body and head, making himself gasp. But he felt as if he were reviving, waking up. He looked at his arms and then realised with a shock that the wristband Keri had woven for him had gone.

'Christ, Mum! Are you all right?' Rose swung her legs over the side of the bed. Jill had felt so shocked to see her that her knees had actually given way and she was sitting on the floor.

'I . . . I thought you were me,' Jill mumbled, wiping her trembling hands over her face.

Rose looked away. She was wearing a white vest and cotton shorts. She ran her hands over her thighs. 'Did Grandma tell you I was here?'

'Grandma?'

'Stephanie – your mother – remember her?' Rose said. Her voice seemed to Jill to be accusing her of something.

'No.' Jill shook her head, trying to clear it. 'I haven't spoken to her. She's in Africa.'

'They do have telephones in Africa – or did you think they still use drums?'

Jill felt chilled at the bitterness in Rose's voice.

'What's going on here, Rose?' she said quietly. But Rose wasn't looking at her. She was looking past her towards the door. Jill felt the back of her neck prickling. She turned her head slowly. Stephanie was standing in the doorway. She held out a hand to help Jill get up.

'Come with me,' she said. 'Rose, get some rest. We'll talk later.'

'Don't tell her, Grandma,' Rose said, her voice cracking.

'I wouldn't do that,' Stephanie said quietly.

Jill felt her body being flooded with some kind of noxious fluid as if the bubble of guilt inside her had sprung a leak. She allowed Stephanie to lead her out of the room.

'I want Nick to come home.' Mila was leaning against Evie, clutching a helium filled balloon. 'I want to give him my presents.'

'I know, sweetheart,' Evie said. 'But we did think he might not turn up today, didn't we? You can still give him your pictures when he comes back.'

'Where is he?' Jack said, frowning, picking up on Mila's disappointment.

'He's on holiday, with Neptune.'

'I know!' Jack's face brightened. 'Dad could go and fetch him.'

Evie and Sophie both laughed and looked towards the cabin where Kyp could be seen with his feet up, talking to the television. He was going through a profound few weeks of patriotism as his beloved country first won the European football cup and was now hosting the Olympic Games.

'I don't think so,' Evie smiled. 'Why don't you both go and tie the balloon to Nick's front door? Then, when he comes back he will have a lovely surprise and you can give him your pictures yourselves.'

The kids ran off, leaving them to nibble at the remains of the paella.

'Are you still enjoying working for Rachel?' Evie asked Sophie.

'Yes, I am. The café is very successful.'

'Mm, well, Rachel is so good at running it – and her cooking is excellent. But what will you do in the winter?'

'I don't know. I keep thinking I'll decide when it comes. But the summer is speeding by.'

'Will you work at the health centre?'

'I don't want to. Every time Jill or Ash brings the subject up I can feel myself thinking up excuses.'

'Maybe you just don't need it any more.'

'How do you mean?'

'Well, sometimes things that attract us like mad suddenly leave us flat. I used to adore travelling – couldn't wait to go. Now I feel I could just stay put here. It's like a different phase with different needs. It probably has a lot to do with having the kids and wanting a stable home. But it's as if I don't need all that anymore. And perhaps you simply don't need all that intensity of delving into other people's hearts and minds. You've moved on.'

'I'd never thought of it like that. I was chastising myself for not caring enough about others. I'd like to feel that I'm moving on, not giving up.'

'Women are good at all that guilt stuff.' She grimaced as Kyp let out a whoop of delight from inside the cabin. 'Men are generally better at doing what they want without too much introspection.'

Evie yawned and got up as the kids dawdled back. Mila looked tearful. 'Bedtime, I think. By the way, Sophie. I don't imagine you'd ever be short of a job here. Jane was asking me the other day to keep an eye open for reliable people. She will need lots of help with all these plans she has. And if you're serious about not wanting to go back to your old career – well.' She put her arms around her sleepy children. 'You could have a chat with her.'

'I thought she was away.'

'She comes and goes. Apparently Marguerite doesn't like to leave the island for too long. I wouldn't be surprised if they end up living here most of the time eventually.'

Sophie cleared the table thinking about all this. If she could work for Jane while Rachel's café was closed that would be perfect. She thought about helping in the gardens, assisting Nick with the planting and greenhouses. Not that she knew anything about gardening. But she could learn. The thought of studying something completely different filled her with enthusiasm. She could go on a course; she'd seen them advertised at the

Botanic Gardens in Ventnor. She finished stacking the dishwasher and went up to Kyp and Evie's cottage to say goodnight to the kids. As she was leaving, she gave Evie a hug.

'Thanks for the meal. And you've given me some fresh ideas.'

A few more days sped past. The weather cooled and the holidaymakers started to complain that the summer wasn't as good as last year. But they were still kept busy in the café. On damp days more people treated themselves to lunch rather than sitting on the beach with a picnic. They also hung around for longer to shelter from the wind. Aidan wanted to work afternoons so he could stay in bed most of the morning recovering from his previous night out.

Sophie spent her afternoons walking. She was on her own again. At first she enjoyed the solitude, time to ponder on all that had happened over the past few months and what she might go on to do. But then she found that she started to miss Nick. She missed the way he used to spot little happenings and point them out. He seemed to have a sixth sense that picked up small movements in the grass or a different bird flying high. She bought a book on the island's flora and fauna so that she could look things up. But it wasn't so much fun. She wondered about calling in at Wraith Cove to see if he was working there, or even finding her way to Puck's Bay. But instinctively she kept away. If he'd chosen this time to have a break he might not welcome her intrusion.

She hadn't heard from Jill, not even a postcard. Sophie found herself missing her too, wondering if she was going through some sort of turning point in her life that she wasn't a part of. Well, maybe this time Jill didn't need her either. She wasn't needed by anyone at the moment.

After work she walked up to the town to do some shopping. She browsed around the Ventnor bookshop and found a beautiful old leather-bound book of photographs of the houses of The Undercliff. There was a picture of the original Wraith Cove Hotel and some more of the grounds. Sophie clasped the book to her. It was expensive but she wanted to buy it for Nick. She hadn't bought him a birthday present, knowing that he didn't want possessions. But this seemed too special to miss. She bought a sheet of shiny gold paper to wrap it in. When she got outside the shop she was seized by doubt. Suppose he didn't want it? Well, he could say so. They said they'd be honest with each other. And to be honest with herself she had to admit that she was still a little disappointed that he hadn't told her he was going away. But then he hadn't even told Kyp and Evie and they were far closer to him than she was.

'Penny for them.' She almost bumped into somebody. She looked up ready to apologise and there stood Peter.

'You're back.'

'I hadn't gone away.'

'What, you mean you've been here all this time?'

'Yes. We had a training course following on from the conference.' He put a hand on her shoulder. 'I was looking for you. I went down to the café. Rachel's boy told me you'd gone shopping.'

You're dead, Aidan, Sophie thought.

'Do you want to walk down to The Mill Bay? We could sit outside and have a drink. I've got some of our financial papers to show you.'

They sat at a table out of the wind. Peter bought a bottle of wine without asking her what she wanted. He had his briefcase with him. He pushed some papers towards her. 'This is a list of all our assets and some of the current share prices. It's not a good time to sell but there we are.'

Sophie shuffled the papers about, trying to look interested. He sat still, looking out to sea. She found herself glancing at him. It was unusual for him to be so quiet. He seemed tired; perhaps he'd been having too many strenuous nights with his female colleagues.

'Have you been to see your solicitor yet?' he asked.

'No, I thought you said to wait until we'd sorted this,' she stacked the papers into a neat pile. 'To be honest, Peter, I'm finding it hard to concentrate. I think I need to take these home with me and study them.'

'Fine. I've made some copies. Take as long as you like.'

She folded the papers and put them in her shopping bag. She began to get up.

'Please stay and help me finish the wine,' he said.

Sophie sat back down, surprised. This must be a first, him saying please.

'Don't you have to get back to your course?'

'Free afternoon. And it's so boring. I could do it with my eyes closed. All that bonding and team building stuff.'

She smiled, imagining scenes from *The Office*.

Peter leaned back and stretched. 'I quite envy you, Sophie.'

'Me?'

'Yes, the way you've made a fresh start like this. You're doing something completely different. I'm stuck in the same old rut.'

'Well, I was stuck for years. It was you that was always into something fresh.'

'I know. Don't rub it in.' He topped up their glasses. Sophie wondered how she was going to negotiate the cliff path. 'It's like we've reversed roles. Now you're the one who is going to have adventures,' he said.

'Perhaps,' she said, non-committally. 'But you're a free man; you can do whatever you want.'

'Trouble is, I don't know what I want. I suddenly feel old and cynical. I feel uninterested in so much that used to excite me.'

Sophie remembered what Evie had said last week about not needing things any more. 'Perhaps you've outgrown the past.'

He laughed. 'Grown up, you mean. You're probably right. It all seems so superficial now.'

'Don't worry,' she said. 'You'll find what you want.'

'Will I?' His eyes searched her face.

'Sooner or later a direction begins to emerge, I think.'

'Is that what you're experiencing?' he asked quietly.

'Just beginning to.' She could feel herself growing wary, waiting for the put-down.

'Can you tell me what it is?'

She shook her head. 'I just have a few ideas. Not clear myself yet.'

'Sorry,' he said. 'Didn't mean to pry.'

They sat in silence for a while watching people come and go, kids playing hide and seek around the large potted palms.

'Audrey reckons we'd have been all right if we'd had children,' he said.

Time for me to go, Sophie thought, taking a large gulp of wine. 'Yes, I've heard that one too,' she said, picking up her bag.

'I respect her opinion, you know. Talks a lot of sense, does Audrey.' His speech was becoming slightly slurred. He'd drunk most of the wine apart from her one topped-up glass.

She got up. 'I must go. I'll send the papers back as soon as I've had a chance to look at them.'

'I'll walk along with you. Some of my colleagues are at a hotel along the esplanade. We're booked in for a meal and a taxi back to Sandown.'

Peter walked slowly, stopping to look at the sea. Sophie wanted to bound along, leave him behind, but found she couldn't. She wondered who was waiting for him at the hotel.

'Those papers,' he said. 'I'm here for another couple of days. I'll call in to Rachel's to say goodbye. If you've looked at them by then I can pick them up.'

They'd walked as far as they could along the esplanade and stopped outside Josiah Tempest's chandlery.

'Okay,' she said. 'I'm there in the mornings.'

When she got to the top of the slope she glanced back, he was leaning against the wall, staring out to sea.

CHAPTER 23

'Tell me about Keri.' Nick heard a woman's voice. It seemed to be coming from inside him. It was soothing, caring; he imagined it would be how Marguerite's voice would sound, if she could speak. He licked his dry lips.

'She was full of life . . . funny . . . loving . . . very loving . . .' Nick often asked her why on earth she wanted to share her life with him.

'Don't make me have to think about it or I might change my mind,' Keri joked. 'Just accept it.'

But he hadn't accepted it – he hadn't understood the full meaning of sharing and trust . . . that night . . . arriving home in the early hours . . . he'd been so engrossed in his search for Robbie that he'd forgotten to phone her. The flat was quiet. Nick crept into the bathroom to scrub the taint of his work from his body before getting into bed with his wife. The bedroom door was closed and Nick wondered briefly if Keri was angry with him. He hated to see that hurt look on her face when she accused him of shutting her out. She'd probably yell at him – he deserved it. But he justified his actions by seeing himself as her protector.

When he was working it was as if his mind shut out everything else, it was so intense. If he put a foot in the wrong pile of shit or mumbled a word with a dodgy intonation he could endanger himself and undo all the acceptance he'd earned in the shadowy world he was burrowing into. He was going deeper and deeper in his search for Robbie. And he was feeling uneasy – he'd noticed an odd look here, a nervous gesture there – maybe he was getting paranoid. If Keri knew, she would give him a bollocking. 'For Christ's sake, Nick. I know the crazy stuff people get into.' But she didn't know. And if there was one thing Nick was sure of, it was that his pregnant wife should remain ignorant about his work. If he could just find Robbie, he'd decided this would be the last time he would work outside his territory. He would stick to the rehab building like the responsible family man he intended to be.

He silently opened the bedroom door and crept into bed. She must be sound asleep; he'd cop it in the morning. Then he noticed the coldness. He reached out his hand. She wasn't there. He leapt out of bed and fumbled for the light switch, his eyes scanning the room as if she might be hiding. He rushed into the lounge – she could have fallen asleep on the sofa waiting for him. Nothing, no sign, empty kitchen. Panic gripped him, paralysing his mind.

'Wait a minute, wait a minute,' he said to himself and sat down. 'Think! Think!' What day was it?

Had she said anything that he'd not listened to properly, about staying away? But she never stayed away. He looked at the wall calendar – she'd had an ante-natal appointment at the doctor's that morning and taken a day off from the leisure centre where she worked. That would be it – she had obviously gone out with her friend, Jessie, and shopped and stayed with her. But why hadn't she left a note? He kept his phone turned off while he was working, but she might have left a message. He fetched it from his jacket pocket – nothing. He rang Jessie's number, not caring that he'd be waking her. He had to make sure that Keri was okay.

'She's not here, Nick,' a yawning Jessie told him, after he'd explained. 'I haven't seen her today.'

'Then where the hell is she?' Nick shouted.

'Don't yell at me. Maybe you should ask yourself why she's gone.'

'What do you mean, *gone*?'

'She's been doing a little private investigation – tailing, I think it's called.'

'Jessie – what *are* you talking about?'

'Look! When a bloke behaves the way you've been behaving, a woman is only going to think one thing. You don't deserve her.' The phone went dead.

Nick stood looking at it feeling shocked. He didn't believe what Jessie had said. Keri would never suspect him of having an affair. She was lying – Keri must be staying with her – there was nowhere else she would go. They'd plotted this to give him a scare – bring him to his senses. And Keri was right – if he wouldn't talk, she had to do something. Nick dressed hurriedly and went out to his car. He'd go over there – bring her back and make everything all right. This was the wake-up call he needed.

His phone rang on the way. He pulled over to answer it. It was Mike – his buddy from the drug squad.

'Found Robbie yet?' Mike asked.

'No. I—'

'They've got a body – the place you said. Wanna get over there?'

'Shit!' Nick thumped the steering wheel.

'Ten minutes,' Mike said.

Mike was waiting for him at the entrance to the row of disused railway arches, beloved by dossers and local fly-tippers. There was a lot of activity – SOCO were setting up their gear.

'Sorry, gave you wrong info,' Mike said. 'You'll be relieved to hear it's female. Wanna take a look? Might be one of your strays – seeing as she was dumped here.'

Relieved that it wasn't Robbie, his mind still half-occupied with Keri, Nick pulled on a protective suit and overshoes and followed Mike into the dark, his nostrils filling with the familiar stench, despite the mask. The team were working to fix up the lights, torch beams flashed around.

‘Who found her?’ Nick asked.

‘Usual. Someone taking a dog for a late-night crap – or so they say.’ Mike shone his torch on the heap of building rubble, spewing bin bags, and other grim detritus. A clump of blonde hair came into the beam, a white face, staring eyes.

‘Know her?’

Nick shook his head. A high whining noise seemed to start up somewhere. Nick looked round to see where it was coming from. When he turned back the light was shining on a bare arm flopped across the rubbish, the veins blue and bruised, a trickle of blood, a bracelet of plaited silk around the wrist . . .

‘Heroin,’ Mike commented. ‘Probably some lousy smack. Not the usual skinny bitch though, is she?’

Nick shook his head again and staggered. He was unbearably hot – or was it cold? He couldn’t breathe. He pulled off his mask.

‘Right. We’ll leave them to it.’ Mike turned away. ‘Christ, Nick! You look like shit. Let’s get out of here.’

‘I’ve got to go and fetch my . . .’ the whining sound in his head had grown so loud it blacked everything out.

Nick woke wondering where he was. He’d been dreaming he was at Iris’s house. He was standing in the kitchen holding the urn containing Keri’s ashes. Iris hobbled over to him and took his face in her arthritic hands. She'd been crying, the bags under her eyes were purple.

'Keep in touch, son,' she croaked.

Son. She'd never called him that before. Nick's eyes filled with tears again. He couldn't believe how much water had trickled out of them these last few weeks. He placed the urn on the table, put his arms round Iris and gently hugged her frail body. Over the top of her head he saw Marley observing him with glistening eyes.

'Don't come back for at least a year, Nick. You gotta lot of stuff in your pig-head that someone might fancy digging out. And don't tell me where you're headin' either – don't wanna know.'

Nick nodded. Mike had given him the same advice. He released Iris and picked up the urn. He knew exactly where to go.

Nick blinked his eyes a few times. He could still feel the plastic urn in his hands. He moved them and the feeling disappeared. He rubbed his eyes and a brass ship's lantern came into focus, hanging above him. Of course, he was still at Neptune's cottage. He lay for a while listening to the sea. It sounded rough, rain spattered against the windows. How peaceful it was – or was it him? He felt rested as if he'd had a deep sleep after a long and arduous journey. And he noticed something else – he was feeling hungry. He swung his legs over the side of the camp bed – they looked thinner. He realised he'd probably not eaten much for some time. He could hear Neptune talking – Marguerite must be here. He pulled on his jeans and one of Neptune's old sweaters which smelled fishy – but he was used to that. He opened the door, letting in a gust of salty rain. Marguerite and Neptune were taking off their waterproofs. She looked at him with an expression of amusement. She rubbed her hands over her face and head and smiled.

'Do you like it?' Nick asked, running his hands over his chin and scalp which were covered in light brown stubble. 'Or, do you think I should shave it off?'

Marguerite shook her head.

'I was going to help you shave last week,' Neptune said, bending down to give Loot a rub with an old towel before he could shake himself over the kitchen. 'Decided it was too dangerous. You wouldn't stop talking long enough.' He filled up the big iron kettle and plonked it on the range. 'We've been shopping to Ventnor,' he said, and went back out to the veranda to collect some carrier bags. He unwrapped a large pork pie, a jar of pickled onions and a crusty loaf. Nick's mouth began to water. Marguerite put plates on the table and Neptune carved the pie into three slices.

'God, I'm starving,' Nick said, between mouthfuls.

'Well, you haven't eaten much lately. You've lost a few pounds I reckon. What do you think, Marguerite?'

She regarded Nick seriously, looking him up and

down. She nodded, holding up her hands, palms close together.

Nick grimaced. 'Not that much, I hope.'

'You'll soon put it back on, the rate you're getting through that lot.' Neptune grinned, his eyes disappearing under his brow.

Nick suddenly put down his pie. 'How long have I been here? I've only just realised how I've dumped myself on you like this.' He felt astounded that this hadn't occurred to him before.

'Two or three weeks or so. Haven't really been reckoning it up,' said Neptune.

'Two or three weeks! That's incredible. Why didn't you throw me out?'

'I tried but you kept crawling back,' Neptune said, sloshing tea into tin mugs.

'I don't know how I'm ever going to repay you two for what you've done.'

'We haven't done anything. Well, I haven't. Marguerite has spent a good few hours doing her healing on you. You did the rest.'

Flashes of memory were crowding into his mind of waking and sleeping, words spilling out of him deliriously. And always they were there – one or the other of them, listening and soothing.

'You must at least let me give you some money for the food and stuff.'

'You haven't eaten enough to keep a fly alive.' Neptune's face was stern. 'I shall get bothered with you if you go on like this. One of these days I might need some help from you. I'm getting old.'

Marguerite put a hand on his arm.

'Anything, just anything. You two only have to ask,' Nick said. 'I feel as if I've tunnelled my way through hell and crawled out the other side. I couldn't have done that without you both.' He tore off another hunk of bread. 'I think I ought to get myself together soon and go back home.'

'When you're ready,' said Neptune. 'No hurry. We were just going out to check the pots and catch a few mackerel – want to come?'

Nick nodded. That's what he could do with, a good lungful of sea air. A spot of exercise, maybe a swim. 'Good on you, Nick,' he could hear Keri say.

Marguerite went outside to put her waterproofs back on.

'I thought Jane was going away for most of August,' Nick said.

'She planned to,' Neptune said. He glanced towards the open door. 'She told me that Marguerite keeps wanting to come back. I'm not happy about her, Nick. Something's troubling her. When you go home would you do a bit of snooping? Ask that neighbour of yours if she knows anything.'

'Do you mean Sophie? Why should she know anything?'

'Because she knows what goes on at that health centre.'

'I don't think she does, Neptune. She doesn't work there.'

'No, but she knows them that runs it.'

Nick felt uncomfortable. This was the first thing

that Neptune had asked him to do and he felt unable to help. 'Of course I'll ask her. But as far as I know, nothing goes on there that shouldn't.'

'All I know is summat's up with Marguerite. That's why she keeps coming back.'

Nick felt his energy turning outwards for the first time since he'd had what he thought of as his breakdown. He thought about Blue Slipper Bay, Kyp and Evie and the Water Babies. Jane, and the work at Wraith Cove. He'd seen Kyp waving from his fishing boat and Marguerite had told Jane he was taking a break. He thought about his cottage – Fair Wind – and Sophie next door. He wondered if she'd missed him on her walks. He pictured her striding along the cliff path with her backpack on, her curly hair springing around her shoulders. He thought about Rachel with her sweet smile. He imagined sitting in the café chatting, joking with Aidan and Patrick. He felt a sudden surge of unexpected happiness. He had so many friends, such a lot to look forward to. He decided to make this his last night with Neptune. Tomorrow he'd help him clear up the cottage and then set off for home.

'Why didn't you let me know you were here?' Jill demanded, ignoring the glass of water that Stephanie was holding out to her. She noticed Stephanie's hand was shaking. She must be feeling shocked too.

'I sent you a card.'

'Well, I didn't get it.'

'I'm sorry.' Stephanie put the glass of water on a small table and gestured towards the only armchair in her room.

Jill flopped down, her legs still wobbly. She put her head in her hands. 'I don't understand what's going on. What the hell is Rose doing here?'

'We arranged to meet in London when I arrived back from Africa. She wanted to come here with me.'

'But why? She's never been here before – she's hardly ever met you.'

Stephanie nimbly sat down cross-legged on the rug. Jill raised her head and looked at her mother. She looked older than Jill remembered – but agile and healthy. Her grey hair was plaited and coiled, fastened to the back of her head with a carved wooden slide. Her slender arms and legs protruding from her loose denim dress were brown and muscular.

'We've always been in touch.'

'In touch? How?'

'We write to each other – have done for years.'

'I've never seen any letters—'

'I send them via a friend. Rose said you wouldn't like—'

'How did all this start?' Jill felt jealous rage well up inside her. Had her mother been influencing Rose all this time?

Stephanie appeared to be lost in thought. 'Well, I suppose it progressed from when I used to send her presents and cards and she used to write thank you notes.'

'Why didn't you tell me?'

'It was up to Rose to tell you.'

'You were the adult.'

Stephanie looked shocked. 'I'm not a child-abuser, Jill. I simply carried on a correspondence with my granddaughter. What harm is there in that?'

Jill felt confused. Her mouth started to tremble. 'I . . . I feel betrayed.'

Stephanie shook her head. 'I don't understand all this animosity. What have I done to deserve so much hostility from you?' She spoke quietly. Jill could see tears glinting in her mother's eyes. 'Why have you always tried to keep me out of your life – obstructed me from seeing my grand-children?'

Jill felt her insides churning – she needed to find a toilet. She struggled to get up from the armchair and stood looking down on her mother.

'You . . . screwed up my life – Mother – I still have difficulty trying to hold on to who I am. Look at me! I can't even decide whether I'm supposed to call you Mother, Mum or Stephanie!'

Stephanie sat perfectly still, her mouth slightly open.

'I didn't want you influencing my children.' Jill gestured towards the wall separating the room from the one next door where Rose was in bed. 'And now I find Rose here. Why? And why is she in bed? Is she ill?'

Stephanie bowed her head. 'You'll have to ask her.'

Jill stumbled to the door and opened it. 'I have to go to the loo.'

Stephanie looked up sharply as if remembering something. 'Why have you come back, Jill? Why now?'

'I just needed to . . . I didn't know you'd be here.'

She stood for a few moments in the corridor breathing deeply, trying to regain control of herself. The door of Rose's room – her old room – suddenly opened and a young man came out. He stopped abruptly when he saw Jill. She recognised him immediately. It was Rachel's eldest son – Patrick.

'Your Peter came in early this morning for breakfast,' Rachel said as Sophie tied on her apron.

Sophie looked at her, surprised. 'He's not *my* Peter.'

'Well, *that* Peter, then. He said he'd call back later to collect some papers, said you'll know what he means.'

'Damn, I haven't got them with me.' That would mean yet another meeting – unless she could send them to him.

Rachel poured her a cup of tea. The café was empty, the day a misty grey. 'He's quite a sad man, really, isn't he?' she said.

'Sad? As in pathetic?'

'No, as in sorrowful. We chatted a bit. I ended up feeling downhearted about him.'

'Don't be fooled,' Sophie said. 'He has methods of buttering up women.'

Rachel laughed. 'Believe you me; I can spot them a mile off. And he is a handsome devil. But I did feel a bit sorry for him, I must admit. I got the feeling that he's had enough of fooling around and wants something a bit more meaningful. He asked me about my life and bringing up the boys on my own. I think he genuinely regrets how he treated you. He asked me whether I thought you were happy.'

'A bit late for him to start caring about me.'

'Do you ever feel though, Sophie, as you get older, that looking back you might have made it work if you'd stuck at it? I mean, I know when I was young I just used to fly off the handle at my old man. Now I wonder – if we could have talked – really talked – whether we could have made it – and the boys would have had their father.'

Sophie felt herself biting back a cynical response. Rachel's face was serious, as if she were looking inside herself. They sat down at a table.

'But, Rachel, you've made such a success of your life, and bringing up the boys, surely you don't regret what happened, not now.'

'It was okay when I was younger. But sometimes I lie awake at night, and wonder whether I'll ever have another special someone. You know, to share the silly things that happen during the day.'

'But you said you didn't want another live-in man.'

'I don't, not rationally. It's just . . . I don't know – in the wee small hours. And the boys will be gone soon.'

Sophie squeezed her hand. She'd never seen her expressing sadness like this before. 'Did talking to Peter trigger this?' she asked.

'I think I must have identified with something in him, that's all. The loneliness that lies underneath all the stuff that keeps us going.'

Sophie sighed. 'I know what you mean, I think about it myself. Maybe everyone does at certain stages in their lives. I love my new freedom but I wonder what it will be like when the novelty wears off. Being alone, knowing that someone is coming home eventually, is a bit different from just being on your own indefinitely isn't it?'

Rachel nodded. 'It's looking ahead that's the problem. If I'm busy and just live from day to day, I'm fine.'

The door opened and two damp families crowded in for coffee and snacks. They got up and smiled cheerfully, falling into their established routine. But all through the morning Sophie was thinking about Rachel and it seemed as if something inside her had clicked into a lower notch, as if the gloss of the holiday had worn off exposing the everyday reality of living with or without love and what that might mean.

When Peter walked in through the door, near the end of her shift, she saw him without the film of resentment and tension that had shimmered between them for years. She saw a handsome man, no longer young, in danger of becoming one of those old but trendy types with an eye for the girls. But there was something different about him, she could see that. He didn't flash his eyes and teeth so vigorously, or give off such an air of self-congratulation. Boyishness, she thought, that's what he's shed. She realised it was the first time she'd acknowledged that he was a grown-up, middle-aged man.

'I haven't got the papers with me,' she muttered as she passed him with a tray of drinks. 'You could have let me know when you were coming.'

'That's what I'm doing,' he said. 'I'm leaving in two days. I wondered if I could have them by then.'

'I'll bring them in tomorrow – but please come after the lunch rush.' He nodded and went out of the café. Sophie delivered the drinks and went behind the counter to organise the kitchen. She might have known he would show up like that. She should have finalised the papers and bought them in. It could have been sorted by now and she would finally be rid of him. She took her apron off and collected her jacket. Outside the wind was buffeting people along the road. Kites were swooping and swirling over the beach. She zipped up her fleece and put on her backpack, looking forward to the walk home. Someone was blocking her path. It was Peter. Damn the man; he must have been waiting outside all this time.

'Can I give you a lift home? You could give me the papers then – if you like.'

'I'd rather not.' She didn't want him to come to Blue Slipper Bay. It was the one place of her own that he had never stepped foot in and criticised. She started walking.

He shrugged. 'Does that skin-head boyfriend of yours live there?'

'Skin-head! Nick! He's not a skin-head.'

'Could have fooled me.'

'And he's not my boyfriend – just a neighbour.'

'Sorry, none of my business, anyway.' He stopped. 'Come for a drink.'

'Peter, I really don't want to.'

'Please, Sophie. I'll be gone in a couple of days. I might not see you again – unless Audrey's kids get married and invite me.'

Sophie smiled, imagining Audrey arranging a wedding with full attention to detail. She held up her hands in a gesture of compliance. They walked along to The Spyglass and sat by a window watching the sea heave and crash. Peter ordered a bottle of wine. She wondered how much he was drinking each day, but decided not to ask. He wasn't her problem any more.

'How's the training course going?' she asked.

'Boring, as ever.'

'What no adoring young colleagues to impress?' Here we go, she thought, same old agenda. It wasn't as if she cared any more. This was just habit.

He ignored her remark and bent down to pick

up his black leather document case. 'I've got something for you.' He pulled out a flat parcel and handed it to her. It felt like a book. She undid the paper – it was a photograph album. She glanced up; he was looking at her intently. She opened the first page. There were photos of when they first met doing courting-couple things – pulling silly faces, hair blowing in the wind, hand-holding, sight-seeing. She glanced through the pages, registering glimpses of her parents and his, their engagement and wedding, a heavily pregnant Jill, Audrey with new babies. She shut the cover quickly.

'Why have you given me this?' she whispered, her heart pounding.

'I was clearing out things. I know you always said you'd get round to putting the photos in an album one day. I thought you might like it as a—'

'As what, Peter? A souvenir of our marriage?'

'I . . . I don't know. I just wanted to do something with them, I suppose.'

'And you thought I'd like them. What about you – why didn't you keep them?'

'I have – I mean, I got copies and did one for me too.'

This took her by surprise. 'You did?'

'Well, yes. I want to keep the memories. It wasn't all bad was it?'

She sighed, looking down at the album. It was expensive, real leather with a gold pattern embossed on the cover and a scarlet silk tassel.

'No, of course it wasn't. Thank you, it was a nice thought. It just seems rather late in the day.'

He pulled the album back across the table, opened it and started to leaf through. He shuffled his chair closer to hers. 'Look, do you remember the day we took Joanna and William to Alton Towers and they were both sick? Do you remember Audrey's face when we got them home?'

She smiled and nodded, not wanting to be drawn.

'And look, the first day in our house, I carried you across the threshold.'

'You didn't. Let me see.' She leaned over the page. The picture was of her opening the front door, grinning with delight. She'd so looked forward to moving into that house. And it was true, she remembered now, after the picture was taken Peter had picked her up and carried her inside and they'd run all through the house and made love on the bedroom floor. She sensed he was remembering that too. A silence fell between them as he slowly turned the pages. She could feel herself responding to the memories as they were triggered and tried to resist the irresistible pull.

'Oh, look,' she found herself saying. The picture was of the old theatre that she'd lived above as a child. It had been turned into a cinema club. Peter and she had gone to find it one Sunday. The exterior with its ornate facade, a replica of a London theatre, had been carefully preserved by a group of people who cherished such things. They'd returned to watch *Casablanca* in the evening, sitting in the red velvet chairs in front of the polished wooden barrier behind which a small orchestra had once played.

'It's still there, you know,' Peter was saying. 'I told Audrey that we ought to take the kids to see it – show them where their mother and grand-parents lived.'

Sophie laughed, 'I bet Audrey didn't jump at that. My sister wouldn't appreciate showing her children their roots. She would rather present them with a detached bungalow in Surrey.'

Peter laughed too. 'I imagine she would.'

'Strange how many of us seem to think we should have been born into a different sort of family. Jill always feels embarrassed by her childhood in the commune and I always wished her hippy mother was mine.'

Peter continued turning the pages. Years rolled by before Sophie's eyes. She could see her face becoming less expressive as the chill of Peter's indifference cooled her inner glow. The photos seemed to get more and more impersonal. The two of them with groups of friends; some of them long forgotten. A wedding in Scotland; another in Cumbria.

'We didn't have many holidays,' she remarked.

'We were always busy working.' Peter closed the album. 'I think that's where we went wrong. We both got too involved in our own lives and forgot about the shared bit.'

'But I was never unfaithful.' She said it in a tired voice. She couldn't raise the energy to go through all that again.

'No. And I'm sorry for that, Sophie. I really am. If I could undo it I would.'

'Would you?'

'Well, I'm trying to be honest. I'll admit I enjoyed myself. But I've changed now and I realise it was at the expense of our marriage. Now I can see that it was too great a price to pay. I might not have been able to see that even a year ago. But I do now.'

'Why?'

He shrugged. 'I don't know. Maybe whatever it was has played itself out in me and I just don't need it any more.'

Sophie thought again about her conversation with Evie. Was it true? Did we have energies that eventually just ran out of steam and evaporated without us having to do anything about them? She sat back and scrutinised Peter. He looked exhausted. His eyes had pouches below them and creases in the corners. His hair showed a trace of grey over his ears. She wondered if he'd been dying it, and it was growing out. He reached out a hand to her. He was still wearing his wedding ring; Sophie had taken hers off. She put her hands in her lap. He rested his on the album.

'Is it too late for us to try again, Sophie?' he whispered.

He spoke so quietly that she truly believed she'd misheard him. She sat and waited.

He cleared his throat. 'I've been thinking, you see. We could buy another place together, see how it goes.'

'What are you saying?' She was having difficulty concentrating.

'Do you think it would be too late for us to have a child?'

'I can't believe I'm hearing this.' She wanted to push her chair back and walk away but her legs were shaking.

'We could start a new life together. Give me a chance to show you how much I've changed.'

'But, I've got a new life. I like it here. I've made good friends.'

'We could live here. I like it too. I know you've always wanted to have kids – and that's what I want now.'

'No! It wouldn't work. It's too late.'

'I'd be such a good father. You can ask Audrey.'

'It's not that. It's you and me. It wouldn't work.'

'We could take it slowly. Get to know each other again, talk about everything. I could even woo you if you like. I'll bring you flowers and chocolates like I used to.'

She found herself smiling at the idea. He grinned back, his mouth trembled a little and his eyes were full of tears.

'I'm not what you want, Peter. I never was.'

'That's not true. You're far more intelligent and funny and wise than any other woman I've spent time with.'

'Well, that didn't count for much when some sexy female fluttered her lashes did it?'

'My brain cells were stuck in the wrong organ. I think they've finally found their way to the right spot.' He reached out again and touched her hair. 'I also happen to think that you are very beautiful.'

His words were having an effect on her despite her resistance. She could feel them inching their way inside her, warming those parts that had been frozen behind *not-up-to-scratch* labels. She flicked open the photo album again to distract him and get herself out of his mesmeric pull. There was a picture of her mother. She felt a rush of emotion remembering her death and her shocked self that morning, nearly five months ago.

'April the first,' she said.

'What was?' He peered at the photo.

'The day Mum died.'

'Was it? I didn't realise that.'

'And the day you left me.'

Peter stared at her. 'Oh, Lord. And you thought—'

'Yes, I did.'

'Did you really believe I could be that spiteful?'

'Yes.' She hung her head. 'I was in shock.'

Peter reached for her hands again but she whisked them away just in time. He sat back in his chair. She could feel his eyes on her.

'For what it's worth, Sophie. Not only was I unaware of the date but I actually left the day before. You just didn't come home and find my note.'

Was that true? she wondered. It could have been; she'd been in such a state of confusion. 'But, you knew how ill Mum was,' she said, lamely.

'What was any different? I phoned the hospital. They trotted out the usual meaningless twaddle about her being as well as can be expected, comfortable, etc. She'd been at that stage on and off for years. How was I to know that she'd snuff it – sorry – during the night? It was almost as if the old girl planned it.'

'Peter!' Sophie sat feeling numb, a bit like she remembered herself that morning. There was no doubt that she was shocked and exhausted – as Audrey had repeatedly pointed out. But how could she have thought Peter would do anything so calculated?

'I may have been a bit of a bastard. But I wouldn't have deliberately done that.' He sounded aggrieved. They sat in silence. She wondered if she should just get up and go, but felt really bad now about her accusation.

'Sorry,' she mumbled. 'I wasn't myself.'

'Well, I suppose I can see why you thought what you did.' He smiled, suddenly. 'Look why don't we put all that behind us? It's full of misunderstandings on both sides. Let's start afresh and remember the good times.' He toyed with the photo album again and then went back to the beginning. 'Do you remember the first time we met?'

Sophie looked at their two young faces smiling at the camera. She was in her nursing uniform, a pale blue trouser suit. She must have been working in the special care premature baby unit. Peter was handing her a cheque – a donation from his company – for new monitoring equipment. He was dressed in a dove grey suit and silver tie. After the ceremony he asked her if she wanted to go for a drink. The unit staff had teased her, the nurses drooling over his good looks. Sophie couldn't believe that he'd picked her. They'd gone back to his flat and made love on their first date. It was so unlike her, she was shy, inexperienced. But she couldn't wait and neither it seemed could he. Where had all that passion gone? Surely that couldn't be resurrected.

'It was so good, wasn't it?' he said.

'Yes,' she managed to say. 'But that was then. We're older and wiser now.' And more cynical, she could have added.

'I know it could never be the same. But it could be good again. We could be two older, wiser people rebuilding a good solid relationship.'

She thought about what Rachel had said earlier about looking ahead to years alone, wondering if things could have been different.

'I really don't know, Peter.'

'Please think about it, Sophie. We could have a good life here. You would still have your new friends and your job at Rachel's, if you want to.'

'What about your business?' She realised as soon

as she said this that it would appear she was showing an interest in what he was proposing.

'I've been thinking about a change. I'm fed up with London. I can work from anywhere in a consultant capacity.'

Sophie drained her glass and put her hand over it before he could refill it. She got up. 'I'm going to go now. I don't know if I can listen to any more of this.'

He handed her the album. 'Take this with you. Let's talk some more before I go. I can stay longer if you want me to. Or why not come back to London for a break? Audrey wants to see you.'

'Enough, Peter. I've got enough to think about.'

CHAPTER 24

Nick stood on the path looking up at Fair Wind, as if he were seeing it for the first time. The sun glinted on the white walls and the faded blue shutters. He spotted flashes of green as lizards darted among the rocks in the cliff. He felt as if he'd been away for years. He walked under the shadow of the balcony to his front door. Something was huddled there in the gloom. For a moment he thought it was Commie, curled up having a shady nap. But it was crumpled and still. He tentatively nudged it with his foot; it moved and began to rise up in front of him as if it were struggling to its feet. He sighed with relief – it was a balloon, half deflated, weighted with a layer of sand. It must have lodged here after a holiday celebration. He caught hold of the balloon. *Happy Birthday!* it said on its smiling clown's face. And then he noticed it was tied to his door knocker. Somebody having a bit of fun. He hoped that was their only prank.

He opened the door, realising that he'd left it unlocked all this time. Would there be a mess upstairs, would someone have had a party, dossed down? No, Kyp and Evie would have kept an eye on it. He went upstairs and lifted the trapdoor into his sitting room. He glanced around, everything seemed as he'd left it. Not that there was much to disturb. The room seemed very bare after Neptune's clutter. But there was something different. A dazzle of light gleamed at him on the table. It was a package wrapped in bright gold foil. He picked it up and read the tag. *Happy Birthday, Nick. Love Sophie*. Next to it was an old shoe box with a note on the top. *Thought you might like to borrow this*.

He pulled out a chair and sat down. His birthday? He knew this was August but had no idea what date. Good heavens, he must be thirty-nine. How had she known? So, the balloon downstairs might have been meant for him after all. He smiled – it was those Water Babies, little scamps. He remembered talking about birthdays with them and they wouldn't rest until he'd told them his. He picked up the parcel. The wrapping crackled and glinted. The colour reminded him of Sophie's shawl – the way it had lit a small fire in the middle of his empty room. He felt an unexpected surge of excitement, like a little boy. He'd not bothered with his birthday for the last three years. He opened his present slowly, savouring the feel of the paper and the ribbon, trying not to damage them. The book inside seemed alive with the atmosphere of the past inhabitants of The Undercliff and the energy they had invested in the grand houses and gardens. What a gift. Where had she found this? He put it down carefully on its bed of gold. This was to be savoured.

He got up and went into his bathroom. He apologetically gathered a large spider from a comfortable corner of the shower, and placed it outside the window. He stood under the water feeling the burn washing away the intensity of the last weeks. He inspected himself in the mirror. Back in his familiar surroundings he realised how different he looked. His face was thinner but softened by the growth of his beard and hair. He wondered if his razor would cope with it. He soaped his jaw and head, raised the blade to his chin and began scraping, but it was too blunted to shave cleanly. He was left with stubble. He lifted the razor to his head.

'Leave it, Nick, it suits you.' He heard Keri's voice behind him. He smiled and looked round, expecting to see her watching him from the doorway. His mind, sensing pain, alerted his habitual defence. But nothing rescued him, no iron curtain clanged down. He accepted her voice and her physical absence with a soft sadness that floated through him but didn't destroy him. He stared at himself in the mirror. Should he leave his hair? Did it suit him? It felt like an acquisition, something to own when he'd tried to detach from so much. He rinsed off the soap and dried his face and head. The light brown fuzz stuck up all over his scalp. Well, he had no choice but to leave it for now.

He dressed in clean jeans and a white tee-shirt and stood in the middle of his bare room. On an impulse he ran downstairs and retrieved the saggy balloon. He washed it in the sink and put it on the table with his book and the gold paper and ribbon. Commie had followed him back up the stairs, bumping around his legs, emitting little rumbles of greeting and was now sprawled on Nick's bed, washing a stretched out back leg with his raspy tongue.

Nick gazed at the orange cat and his little pile of gold and felt wealthy. He ran back down the stairs and stood outside Sea Spray. The French doors onto Sophie's balcony were closed. He tapped at her lavender door but there was no answer. He looked across to Sun Spot, Kyp and Evie were nowhere in sight. He turned to look at the sea. The tide was coming in; the waves gulped and gurgled against the rocks. He took a deep lungful of the briny air. Never mind, he would just ease himself slowly into Blue Slipper Bay.

He walked mindfully back upstairs, treating it as a meditation, feeling the bend and contact of each foot on the wooden steps. He picked up Sophie's miracle box and took it outside onto his balcony. He hardly dared open it. It seemed as if he was holding something infinitely precious. Maybe she had never let anyone see this before. He wondered why she had entrusted it to him. Something was written on the lid in a faded childish scrawl.

Miracles happen when droplets of truth seep through the membrane of the dream.

Nick felt astonished. That wasn't childish. It sounded like something a spiritual teacher would say. But hadn't she said that her friend Tiggy had told her things to write down? He lifted the lid, noticing his hands were trembling slightly. The box was full of scraps of paper, all different colours and shapes. There didn't seem to be any order to the contents – maybe it was something to dip into. Nick closed his eyes and put his hand into the nest. He let it rest there for a while until he became aware of the one that was waiting at his fingertips to be chosen. He pulled it out. It was folded in half, a piece torn out of a school exercise book, browning slightly at the edges.

Deep inside you, your innocence glows and can never be lost. It is your very essence and was never born, neither can it die. Rest in this place.

Sophie's glow-worm. Nick felt tears running down his cheeks and he didn't brush them away. He'd heard similar sayings – pored over them, trying to understand. But never before had he felt so moved – as if, indeed, something inside him was glowing with recognition.

Jill felt as if she were stuck in some sort of Alice in Wonderland fantasy. She ran outside and headed for her car and then realised she had left her bag and her keys back in her room – Rose's room – or Stephanie's – she couldn't remember.

She paused, getting her bearings, and then scurried round the side of the house where she seemed to remember there was an outside toilet. It was still there, thank goodness. She relieved herself, then washed her hands and face in the cracked sink. She reorganised her hair into its clasp and studied her strained face in the grimy mirror. Her mother looked healthier than she did, and Stephanie must be getting on for seventy. What a weird experience it had been seeing Rose asleep in her bed – like a fairytale – seeing her young self lying there – her *doppelgänger*.

She went outside. The rain had stopped; the hot sun was drawing vapour from the ground, releasing a strong earthy smell. What should she do now? She had intended to drive away but she would have to go back inside the house and retrieve her bag. And she couldn't just leave without understanding all this. Rose had looked horrified to see her – had sworn at her. She'd never done that before. She was a well-mannered girl. But she must have been equally shocked. Jill shook her head in disbelief – she'd hoped to have a quick snoop, purge her fear of her old home and all it represented. But not this confrontation with her mother. And that boy, Patrick. What was he doing here? Maybe Rose had brought all her friends down for a party. Who else was going to turn up? She'd bump into Ash and Fleur and Tom next.

Jill found herself walking along the path that she

thought led to the walled garden and the stream. She opened the gate to a well-tended vegetable plot. She could remember people digging here, planting and hoeing, the women with their bare breasts swinging – why did she always picture the nudity? Surely everyone must have worn clothes most of the time. It was always so bloody cold. She walked past the greenhouses – there were a couple of women working inside who waved to her. She let herself out of the far gate into the field which led to the stream. Sheep still grazed the lumpy grass. Jill took off her sandals and padded barefoot to the water. It was running low, but it could be quite a torrent in winter. She remembered a couple of little kids getting into serious trouble here. There was a slate bridge across it. It felt warm and damp under her feet. She sat down at its centre and looked around. It was the first time she had raised her eyes since she'd arrived. The view was astounding. Green hills sloped up to meet misty blue mountains. Birds were soaring high – she loved that mewing sound of the buzzards calling. This truly was a beautiful spot. She hadn't appreciated it when she was a child. She sat watching the dippers bobbing on the stones further downstream, feeling calmer. Getting up, she followed the stream to where it pooled. She remembered building a shit-pit here with the other kids, so they could have a rave-up without using the toilets in The Morg which were always rationed because there was something wrong with the water supply. They'd had such fun painting that pit in psychedelic colours.

Okay, so it may have been a wild and free childhood in idyllic surroundings. But who was there to keep her safe? Where were the adults? All in each other's rooms, shagging? How naive those so called grownups were. They thought they were so progressive – open and allowing – all that vast space for children to grow and expand. God, if they only knew how the kids had laughed behind their backs. Tammy – she was the worst – always egging Jill on. A vision flashed into Jill's mind of being tangled together with Shakti and Tammy, comparing the colours of their naked bodies – Shakti's light brown, Tammy's black, and her own pink skin. How they'd explored each other! Well, that was all right, wasn't it? Normal adolescent activity. But Jill was only just fourteen compared to Tammy's sixteen and Shakti must have been in her twenties. Then Shakti had encouraged the boys to join in, and the sexual activity changed into something more compelling – setting up competition between the girls.

And how did they ever get through school? The amount of dope and alcohol that was smuggled into the forgotten garden, along with the village kids, was unbelievable. They even used to go up to Si Evans's farm and mess about with the lads in the barn. Jill and Tammy had a whole list of invented places where they told their mothers they'd be – studying nature for school projects was a favourite, or going to the pottery classes that some arty couple ran in their converted stable studio. All this dangerous deception was going on while saintly Stephanie – the self-appointed guardian of the residents' morals – routinely condemned the use of pleasure drugs and bad language in the presence of the children. What plane of existence was she on?

Jill briefly thought about her own daughters. Fleur was still young and protected but Rose – what did she really know about Rose and what she was into? But Rose had always been such a good girl – and Jill had always been so bad. That feeling of badness had stuck inside her, seeming to attract more, as if it were a magnet. And men like Peter knew it. Ash was the first man she had met who seemed not to recognise the badness in her and had loved her for other qualities. Also Sophie – who seemed to possess something genuinely different. Jill didn't know what it was at the time – but she wanted it. She needed Ash, and she needed Sophie too.

'Jill!' She could hear Stephanie's voice calling her. Jill moved out of the shelter of the willows. She could see her mother walking across the field. Rose was with her and they were holding hands.

Sophie got back late to Blue Slipper Bay after having been dined, but not wined, by Peter. She'd driven to his hotel and stayed alcohol free despite his offers of taxis – or staying the night.

'We are still husband and wife,' he'd whispered in her ear, stroking her arm. She'd felt all kinds of conflicting emotions struggling inside her. He looked handsome in the candlelight and she recognised the pulse of desire that his intense gaze could trigger in her. But she knew it would be stupid simply to fall into bed with him. He would regard that as her acquiescence to all his plans. She returned the conversation to settling finances. She needed more time alone to think this through.

She parked her car and walked down the steep lane, glad of her torch. She picked her way carefully round the wet path, slippery with shingle thrown up by the tide. She stopped, looking at the three little cottages huddled against the cliff. It took her a few moments to disengage her brain from her evening with Peter before she realised that a light was on in Fair Wind. She felt a surge of delight. Nick was back.

It wasn't until she'd knocked on his door that she remembered how late it was and immediately felt awkward. He might be meditating or going to bed. But she heard his footsteps bounding down the stairs and the door flew open. She stepped back; the light was dim and for a moment she thought it was someone else.

'Nick?'

'Sophie?'

'You look . . .'

'Scruffy?' He ran his hand over his chin and head. 'I've been living wild. Coming up for tea?'

'It's a bit late . . . I was just glad to see you're home.'

He opened the door wider and stood back. She followed him up the stairs. They stood in his sitting room, glancing at each other.

'You look lovely,' he said. 'Have you been out somewhere? I haven't seen you in a dress before.'

'I hardly recognised you,' she stammered. He looked thinner; his hair had grown into a light brown crew-cut, his chin covered in stubble. He seemed younger, softer.

'Is it awful?' He put his hand to his head again.

'No, no. I like it. It was just a bit of a shock, that's all.' She smiled. 'I thought perhaps you had a brother staying.'

Nick grinned and offered her a chair. He made tea and they sat by the window. She noticed thc book she'd given him for his birthday, open on the table. And her miracle box – closed. Maybe she shouldn't have . . .

'Thank you for my present,' he said.

'Don't feel embarrassed if you don't want it. I know you don't like . . . things.'

'I like these things . . . very much.' He laid one hand on the book and another on the miracle box.

She felt slightly sheepish, wondering if he'd looked inside and decided she was weird. She saw the gold wrapping paper was folded beside the book, with Jack and Mila's flat balloon. She giggled. 'You found it then. Did the kids have it right – about it being your birthday?'

Nick nodded. 'Were they disappointed that I didn't show?'

'A little, we had dinner together but warned them you were away on holiday. They've painted some pictures for you. You might have to hang them up.'

Nick glanced around the room. 'Well, this place could do with a bit of colour.'

'Did you do some good fishing with Neptune?'

'I did. He taught me some old fisherman's lore.' Nick took a deep breath. 'To tell you the truth, it wasn't just a holiday.'

'I had wondered . . . the way you disappeared like that . . . not that it was any of my business.'

'I hadn't planned it. I wouldn't have gone without telling you – but things happened suddenly.' He turned his head to look out at the starlit sea. She could sense him making a decision whether to tell her anything more. He swallowed. 'I went to pieces, just fell apart. I had to stay there to recover.'

She caught her breath. 'At Neptune's?' Nick nodded. 'My God. How are you feeling now?'

'Better, sort of soft-bellied, like I've lost my shell.'

'How did it happen? If you want to talk about it, that is.'

'I think it was triggered by Neptune telling me about his partner who he suspects was murdered. He said he was almost destroyed by guilt and grief and couldn't see any point in life. He told me how he was healed by the love of Marguerite's family. And then I found myself spilling everything out to him and Marguerite – about Keri's murder and my baby, and my guilt and self-hatred. I went crazy. I nearly drowned at one stage. They rescued me. And they simply let me talk, howl and sleep until it had all run out and I started to get myself back together again.'

'Oh, Nick.' Sophie realised she was clutching his arm.

'I had no idea of the days or nights passing. I think Neptune even washed me. I kept surfacing and finding Marguerite sitting beside me with her hands on my chest.' Nick sighed deeply, shaking his head slowly from side to side. 'I don't know how I'm ever going to repay those two.'

'It sounds like you had a real catharsis.'

He nodded. 'It was like you said. It was the right time and I did handle it. Although at first I didn't think I would. I just wanted to die.'

'I'm so sorry I wasn't able to help you.'

'No, don't think that for one moment. I was with the right people. Who knows what might have happened to me in some other time or place? I might have killed myself, or been hospitalised. Anyway, I know I can talk freely to you now without spewing my past all over you and maybe ruining our friendship.'

'I still feel I wasn't much of a friend—'

'But you were. Don't you see? You were truthful with me. And that's what I needed. You made me crash up against my own iron curtain and then Neptune blew a hole through it by telling me his similar story.'

Sophie was glad he felt like this. She guessed his experience had far more suffering attached to it than he was telling her, or could even remember. But he'd got through it, that's what mattered. It could so easily have ended in disaster. Neptune and Marguerite must have made him feel so safe.

'Keri had a lot to do with it too.' Nick rubbed his head, as if he couldn't quite believe he had hair. 'She always was a get-off-your-arse kind of girl.'

Sophie laughed. It was good to hear him mention her casually. 'So, where do you go from here?'

'Nowhere, I hope. At least not yet. I just feel like being here with my new soft belly, learning to live with it exposed.' He placed his hand on the miracle box. 'This seems a good place to do that.' He got up to close the window. A chilly night breeze was sneaking in. The sea was picking up moonbeams, shivering in the light. 'So, tell me what you've been doing while I've been turning inside out.'

Sophie sat back in her chair to collect her thoughts. There was so much more she wanted to ask him about what he'd been through. But he'd probably said as much as he could for now. Hopefully he would tell her more in the coming weeks when they'd got back into their friendship, maybe walking together. But did they have a few more weeks? Would she be here? She glanced around his room, but was seeing her own room in Sea Spray, next door. She'd grown so fond of her little home. It would be hard to leave it.

'Sophie? Are you okay?'

'I was just thinking about what I've been doing. Working mainly. The café's been very busy. I'm doing the morning shift, while Aidan drags himself out of his adolescent stupor. We're usually all there at lunch time. Rachel's working without ceasing. Patrick was going to lend a hand, but he suddenly took off for a holiday before he takes over at Wraith Cove.'

'Yes, I must go there to see Jane.' He brushed the sleeve of Sophie's dress. 'This is pretty. Have you been out with Jill?'

'No, she's still away.' Sophie smiled. 'I've been abandoned by all my friends. Except Rachel of course, but she's always up to her elbows in flour.' She realised she was avoiding telling him about her meetings with Peter. She remembered when Nick had met him on her birthday and how rudely Peter had acted, how she'd felt diminished and their celebration lessened by his intrusion. She didn't want Nick to think she was being foolish. But she needed to talk to someone. She was missing Jill who would have helped her get some clarity. In fact, knowing Jill's feelings about Peter, she would more than likely have told her to get a brain transplant.

'Actually, I've been out with Peter.'

'Peter?'

'My ex. He's been working on the island and we needed to sort out our finances and divorce.'

'Has that been difficult?'

'Yes. We've met a few times.' She could feel her eyes sliding away from his interested face. 'He wants us to get back together – to try again at our marriage.' She glanced at Nick's face. A look of surprise passed over it, his eyes widening.

'I know he must have seemed a real bastard to you – that time you met him. But, he's changed. I didn't believe him at first. But it's genuine, I can see that now. It's as if he's worn out his old patterns. He's full of regrets and desperately wants to settle down – maybe have a child.'

'With you?'

'It is still possible.'

'Sorry. I didn't mean to pry.'

She smiled. 'It's okay.'

'You really think he's changed that much?'

Sophie nodded. 'Audrey talks about it too – he sees a lot of her and her children. Even Rachel thinks he's not a bad bloke when you get to know him. I think she identified with him a bit.'

'But what about you? How do you feel about him?'

'I'm still very wary. But, I have to acknowledge that I do still feel something for him. We were together a long time.'

'But he treated you so badly.'

'I wasn't exactly a scintillating companion. I was always distracted by my workload and obsessing about patients. We forgot how to communicate. It takes two, doesn't it?'

Nick nodded. 'A common scenario, I guess. Sophie, I know I have no right to ask you this, but do you still love him? Are you sure this isn't just a bit of rekindled excitement – an opportunity to have a family?'

She hung her head for a while, unable to meet the directness of his gaze, while all her doubts tumbled around inside her.

'I don't know. I've been intrigued – and flattered – by the change in him. I've been force-fed with all the good times we had – which are now more in focus than the bad.' She threw her head back, rolling it from side to side dramatically. 'And I'm tempted by thc thought of family life.' She sat upright. 'It's as if all I ever wanted has returned and been offered to me. It might be my last chance. How can I know, Nick? What if I turn my back on this and regret it for the rest of my life?'

'But do you love him?'

'Love changes, doesn't it? It's not like the honeymoon stuff. But roots grow down, shared experiences, family histories knit together. He knew my parents, I knew his. He's fond of my sister. I don't know, we have a past, I suppose.'

'Is that enough to build a future on? Enough to support the demands of a child?'

'I just don't know. How will I know unless

I try?' She groaned. 'And then it might be too late.'

'Look, don't rush too far ahead. You're not committed to having half a dozen kids by next week. Why not try to concentrate on your feelings about Peter? Try not to get carried away by intoxicating fantasies and—'

'Lust?' She laughed. 'I've managed to stay clear of that, so far.'

'Has he been here – to Blue Slipper Bay?'

'Why do you ask that?'

'I'm trying to think . . . I suppose it's because I know that having your own place means so much to you and I'm feeling protective. I don't want him to come here and make his mark. It's a bloke thing.'

'I understand that. It must be territorial. No, he hasn't been here – I haven't wanted him to.'

Nick reached out his hand to cover hers. 'What does that say?' he said quietly.

Sophie pushed her hair back, feeling tired. This was all so complex. But Nick was right. Her feelings for Peter were what she needed to concentrate on. That's what Jill would say too – after she'd kicked Sophie up the backside.

'I'm going up to London with him for the weekend. I'm staying with Audrey. I need to collect my things that's she stored for me and I want to experience how I feel being back there. After living here, I'll probably realise how awful it is and come rushing back.'

'Or you might decide to stay,' Nick said.

'Either way, I'll need to come back to sort out things here.' She got up. 'I must go, Nick, I'll never get up for work in the morning. I'm so glad you're back.'

He got up and put his arms around her. They swayed together in the middle of his room. It felt good, resting against a masculine chest, strong arms around her. She drew away. He kept his hands on her shoulders.

'Will we have time for a walk before you go to London?'

She shook her head. 'Peter's picking me up from work after my shift tomorrow. Maybe next week.'

Nick nodded; his hands fell from her shoulders. She leaned forward and kissed him on his stubbled cheek. 'Don't shave your hair off, it suits you,' she said.

CHAPTER 25

Nick woke gasping for air. His mind struggled to make sense of where he was. Was he still at Neptune's? He felt something thump against his side with a throaty grumble. It was Commie. He was in his own bed at home, at Fair Wind. He sat up and swung his legs over the side, his heart still thudding. He'd been dreaming about drowning. But it wasn't him this time. He'd been trying to save someone else. He tried to recall the anguish. Was it Keri he was straining to reach, her fingers tantalisingly close, impossible to grasp? Her hair streamed and floated like seaweed. But it was dark, dense, waving through the water as she drifted away. It was Sophie.

Nick padded to the kitchen and poured himself a glass of water. Through the window he could see a pale shade of dawn brushing the cliff face. He recalled the feelings that had shifted about inside him when he'd been listening to Sophie earlier. He'd wanted to take hold of her slender arms, her thin hands which twisted in and out of themselves. He wanted to tell her not to go backwards into her life that might have been. What was the purpose?

You couldn't recapture the past in any meaningful way. It came trailing chunks of old memories ready to trip you up like boxes stored in a dark attic.

And what had stopped him – what had prevented him blurting all this out to her, passionately, so that she would hear? It was the same old reason. How could he know what was right for anyone else? For all he knew, Peter had metamorphosed and he and Sophie might live the rest of their lives together in bliss. So he'd kept quiet. Once again he'd decided to say nothing, respecting someone else's integrity over his own. Or was it just cowardice? After all, Sophie didn't have to take any notice of his opinion, however impassioned. He just didn't want to feel responsible for influencing anyone, for changing the course of someone else's life. Arrogant, that's what he was. Thinking he had the power to do that. He had vowed to himself at Neptune's that he would always speak up, he would never again hold back his feelings or be dishonest. And the first time an opportunity had arisen he'd backed off. What was the matter with him?

And then he realised it was because he hadn't wanted Sophie to think badly of him. He'd been scared that if he had followed his instincts he might have pushed her away, risked losing her friendship. At least he was beginning to see himself more clearly now, his own motives. He supposed it was because he'd demolished his iron curtain. Everything seemed to stand out starkly in the dawning light. He was falling in love with Sophie.

He stood in front of the sitting room windows, looking out on another day. He could leave now. He could pack up and return to New Zealand, finish his world trek. It was too soon to face another life crisis. His soft belly wasn't acclimatized yet.

'Deal with it. Nick,' he heard Keri say. 'You can't run for ever.'

Rose stood looking at Jill. 'Come and have some tea, Mum. You look awful.'

Jill stared at her, not knowing what to say. Rose looked very pale and tired.

Stephanie held out a hand. 'You mustn't drive away feeling like this. We all need to talk.'

'Grandma's right, Mum. Look. I'm sorry I swore at you – didn't expect to see you here.' She smiled shakily. 'I gather you saw Patrick too – he's making the tea. Come on.' She turned to go. Jill lifted a foot and managed to get herself walking.

They walked in awkward silence back to the house. Stephanie led them round to the terrace where Patrick was waiting for them. He disappeared inside to fetch the tea. They sat down at a wooden table. Jill remembered this terrace, weeds pushing through the cracked paving slabs. She and her friends had danced out here, their music blaring out through the huge French doors. She wondered where all those kids were now – had they all coped with life outside The Morg? Or were they all as fucked up as her?

'Didn't expect to see you here,' Jill said to Patrick

as he placed a tray on the table. He smiled, he was a very handsome young man, Jill thought.

'No,' he replied. 'Isn't it odd – unexpectedly seeing someone you know in a completely different setting – strangely disorientating.'

Confident too, thought Jill. But then he has been to university.

'So you grew up here?' Patrick continued. 'What a wonderful place to spend your childhood.'

Jill saw Rose put a hand on his arm. He looked from face to face. 'I'm going to take a walk,' he said and bounded athletically down the terrace steps. Stephanie poured the tea and pushed a mug in Jill's direction.

Jill was studying Rose's pale face. She looked different, closed and sullen, avoiding Jill's eyes.

'Are you all right, Rose?' Jill asked. Rose nodded and started playing with a teaspoon. 'Are you and Patrick – seeing each other – or whatever you call it these days?'

Rose nodded.

'How long?' Jill continued.

'Oh, for Christ's sake, Mum. Don't start interrogating me. I'm eighteen! I can make my own decisions.'

'All right. I was just interested, that's all.' Whatever had got into her? Stephanie sat quietly, sipping her drink as if this were an everyday tea party.

Rose put her hand to her forehead. 'Sorry, just didn't want to hear all the criticism.'

'What criticism?'

'You know. All the crap about being too young – he's not good enough for you – what about your career—'

'Hold on. You don't know that—'

'Oh come on, Mum. Dad would be horrified – his perfect Rose going out with a café owner's son.'

'That's unfair—'

'Is it? Face it Mum, you and Dad are snobs. You've had my life mapped out for me ever since I was big enough to get my sticky little fingers on the violin strings—'

'It wasn't *for* us! We thought that was what *you* wanted.'

'Did anybody ask me?' Rose's eyes were blazing.

'You never said . . . we thought—'

'You never listened!'

Jill felt shocked. This wasn't the same girl that she'd seen a few weeks ago. What had happened to her? 'Okay,' she said, 'I'm listening now. Tell me what you want.'

Unexpectedly, Rose burst into tears. Jill reached for her but Stephanie put a surprisingly firm hand on her arm.

'I tell you what I want!' she sobbed. 'I want to live my own life and find out who I am. I don't want to be a concert violinist. I don't even want to be first violin in an orchestra. I want to play in a folk band – the sort of music I love and have always loved. I want to visit Grandma and do things openly instead of secretly, like you and Dad have forced me too.'

'But why have you never said?'

'I didn't know I had a choice until I left home and learned from others.'

'From Patrick?'

'Don't start pinning things on him! From all kinds of people.'

Jill suddenly swung round to face Stephanie. 'You?'

'Don't blame my Grandma!' Rose shouted. 'Don't you realise, Mum! I made my own choices.' She jumped up from the table. 'And if you want to know, I've dropped out of uni. I'm going to Africa with Grandma when she returns.' She started to walk away in the direction that Patrick had gone. 'And just for the record, I came here to recover from an abortion.'

Sophie had forgotten the texture of London air. Choked with its own pollution, it didn't have much to offer when inhaled into a pair of human lungs. Peter kept glancing at her as if monitoring her response to being back in the buzz and fidget of the streets. He pointed out a new book shop, another themed wine bar, an aromatic delicatessen. Sophie feigned enthusiasm, appreciating the choice that only a big city can offer, but noticing the shove of the crowds, the aggression of the traffic, the tension of over-stretched resources. She had to look up to remember the sky was still there, under its rheumy haze.

Peter dropped her at Audrey's and went to his flat to organise himself. Audrey seemed pleased to see her, dragging her in the door as if once over the threshold she could start to pin her down like Gulliver. Peter was returning later to have dinner with them and Sophie wasn't allowed in the kitchen. She suspected Audrey was worried she might offer to do something and wreck her management plan. John had taken Joanna and William to visit his mother so that Sophie could have a quiet soak in the bath – *after all that travelling* – even though she'd already showered before she left.

Sophie lay in the tub, perfumed bubbles exploding under her chin, staring at an expanse of flawless white tiles. She closed her eyes, trying to imagine the hum of traffic was the drone of the wind on the sea. She replayed her talk with Nick last night, wishing she could have gone for a walk with him before she left. He'd touched on some interesting insights, given her some clarity about her future. He was right; she didn't have to decide everything at once. She realised how much she was starting to value his opinions. She'd missed him while he was away and she missed Jill. Ash's parents lived in Dulwich. She could phone them to find out if Jill was there, if she had time – Peter had activities arranged for the weekend.

'Isn't this wonderful – all back together again?' Audrey's eyes and mouth flickered at the corners, fuelled by her unquenchable flame of hope. She sent her meaningful gaze around the table so that each of them was obliged to smile back in turn.

'Mummy, is Aunty Melissa coming?' Joanna asked.

'Joanna! You know perfectly well – I've already explained that to you.' Audrey's cheekbones turned pink. 'Say sorry to your Aunty Sophia.'

Joanna frowned, obviously trying to fathom this obscurity. 'She was going to put plaits in my hair for me. She promised—'

'Joanna! Do you want to leave the table?' Audrey was scrunching up her white linen napkin, widening her eyes at John for parental support. John, realising something was expected of him, looked surprised to find himself there at all.

'Anyone been watching the Olympics?' he asked.

Peter and Sophie both started to laugh. Audrey looked confused and began collecting up the avocado dishes.

The conversation felt strained as they ate their way through Audrey's exquisite creamy chicken, which probably had an exotic name that she was dying for Sophie to ask so she could berate her ignorance. The children were subdued, scared of saying the wrong thing after Joanna's apparent slip. John, Peter and William discussed sport. Sophie could see Audrey trying to steer the conversation back to the high priority topics at the head of her mental list.

'So,' she said, basking centre-stage, after they'd all lavished praise on her home-made chocolate mousse. 'Are you going to see that house tomorrow?'

'House?' Sophie ventured. Now who was putting their scheming little foot in it?

Audrey put her hand to her mouth. 'Sorry – I thought you knew.'

Peter wiped his mouth with his napkin. 'I was going to tell you – I've seen a house – a bit like our old one. It's been beautifully refurbished and the price is good.'

'But I'm not—'

'Only out of interest, that's all. I've been thinking about getting back into the housing market before it's too late. Thought you might like to come and take a look with me.'

'You can go and watch television if you want to,' Audrey said to the kids. They looked at each other as if the Hogwart's Express had just steamed up outside. They fled before she could change her mind.

'I'll see,' Sophie said. 'I need to sort out my stuff and re-pack it to take back.'

'No hurry for that, you can leave it in the spare room for as long as you like. Can't she, John?'

'Absolutely. No problem.' John looked as if he wished he'd escaped with the kids. 'How about a brandy?'

Sophie passed on that. She didn't want to get her head befuddled and find herself agreeing to something she might regret tomorrow. She felt curious about this house. What did Peter have in mind, why hadn't he mentioned it?

'What else have you planned?' Audrey asked.

'I did think I might go and visit Ash's parents to see if Jill and the kids are there. I want to know when she's coming home – to the island that is.'

Audrey took a tiny sip of brandy and screwed up her eyes. 'Couldn't you just phone?'

'I'll phone first. But I'd like to see them. You remember Ash's mother and father, Peter? So conservative – the complete opposite of Jill's mother.'

Peter pulled a face. 'And look how Jill turned out.'

'Jill turned out fine,' Sophie said, protectively. 'She speaks her mind, that's all.'

Audrey, predictably, took the opportunity to gripe about Jill. 'If you can call that fine – I call it rude. It's all that psychological stuff – and she's always encouraged you—'

'Audrey, let's not go there again. Jill's always been a good supportive friend to me.'

'Are you sure about that?' Peter said, his voice sharp.

Sophie looked at him in astonishment. He had a strange expression on his face – almost a sneer. 'What do you mean?' she said.

'Think about it. Jill never exactly championed our relationship did she?'

'But . . . she was the one that encouraged us to stay together in the early days when everyone else seemed to think we were doomed to fail.' Sophie was beginning to feel outnumbered.

'Then why didn't she encourage you to work at it later on?' Audrey's face looked flushed. John was gazing into his brandy glass as if he hoped the future might become clear.

'Because . . . I don't know—'

'Because she never liked me, that's why,' Peter said. 'And she claims to be so knowledgeable about human beings. But I'll tell you something, your friend Rachel has more understanding, and she doesn't charge exorbitant prices for her advice.'

'Oh, that's ridiculous, Peter.'

'Is it? Well I think Jill has a lot to answer for. Audrey and I have talked about this. Jill coloured me with the same brush as your father. That's what all this has been about, hasn't it? She had it all worked out to fit into her neat psychological theory that girls marry their fathers, and convinced you that's what you'd done.'

'As a matter of fact I worked that out for myself. Jill always reckoned it was a myth that Dad was unfaithful, it was just his Italian, bottom-pinching ways.' She turned to Audrey. 'Jill thinks that Dad was crazy over our mother and as faithful as an old dog. It was just a game they played. She enjoyed being the wronged wife and letting him make it up to her.'

Audrey stared uncomprehendingly as if her life script had been ripped up and she might have to write another one.

John suddenly threw his head back and roared with laughter. Sophie thought his chair was going to tip over and he might crack his head open on the sideboard.

'What a load of old bull-shit.' The wine and brandy had certainly loosened him up. She'd never seen him behave like this before. He rocked forward, jogging the table. 'Do you know what I think? You're all talking out of your arses. And I don't know or care if Freud said it first.'

'John!' Audrey started to cough and reached for the water jug. Sophie wondered if she might try to douse John's surprising bout of eloquence. She hoped she wouldn't. Sophie was enjoying this.

'Look,' he continued, waving a finger in the manner of inebriates. 'There's no formula. We aren't robots. You either have a bash at getting on together or you don't. No good blaming your parents or your friends. They're by and large just as fucked up as you and me.'

'John!' Audrey spluttered.

Sophie started to laugh uncontrollably, wiping her eyes on the stiff napkin. Audrey would have some starching to do tomorrow. Peter was looking at her, his lips quivering, his belly heaving as he tried to resist joining in. Then he gave up, letting out a shout of laughter that brought Joanna and William running in. Audrey got up, smiling uncertainly, as if she were thinking that everything must be okay if they were having such a raucous time.

'I'll, er, go and make the coffee,' she said.

'Please, don't go to see Jill.' Peter caught hold of Sophie's arm as they were walking back to his car after viewing the house. It was indeed a lovely place, restored back to its Victorian splendour, expensively fitted out. Minimally furnished with show house items, fluffy white towels piled on bathroom shelves, an exotic flower here and there, no trace of a dog or child. Sophie suspected the estate agent had wafted a few vanilla pods around the place before they arrived.

'Good family-size house,' Peter had commented. The estate agent looked at them shrewdly, trying to assess how old this family might be. Then he pointed out relevant features – a decent sized walled garden, kitchen big enough to be a family room, and a spare downstairs room for a playroom or study. He was good at his job. Sophie began to visualize bright toys scattered over the wooden floor, little hats and coats hanging in the hall, a tabby cat sprawled on the window sill amongst a jumble of jars and geraniums. 'We'll be in touch,' she'd heard Peter say to the agent as they left.

Sophie stood looking at Peter; his face was thrust towards her, pleading.

'Why don't you want me to see Jill?' she said.

'Because I want you to give us a chance without running to her for advice.'

Sophie had phoned Ash's parents. Jill was supposed to be back with them the next day, to stay for a while before returning to the island. Sophie longed to see her. But maybe Peter was right. It was him she should be talking to, not Jill. She looked away from him, reluctant to agree to his suggestion. He was still holding her arm, rubbing his thumb gently over her skin.

'Anyway, I've got lots of exciting things planned for us, for Audrey and John and the kids too.'

'What things?'

'You'll have to wait and see, won't you?' He smiled, teasingly. 'Plenty of fun to be had in London, remember?'

She did remember. She could recall all sorts of thrilling excursions once she'd escaped the restraints of her family and before she'd got herself overwhelmed with her work and her mother. And then London had become a confining place, and she'd drifted into martyrdom. She didn't know whether she'd ever be able to view London again without the veil of bleakness that she'd managed to smother it with.

'I don't know whether I could live here again,' she said.

'No-one's asking you to. I'm just suggesting a bit of fun, that's all.'

'But,' she gestured back at the house, 'I thought you had your heart set on it.'

'It's just a house, Sophie.' His hand moved up to her shoulder. 'We're the important issue here.' His hand brushed her cheek. 'Please spend this time with me.'

I can see Jill next week, she thought, when I get back to the island.

CHAPTER 26

Nick was having lunch at Wraith Cottage with Jane and Marguerite. He felt he owed Jane an explanation of his unannounced absence from work but she was unperturbed about his time away.

'It was fine by me, Nick. You deserved a holiday and sometimes they're all the better for being spontaneous.' She pushed the glass jug of elderflower cordial towards him. 'Marguerite and Neptune told me you were doing a bit of heart and soul-searching. Everyone needs to do that from time to time.' She smiled at Nick. Her direct gaze always made him feel as if the world held nothing that couldn't ultimately be coped with.

'I think I'd never really let go of Keri,' he said simply.

Jane sighed. 'Death is never simple is it? It leaves us with all sorts of issues to deal with – grief being just one of them.'

Nick nodded. 'It changes everything.'

Jane sat back in her chair and looked around the cluttered room. 'When I first came to Wraith Cottage, my Aunt Emmeline was living here with

Marguerite.' Jane reached for her sister's hand. 'She was a wise old soul. She always used to say that if one person changes everyone else connected with them has to change too. And ultimately we are all connected. I suppose some would say that's how evolution works.'

Nick smiled. 'You know, I don't think on all my travels, I've ever met a wiser bunch of people.'

'Perhaps you weren't listening to the women.'

Marguerite made some rapid signals at Jane.

Jane laughed. 'Okay. We'll make an exception for Neptune.'

'Absolutely,' Nick agreed. 'So, do you still need me on the hotel project, or has Patrick got it all in hand?'

'Nick, there will be work there for years. Patrick isn't back yet, but the others are doing a great job with the foundations – the place is churning with concrete mixers. Look – you are the one with the vision, the big picture. We need you for as long as you can stay – and please take time off when you want to. There's no hurry. Chas calls it my little hobby.'

Marguerite threw up her hands, shaking her head so that her silver hair rippled over her shoulders.

'Marguerite thinks Chas has got an odd sense of humour,' Jane said.

Nick cut himself another chunk of homemade bread. He'd been ravenous ever since his return from Neptune's.

'To tell the truth, I had thought about moving

on.' Nick briefly wondered what Sophie was doing in London with Peter. He noticed his thoughts were often pulling him that way.

'But?' prompted Jane.

'I decided I need to stay here, to deal with life as it is right now. Besides, I would miss you all – and this place.'

'Well, we're glad, aren't we, Marguerite? We hope you'll stay for a long time.'

Marguerite nodded and then jumped up and went outside as if she'd heard something. Nick still wasn't sure how much she could hear.

'That's Neptune,' said Jane. 'He's taking her into Ventnor this afternoon.'

'To Cormorants?'

She nodded, frowning.

'Are you and Neptune still not happy about that?'

'Neptune's not. I'm more resigned. I think Marguerite needs to be allowed to do what she wants. God knows she's had little enough choice. I hoped she might enjoy travelling but she seems distracted when we're away, as if she's listening for something way beyond what any of us can hear.'

'And you think it's to do with Cormorants?'

'Ash, to be more precise.'

'Do you think this is an infatuation?'

'That's my fear, yes. And because she's an adult, I'm unsure how much to interfere.'

'But a vulnerable, inexperienced adult.'

'That's what Neptune says. But,' she leaned forward across the table, 'she's also very astute, Nick. She's the clearest person I've ever met.'

'I agree.' Nick remembered the time she sat with him through his grief and pain, as if she knew exactly what she was doing. 'But maybe there are some areas of life she has no knowledge of.' Nick thought about sex. Marguerite was a beautiful woman who had spent her life secluded from men. How would that affect her if she'd suddenly fallen for someone?

'Nick . . . how would you feel about talking to Ash – I mean man to man?'

'I hardly know him. Ash and Jill – they're really Sophie's friends. I have talked about it with her. She said Ash had sorted out whatever was going on – some sort of new-fangled therapy as far as I could make out.'

'Yes, and I think it was better for a while. Marguerite certainly seemed less preoccupied. But I don't know. She's still disturbed by something – and I'm not sure it's altogether healthy.'

Nick nodded. 'Look, Sophie will be back soon. I'll talk to her again and report back to you. Have you ever asked Marguerite directly?'

Jane put her head on one side. 'It's the only thing that she seems unable, or unwilling, to share with me. That's why I'm so diffident. I'd hate her to think I was intruding in her private life. We're all entitled to that, aren't we?'

* * *

Nick spent the afternoon re-familiarising himself with the hotel gardens. A lot of trampling had gone on with the arrival of the building team. But that was inevitable. He wrote down a list of projects. He wanted to resurrect this garden as best he could. And he had friends to be involved with, to care about. He'd been supported and nourished by others who were concerned about him and his life. He felt that he mattered to this place and these people. He wanted to tell Sophie.

'You must stay the night,' Stephanie said, handing Jill a wad of tissues to mop her tears. 'I won't let you drive in your state.'

'Where . . . where will I sleep?' Jill sobbed. 'Rose has got my old room.'

'You can have my bed. I can sleep on the floor, I'm used to it.'

'Is she sleeping with Patrick here?'

Stephanie shrugged. 'That's her business.'

'Well,' Jill let out a scornful laugh. 'At least they won't be having sex at the moment. I won't have to listen to *that* next door.'

'Jill!' Stephanie's face looked shocked.

'That's one of the things I remember, you see – about this place. Hearing people having sex. I didn't realise what it was at first, I was too young. But I soon grew up.'

'Jill,' Stephanie looked anxious. 'I know this wasn't the ideal place for a little girl – I didn't realise—'

'But you should have. You were the parent, not me. You were always busy with some good cause or other – women's clinics, women's rights—'

'And you think I neglected you? What about all the freedom you had growing up in this wonderful place? And what about the experience of having lots of different adults in your life, broadening your mind. You grew up without any kind of indoctrination—'

'What? You are joking! I was indoctrinated into sex and drugs and—'

'Probably no more so than if you'd lived in a city.'

Jill could feel something inside her about to explode. 'Let me tell you a few home truths, Mother. After you ferried us commune kids home on my fourteenth birthday from the cinema, some of us went up to Shakti's attic rooms and got initiated into group sex after smoking dope. And that wasn't my first sexual experience by far. Ever wondered about all those waifs and strays that you landed us with – nice break for them from their terrible lives? Did you ever consider what all your men friends were up to – the ones that loafed around the place while you were delivering some lecture or other to the disadvantaged? How I managed to escape getting pregnant or some horrible disease I will never know.'

'But . . . drugs were banned, 'Stephanie said feebly, obviously not ready yet to take on board the issue of underage sex.

'Oh, very funny! The place was so steeped in

patchouli, you wouldn't have been able to smell a joint if it was burning under your nose.'

'I always made sure you were with the older children. I knew what activities you were doing – pottery and the art—'

'But I wasn't. It was so easy to fool you because you were always so engrossed with saving with world.'

'So you were lying to me – about where you were.'

'Of course I was lying. What child wouldn't? God! What went on was terrible and shocking. But it was also fascinating and riveting and wonderful. But I didn't understand. I was a child!'

Stephanie put her hands over her face as if she were trying to shut Jill out.

'I grew up with crossed wires. I never understood how relationships worked in the outside world. I thought it was a free-for-all. I thought that if one of my friends was interested in someone then I could muscle in and have them too. I had no idea about love and respect.'

Stephanie took her hands from her face. Her eyes were wet. But Jill couldn't stop now. 'You've no idea how many friendships I ruined. I tried to control it – tried to understand myself. Why do you think I studied psychology? It wasn't until I met Ash that I found some stability in my life. Even then I still . . .'

'Still what?' Stephanie whispered.

'Still . . .' Jill shook her head. 'It doesn't matter.'

* * *

Rachel bolted the café door after having closed the shutters early. Sophie had worked all day to pay Aidan back for filling in during her trip to London.

'Right,' she said, 'bugger the punters. Tell me everything.'

Sophie poured fresh tea and cut generous hunks of treacle tart for them both. 'I had a good time. I didn't think I would – I was determined to collect my belongings and get back here as quickly as possible. But Peter made such an effort – he'd arranged lots of outings for us – Audrey and John and the kids too.'

'Outings?'

'London Eye, Regent's Park Zoo – fun things. And, he took me to see a smart house that he's got his eye on.'

'He's serious then. So what's the deal?'

'He wants us to try again – he would like us to start a family before it's too late. He swears he's changed.'

'And you believe him?' She sounded sceptical.

Sophie nodded. 'I'm sure he has. There's no reason for him to pretend.'

'Have you spoken to Jill?'

'She's not back until the end of the week – why?'

'It's just that, you've always said she gives you a sense of balance – makes you see reason.'

'That's true. I planned to see her while I was in London but Peter persuaded me not to. He wanted me to give him a chance without running to her. As it happened, Ash's parents said she was staying away a bit longer than she planned.'

Rachel looked thoughtful. 'I can see Peter's point. I expect Audrey was his number one back-up, wasn't she?'

'Oh, yes. I was enticed back into the family thing. I did feel I belonged – they are all I've got.'

'And now you've got the possibility of adding to that family.'

'Well, who knows? It might not happen easily at my age.'

'I presume all your bits are in working order?'

'As far as I know. I suppose I could have my hormone levels tested.'

Rachel looked at her thoughtfully. 'You're serious about this?'

'Yes – I told Nick – it feels like I'm being offered all I ever wanted.'

'I thought you wanted to stay on the island.'

'Well, Peter reckons we can afford to buy a holiday home here. He earns big money these days.'

'He really has got all exits covered.' Rachel shook her head.

'But you said yourself that he isn't bad when you get to know him, that I might regret it.'

'I know. But I was being a bit maudlin about my own situation. I honestly didn't think you would be tempted by him.'

Sophie sat twisting her fork over and over. She could tell Rachel wanted to say more but felt unsure. Eventually Rachel laid her hand on Sophie's.

'Make sure you're not being seduced by what he's offering. It's how you feel about him that's important.'

'I know, Rachel. You're right. But I'm having great difficulty separating that out from the package.'

'When have you got to make a decision?'

'As soon as possible – he wants to make an offer on this house and it will be too big for him if I say no.'

'Don't let that pressurise you. Wait for Jill to come home. Talk to her. Talk to Evie, talk to Nick.'

'I've already talked to him.'

'And?'

'He says the same as you, to concentrate on my feelings.'

Rachel poured more cream on her tart. 'Do you like Nick with hair?' she said.

Sophie took the jug from her. 'Mm, it was a bit of a surprise, but I do prefer it. I think it makes him look softer.'

'I preferred him bald. Couldn't you just imagine that lovely smooth head between your—'

'Rachel!'

'Well, just think about it.'

'Not while I'm eating treacle tart and cream, I won't.'

Rachel giggled. 'Later then.'

'Anyway, to get back to the subject of Peter, he'll

be here in a couple of days. I just hope Jill returns before him.'

Sophie walked slowly home along the cliff path, enjoying being alone again. She held her face up to the warm evening breeze, waiting for the relaxation the smell and the sound of the sea gave her. But it didn't come. She wondered if part of her had already made the decision to leave and removed itself back to the drone of traffic and absence of sky. She wanted to be back here, fully present, but she knew she desired other things too. Perhaps this had just been a brief time-out from the course her life had already chosen. An interval to make Peter and her both realise what they really wanted now they were older. She felt the unsevered bonds between them, different now, but with the possibility they could deepen, strengthened by the depth of their new understanding.

When she rounded the corner to Blue Slipper Bay she could see Kyp and Evie sitting outside the cabin talking to Nick. The Water Babies were playing on the beach with some holiday children. The tide was out and gulls were pecking in the rock pools. Deckchairs were scattered about. Evie had strung coloured lanterns along the awning above the tables. Sophie stood for a while watching. She would miss this place. But – as Peter kept pointing out – what would it be like in the winter? Kyp and Evie would fly away to Greece. Supposing Nick went off on his travels too? She couldn't live here alone. What if a storm came and the cliff started to slip? Would she cope with the waves sweeping in beneath Sea Spray? Rachel had said Sophie could move in with her but now there was a good chance that Patrick might stay at home. How would she support herself? She might have to reconsider working at Cormorants. She suddenly felt tired. She'd pondered over these questions so often her mind was seizing up. She waved across the beach to the others and let herself into her little cottage and shut the door. She staggered up to her bedroom, threw herself onto her bed and fell into a deep sleep. When she awoke it was dark. She went down to the sitting room and looked out of the window. Kyp and Evie had cleared up after their guests. The lanterns went out as she watched. She'd intended to call on Nick to catch up with him. Never mind, tomorrow would do.

CHAPTER 27

Nick felt disappointed. He'd been watching for Sophie to arrive home from work. He anticipated her coming over to join him and Kyp and Evie for a drink, eager to tell them about her long weekend in London. But she'd simply waved and gone into her cottage. He found himself glancing up at her balcony all evening, feeling a little like Romeo. But her windows stayed closed and no lights had gone on at dusk. She'd missed the most spectacular sunset. He wanted her to see it with him; layers of pink and gold tinting the sea lilac.

He guessed she must be tired after her travelling and then working all day. What if she were ill or upset? But she obviously wanted to be alone. He remembered that he'd promised to acknowledge his feelings, not try to shut them out. So he was going to deal with this. He wanted to be with Sophie and she didn't want to be with him right now. He sat cross-legged on his bed and felt the clench of loneliness in his solar plexus. He breathed deeply into his abdomen, noticing the tension. He didn't have to deny it or do anything about it. All that was required of him was to accept its presence. That's what he'd been taught. His mind was used to grabbing hold, rationalising, berating, denying. But tonight he simply let it be and after a while he was aware of his belly softening and the presence of a background feeling of peace. It didn't arrive, or sneak in bit by bit. It was as if it had been there all the time and he'd never really noticed. It felt both normal and sacred, as if this was how life was meant to be, under all the fear of loss and pain. He thought again of Sophie's glow-worm and something he'd fished out of her miracle box earlier.

Weary child, let words fade like the darkening day and come home to rest a while.

Jill spent a few days exploring every inch of Morgan's Hall that she could access without incurring anyone's wrath. She felt as if the ghosts of her past were following her, increasing as she peered into every room and outbuilding until she felt like the Pied Piper. The place that had the deepest impact on her was the attic – it was here that most of the trysts with Shakti and her disciples had taken place. Shakti let it be known that the attic rooms were her sacred place that she used for her spiritual practices. The adults respected her privacy. She had come from an ashram in India where free expression of sexuality was encouraged. But not for children – Jill had researched the ashram later and found out that no children were permitted to live there. She realised now from her adult perspective that Shakti had been a damaged person, but Jill had thought her the most marvellous, beautiful being that she'd ever encountered. She was first in line to experiment with everything Shakti had to offer. And of course the boys – especially the older ones were smitten. And it wasn't only the commune kids – adults and visitors had been involved too.

Jill sat on the floor of the attic room that had been Shakti's inner sanctum. There was still an old mattress on the floor and Jill could swear the smell of patchouli still hung in the air. She imagined Shakti lying on the mattress in a puff of orange gauze, her breasts bare, smoke drifting from her nostrils, heavy eyes half closed, lips parted. Everything about Shakti was open, beckoning. And Jill had wanted to be her – tried to emulate her. And there was no-one to tell her that Shakti's choices were not appropriate for a little girl.

Jill ran down the stairs and out of one of the back doors and began another circuit of the grounds. Everything looked a bit neater than she remembered – the forgotten garden that some of the women had worked to restore was now more wild than neglected – the tiny pagoda still there. Some of the barns had been nicely refurbished and were being used as a conference centre. She walked through the orchard and up the steep hill to Windy Ridge where the reservoir was situated. She sat on a stone and looked down on Morgan's Hall, basking like an old dinosaur in the sun. It was a beautiful place. Suddenly a flood of warmth seemed to flow through her. There was no doubt that she had intoxicating memories of growing up here. It wasn't until she left and tried to adapt to living in a more conventional world that she understood how disastrous it had been for her.

She could see a small group of people emerge from the house and stand looking around. It was her mother and Rose and Patrick. Jill had told them that she didn't want to talk about anything until she felt ready. She got up and stretched. Maybe now was the time.

Peter phoned Sophie at the café to say he would be arriving later that afternoon.

'Is this decision time?' Rachel asked. She wasn't smiling.

Sophie nodded. She'd spent last night battling with herself. She had to decide without further influence from anyone. She felt pulled apart. On the one hand there was all the comfort of her family and relationships forged over years, the familiarity of people and places and life-style. She could sink back into that, hopefully wiser, mature, with more to give. And, on the other hand she'd tasted independence, possibilities of a different life with no idea of where that might lead. She could end up childless, single, estranged from Audrey. She veered from one scenario to the other until she felt her head might burst. But in the end she knew she couldn't let go the possibility of having a child of her own.

Rachel was still looking at her. 'You're going back to him, aren't you?' she said.

'If I don't give it a try I'm never going to know, am I? I could end up full of regrets – a childless, bitter old loner.' Her attempt at light-heartedness sank like a coin in a wishing-well. She walked home at lunchtime and found herself wandering around Sea Spray, sadly watching the sea as if she were trying to let go of it. She showered and dressed and returned to Ventnor in her car so she would have the means to get back independently later. She still didn't want Peter to come to Blue Slipper Bay. She needed to keep this small interlude of her life separate – a bracketed memory of her attempt to live for herself.

She parked at the east end of the esplanade and walked slowly towards the café, threading her way through the holiday crowds, out en masse today. The school holidays were drawing to a close and families were soaking up the sun and sea as if they needed to store as much as possible to last them over the winter months until they could slip out of city life once more. Sophie stood and watched for a while. The sea was frisky, children shrieking as it washed their legs. Dads and mums waded and watched and took photos. She wondered what sort of parents Peter and she might turn out to be – if it happened. And if it didn't happen – would they be the ones sitting in the striped deckchairs, content to watch?

She looked along the esplanade towards the café and realised that Peter was sitting on a bench watching the crowd, early like her. He kept glancing up towards the far car park, craning his neck, obviously expecting her to appear from the opposite direction. Sophie stood and watched him. He had one arm spread along the back of the seat. He was wearing navy jeans and a blue and white striped tee-shirt, looking as if he'd just moored his yacht in the harbour. It would be fun to have a holiday place here, perhaps a small boat. That way she could keep in contact with Jill and Rachel and her new friends at Blue Slipper Bay. It would be so hard to leave. She could feel a constriction in her chest at the thought of it.

But she knew that today was the day. She couldn't expect Peter to wait any longer for her decision. She felt reluctant to move towards him now, as if this were the last few moments that belonged entirely to her. She stood still, watching him watching. His head turned, she wondered if he would spot her but his gaze was following a young woman with a poodle on a lead. She stopped while her dog sniffed around the legs of the bench Peter was sitting on. Sophie wondered if this was by design. She was slim and leggy, wearing tiny frayed denim shorts and a minimal strappy top. She bent forward to ruffle the dog's topknot, allowing dark hair to swing forward and breasts to tremble. She said something to the dog and glanced at Peter. He reached out a hand and started to stroke the animal, smiling up at her as if poodles were the best thing that ever graced four legs. Peter was not a dog lover. His attitude towards them was similar to that of small children. He could never understand why people doted on something which crawled over their chairs and carpets making a mess, let alone talking to them as if they were meaningful companions. But this poodle was obviously different. Peter sank two hands into its white curls, he was talking to the dog now while the woman laughed and posed. Sophie saw Peter look at his watch and glance towards the car park again. The dog had its two front paws on Peter's knees now and he was smooching like a man besotted.

Sophie turned away – she didn't want to spy on him. She was used to this scene, this easy way he had of chatting to females and their predictable flirty responses. It was most likely harmless; it was embedded in his nature. But she knew that she wouldn't be able to take another step towards him, not today. She walked back to her car and drove home.

Sophie sat on her sofa with Commie pressed comfortably against her thigh. She could hear nothing but the rush and drag of the sea and the occasional cry of a gull. She thought carefully through all her recent meetings with Peter. She thought about the confessions and remorse and promises. She thought about the perfect house in

London offering to fulfil the family dream. She was waiting, expecting a flood of emotions to rise up, a tidal wave of disappointment and frustration. But nothing happened. Where had it all gone – that fear of spending the rest of her days lonely and regretful?

She began to dredge up the past. She delved into the sludge of betrayal and humiliation. She remembered the excuses and blatant lies and deception, her confusion that maybe she was after all the one in the wrong. So many years of her life had been dominated by uncertainty and an undermining of her own integrity.

She thought and thought until she couldn't think about anything else to think about. She must be in denial. Where was all her anger? Why didn't she go into catharsis like Nick? She thought vaguely that Peter – and Rachel – would wonder why she hadn't shown up this afternoon. She had no idea of the time. She got up stiffly and went out onto the balcony. The beach was quiet, just Nick walking barefoot on the sand. He glanced up and waved. Sophie felt a little burst of warmth inside, like a small flame igniting. She gestured for him to come up.

He had shaved his face but left the hair on his head. It stood up in little mink-brown tufts, as if unsure which way to grow now that it had the choice. He stood looking at her, his face puzzled. She felt her eyes brimming with tears but no convulsive sobbing followed.

'What is it?' he said.

She found herself telling him about all her indecision and how, having made up her mind, everything had unravelled at the speed of light just because she'd seen Peter drop back into the habit of a lifetime.

'Just because . . . are you saying that you shouldn't have any feelings about it – that it doesn't matter?'

'No. What I'm realising is that I really don't have any feelings about it. I expected to. I thought I was making excuses for him, telling myself it meant nothing. And then I thought I must be denying how I felt. I tried to release my anger and . . .'

'And?'

'It's beginning to sink in that I just don't care. All that turmoil I've been caught up in ever since Peter's avowal that he'd seen the light and all will be well. I realise now I've been awash with nostalgia and memories and family fantasies. I've allowed myself to be seduced by it all.' She shook her head, trying to clear her tunnel vision. 'Oh, I'm sure he means well and that he has changed. But so have I. I'm a different person too. I can't go back to that. I know it now.'

She felt a sudden ripple of laughter surge up in a glorious rush of freedom. She turned to Nick and threw her arms around him. He looked astonished. 'Oh, thank God,' she cried, 'thank God that bimbo got to him before I did. I never thought I'd be glad to say those words.'

She felt elated and energised. She kept hold of Nick and began to sway. He was laughing now and they started to dance. She hummed a Strauss waltz and he joined in and then they were whirling around the room. Commie sat up staring with curiosity. Sophie hung her head back with abandon and saw with surprise the door open and Peter step into the room. She stopped abruptly, letting go of Nick. He toppled onto the sofa. Peter stood wide-eyed, mouth open.

'I need to talk to you,' Sophie stammered.

Peter jabbed a finger at Nick. 'I thought you said he wasn't your boyfriend.'

'He isn't—'

'I hope you don't expect me to believe that. What were you doing? Stringing me along? Getting your own back? You might at least have had the decency to be honest with me.'

Sophie hung her head and felt the corners of her mouth twitch and wondered if she was about to burst into tears or dissolve in helpless laughter. She wished Jill was here – she would appreciate this. She shook her head. 'Truly, this has nothing to do with Nick. I've been thinking for hours and made my own decision. I'm sorry, Peter. It was never going to work for you and me. I'd already made up my mind when Nick—'

'You'll regret this. You never gave us a chance.'

Before she could say anything else he was gone, slamming the door. Sophie heard his footsteps running down the stairs as if he couldn't get away quickly enough. Then suddenly she heard his voice calling her from outside. She went out onto the balcony. He was standing on the path, shouting up at her.

'Oh, and by the way. You can tell Ash if he wants to have sex in his consulting room he should do it more discreetly.'

Sophie didn't want to hear any more. She went inside, shutting the windows. Nick was standing up now and she could tell by his expression that he'd heard.

Nick wondered what might happen next. Sophie seemed to be looking through him as if she were overwhelmed by events. He grasped her gently by the shoulders.

'Why don't you go and have a shower and I'll make us some supper?' She continued to look blankly at him. He propelled her into the bathroom, listened until he heard the water start to run, then went into the kitchen and leaned against the sink. He was aware that his heart was beating rapidly and his mind racing. He took a few deep breaths, telling himself not to get carried away. He knew that part of him was elated that Sophie had decided not to go back to Peter. Her feelings had seemed to come from the very depths of her as if she had been set free from all her doubts. When she'd swept him into that spontaneous dance he wanted to press her to him and kiss her and tell her about his deepening feelings. His desire for her had seared through him as if it had been released from captivity. But he also knew that it would be foolish to do such a thing. If she'd responded he would never know whether it was just on the rebound from Peter. He had to be the responsible one here. He knew all about vulnerability and crisis states. Perhaps she was on the verge of collapse like he'd been and her abandoned dancing had been a reaction. But she'd seemed to be enjoying herself, alive with a lightness that he hadn't seen in her before. It was Peter's parting shot that had floored her. The problem of Ash and Marguerite kept intruding into their lives.

Nick opened Sophie's fridge. There were a few plastic boxes in there containing Rachel's delicious pastas and salads. He found cutlery and laid the table with blue and white mats and napkins. He filled some of Sophie's bright ceramic bowls with a selection of the food, poured grape juice into a glass jug and uncorked a bottle of red wine. He stood back to admire his work. How bright everything looked. He usually ate off a chipped white plate with a bent fork. It would be nice to get some cheerful tableware. It made the food look more appetising. As an afterthought he took a huge lemon candle off the mantelpiece and placed it in the centre of the table. He lit its three wicks, even though it wasn't yet dark.

He heard the water stop, and stole a glance as Sophie flitted, towel-clad, up to her bedroom. Little darts of pleasure were waking up parts of his body. 'Take it easy, man,' he whispered to himself. He sank down on the sofa and picked up a book, pretending to read.

At last she emerged, smelling of something exotic, looking damp and wild-haired in a honey-coloured vest and blue jeans. Her brown feet were bare. Nick felt as if he'd never truly seen her before. She walked over to the table.

'This is nice,' she smiled at him. 'Thank you.'

Nick thought she seemed calm, not on the verge of cracking up at all. 'Well, I wish I could claim to have spent hours in the kitchen but I guess that's due to Rachel.'

'I've hardly cooked a thing since I started working at the café.'

They sat down at the table. Nick poured the drinks and they loaded their plates. He wasn't sure whether he was hungry or not. He just wanted her to speak to him so that he could sit and look at her. She picked up her glass.

'Well, here's to . . . I don't know what . . .'

Nick clinked his glass against hers. 'I'll drink to that,' he said. Their eyes met and there seemed to him to be a moment of utter peace that descended as if something had fluttered down and wrapped a barricade of wings around them. And then there came a rapping at the door.

'He's come back,' Sophie whispered, her eyes widening.

'Do you want me to go down and tell him to go?' Nick said. Then came the sound of the front door opening and footsteps coming up the stairs. He got up and went to the sitting room door. There was a few moments silence and then a gentle tapping.

'Sophie? Are you there?'

'Rachel!' Sophie pushed her chair back as Nick opened the door. Rachel stood there looking anxious.

'Thank God, you're all right.' Rachel rushed into the room and the women hugged each other. 'I've been so worried about you. I've had Peter storming into the café and behaving like a mad man, Jane's been running around searching for Marguerite, and then Ash came in looking demented. What the hell's going on?'

Nick pulled up a chair for Rachel and poured her a glass of wine and sat back to listen while Sophie told her what had happened between her and Peter. It seemed to him that Sophie had no doubts that she had made the right decision.

'It was such a revelation, Rachel. I could see everything so clearly. I'm sorry for Peter, but I don't have any doubts now. I got caught up in nostalgia and memories and wishful thinking and I wanted it to be true. I wanted to believe that it could work. But I realise now that I was fooling myself. Peter's my past and it's over. Those old original feelings can't be resurrected.' She paused and sighed deeply. 'Even with the promise of a family,' she added. And Nick could feel the weight of her underlying sorrow.

Rachel reached out and put her hand on Sophie's

arm. Nick envied the ease with which women could express their empathy. He supposed it was the absence of ambiguous sexual undertones that allowed it. Or did women possess something that men didn't recognise or couldn't allow? He felt a slight resentment towards Rachel for stepping in when he wanted to be the one that Sophie turned to. But Sophie was talking to him just as much as to Rachel, including him with her eyes and the sweep of her gestures. Silly to be jealous of such a good friend.

'Well, I must be honest,' Rachel said. 'I was almost taken in by Peter. He hung around the café sometimes when you weren't there. He's hard to resist – he has a certain something. When I saw you softening towards him I wanted to test him out. I behaved quite badly, I know. But I started to flirt a little and I knew right away that I only had to say *upstairs* and he would have been straight up there – excuse the pun.'

Sophie smiled ruefully. 'Is that when you changed your attitude towards him?'

'Uh, huh. I was trying not to influence you. But I got seriously worried when I saw you starting to get hooked. I thought I might really have to lure him upstairs and take a video or something.'

'I'm glad you didn't have to go to those lengths. So what did he say when he burst into the café this afternoon?'

'He'd been in earlier wondering where you were. He wanted to know where to find you but I refused to tell him. He went off in a temper – I can only think he must have gone up to see Ash. And then when he came back later he was in a real lather – accused me of knowing you had a lover all along.'

'Poor Nick, wrongly accused. I'm so sorry to have dragged you both in like this.'

'Please don't be,' Nick said. 'I don't mind being accused of being your lover.' He felt his face flush, had he given himself away?

'Well, it's been just like *EastEnders* in the café,' Rachel said. 'But I don't mind, as long as you've made the right decision. Have you got another plate? This food looks good enough to eat, even though I made it myself.'

Nick felt hungry now. He started eating his pasta and found himself wondering if Peter had made his final exit.

'So, then Ash barges in looking for Peter,' said Rachel, continuing the drama as if she were truly writing an episode for a soap opera. 'He said he'd come out of his consulting room to find Peter in reception rifling through the address book. He was seething. I've never seen him behave like that. I hope Jill comes back soon and takes him in hand.'

Nick looked up sharply. 'Jill's still away?'

Rachel put her fork down. 'I'm missing something here, aren't I?'

Nick saw Sophie pause in her eating.

'Come on, out with it,' Rachel demanded. 'I might as well know the full story seeing as my café seems to be the place where everybody blows up.'

Nick could see Sophie struggling between friendship and professional confidentiality. Same old problem. But this was friendship, wasn't it?

'Look, Sophie,' he said. 'I know this is difficult. But how can we help if we don't all speak up and do something?'

'Don't tell me then,' Rachel said. 'Let me work it out. Ash was over the top furious – as if Peter had nosed into more than his address book. So, knowing men it must have something to do with sex.' She looked at each of them in turn. 'I can tell by your faces that I'm on the right track.' She looked mischievous. 'Perhaps Peter caught Ash canoodling with a patient in the consulting room?'

'You're right,' Sophie said. 'And it's no secret now anyway. Peter shouted it for the world to hear before he left.'

Rachel gaped. 'I was joking! Surely not Ash. Not our respectable Bone Man. Are you sure Jill hasn't come back early and they were having a fond reunion – you know, a little medical fantasy on the couch, while the kids were locked in their rooms upstairs?'

'Possibly,' Nick said. 'But, it's doubtful. You said earlier that Jane was in trying to find Marguerite.'

Rachel was looking puzzled. 'I'm not sure where this is going . . .'

'Okay,' Sophie said as if she were getting down to business. 'This is what we know. Marguerite is obsessed with Ash and has been behaving in a disturbed manner. Jane is worried and has been trying to get her away all summer but Marguerite insists on coming back.' She glanced at Nick as if deciding how much more to say. 'Ash has also been acting strangely and I walked in on him having some kind of sexual encounter—'

'No! Not with Marguerite! Please tell me that's not true.' Rachel's fork clattered to the floor.

'I didn't see who he was with. But, well, we don't know what to think, do we, Nick?'

'Does Jill suspect?' Rachel's voice had lost its humour.

'She knows he was distracted by something but she doesn't suspect that, no.'

'My God.' Rachel shook her head with disbelief. 'I can't believe Ash would do that. Marguerite's beautiful but she's like a child. She isn't worldly-wise at all.'

'We know. But it's difficult to know what to do.'

'You have to confront Ash, that's what,' Rachel said.

'You're right,' said Nick. 'And we have to do it before Jill comes back.'

CHAPTER 28

Sophie didn't want to do this. She needed time to digest everything that had happened. She'd felt exhilarated after everything became clear to her. Poor Nick, she'd swept him into her liberation without considering his precarious state of mind. He'd had a breakdown. People took a long time to recover; relapses could be triggered by any excitement. It was unfair of her to drag him into her drama. In that moment, when they'd danced, she'd felt so free she could easily have fallen into bed with him. But she was glad that hadn't happened. She didn't want to be responsible for more misunderstanding.

And now she was drawn back into the saga of Ash and Marguerite. Just as she thought everything had settled. It seemed she wasn't going to escape. She was going to have to participate in this – like it or not. Where was this heading? How would it affect her relationship with Jill and Ash? But how could she stand by now after what Peter had shouted? Marguerite might be a beautiful, gifted adult but she was an innocent. Maybe she should just tell Jill and leave it with her. But what would she tell her? She didn't really know anything for sure. No, she would have to speak to Ash first. After all, he had begged to talk to her before. She should have listened. She'd been selfish and naïve to think it would all go away. If she didn't intervene now, Ash could land himself in serious trouble, might even be struck off his professional register.

Sophie didn't want to do this on her own. She wasn't sure whether she was up to dealing with Ash's wrath if she was wrong. Jane would feel difficult about betraying Marguerite if she got drawn in, and Rachel's presence wouldn't be tolerated by Ash, she felt sure. Neptune would most likely go for Ash's throat if there was any confessing to be done. It had to be Nick. Nick was involved. He didn't know Ash that well; he could be more detached. She needed the support of another male and she trusted Nick to stay calm.

They walked over the cliffs the next evening, psyching themselves up for the meeting. She felt like holding Nick's hand as they talked, as if she needed to physically feel his support, but after all the grabbing of him she'd done recently she thought she'd better restrain herself.

'What if Jill's back?' Nick asked.

'Her car will be in the drive at Cormorants. I'll sneak into the centre to see if he's down there. If he's up in the house we'll have to retreat and think again.'

There was no sign of Jill and the kids. They went into the health centre. Solveig was tidying the reception desk, a couple of students sat writing up their notes.

'We are just closing,' Solveig said. 'Did you want to make an appointment?'

'I wanted to speak to Ash. Is he still here?'

'You're Sophie, Jill's friend, aren't you? He is seeing a patient. Can you come back tomorrow?'

'We'll wait,' Nick said, sitting down.

Solveig adjusted her glasses and glared at Nick. 'He has had a long, hard day.'

Sophie smiled and sat down beside Nick. 'Oh, he won't mind us. We're friends.'

'I will have a word with him, when he's finished his work,' Solveig said, imperiously. She sat down behind her desk, on guard. Sophie was glad to see her control though, after the shambles that Jill had reported before. The students put away their notes, took off their white coats and left. Muffled sounds could be heard from behind Ash's consulting room door. A patient emerged, made another appointment with Solveig, wrote a cheque and left. Solveig went into Ash's room. A few moments later he appeared, a quizzical look on his face.

'Oh, hello,' he said. He turned to Solveig. 'You can go now, I'll lock up.'

She left, reluctantly, Sophie felt. She certainly needed to be in command, this woman. Ash took off his white coat and put it in the dirty linen cupboard.

'This is a surprise,' he said. 'Social visit or medical?'

Sophie glanced at Nick. They'd decided she would start the talking. She got up. 'Neither actually, Ash.'

He looked around as if checking there were no stray students hanging about. He grinned and shrugged. 'So?'

'So – this is difficult – you remember a few weeks ago, you spoke to me about some disturbing things happening here—'

Ash held up his hands. 'That was in confidence, Sophie.'

'Yes, yes, I know. But other people have become involved and spoken to me too. Jane has voiced her concern to Nick. And Peter came to Blue Slipper Bay – believe me he made no secret of it. That's why we've come. We want to help.'

'Peter! I could have had him arrested for theft. What's he been saying?'

Nick stood up. 'The point is, Ash, however much Sophie and I have tried to keep quiet and pretend this is resolved, it keeps coming back. Jane knows, Peter knows, and even Rachel guesses there's something going on. We do want to help, if we can. If you tell us to go away and mind our own business then that's up to you. But it doesn't necessarily mean we won't take action if someone is at risk here.'

Ash stood staring at them. His face looked shocked. He staggered to a chair and collapsed onto it. 'What are you saying?' he whispered.

'Ash, you and I know what I saw when I came

down that evening. I should have listened to you, should have heeded your request for help. Jane and Neptune are both very concerned because Marguerite is obsessed with you. Peter let it be known – very vociferously – that you were having sex in your consulting room when he called in. And Rachel – well she just uses her instincts. I know that Jill thinks it's all to do with regression-therapy – that you got in over your head and that it's resolved. But it isn't, is it?'

Ash buried his face in his hands for a few moments. When he took his hands away they were trembling. His face looked haggard. His voice was harsh. 'I don't believe this. You think I've been having sex with Marguerite?'

'You've been having sex with someone.' Nick gestured with his arm. 'Here, in your professional place. Marguerite is very disturbed. Jill is away.' He glanced towards Sophie. 'We have been drawn into this.'

Ash glared at Nick. 'Then you can damn well draw yourself out of it.' He got up out of his chair, looking menacing. 'Get out! Get out before I throw you out.'

'Then give us an explanation. You owe us that. Tell us we are mistaken and we will go,' Nick said, without flinching.

'I owe you nothing,' Ash growled.

'But you do,' Sophie said. 'We didn't want to be involved in this. You owe it to yourself too. And Jill and the children. Sort it out now, with us, with friends, before it's too late.'

'Friends! You call yourselves friends – yet you could believe that of me.' His voice broke. 'Where were you when I needed you, Sophie?'

'I couldn't handle it then. You know that. And when I felt stronger, it seemed to be resolved. You told me yourself that it was.'

Ash slumped back into the chair; his hands hung limply down between his knees. He looked hunched, defeated.

'At least tell us why Marguerite is so disturbed and obsessed with you and this place. Put our minds at rest about her. We can reassure Jane and we'll leave the rest up to you.' Nick spoke quietly. The silence gathered in the room. Eventually Ash raised his head.

'Marguerite knows,' he whispered.

'Knows what?' Sophie said.

'She knows what's been going on. I swear I haven't touched her. I wouldn't dream of doing such a thing. I can't believe you'd think . . . but I can see how it looks.' He sighed. 'I know she cares deeply about me and about her work here. She's been trying to help me and I want to let her, but . . . I can't.'

'Why?' Sophie drew a chair close to him and sat down leaning forward.

'I'm in too deep. I don't want to drag her into this any more than she already is.' He raised his head to look at them. 'I'm finished.'

Nick was leaning towards him now, his hands on his knees. They formed a focused triangle of bent backs. 'Tell us, Ash,' he said, quietly.

'It did start with the regression stuff. I told Jill that Solveig had introduced me to it. But that wasn't true. We had a student who was dabbling in it. Solveig is very knowledgeable and told us how powerful it can be and not to mess with it. But this student was really hooked and persuaded me to try it out with her. It was amazing. I've told you this, Sophie. Then Solveig realised what was happening and gave me the lecture of my life.'

'But?' Sophie prompted.

'But the student who started it, she insisted that we should carry on with it. She said she recognised me from a previous life and we had unfinished business. She'd come down here in the evenings and we'd get into all this sexual stuff.' He paused, thinking. 'I was going through a rough patch – really depressed after Rose left home – and Jill didn't understand. No! What am I trying to do here, blame my family? I got hooked – that's the bottom line. I was a weak idiot, risking everything for a hot young body.'

'So it didn't stop?' Nick said.

'I tried. Solveig was vigilant and I pulled myself together. But when I told the student it was finished she refused to accept it. She said we hadn't worked through all our stuff yet and it would be dangerous not to.'

'And you believed her?' Nick said.

'She discovered a weakness in me that I didn't know I possessed. I struggled with it as best I could and told her again and again it was over, but she said she would report me to the authorities alleging sexual misconduct if I didn't see it through.'

'And this is still going on? That's what Peter walked in on?' Sophie asked.

'As I said, she found my weak spot. I've always been highly disciplined with female patients. I've trained myself to see the bones beneath the flesh. I don't know what got into me – I felt out of control. That's why I've so appreciated Marguerite's assistance and Solveig's discipline.' He grabbed Sophie's hand. She tried not to pull back, struggling to control her sadness for Jill and Tom and sweet Fleur. How was this family going to survive?

'This student,' she ventured, 'are you sure about her motives?'

'How do you mean?'

'This past life theory. Are you convinced by it?'

'Oh, yes. It all happened so spontaneously. It surprised her as much as me. She says nothing like this has ever happened to her before.'

'There is such a thing as self-deception, Ash. In my experience of dealing with this sort of thing, sometimes it's genuine, sometimes it's a wish-fulfilling prophecy.'

'I don't understand.'

'We all know how students fall for their teachers – and vice-versa. Clients transfer feelings onto their therapists. But it's up to the practitioner to be the responsible one. You know that.'

'But this seems different, so powerful. We didn't plan it.'

'The unconscious is a tricky thing. You can't be sure what's happening beneath the surface – unless you look pretty thoroughly. Did you have any of your own past-life re-call with this student?'

'I didn't at first, but—'

'She convinced you.'

'Are you saying it might not be genuine?'

'I don't know. But whatever it is, it's causing harm.'

'Do you think I don't know that? What the hell should I do?' He dropped Sophie's hands, shoved his chair back and stood, a helpless, desperate figure.

This is it, Sophie thought. She looked at Nick. He was leaving this to her – this was her field. And it was up to her to make the decision whether to offer help. She closed her eyes and felt inside herself for the familiar resistance but none came. The frozen block she'd carried inside was melting fast. She wondered if it was because she'd finally severed the link with Peter and freed up her energy.

'Ash?' her voice was firm. 'Would you like me to try and help you both?'

He swallowed hard and nodded. 'I need help, I know.' He began to pace up and down. 'I beg both of you not to tell Jill. My God, I hope Rachel and Peter keep quiet. And I'll talk to Marguerite – she knows I've been evading her help. I've hurt her and she deserves better.'

'When is Jill coming back?' Nick asked.

'Sunday.'

'Two days. Can you get your student here tomorrow evening?' Sophie asked.

'She won't come if I tell her someone wants to question her.'

'Tell her I'm interested in past-life experiences. Tell her I'm researching for a book. If she's that fascinated with it all she'll want to talk. Just get her here.'

Nick and Sophie walked slowly home along the cliff tops. They didn't talk much; just let the soft breeze and the rhythm of the waves below accompany them. This time Sophie reached for his hand and his grasp was firm and constant.

Nick watched Jane's face sag with relief. She'd been looking like a fifty-year-old woman recently instead of the indeterminate-aged, energetic person that he'd first known.

'But what I don't understand, Nick, is why Marguerite is involved in this. Why doesn't she just let Ash and this student sort it out themselves? I've never known her to judge anybody morally or expect a certain outcome. Is it jealousy do you think? Is she in love with Ash?'

Nick shook his head. 'I can't answer that. Sophie thinks it's because Marguerite knows something that Ash doesn't and she's trying to get through to him. He won't take any notice of her because he's too obsessed.'

'But if Ash is resisting Marguerite's help, what can Sophie hope to do?'

'Ash is falling apart. Now he's been confronted he's acknowledged that he needs help.'

'And the student?'

'Sophie says she simply wants to talk to her – to find out where she's coming from.'

'Can't Ash just tell her to go?'

'The problem is she's threatened to report him for sexual misconduct.'

'Who to?'

'I'm not sure. The police? His governing body? Whatever. He'll get struck off for sure.'

'Oh, my God. It's blackmail then.' She looked thoughtful. 'Do you believe in past lives, Nick?'

'Not sure. I was pretty convinced by my eastern mystical friends. Reincarnation does have a certain logic. How about you?'

Jane laughed. Nick hadn't heard her laugh for a long time. 'Nothing surprises me after living with Marguerite for this last year. My old belief system has become flimsy and unreliable. Anyway, I'm going to pick her up from Cormorants later. Why don't you come with me? We could sit outside while all this is going on and rush in if violence breaks out.'

'Like a sort of back-up team?' Nick smiled. 'Yes, I was planning to be on hand. I'm concerned for Marguerite and Sophie. Ash is quite unstable really, and we have no idea how this student is going to react.'

'I'm being nosy now. But, you and Sophie . . . sorry, it's the novelist in me creating stories.'

Nick laughed. 'I'm trying to restrain myself from falling in love with her, without much success.'

'Why the restraint?'

'Sometimes I fear for my sanity – I've been so locked up these past three years. I wouldn't want to inflict myself on anyone just yet. And also, she's only just made the final decision to split from her husband. I'm so tempted just to fall on my knees in front of her. But . . .'

'You don't want to frighten her off?'

'Yes, or catch her on the rebound. We get on really well and I want to try and nurture that.'

'You're a good man, Nick. Don't let her slip away.'

'Please don't tell Dad about the abortion.' Rose's eyes were luminous with tears.

Jill shook her head. 'I promise. As long as you're feeling okay about it and recovering – that's my concern. But you'll have to tell him something – at least about your decision to take a year out.'

Rose sighed. 'He'll kill me.'

'Of course he won't. He loves you.'

'But,' Rose wrung her hands, 'that's the problem, isn't it? He doesn't love the real me – he loves the Rose he thinks I am.'

Jill sighed and sat back in Stephanie's old armchair. 'You're right. That's the problem for all of us. We've created a fiction about each other and none of us wants to break the spell.'

'The spell has been broken, Mum. There's no going back. But doesn't it feel better?'

Jill gazed at her daughter. How did she get to be so wise?

'It's really difficult – being honest – we might not like it but at least it's real and we know what we're dealing with.' Rose leaned against Stephanie's shoulder. 'Look what's happened between you and Grandma. So painful – but it's been said and now you both know how it was for each of you.'

Stephanie smiled sadly. 'We're beginning to, I think.' She kissed Rose on the cheek. 'Look at us – three generations of women talking – that's something special. She held out a hand to Jill. 'I know I made huge mistakes and you paid the price. I can't undo that but I can at least learn from it – even though I'm an old woman. I know I can't give your childhood back to you, but I can make amends in other ways.' She squeezed Jill's hand. 'I want to be part of your family – a good grandmother – please don't shut me out.' Her voice was cracking. 'I'm not all bad.'

'Grandma!' Rose sounded shocked. 'You're not one bit bad. You're the best person I know.'

Jill felt the impact of this like a blow to her belly. It astonished her that Rose had a completely different viewpoint on Stephanie. But why wouldn't she? Rose's grandmother was an interesting, adventurous, intelligent woman who risked her life to help others. Jill could feel the love and admiration pouring from Rose towards Stephanie. What was it all about this love – did it skip generations?

'Maybe,' Jill stammered, not knowing what she was going to say. 'Maybe we don't realise how powerful parenting is.' She looked at Stephanie, feeling she was meeting her gaze at last. 'You allowed me too much freedom and ended up neglecting me. And,' she looked at Rose, 'your father and I – we have been too restrictive – forcing you to be secretive and turn to others. I can see that now.'

'But you were never restrictive, Mum. It's Dad. If you'd been a single parent – like Grandma – I'd have been a street kid by now.'

'Oh, Rose—' Jill protested.

'I would! You don't realise – I've got a really wild streak.' She grinned suddenly, reminding Jill again of her young self. 'Got that from you,' she added.

'So perhaps we three have more in common than we thought,' Jill said.

'And Dad has been the one that has kept us two in check.'

'I would agree with that,' Jill said. She laughed suddenly. 'He's not a bad old bag of bones, is he?' She wiped her hands over her hot face, then lifted her hair off her neck.

'Mum, there's something I've always wanted to ask you,' Rose said.

'Oh, God,' Jill groaned, 'more skeletons?'

‘If you feel the heat so much, why do you always wear those awful black clothes? And that dark lipstick – a bit gothic.’

Jill felt momentarily insulted. ‘I like black,’ she snapped. ‘It’s dramatic.’

‘You’re dramatic enough!’ Rose said.

‘It gives me the chance to wear brightly coloured accessories.’

‘Then why not wear bright clothes?’

‘Colours don’t suit me.’

‘You could wear white,’ Stephanie said.

‘Makes me look like a whale.’

‘Red, then,’ Rose suggested.

‘Prostitute,’ Jill countered.

‘Pink?’ Stephanie ventured.

‘Lobster. Look, I like black, okay? It suits my pale skin and titian hair!’

Rose suddenly burst out laughing and Jill felt her face break into the first natural smile since she’d arrived at The Morg. Stephanie clapped her hands and giggled.

Jill heaved herself out of the armchair. ‘Anything else you want to get out in the open before I leave? You hate my jewellery? You disapprove of the books I read? You don’t like me playing my blues music?’

Rose was doubled up with laughter. ‘Jewellery is a tad iffy. Books – a bit chick-lit, for your age. But I like the blues – that’s always been great. I felt you were on my side against Dad’s attempts with the cello, and Fleur and Tom’s wonky scales.’

Jill laughed. ‘Glad I got something right. That

reminds me – I have to go home. I have two other children to try and get it right with.'

Rose, Patrick and Stephanie came out to the car to say goodbye.

'Promise me you'll come home before you set off for Africa,' Jill said to Rose, hugging her. 'It will cheer your dad up before you deliver the next blow. And Tom and Fleur miss you.' She kissed Rose on both cheeks. 'So do I.'

'Oh, Mum, of course I will. Patrick has to start work at Wraith Cove next week. He's bought a motorbike and he's dying to give it a good hammering.'

Jill shuddered. 'I didn't hear that,' she said.

'Don't worry,' Patrick said, putting an arm around Rose. 'I'm not taking her on the back until I'm used to it.'

'That's a relief.' Jill turned to her mother. 'I was wondering . . . would you like to come for a visit?'

Stephanie's eyes filled with tears. 'Do you really want me to?'

Jill nodded. 'Yes, really I do.'

Stephanie put her arms around her. 'Why now, Jill?' she murmured. 'Why did you come back now?'

Jill hugged her mother back, her throat constricting. 'Everyone's changing,' she whispered.

CHAPTER 29

Sophie was surprised when she saw the girl. She'd expected someone more overtly sexual with the immature gullibility that she'd seen in previous teacher/student relationships. But Yasmin was slim and graceful. She had black hair cut in a straight bob just below her jaw-line and dark eyes accentuated with eye-liner. Sophie was sitting at Ash's desk in his consultation room when she walked in. She stood, looking down at Sophie.

'Ash said you wanted to talk to me,' she said.

'Please, sit down,' Sophie said, pulling another chair across to face her. 'Ash tells me that you and he have been doing some regression work. I'm interested in how some cranial and other healing techniques can trigger childhood and even deeper memories. I wondered if you would be willing to tell me about your experiences.'

Her eyes flicked from side to side. 'Who are you exactly?'

'My name is Sophia Lucci.' She surprised herself by using her family name. 'I work in mental health. I've worked with quite a few people who claim to have past life experiences.'

'Then why do you want to know mine?'

'I'm building up a body of knowledge so that it can be recognised. A bit like near death experiences.'

'Will it be confidential? No names?'

'Oh, absolutely.'

'What do you want to know?'

'Maybe we could start with how you got interested in this?'

'Through a hypnotherapist, in London.' Sophie wondered if she was going to answer all her questions with the minimum information in this monotone.

'Why did you go to see the therapist?'

'Because I wanted to give up smoking.' She seemed reluctant to say more. She sat staring, unblinking.

'Was it successful?'

'No. As soon as he started working with me, I found myself back in another life. I had no idea what was happening.'

'And your therapist – did he handle it well?'

Yasmin pouted her lips, as if assessing how much to tell, then appeared to let go her reluctance. 'He was as amazed as me. Said he'd never experienced anything like it before. We went on to have more sessions. It was fascinating.'

Sophie wondered what kind of *sessions* she meant. 'Will you tell me more about the past life?'

'I was an Egyptian princess – I know that sounds old hat. But I was being trained as a priestess. I was passionate about the spiritual path, receiving advanced initiations. I vowed to be celibate of course. But I was lured by an older man, a physician, and I fell back many lifetimes.' She stopped abruptly.

'Go on,' Sophie prompted.

'That's about it really.'

'You didn't continue seeing the hypnotherapist?'

'No. I got scared. I kept having flashbacks in my ordinary waking consciousness.'

'But you started it again – when you came here as a student?'

'It was when I met Ash. I recognised him straightaway.' She was starting to get restless, stroking her hands down her thighs, her eyes moving from side to side as if she were looking for him. 'How much has he told you about this?'

'A little—'

Suddenly, she leaped up. 'You're lying. He's told you everything, hasn't he? You're investigating me, you deceitful bitch.'

'Okay. Time to be honest, Yasmin. Your involvement with Ash is putting your future, his future, his family and this healing centre in jeopardy. I think that deserves some investigation, don't you? Before any of the authorities get involved.'

She rushed to the door before Sophie could stop her. She flung it open so that it crashed against the wall. 'Ash!' she yelled.

Sophie could see Ash sitting in reception with Marguerite. He hurried into the room, looking haggard with tension.

'You lied to me,' she spat the words out and hurled herself at him. He caught her by the wrists. 'Why do you always do this to me?' she implored. 'Just when we're on the point of resolving it all – you cast me away again.' She started to cry, her body slumping against him. He put his arms around her and rocked her. As Sophie watched, Yasmin turned her face up to his, their eyes seemed to lock together.

Oh, God, Sophie thought. She could just picture the two of them in Egyptian dress. Ash had the perfect physique to play the imposing priest. If she wasn't here they'd have sex right now. Ash definitely needed to avoid looking into those eyes.

'Ash!' Sophie spoke sharply. He jumped and looked at her. His eyes seemed unfocused. What was going on here? It was almost as if they were both drugged. 'Come and sit down. Both of you,' Sophie commanded. They sat down as meekly as small children. She had no idea what to do next. She thought back to the last thing Yasmin had said.

'What is it that needs to be resolved?' Sophie asked.

'Our passion,' Yasmin whispered. 'It has to burn itself out otherwise we will carry on doing this life after life. And I will never become an initiate.'

Sophie had heard this story many times. The Egyptian initiate was a common theme. Yasmin was gazing at her intently. Sophie could feel the pull of her powerful eyes. She appeared to be a natural hypnotist, that was the problem. What Sophie was unsure of was how much Yasmin was aware of her power. Was she using it deliberately or was she a victim of her own abilities, not realising what influence she was having on others? On one level she was childlike, caught up in her own fantasy; on another she was dangerous with the power of destroying lives. Sophie needed to know how much she was in control. She pulled her gaze away with some difficulty.

Ash's eyes were fixed on Sophie too, as if willing her to do something. Yasmin seemed to sink down in her chair, like a little girl again. Sophie had an overwhelming feeling of compassion for her and her dilemma.

'Yasmin,' she said, gently. 'I want you to close your eyes for a while and relax.' She did exactly as Sophie said. Her hands uncurled and she started to breath slowly. She seemed to be at the mercy of her own and others' commands, without being free to choose. 'Now, when you feel ready I want you to tell me again how all this started.'

'I told you,' she mumbled. 'I went to a hypnotherapist.'

'And you had never dabbled in anything like this before?' She didn't answer. 'Had you read any books about it?'

'Not about hypnotherapy, no.'

'What about Egyptology then?'

'A bit.'

'Where?'

'My father – it was his passion.'

'And you read his books?'

Yasmin nodded. 'And he read them to me – when I was little.'

'And this story – about being a priestess, an initiate?'

She sat silently. Sophie wondered if she was on the wrong track here. She closed her eyes and tried to tune into her own intuition, beyond her thoughts. She could sense a growing resistance in Yasmin. Something was building up. Sophie opened her eyes. Yasmin was sitting upright, her eyes wide open, seeking to latch onto hers.

'My father wouldn't lie to me.' Her words seemed to force themselves through her clenched teeth. 'He saw what I was. He told me what I had to do.'

'Yasmin! How many men have you acted out this story with?'

Her eyes were blazing; Sophie couldn't look away. She felt as if something was being pulled out of the centre of her. She wondered if she was going to pass out. This young woman's psychic strength was beyond anything she had experienced before. And it was a long time since she'd worked like this. She should have prepared herself – not been drawn in by the needs of others. She wasn't ready. She felt herself begin to sweat. And then the tension broke as suddenly as it had built. Sophie's eyes snapped away and she was able to draw in a deep breath. Marguerite was standing behind Yasmin's chair, holding her hands over the top of the girl's head. Yasmin's eyelids drooped and she seemed to fall asleep. Marguerite moved around to the front of her and swept her hands up and down the centre of Yasmin's body without touching her. Finally she gestured to Ash to bring a glass of water. Yasmin opened her eyes and sipped the water, looking around as if she didn't know where she was. Marguerite stroked strands of dark hair back from Yasmin's face and smiled at her. Yasmin smiled sweetly back. Ash and Sophie sat and watched.

Yasmin gave a little shrug. 'Have I been saying awful things?' she said.

'Confused things,' Sophie replied.

'I can't seem to stop this,' she said, and her eyes welled with tears. Sophie wanted to hug her and tell her everything would be all right. But she knew she was in for a long haul.

'You have a very powerful psychic ability,' Sophie said. 'But you have no boundaries at the moment and you can easily control others weaker than yourself.' Sophie glanced at Ash to see if he was taking this in. 'It's vital that you heal yourself and harness this power. You can learn to control it, Yasmin. But you need expert help.'

She shook her head. 'Nobody understands,' she whispered. Sophie could feel her loneliness.

'You're right. There aren't many who understand. But you don't need many. You just need a few you can trust. I will help you if you want me to.' Sophie glanced up at Marguerite; she nodded and took hold of Yasmin's hand. 'And Marguerite will help you too.'

Yasmin wept quietly for a while. Then she whispered to Ash. 'I wouldn't have reported you.'

'Yasmin, please,' Ash said. 'I'm the one to blame. I should have been strong and responsible and all the things that I'm not.' He held out a hand to her.

'Ash,' Sophie warned. She got up, pushed his arm away and knelt down beside Yasmin. 'Where do you live?'

'I'm lodging in Solveig's house.'

'Ash,' Sophie said. 'Go and phone Solveig. Explain as best you can and ask her to come and fetch Yasmin.'

Ash cast a doleful look at Yasmin. Sophie put her hand on his back and shunted him out of the room. 'And then go up to the house, have a shower and don't come back.'

'I don't know what to say to you,' he began.

'Just don't go anywhere near her ever again and don't let her within a mile of this place. I'll arrange to see her at Solveig's tomorrow, with Marguerite.'

He nodded. Sophie hoped he wasn't going to cry all over her. She didn't feel as compassionate towards him as she did to Yasmin.

'Jill,' he murmured. 'She'll be back soon.'

'Yes, she will.'

'I'm going to tell her everything, Sophie.'

'I think you're going to have to.'

* * *

Marguerite and Sophie watched as Solveig drove away with Yasmin. Sophie mentally thanked her intangible God. She didn't know what she'd have done without Solveig. She would have to have taken Yasmin home with her, simply to put distance between two sets of uncontrolled hormones. She turned to Marguerite. They both let out long slow sighs and smiled at each other.

'Can we work together with this?' Sophie asked her.

Marguerite nodded vigorously.

'It could take some time; she's a very disturbed young woman.'

Marguerite looked out towards the sea for a while, moving her lips. When she turned back she was smiling. She shook her head.

Sophie smiled. 'I have a feeling that your completely baffling method of healing is going to speed everything up.'

Marguerite nodded and threw back her head with silent laughter.

Jane drove them home. She kept patting Marguerite's leg on the journey as if she was relieved to have her back in one piece. Nick and Sophie sat in the back. It was nearly dark when Jane dropped them off. They picked their way down to Blue Slipper Bay. Sophie felt energised by the positive outcome of the evening and the prospect of working with Marguerite to help Yasmin.

'Would you like to come in for a drink,' she

asked Nick. 'I'll tell you all about it – as much as I can anyway.'

'Can't wait,' he said.

When they rounded the corner to the bay, Sophie stopped in her tracks. A light was on in her cottage.

'Perhaps you left it on when you came out,' Nick whispered.

'I'm sure I didn't. It was broad daylight.'

'Did you leave the door unlocked?'

'I must have. I don't bother to lock it most of the time.'

'A thief?'

'Nothing worth taking.'

'Peter?'

'I'd rather it was a thief.'

They walked to the front door. It was ajar. Nick started to creep up the stairs. Sophie followed close behind. They listened at the sitting room door but couldn't hear a sound. Nick threw open the door quickly. There, sprawled on the sofa, was Jill. She'd obviously been dozing. She came to with a start.

'My, God,' she said, 'you scared me.'

'We scared *you*!' Sophie cried. She rushed over to her and hugged her. 'What on earth are you doing here?'

Jill pushed her away and staggered up. Sophie wondered if she'd been drinking, but there was no glass in sight.

'I came back early, left the kids in London. I needed

to talk to Ash but he was still working, so I walked over here. I want to talk to you.'

Her face was serious but she seemed calm, composed. She looked at Nick. 'Would you mind?' she said.

'Of course not,' Nick turned to go. 'I'll see you tomorrow, Sophie.'

Jill sat down again. Sophie sat beside her.

'What is it, Jill?'

'Peter came to see me yesterday—'

'Peter!'

'Yes. Nice of him, wasn't it? He came to Ash's parents' house. Said he'd been over here for a visit and he couldn't wait to tell me that he'd caught Ash having sex with someone.'

Sophie put her head in her hands and groaned.

'I take it this isn't news to you?' Jill said, coldly.

Sophie shook her head.

'It's Marguerite, isn't it? I should never have believed his stupid stories about esoteric stuff. And I even kidded myself that he was missing Rose. Well, at least now I know.'

Sophie caught hold of her hands. 'Jill, it isn't Marguerite.'

'I don't believe you.'

'I swear to you. I know who it is and it is not Marguerite. I can understand why you think it is. We all thought it. But Ash was shocked when he found out what we were thinking.'

'We? Who are all these people?'

'Jane, Nick and Rachel.'

'Oh, great.' She wrenched her hands from Sophie's and turned away. 'I suppose none of you thought I might need to know.'

'It's not like that, Jill.'

'What is it like then?'

Sudden rage seared up inside Sophie. She jumped up. 'I've had enough of this! Ash is bloody well going to do the explaining. Get up! I'm taking you home and I don't want to see you again until you and he have got everything out in the open.'

'But I wanted to stay here tonight!' Jill's voice sounded panicky.

'I'm not prepared to sit up all night listening to you accusing me of sabotaging your marriage. You once told me not to be a victim. Now get up and go and face the person who should be telling you the truth.'

Jill looked at Sophie, her expression shocked, her mouth slightly open. 'Peter also told me that you and he were going to get back together, but then he caught you in bed with Nick. What the fuck's been going on here since I've been away?'

'And Peter's worth listening to?' Sophie snapped.

Jill got up slowly and picked up her bag. Sophie grabbed her torch and keys and stormed off ahead, leaving Jill to negotiate the path through the rocks and up the lane to the car park. She drove fast to Ventnor, refusing to answer any more of Jill's questions. She dropped her outside Cormorants, which was in darkness, and sped back along the road home.

* * *

Nick lay awake worrying about Sophie. He'd seen her hurry past with Jill and assumed she was giving her a lift home. But the wind was gusting, the tide was in and he hadn't heard her come back. He wondered whether she would be scared making her way down to the bay in the dark with the sea pounding. At least the moon was bright. He hoped she wouldn't get caught up again in the turmoil at Cormorants. It looked like there was going to be another confrontation tonight.

He pushed Commie off his chest and got out of bed. He sat in the dark watching the moonlit sea surging across the sand, hitting the rocks, sending silvery spray into the air. Why was it that whenever he was anticipating some time alone with Sophie, someone burst in on them? Peter, Rachel, and tonight – just when he wanted to talk to her about the evening – up pops Jill.

Poor Sophie, all she wanted was a quiet, ordinary life without this constant involvement in other people's problems. But somehow she always seemed to get sucked in. Nick thought that people saw her as someone they could talk to, rely on. Empathy seemed to transmit itself from her even when she didn't say very much. He could imagine that she had been a wonderful nurse and counsellor. He'd love to have had his fevered brow stroked by her. But still, she'd seemed fine on the drive home tonight, as if everything had gone well.

He ought to get some sleep. It was gone midnight and tomorrow he planned to help the building gang raise the rafters on the stable roofs. He looked at the old shoe box on the table. Perhaps one of Sophie's miracles would relax his mind. He yawned and rubbed his eyes. Then he saw a shadow flit by outside. It was her. She didn't pause or look up at his window. That was okay, as long as she was safely home.

Jill expected Ash to be in bed – the house was in darkness. But as she walked up the path she saw him standing on the balcony looking down at her as if he was waiting. Jill walked into the living room, switched on a lamp and sat on the sofa. After a few minutes Ash let himself in through the French doors. They stared at each other. Ash's dressing gown hung on him as if his shoulders were a coat hanger. His face was gaunt.

'I think we need to talk, Bone Man,' Jill said quietly. 'Peter came to see me.'

Ash winced then cleared his throat. 'What did he—'

'I don't want to hear any bullshit. I want the truth – straight.'

Ash tottered to a chair, sat down and pulled his dressing gown over his knees.

'Believe me, Ash. You aren't going to be the only one telling some truths tonight.'

Jill felt as if she were being physically wounded as Ash stumbled through the story of Yasmin. She knew he wasn't lying – even though he'd been deceiving her for so long. By the time he'd finished he was curled on the rug in the foetal position, crying. Jill made no attempt to interrupt him or hurl accusations, or to comfort him. She sat perfectly still and listened. She couldn't bring herself to reach out and touch him. Of course she felt betrayed and repelled. Her Ash, her bedrock, her saviour, had fallen from grace. She couldn't imagine him expressing great sexual passion for this girl – even though he'd confessed it. She couldn't even muster feelings of jealousy. She felt all kinds of conflicting emotions darting through her, piercing and stinging. But she also felt a sense of relief – she was no longer the bad one – they were both bad.

Ash continued to lie on the floor, his sobs grew quieter and Jill wondered if he'd fallen asleep. She pushed him with her foot and he jumped.

'Get up,' she said. 'Sit in the chair. We haven't finished yet.'

'Do . . . do you want a drink?' he rasped.

Jill shook her head. 'All I want is the truth – to get it over and done with.'

'But, I've told you the truth.'

'I know. And now I'm going to tell you mine.' She was amazed at how calm she sounded. But wasn't this what she wanted after all these years? 'And I don't want you to say a word until I've finished.'

Ash nodded and sat in the armchair, primly crossing his knees, his red eyes downcast.

'I've been unfaithful too.' Ash glanced up but didn't say a word. 'It seems to be part of my nature – something inherent that I've never understood. I've just been back to Morgan's Hall – to see if I could get some insights. I had it all out with my mother. I'll tell you the details another time. But I'm beginning to understand now why I felt compelled to have sex with so many men – sometimes strangers – even men I didn't like. I recognised something in them that I had grown up with – a sick kind of desperation, I think.'

Ash groaned. 'Oh, Jill,' he mumbled.

'Be quiet! I don't know how we're going to cope with this. I just know I have to tell you.' Jill unwound her pink scarf from her throat, feeling as if something was threatening to choke her. She swallowed noisily. 'I started having sex with Peter as soon as you introduced him into our lives. We recognised that thing in each other straight away. He was only one of many – but he was the one I despised most. And he despised me – we were equals. Neither of us could stop. When he met Sophie, I felt straightaway she was different from his other shallow women. I thought if I could encourage them to stay together I could start to take control.'

Ash shot up out of his chair. Jill jumped, surprised, wondering what he was going to do. He towered above her, his arms flailing.

'Do you think I don't know this?' he hissed. 'Do you really think I had no idea about your infidelities – all your fabricated seminars? Do you think I never checked them out? I'm a man remember – we understand how it works. And I learned a lot from watching Peter lead his sordid little life.'

Jill was aghast. She couldn't believe that he knew. He must be saying this to protect himself. How could he know and never let on? 'Why?' she blurted out. 'Why did you never say anything?'

'Because I wanted to keep you. I wanted to keep our family together. We had Rose to think of.'

She had to say it, say it now, the force of it seemed beyond her control. 'Did you ever consider she might not be yours?' she whispered the words, thinking this was the cruellest thing that she had ever said to him.

Ash gave a harsh laugh. 'How could I not?'

Jill stared at him. How could he have lived with her all these years harbouring that suspicion? She picked up her bag. With shaking hands she unzipped the inner compartment and pulled out two plastic envelopes. 'Then maybe we should have a paternity test done.'

Ash snatched the envelopes from her. 'What are these?'

'Samples – from Peter – hair, and some material – with semen on.'

Ash flung them down. 'You disgust me,' he spat. 'How could you bring those into our home?'

'Rose is in our home,' Jill said, determined to see this through.

'Rose is my daughter,' Ash said slowly.

'Do you see any resemblance?'

'She may look like you, but she's more my child than yours. You've always been indifferent to her – uncaring.'

'No!' For the first time Jill felt tears springing to her eyes. 'Selfish and dishonest I may be. But not uncaring. I care so much about you—'

'About me!' Ash dropped to his knees on the rug and stared up at her. 'You think I'm the most stupid man that ever lived.'

'No! I don't—'

Ash searched around on the floor and retrieved the envelopes – he opened the door of the wood burner and threw them into the dying embers.

'No!' Jill flung herself at him, but it was too late, the flame ignited and the plastic shrivelled.

'Oh, God!' She felt her last chance of knowing the truth had gone.

Ash pushed her away and got up. 'I had the test done years ago – Rose is my daughter. I have the report filed away, if you want to see it. And in case you're wondering, I've had the tests for Tom and Fleur too.'

CHAPTER 30

'Rachel, I need time off. I've got to sort out a few tricky things.' Sophie clasped her hands together in mock prayer. 'And I have to find out where Solveig lives.' 'That's easy, I know where she lives.' Rachel was drying her hair. Sophie had arrived at the café so early she was only just up. 'You can certainly have time off – as long as you can get Aidan out of bed – that's the penalty. I suggest a mug of black coffee. If that fails, a bucket of cold water.'

Sophie told her briefly about the previous evening, careful not to break too many confidences. She'd acted as a therapist last night and now was back in her familiar dilemma. But Rachel had a right to know certain things.

'I know you can't tell me everything,' Rachel said, tapping Sophie's arm. 'I'm just glad that Marguerite hasn't come to any harm. Perhaps Jane will lighten up now and get on with her novels. They're good – you should read the latest.'

'I intend to, when I get a moment.' Sophie heaped coffee in the largest mug she could find and took it into Aidan. His room smelled of adolescent activity. He raised his tufty head off the pillow, scrunching up his eyes. 'It's an emergency,' Sophie told him. A hand emerged from under the duvet and embedded itself in Aidan's hair. It was a small hand with purple fingernails. 'Your mother needs you,' Sophie said, and scuttled from the room.

Solveig's three-storied Victorian house was in a side street up in the town. Sophie hoped to catch her before she left for work.

'I'm glad you've come,' Solveig said, leading her into her kitchen. 'Yasmin is still asleep and I've talked with Ash. He and Jill are going away for a few days before they collect the children. School starts next week.' She switched on the electric kettle. 'I've arranged for a locum to take over Ash's cases until he is fit to work again.'

'Goodness, Solveig, have you been up all night?'

She smiled, her stern face relaxed and her eyes crinkled. 'I'm very good at organisation,' she said. 'And I care about what happens at the centre. I know Ash has been a foolish man but I've seen the wonderful work he does with people. He has helped me so much. My orthopaedic consultant told me I should be in a wheelchair by rights, after my car crash. And you should see how Ash encourages Marguerite. He's a patient teacher; the students who come here do very well. I think he deserves a chance.'

Sophie felt chastened. Her concern had been for Yasmin, and Jill and Tom and Fleur. 'I just hope . . .' she faltered, not knowing how much Solveig knew.

'I know,' Solveig said, pouring tea. 'We all hope.'

The door opened and Yasmin shuffled in. She was wearing a long white nightgown, grubby and shapeless. Her hair was dishevelled and her eye makeup gone. She looked pale and lethargic. Sophie wondered if she was a drug user.

'How are you?' Sophie said.

Yasmin's eyes flicked towards her. She reached for a mug of tea, her hands trembling. 'Is Marguerite here?' she said.

'No, but she's coming later,' Sophie said.

'I don't want to go to the centre,' Yasmin said, her eyes turning towards Solveig. 'I don't want to see him ever again. I'm leaving here today.'

'Not today, you're not,' said Solveig briskly. 'Not until you're feeling better and we've decided between us the best thing to do.'

'I'm not a child. You aren't my mother,' Yasmin said without much conviction.

'No, thank goodness,' Solveig laughed. 'I might give you a good hiding if I was.'

Yasmin pouted and hunched over her tea like a moody teenager. Sophie had the feeling that this banter was familiar between them and that it made Yasmin feel safe.

'I think it is important that you go away from here,' Sophie said, after Solveig had dished up eggs on toast. 'Marguerite and I can do some healing sessions with you over the next few days, if you'd like us to, and we can take you somewhere before Ash returns.'

'Where?' Yasmin demanded.

'I know of a good psychic healing centre in Dorset where they understand these things,' Solveig said. 'There aren't many places that do. You will be lucky to escape the psychiatric hospital if you carry on like this.'

Well, that was blunt, Sophie thought. But she was right. And Sophie knew the place – she'd been involved with it. It was one of the very few residential places where psychotherapists and psychic healers worked together. It would be perfect but very costly.

'Ash will foot the bill,' Solveig said, matter-of-factly.

'He doesn't owe me anything,' Yasmin muttered.

'Oh, yes he does, my dear. He's getting off lightly and you have no choice.'

Solveig reminded her of Rachel with her no-nonsense approach. Maybe those two could get together and get this crazy situation resolved. She was feeling redundant here.

'Right, go and have a shower before Marguerite gets here,' Solveig said. Yasmin obediently left the room. Solveig sat down at the table. 'She has been badly abused by her father, you know; her mother did nothing to stop it, usual story.'

Sophie nodded. 'Did she tell you about it?'

'Yes, not the details . . . that's up to you. But enough to horrify me. She's a bright girl – good degree, high IQ. Sometimes she acts like a grown woman, other times – well, you can see for yourself.'

Solveig's eyes filled with tears and Sophie wondered what was in her past that fuelled her intense involvement in mothering these students. Solveig brushed her hands over her face. 'I don't know Jill very well,' she said. 'She keeps herself apart from the rest of the staff. She sees her clients and then goes. I think it would be better if she was around more. Ash would appreciate that too.'

'She's very busy – there are the children—'

'But it's not that, is it?'

Sophie shook her head, reluctant to speak of Jill, but she trusted Solveig, her concern seemed so genuine. 'She has difficulty with certain aspects of—'

'Marguerite?'

Sophie nodded. 'But that might resolve itself now.'

'I do hope so. Marguerite is such an asset.' Solveig sighed. 'I suppose it all depends on whether Jill and Ash can see this through.' She got up and began clearing dishes. 'Well, we can help by getting Yasmin sorted and on her way.'

'You really care about her, don't you?'

'Yes. And I care about what happens here too. If Yasmin doesn't get the right help she could reappear and cause a great deal of damage.'

Bearing this in mind, Sophie spent the next two hours closeted with Marguerite, beginning to fathom her methods of communication as she sketched out pictures of Yasmin and her traumatised energy patterns. Sophie understood some of what she was showing her – the way they both saw the movement of colour was similar. But the rest was too intricate and Sophie was intrigued. It was as if Marguerite was filling in missing links and, on Sophie's side, she had her experience and methods of communication which could enable her diagnostic insights to be communicated to Yasmin. She felt excited by this work as she hadn't been for years, and eager to discover more.

Finally they felt ready to work together and decided to use Solveig's sitting room. Yasmin was back to her slinky Egyptian style with elongated eyes. Her straight black hair was brushed and gleaming. Sophie started with a straightforward counselling approach which Yasmin resisted until Sophie got her to relax, which she did easily and deeply and her words and feelings flowed. She talked about her father with very little prompting, as if she were right back in that time. He had used her to act out his own Egyptian fantasies. Sophie could see how easily she would be able to mistake past lives with her own confused childhood. Finally she slipped into near sleep and Marguerite took over with her healing passes. It was beautiful to watch, like a dance. Sophie felt her own energy responding to the rhythm. Yasmin emerged looking rested and soft-eyed. It was a good start.

'Same time tomorrow?' Sophie asked. Yasmin smiled.

Sophie phoned Jane to say she'd bring Marguerite home. She didn't want to go near Cormorants until she knew Jill and Ash had definitely gone. When she got back to Blue Slipper Bay she felt calm and peaceful. Kyp and Evie were sitting in deckchairs on the beach, holding hands, watching the Water Babies playing with a beach ball in the shallows. Without thinking too much, Sophie walked down to the sea, stripped off her jeans and shirt and waded into the waves. For the first time she allowed herself to sink right down in the water. She didn't feel her usual fear. She welcomed the chill and felt as if the water was supporting her. She lifted her feet off the bottom and took a few tentative strokes. Her feet flipped out behind her. Suddenly she was surrounded by laughter and Jack and Mila were beside her. This was such fun, why hadn't she taken the plunge before? She wondered if some of Marguerite's healing was still affecting her.

She looked back towards the shore. Nick was standing there in his working clothes. Well, now she would have to face him in her bra and pants. So what? They weren't much different to a bikini. He waved and began stripping off his clothes. He splashed out to join them in his underpants. Jack threw the ball to him. This is what it would be like to have a family, Sophie thought.

Nick struggled out of the waves with a Water Baby under each arm. He dumped them squealing on the sand at Kyp and Evie's feet and disappeared inside his cottage to fetch towels and to give his body a chance to calm down from the sight of Sophie in what he suspected was her underwear.

'Down boy,' he said, wrapping a towel around his waist. He'd been so amazed to see Sophie swimming when he got home that he wasn't able to resist plunging in after her. Of course he'd pretended to be playing with the kids – just like a bloke. To give himself time to divert his thoughts, he poured orange juice into his new green glass jug, tipped in the contents of the ice cube tray, set it with its matching glasses on a shocking-pink plastic tray and carried it outside.

Sophie was sitting on the sand talking with Kyp and Evie. She was wrapped in a large orange and white striped towel. Just as well, he thought, trying to ignore his disappointment. He handed around the drinks.

'Lovely glasses, Nick,' said Evie.

'I got fed up with polystyrene,' he said.

'About time. Good food and drink deserves better,' Kyp commented from under his peaked cap.

'Oh, by the way, Jill was down here this morning looking for you, Sophie,' Evie said. 'She said you weren't in the café.'

'No, I had to go somewhere.'

'She said to tell you she was going away again and would come to see you when she got back. I must say she looked pretty awful.'

Nick saw the laughter fade from Sophie's face. Damn, he thought, here we go again.

'She is going through a bit of a bad patch,' she said.

'Briar patch by the look of her,' Kyp said.

'Don't be mean, Kyp.' Evie looked concerned.

'We did hear what your ex shouted out the other day, Sophie. Is it true?'

'When Peter's angry he diverts it by accusing someone else of doing what he's so good at. He's always behaved like that.'

'How childish. Thank goodness you didn't get back with him.' Evie shuddered.

'You need a mature man, like me,' Kyp said, heaving himself up from his deckchair, patting his paunch. 'Well rounded and seasoned.'

'Yes, but you're mine,' Evie giggled.

'Don't take me for granted, woman.' Kyp wiggled his hips. 'I'm going to cook up something delicious and aphrodisiacal, so watch out.' He winked at Nick and Sophie. 'If you two would like to join us – for the food, I mean – you would be most welcome.'

Nick looked at Sophie, she was smiling and nodding. 'That would be nice,' he said.

Sophie spent the rest of the week working a few hours in the café and dashing to Solveig's house for sessions with Yasmin and Marguerite. Rachel told her not to worry about shifts. The girl who owned the purple finger nails was joined to Aidan's hip, clearing tables and serving at the same pace as him. But Sophie needed to keep in touch with the café. She needed the grounding that came with providing food, and she needed Rachel's common sense and humour to balance the tragedy of Yasmin. The healing work was intense, too much too soon in normal circumstances, but it was necessary to get Yasmin away before Jill and Ash returned.

Yasmin coped well. Marguerite waved away Sophie's concerns that they were going too fast. Sophie realised they were working with a completely different set of rules. She had to trust that Marguerite could see deeper than her and that all would be well. Solveig had booked a place for Yasmin at the Dorset centre and Sophie had spoken to the people who would be responsible for Yasmin's care and written a detailed report. Solveig wanted to drive Yasmin and see her settled in. Sophie and Marguerite waved them off on Sunday morning, breathing a sigh of relief.

'I have this terrible image of them meeting Ash and Jill on route, cars screeching to a halt and Yasmin and Ash having sex in the middle of the motorway,' Sophie said to Marguerite, now that she'd experienced her sense of humour. Marguerite swayed and did her silent laugh. Sophie would have loved to hear her voice, imagining it would be as silvery as her hair. But then again it might be quite raucous – she was full of surprises, this woman. Marguerite had told her, using her unique signs, that she had a gentleman friend – one of the gardeners working at Cormorants. She shared sandwiches with him during their lunch break and they sometimes went for a walk. They planned to go and visit some of the island gardens together.

If only Jane had known, Sophie thought, and Jill for that matter. Although Jill still had Ash's appalling confession to contend with. She wondered how they were coping with their few days together. Perhaps Jill wouldn't come back. Perhaps she would leave Ash and stay in London – but what about uprooting the children? It was all so complex, but hopefully, they were being truthful with each other at last. Jill was always brutally honest. Now it was her turn to take it. They would have to work it out from there.

Sophie took Marguerite home and went back to Blue Slipper Bay to relax. She had the rest of the day to herself. She showered and sat on her balcony with Jane's novel. But she couldn't read. Her gaze kept being drawn to the sea and the people on the beach. Next week it would be quieter when the school holidays finished. All those reluctant little bodies would be confined to uniforms and wooden seats, and brains would grapple with the mysteries of algebra and conjugation.

September. It had come around so quickly. She would have to decide soon what she was going to do. Another month and Rachel would be opening her shutters on bright days only, until finally they stayed closed for winter. Sophie wondered – if Jill and Ash recovered – whether the offer of a job at Cormorants would still be an option. It certainly wouldn't be full time. If she worked with Marguerite on the special cases, they would only crop up now and again. Jobs were scarce on this holiday island in the winter. Sophie stretched and yawned and put her feet up on the balcony rail. She would talk to Nick about it. She realised he was becoming part of her life. She wondered what his plans were and if he was considering travelling this winter. She felt a strong pang of disappointment at the thought of his going. But he'd always said he intended to go back to New Zealand to visit Keri's family and return to Lake Tekapo.

Sophie wondered to what extent he'd recovered from Keri's death. To lose a wife and child through murder must be one of the most horrendous experiences to get over. He'd told her in more detail the circumstances of Keri's death and Sophie recalled reading about it in the papers at the time. She remembered the discussion at work about the dilemma of health workers and the *damned if I do, damned if I don't* situation they often found themselves in. Nick had described how he'd tried to recover by pursuing his monastic vision. He said he was enjoying the writings in her miracle box and how they were reminding him of some of the beautiful teachings he'd heard on his travels. And Sophie knew that given time he would tell her more. He seemed more relaxed and open after his time with Neptune. Sophie smiled, thinking about magical Marguerite. It was quite uncanny, this ability she had to speed up the healing process. If her secret could be unlocked the world could be licked into shape in no time.

She closed her book and put it on the table. She didn't want Nick to go away. She believed that he was well into his healing process and so was she and it felt good to trust that. She allowed the realisation that she was falling in love with him to surface slowly. And it wasn't on the rebound from Peter. There was no rebound from him because she had never really gone back to him – not deep inside. She'd wanted what he was offering, that's all.

But what did this mean? She couldn't rush round to Fair Wind and confess her feelings to Nick – he was working all weekend, trying to finish off the stable block before the weather changed and the students started to drift away. Cool down, Sophie, she thought. This could be the end of a beautiful friendship. She'd always known Nick was a free spirit and could take off at any moment. They got on well and she knew he enjoyed their walks and talks. He'd never professed love for her or made any sort of pass. It'd been her that had thrown herself into his arms on various occasions. Poor man, he must feel like her safety net.

She needed to tread carefully here. She didn't want to lose him, she was sure of that. She needed to be adult and sensitive and spend more time getting to know him. Oh, God. Why was love so difficult? She needed Jill. But Jill's life was in crisis now. She could talk to Rachel though. Rachel always saw things clearly. Tomorrow she'd invite her for a drink after work.

Sophie felt restless now. She got up and wandered around the cottage, moving things and putting them back again. Finally she picked up her mobile phone and walked up to the road to try and find a signal.

She hadn't phoned Audrey for ages. She would be in for a lecture.

'Sophia, I'm so glad to hear from you.'

'Sorry, Audrey. I've been really busy.'

'That's all right,' she said. 'I expect you've been rushed off your feet in the café.'

Sophie wondered if this was sarcasm. 'School holidays,' she said.

'Absolutely,' Audrey agreed. Perhaps Sophie had dialled the wrong number and it wasn't her at all.

'Sophia?' her voice sounded thin.

'Is something the matter?'

'I feel I owe you an apology.'

'What on earth for?'

'For trying so hard to get you and Peter back together.'

'Don't worry, Audrey. It's all over. It's not going to happen, I'm sorry.'

'No, don't be sorry. You were right. He's seeing someone else already. She's just like the others. I didn't know whether to tell you but thought it might settle things once and for all.'

Sophie laughed. 'It was all settled anyway.'

'John says he's an absolute shit.'

Sophie couldn't believe her ears. 'Audrey, I never thought I'd live to hear you say that word.'

'Well, it sums him up nicely, doesn't it?'

'It does, indeed.'

'Have you decided what you're going to do?'

'Stay here for a while longer.'

'I don't blame you. Why would you want to come

back here? Anyway Joanna and William like having their aunty at the seaside. They want to come and see you again soon.'

'Oh, Audrey. You can come any time, you know that.'

'Yes. And one day I'll come on my own and we can have a good time.'

Was this really her sister? 'That will be wonderful,' she said.

'I'm sorry I'm such an old stick in the mud. Sophia, I do love you.'

'I love you too. You're the only sister I've got.'

Sophie wandered slowly along Undercliff Drive pondering on the people around her and the various kinds of love they had for each other. What was the best kind, the truest kind? She supposed only perfect people could offer perfect love without needing something back. Maybe a parent for a child, until the child became too aware of its individuality and made unreasonable demands. Perhaps it was okay to be a good enough lover, just like being a good enough parent. We picked it up as we went along. And most of us got by. Even people like Yasmin survived.

And Nick. How did she love him? She enjoyed his company. He interested her with his philosophy of life. She wanted to be with him, to find out more about him, to share things with him. She wanted to give to him. She wanted him to recover from his grief and be able to remember his wife and child with love untarnished by guilt. She wanted to laugh and swim and walk the island with him. And, she admitted, with a flash of desire, that she wanted to make love with him, curl up to sleep with him and wake up in the morning with him beside her.

She stopped, reeling at the intensity of her thoughts. She leaned on a stone wall overlooking a meadow humped and dipped by landslides. And what about your other desire, Sophie, she asked herself. What about a child? Sooner, rather than later, she was going to have to take a long hard look at that question.

Nick forgot about his fishing line. He was dazzled by the crimson and blue stripes of the sunrise. It seemed to hang above him like a vast blanket. He felt like a tiny speck bobbing out at sea, but if he allowed his mind to be quiet and stop thinking up unworthy adjectives, he seemed to expand with awe.

'I think you've got a bite there,' Neptune remarked. Nick brought his attention back to his line, which had pulled taut, and started to reel it in. He could see before it broke the surface that there was the usual clump of vegetation on the hook. Neptune had taught him so much but the fish still weren't eager to bite for him. He wondered if it was because they sensed he was a reluctant fisherman. He still cringed when he pulled hooks out of soft white mouths. If you're prepared to eat them you should face up to the killing, he kept telling himself. He cleared the weed and recast his line.

'Do you feel happier about Marguerite now?' he asked Neptune.

'Yup. I still wish she'd quit working at that centre. But if that trouble is over I suppose she won't come to no harm.' He tipped his cap back and screwed his eyes up at the sky. The sunrise tinged his face red. Nick saw that he was smirking.

'What's the joke?'

'She's got a fellow, it seems.'

Nick sat down. 'Really?'

'Nice enough chap – a widower – got a grown up deaf son. Does some gardening at Cormorants.'

'Have you met him?' Nick smiled. 'Did she bring him home for you and Jane to vet?'

Neptune shook his head, still grinning. 'No, I saw her with him. They sit on the beach and share their lunch sometimes. He can sign – their hands were flying about all over the place. I did a bit of checking up – you know – asked around.'

'Spying, I think it's called, Neptune.'

'Had to be done,' he said. He squatted down, inspecting the few fish they'd caught. 'And how are you getting on, with your lady friend?'

'Been spying on me too?'

'You can take care of yourself. She's a nice lass.'

'Yes,' Nick sighed.

'Oh, love is it?'

'I believe it is. I've been thinking about asking her to go out with me.'

'Thought you already did.'

'I just mean, more seriously.'

'Like courting?'

'That's it. It's so long since I did it – and I already know her quite well – I don't know how to – sort of move it forward.'

Neptune looked thoughtful, his mouth puckered. 'Do you feel steady enough for this?'

Nick recalled the dream he'd had last night. Keri had been leaning over him saying goodbye. He woke crying but knew it was time. 'I'm feeling all right.'

'Sure you don't need to have a few flings before getting too serious with someone?'

'I don't think I'm a flingy sort of guy. I wouldn't be any good at it. Anyway I'm too old for all that.'

Neptune nodded. 'No, you're more like me – all or nothing. Too sensitive for your own good.'

'So, what shall I do? Flowers, dinner, do you think?'

'Nah, that's what that playboy bloke of hers would have done. What does she like to do?'

'She likes to walk and talk and share a pub lunch, that sort of thing.'

'Well, that's best then, isn't it?'

'But that's what we do anyway.'

'You'll know what else to do when the time's right.' He got up to reel in another fish. Nick's line was limp. 'Plenty here,' he said. 'Let's head back and cook these for breakfast.'

Nick had two days off after working all weekend. There wasn't much he could do at the moment. The roofers were doing the tiling today and the drains around the hotel were being excavated.

He towelled himself down after his shower. His muscle tone was building up again, his energy returning. He looked at his little row of bottles on the bathroom shelf. He had shower gel now and proper shampoo, aftershave and deodorant. It definitely made life more complicated. He hadn't had to make choices when he just used a bar of soap for everything. He imagined his Buddhist friends laughing at him. As long as I can smile at myself, he thought, patting a little aftershave on his chin. He didn't want to smell of fish.

He pulled on his jeans and went into the sitting room. He contemplated the two blue loungers and the orange and white striped rug that he'd bought. He surveyed the terracotta bowl of fruit on the table, the books he'd borrowed from Jane stacked on the shelves along with pebbles and shells. Mila and Jack's birthday paintings were tacked on the wall. He thought how cheerful everything looked. He walked over to the fireplace and picked up the photo he'd framed of Keri and himself at Lake Tekapo. He smiled at her and put it back beside the Buddha.

He sat down at his table and wrote a note to Sophie asking her if she'd like to go for a walk and have a pub supper when she got home from work. He ran down the stairs and slipped it under her door.

CHAPTER 31

Sophie worked all day at Rachel's so that Aidan could top up his sleep and sex quotas.

'My God,' said Rachel. 'It's like a pressure cooker upstairs. I have to keep the windows open to let the steam out.'

Sophie laughed. 'I couldn't imagine doing that in my parents' house. Even when Peter and I were married I felt we ought to sleep in separate beds when we stayed there.'

Rachel untied her apron. 'Right, let's get out of here and catch up on important things.'

They went to The Spyglass so they could watch the waves while they ate.

'Any sign of Jill and Ash?' Rachel asked.

'I was about to ask you the same thing.'

'Well, there were no lights on up at Cormorants last night.'

'They'll have to come back soon. School starts in two days.'

Rachel poured more wine into their glasses. 'What do you think she'll do?'

'I've really no idea. I just hope we can stay friends.'

'Why should she blame you for any of this?'

'Because she so desperately wanted me to talk to Ash before. And it's bound to come out that I withheld information from her.'

'This isn't a police trial. She should understand that you had no choice.'

Sophie shrugged. 'People do strange things when they're under such pressure. They hit out at anyone involved. It's a sort of defence against facing up to the truth.'

'But she's a psychologist, for heaven's sake.'

'That can make it even harder. Sometimes others have expectations of some greater understanding in a counsellor or therapist. It's like a double failure – that's how I felt when Peter left me.' She buttered a piece of roll, suddenly not feeling very hungry. 'I can't imagine life without Jill around. It would be weird if she moved away and I ended up staying here.'

'Are you going to stay?' Rachel asked.

'I'd like to. I'm still uncertain how I'm going to earn a living and if I can cope with Blue Slipper Bay in the winter.'

'Well, concerning the first part of that – I've got a small business proposition for you. A chef in one of the hotels along here has approached me with a plan about using my café as an Italian restaurant in the evenings. He would use the facilities to do the cooking, pay rent, and give me a share of the profits. If it is a success – and it might well be as Ventnor is picking up nicely – he would run it all year round.'

'Wow, that sounds exciting. Are you up for it?'

‘I am interested. But the kitchen will need to be modernised and I’d have to buy new tables and chairs – Italian style – and apply for a licence.’

‘Wouldn’t he pay for the equipment?’

‘He can’t afford to. And I want to maintain complete ownership of the premises. So, I’m looking for someone to go in with me as a permanent partner in this venture. I thought of you.’

‘Me? I don’t know anything about Italian cooking.’

‘You wouldn’t have to. You would invest and have a share in the profits of the place – daytime as well.’

‘Would it make enough money?’

‘We’re having a business plan drawn up – Jane’s husband, Chas, is doing it. He’s interested in it too. But I said I wanted to give you first refusal.’

Sophie sat back. ‘Well, Rachel. I’m honoured. I’m certainly interested. I’ve got the money through from the sale of my house and soon I’ll have half of our investments.’

‘Don’t touch your house money. It might even be a good idea to buy a place. Why don’t you have a word with Chas – he’s top drawer when it comes to this stuff.’

‘This could be the answer,’ Sophie said. ‘I could do part time things – occasional consultations at Cormorants, work here when you need me, a bit of manual slog at Jane’s. It will stop me getting too intense.’

Rachel smiled. ‘We don’t want you getting intense, my girl. So, you’re not having any regrets about Peter?’

'None. I feel absolutely clear. My judgement was entirely clouded by my desire to have a child.'

'Did he manage to lure you to bed?'

'Nope. I have to admit I was tempted. But I controlled my vino intake and kept my chastity belt on.'

Rachel sat back. 'I'm full of admiration. I don't think I could have held out that long. Especially with no-one to fall back on. Or is there?'

'I take it you mean Nick?'

'You can tell me.'

'Nothing to tell. But, I have to admit I'm getting very . . . you know.'

'Horny? Sex-starved? Desperate?'

'Rachel! Well, all of those, yes. But, I think I'm falling in love with him.'

'Seriously?'

'Yes. Can't stop thinking about him, dreamy, eating less—'

'Could have fooled me. Have you told him?'

'No. I've hardly seen him. We've both been working flat out.'

'Tell him. Have the day off tomorrow. Get him into bed before he knows what's hit him.'

'Rachel! Stop it. It's not that simple. I don't know how he feels for a start. And you know what men are like – they always want somebody younger. He's only just—'

'Yes, yes, I know all that stuff. But, I've seen the way he looks at you. I've been waiting for one of you to succumb for ages. I was beginning to give up hope – especially when your ex tried to muscle in.'

'But, there's also the question of being responsible. Since I finished with Peter I've been faced with the same old question about having kids.'

'Ah! Isn't that rather jumping the gun? Why not see how things work out between you before arranging the christening?'

'You see, I don't want to get into a long-term relationship without being absolutely clear what I want. Or what he wants. Not at my age.'

'Then you'll have to talk to him.'

'This is my dilemma. How could I possibly ask him – or anyone – for that matter, about such things? Before even getting started on a relationship.'

'I suppose you have to make a choice. You'd have to ask right at the start what are the prospects, or you go for the love thing and hope that it works out.'

'And then it could be too late.'

'Possibly. But you might settle for love. That must be worth something.'

'Yes, of course it is.'

'Or, you could put the baby thing first and go it alone. And then someone might turn up anyway.'

'Go it alone?'

'Yes. Plenty of women do these days. Sperm banks, donors and that stuff.'

'Be a single parent? Jill has talked about that. Would it be fair on a child?'

'You've always said I've done okay. Although

looking at my two sex machines, I begin to wonder.'

'I don't know much about it. I wouldn't know where to start.'

'Internet probably. I could ask Patrick to find a few websites if you like. He's due back any day. It's worth finding out the facts. Then you could plunge in with Nick and keep your options open if it doesn't work out.'

Sophie felt full of misgivings about this. But Rachel was right. It would do no harm to find out. She couldn't get pregnant by downloading a bit of information.

They wandered back towards Rachel's and paused to look at the brilliant sky, glittering with a zillion stars. They'd had quite a lot to drink and Sophie was going to sleep in Patrick's room.

'It's all clean and testosterone free,' Rachel assured her. 'Patrick is moving into one of the caravans at Wraith Cove to start his job. I wish Aidan would go with him – you'd better put a pillow over your ears when he rolls in.'

Nick had been staying over at Wraith Cove as well, helping with the roofing. Sophie wondered if he was back at Blue Slipper Bay tonight, perhaps he would be looking out for her.

Rachel nudged her in the ribs. 'I know who you're thinking about,' she teased. 'Shall we go for a stroll along the harbour walkway?' She pushed her arm through Sophie's. They walked to the end and turned to look at Ventnor. The little town was lighting up, sparkling like a fairy story, its shabby bits romanticised by nightfall.

'Look,' Rachel pointed to the hill above her café. 'Up there. The lights are on at Cormorants.'

Nick wished he could retrieve the note he'd put under Sophie's door. But they'd decided to lock up while they were out, just in case Peter returned. Sophie hadn't come home and it was obvious she'd been out all night. He felt disappointed, trying not to keep watch on her cottage, feeling like a spy.

He'd tried to acknowledge his feelings, simply letting them be, telling himself, 'that's life, mate,' as Keri would have done. He'd passed the time organising a game of cricket on the beach for Jack and Mila, encouraging the holidaymakers' children to join in. It had developed into quite a match with competitive dads pitching in. Kyp and Evie had set up a barbecue later and it had been a good time. Except he always had a part of his mind on alert for Sophie's arrival. Well, that's what love is like, he thought, remembering how distracted he was when he first met Keri.

But he felt awkward about the note. He tried to remember the exact wording. Did it sound as if he was taking too much for granted? Of course it didn't. They'd been for walks and pub meals before. But it was different now. Now that he was in love. He'd hung around all morning expecting her to turn up, but she must have stayed with Rachel and gone straight to work. He decided to walk over to Ventnor. It would be nice to wander through the Botanic Gardens and along the esplanade. Maybe he could call into Rachel's for lunch.

The café was full. He managed to grab a small table in the corner as someone left. He could see Sophie and Rachel in the kitchen area, busy with the dishing up while Aidan swanned about the café taking orders. There was a gothicky-looking girl washing dishes. Aidan came over and took his order and then Sophie appeared. She glanced over at him without recognition as if she was just registering another customer. And then she seemed startled and her face flushed pink.

'Nick!' she said. 'What are you doing here?'

'Hoping to eat,' he smiled.

'I mean . . . no work today?'

He shook his head. 'Day of rest.'

'Lucky you. I must get on.'

The two plates of pasta she was holding seemed dangerously tilted towards Nick. 'It's all right, I know you're busy,' he said. He tried not to watch her as she worked. She seemed a bit flustered, constantly tucking strands of hair behind her ears and adjusting her striped apron. Rachel came over to say hello.

'Nightmare day,' she said. 'Had to yank Aidan out of bed by his throat.' She glanced around as more people came through the open door. 'Why do people need to eat all the time? I'll be glad when the holidays are over.'

'You love it,' Nick said. 'Is Sophie working all day?'

'If the crowds don't abate she will. I'll chain her to the sink. Will I do instead? Don't answer that.'

Nick laughed. 'Just thought she might like to go for a walk.'

'She won't have any legs left by the time she's finished here. Must go.'

Nick ate his crab salad as slowly as he possibly could. At last he got up to pay his bill. He caught Sophie's eye.

'Walk later?' he mouthed.

Her face was still pink from the heat. 'I'll call in when I get home,' she said, before disappearing in a cloud of steam.

Sophie couldn't wait for the café to close. The last customers seemed to take one sip a minute from their drinks. She took in the menu board and began stacking the outdoor chairs. Rachel rolled in the awning. And still they sat, staring into space. Eventually Rachel shut the door and put up the closed sign. The couple took the hint and grudgingly departed.

'Yes!' said Rachel, raising her arms in the air.

Sophie shrugged on her backpack and let herself out of the café. The air had cooled and she closed her eyes, letting the breeze blow on her hot cheeks. She'd felt herself boil up when Nick had appeared and the flush refused to go even after he'd gone. Whatever must he have thought of her, looking like a lobster, hair a mess, bumping into tables, sending cutlery skidding across the floor? She'd completely lost her concentration and he seemed so cool sitting there eating his salad. Why couldn't he have come in when the café was quiet and she could have sailed around looking calm and efficient?

'Sophie?'

She opened her eyes wondering if she'd misheard. There in front of her stood Jill.

'Hello,' she said. 'Come for a drink?'

'Well, I,' Sophie gestured lamely toward the cliffs. Oh, no. All she wanted was to get home, have a shower and see Nick.

'Please,' Jill said. 'Promise I won't attack.' She smiled. Her mouth trembled and Sophie could see her eyes were full of tears. She looked desolate, her hair was lank and she wore no makeup or jewellery. Sophie couldn't ever remember seeing her without a pair of significant earrings. Her clothes looked creased and saggy, as if she'd slept in them. This wasn't her Jill. Sophie's heart lurched.

'Come on,' Sophie said, taking her arm, leading her towards The Spyglass. She sat her down at one of the outside tables and ordered orange juice and lemonade. She wanted them both to stay clear.

'Ash has gone to collect Tom and Fleur,' she said. 'They'll be back late this evening.'

Sophie didn't know what to say. She reached across the table and put her hand on Jill's and waited. Jill sipped at her drink and then raised bleak eyes.

'He told me everything.'

Sophie nodded, encouragingly.

'I'm glad he did. I wanted him to.' Tears welled up and spilled over Jill's bottom lids. 'At least I know now.' She rummaged in her pocket for a tissue. 'But it hurts like hell.' She blew her nose. It looked red and sore. Sophie guessed she'd done a lot of crying.

'Where did you go, you and Ash?'

'Oh, we just drove and stopped at the first hotel on the mainland that looked a bit isolated. We've been talking non-stop.' Her eyes looked glassily out to sea. 'At first I felt relieved that it wasn't Marguerite, but then it sank in that it was a student that he'd been fucking. A student! Can you believe that, Sophie?'

'She was a very powerful student,' Sophie said after a long silence.

'Don't make excuses for him,' Jill growled.

'I'm not. I don't excuse him. But I just wanted you to know that this was someone exceptional. She nearly sucked me in with her hypnotic ability and I've had some experience. If it hadn't been for Marguerite's intervention I think she would have pulled me under – psychically speaking.'

'But he should have got rid of her right at the start before she got a hold.'

'Yes, he should have,' Sophie agreed, wondering how easy that would have been – like an iron filing avoiding a magnet.

'I'm not having a go at you, Sophie. But I just want to know – that time you asked me if Ash was having a fling. You'd caught him out, hadn't you?'

'I . . . I wasn't sure. I heard some noises, that's all. You know the sort of grunts people make when Ash is manipulating spines? It could have been that.'

'Please don't lie to me. I feel betrayed enough as it is. Ash told me you walked in on him and he begged you to help.'

'Oh, God. I'm so sorry, Jill. He also begged me not to tell you. And I didn't see anything or anyone. I only suspected it was Marguerite because I saw her outside Cormorants late that night, staring up at the house. I didn't even know who she was until I saw her again in the café.'

'Poor Marguerite. She was desperately trying to help him. I know that now.'

'That's one of the reasons why I wanted to move out. Ash put me in an untenable position. Whichever way I turned I was going to betray someone.'

'I wish you had put me first.'

'Ash told me it was all over – whatever it was. And you told me everything was all right.' Sophie's throat was getting tight; she tried not to let her voice rise. 'Would you really have wanted me to jeopardise it at that stage and tell you that, actually, I was sure Ash *was* having sex with someone? What would you have done?'

Jill shook her head. 'I've asked myself that over and over. The truth is I'd probably have done exactly the same. Honesty would have been impossible.' She got up. 'Got to have some alcohol.' She disappeared inside the pub and came back with two large glasses of red wine. Sophie wasn't in the mood for drinking. She watched Jill gulping hers. So much for her alcohol-free retreat.

'I did try,' Jill said, as if reading Sophie's thoughts. 'I went to Iona and Findhorn. Not really for me – one too traditional, the other too New Age. Don't know where I fit in.' She shrugged and ran her hands through her hair. 'I don't know whether I can forgive Ash for this. He put his family, his professional reputation, and our livelihood all at risk. He's bloody lucky that he hasn't been struck off.' She rummaged in her bag for more tissues. 'And how do we know that it might not still happen? How do we know that this Yasmin woman might not still flip and report him? She's a real nutter by the sound of her.'

'I agree; it is still uncertain. But I did a lot of work on Yasmin – with Marguerite.'

'Did you?' Jill sounded plaintive.

'She was very responsive. She seemed genuinely to want to get over this obsession. I know that doesn't mean she will, but she's in good hands now – the best.'

Jill's eyes scanned Sophie's face. 'I didn't know you'd done that. And Marguerite too? I owe her an apology.'

'And Solveig was marvellous. Just like a good mother. I have a strong feeling that Yasmin will come through this.'

'If she shows her face back here I will kill her and bugger my training,' Jill said.

'Well, that would certainly help things.'

'If it wasn't for Tom and Fleur I'd leave,' Jill

continued. 'But, we've agreed we owe it to our kids to try and keep things going.' She drank some more wine and rubbed her hands over her face. 'Oh, God. How do I know he hasn't contracted some horrible disease? He didn't consider that when he was playing chase me round the pyramids. He'll have to have tests. Although I can't imagine us ever having sex again.'

'Give it time. At least it's all out in the open now. Truth is a good place to start rebuilding from.'

'Is it, Sophie?'

Sophie suspected this wasn't Jill's first glass of wine of the day. She was looking distinctly wild-eyed. Perhaps she should get her home and then she could escape and see Nick.

'Truth is a good place . . . okay – I have something to confess.'

Sophie had a sudden premonition of the sea rushing towards her; a mighty wave slapping her in the face. She shivered. 'I'm listening.'

Jill took a deep breath. 'I've had sex with Peter.'

The words seemed to Sophie to be suspended in the air, as if they had nowhere to land. 'What?'

'I think you heard me,' Jill muttered.

The words seemed to be shuffling themselves about now, as if trying to make sense. 'You mean . . . before he and I met—'

'No!' Jill shook her head wildly. 'Yes! I was having sex with him before you came on the scene – but it carried on after—'

'I don't believe you!'

'Peter and I – we're two of a kind.'

Sophie stared at her, astounded. 'I don't understand—'

'We both have the same need for illicit sex. I'm not going to excuse myself and give you all the spiel about my promiscuous upbringing. I'm telling you because I need to get clear of all this – even if it costs me your friendship—'

Sophie shook her head. 'No! You're my best friend. I would have known—'

'I wanted you to hear it from me because Peter said he was going to tell you. He's really bitter about you not getting back together. He's determined to wreck everyone else's marriages out of spite. Audrey is the only one he can't lay anything on.'

Sophie continued to shake her head. Why was Jill saying this? Had she gone mad? 'You couldn't have hidden that from me.'

Jill shrugged in a defeated way. 'Oh, yes I could. Believe me, I'm not to be trusted, even by my best friend.'

Sophie felt as if she'd been presented with a puzzle that was unsolvable. 'But . . . why . . . you encouraged me to marry him . . . and then you couldn't wait for me to leave him.'

'I thought – the sex – would all stop when you came on the scene. You were different.'

'But it didn't stop?'

Jill shook her head.

'Why didn't you tell me then?'

'I didn't want to lose you. Neither did Peter.'

'You manipulated me – you both—'

'But then I decided that I would have to lose you – that's when I tried to turn you off him – more overtly.'

'But why? I'm still not getting this.'

'I got pregnant.'

'You got pregnant – but surely that would have made things better. You and Ash wanted kids. Didn't that change everything?'

'But I didn't know whose baby it was.'

Sophie slumped back in her chair. They sat and stared at each other for a few moments. 'Did you have a termination – or are we talking about Rose?' she whispered.

'We're talking about Rose.'

'But that's utterly ridiculous! Rose is so like Ash!'

'She looks just like me.'

'Yes, but she has Ash's bones – all your kids have them.'

Jill nodded. 'Couldn't see beyond my own guilt. I was so frightened by Rose that I didn't want any more kids. Until I came to the island – away from Peter – this place has kept me in check.'

'But you go back – for seminars. Does that mean . . . you and Peter . . . ?'

Jill nodded. 'It's over now – too late I know.' She emptied her glass. 'I was going to arrange a paternity test, but Ash says he did that years ago. Rose is his.'

'Ash knew? Everybody knew about this, except me?'

'Peter never asked. It's been hell – especially knowing how much you wanted a baby. I've been obsessed these last few years about getting you away from Peter before it's too late.'

'Too late?'

'For you to have a child with someone else – or on your own.'

'In order to alleviate your guilt?'

Jill bit her lip and nodded.

Sophie wanted to get away from this person – this stranger who was pretending to be her friend. Jill toyed with her empty glass and then looked at Sophie's.

'Can I—'

'Well you seem to need everything else of mine, why not?' Sophie picked up the glass of wine and threw its contents in Jill's face. She stood up. 'Just for your information. I made my own decisions about my life. I chose to stay with Peter because I needed to.' Sophie lowered her voice, people were beginning to stare. 'How dare you think you can control my life.' Jill blinked up at her for a few seconds then lowered her dripping head to the table.

Sophie walked out of the pub and took the nearest set of steps down to the beach. She slumped down on the sand, leaned against the wall and closed her eyes. Her mind was seized up with unanswered questions. Had Jill been her friend or her enemy all these years? When exactly had the sex with Peter stopped? Sophie always knew that Jill was a compulsive flirt. She'd seen how she behaved at the seminars they'd attended together. She often wondered how far she would go on the ones she went to on her own. And Ash knew about all this! How could he have borne it? Sophie felt her face flush with humiliation. And all these years that Jill had been encouraging her to leave Peter and go it alone – Sophie had thought it was because Jill cared.

Sophie sat until her bottom grew numb. Things were starting to make sense now. All the confusion she'd lived with about Jill and Peter's antagonism. She couldn't understand why she'd never realised. She was such a fool, focusing on Peter's betrayals and listening to Jill's advice. That's what hurt most. She knew about Peter – that some of his philandering was simply male strutting – just like her father. But it had been her choice to live with that, rather than face life alone. But Jill – that's where the deepest pain was – how could she have deceived her for all those years? Jill had said she didn't want to lose her, but Sophie couldn't understand that. Surely Jill's life would have been simpler without her around. Had Sophie just been an unwitting accomplice, adding to the thrill of illicit sex, as Jill had put it?

Night was falling, the beach empty – she must head for the cliff path before it got too dark. Her enthusiasm about seeing Nick had drained. If she saw him she would probably blurt it all out. She didn't want him to think he'd made a friend of a woman who came trailing a new relationship problem every day like a soap opera character. She got up stiffly and walked up the steps and past The Spyglass, relieved to see that Jill had gone. Unless, of course, she was under the table.

Stephanie had listened to Jill's hysterical babbling without interrupting or giving advice. Which was just as well, Jill thought, knowing how much she would resent any suggestions her mother had to offer.

Jill felt uncontrollable giggles start to rise again. 'Well, if Ash thinks I'm dressing up as Nefertiti he can dream on.' Stephanie wasn't laughing. 'Seriously though, Mother, it's all psychological, isn't it? Beloved, adoring daughter leaves home – sensuous young woman fills the gap. All that forbidden unconscious father-daughter stuff.' Jill suddenly felt sick. 'I need some food,' she said.

Stephanie grasped her hands and hauled her out of her chair. 'What you need is a cold shower. Come on, let's get you cleaned up and sober before Ash gets back with Tom and Fleur. You have to put on a brave face for them.' She shook Jill's shoulders. 'You've got to start somewhere.'

'Being the good mother now, are we? Bit too late for that.' She suddenly slumped against Stephanie, nearly knocking her over. 'I'm glad you're here,' she wailed.

CHAPTER 32

Nick wondered if Sophie was avoiding him or whether she had other things on her mind. She'd seemed distracted in the cafe and then she hadn't come home – again. At least not until late. Maybe she'd met someone else. Why shouldn't she? There were enough men coming and going all day in and out of the café. Surely it would be easy to get chatting to someone and maybe asked out on a date. Perhaps he'd left it too late with all his caution about not wanting to crowd her. He felt his spirit start to sink. But it might not be that at all. Perhaps she sensed his eagerness and just didn't want him to get ideas.

He put down his cutters. He'd been trying all morning to get some semblance of a shape in the ancient rambling roses that had created their own wild design. Jane wanted to preserve them. His arms were scratched and sore. He went into the portable cabin which acted as a canteen for the team and rinsed his arms under the tap. They stung like mad. It was hot and smelly in the small wash room. The students lounged in the seating area, eating their lunch and playing loud music.

He could hear Patrick's voice above the rest; he sounded so like Aidan. Today something hilarious was obviously happening by the exuberance of their laughter. Normally Nick would be amused by their youth and their quick-witted humour – but today he just wanted some peace. He thought he might take his sandwich outside.

'Look at this,' Patrick was saying, 'you have to be really careful what you put into a search engine. Before you know it, unstoppable porn downloads by the shitload.' There followed hoots of laughter. Nick peeped around the door; they were handing around sheets of paper.

'You wanna be careful,' someone said, 'you can get arrested for having this gear. What were you trying to find, anyway?'

'Oh, info for someone, about fertility and stuff. Sperm banks and how to get pregnant without a man.'

'Weird. How does that work?'

'Lesbians. They pay some poor sod to wank in a jam jar and then syringe it up,' one of the girls said.

'No,' said Patrick, 'it's legit. They have proper donors. Students do it – get paid, I think.'

'They'd have to pay me thousands for the privilege of my golden bullets,' someone said. 'So, who is this for? What poor cow can't get it any other way? Tell her I'll give her one for nothing – don't care what she looks like – put a bag over her head.'

'It's some friend of my mum's. Split up with her

husband – had enough of men by the sound of it. She's not bad looking – bit old, but I wouldn't say no.'

Nick felt his body go rigid. He walked into the room. Patrick glanced up.

'Hi, Nick.' He began sorting out the printed sheets. Could you deliver this to your next door neighbour? It's some info Mum asked me to look up.'

'Did she ask you to share it around with your mates first?'

'No, that was some other stuff. Got mixed in with it, that's all.'

'It might be confidential. You could have put it in an envelope.'

Patrick looked awkward. 'Mum didn't say it was.'

'Right, well you'd better give it to me. I'll see she gets it.'

This caused sniggers all round. 'Sounds like that's what she needs,' someone ventured.

Nick took the bundle of papers outside with him and sat on the grass to eat his lunch. He felt himself shaking with rage. How dare these youngsters have so little regard for someone's privacy? And what was Rachel thinking of asking Patrick to download this stuff without telling him to keep it confidential? It wasn't like her. He hardly let himself dwell on what the material implied. Was this why Sophie was avoiding him? Had she decided to put a child above all else and go it alone? She didn't want another partner then. She didn't want him.

What a fool he'd been, thinking she might be interested in starting up another relationship after having escaped from a shallow man like Peter. He put his head in his hands. Thank goodness he'd had this revelation before he'd made a real exhibition of himself. He would have to back track now and try to remember what it felt like to have Sophie as a friend.

He didn't want to hand her this information. He would have to find a way of delivering it when she wasn't there. Or early tomorrow morning – before she was up. And he could work late tonight and then drop in on Kyp and Evie, to gain some time to adjust. He must pull himself together, or the next time he saw her he might give way to his feelings.

At last Sophie had a day to herself. She felt exhausted physically and mentally. She hadn't allowed herself to dwell further on her meeting with Jill and all its implications. She certainly wasn't ready to talk about it with anyone. She and Rachel had spent yesterday afternoon and evening scrubbing out the café from top to bottom and she'd been glad of the hard practical work. And now, waking early, she lay in bed listening to the sea sounds and Kyp starting up his fishing boat. She thought she heard Nick going off to work but it was difficult to tell with the wind buffeting around the cottages.

She drifted in and out of sleep, letting events come and go in her mind until eventually the sad image of Jill crept in. This wasn't the end of their relationship, she knew that. Too many years of deception lay between them to be ignored and let go. Their lives were entwined, their histories bound together. What a lot of unwinding and separating out they were going to have to do if they were to move forward stronger and wiser than they'd been. And would Jill want to anyway? Yes, she would, Sophie knew she would, she was a tenacious woman. She would even respect Sophie for the red wine incident. And Fleur was Sophie's beloved goddaughter.

Sophie sighed and decided to shelve the problem of Jill for now. Today it was going to be her turn to put a note under Nick's door to invite him for a walk and a meal after work and explain why she hadn't called in. They kept missing each other – he wasn't home again last night when she'd arrived back, which was just as well, given her fragile state. But now, she couldn't wait to see him; it seemed ages since they'd spent time talking. She wondered if tonight might be the night they ventured closer, perhaps hold each other, maybe kiss. A dart of desire flashed through her body. She would have to restrain herself, didn't want to scare him off. She smiled, God, Sophie, she thought, you're behaving like a silly girl. But, that's exactly how she felt. She wanted to spend hours grooming herself, shaving her legs, taming her hair, making every part of herself soft and scented. She wanted soft lights and seductive music and delicious food and wine.

She could hear Jack and Mila chattering. They were going back to school today. The beach would be emptier – just older couples sitting in deck chairs, reading and dozing. She heard Evie calling to them to hurry up. Everyone was getting on with their day and here she was lying in bed, indulging herself with thoughts of Nick.

She realised she felt disappointed that she hadn't been able to share her happiness with Jill. She would have liked to talk about Nick with her. But that was before Jill's confession. Right! She was getting back to the subject of Jill again and she didn't want to do that.

She got out of bed and spent the morning cleaning her cottage. Not that it was particularly dirty; she'd hardly been home recently. But it gave her something to concentrate on. She was in danger of daydreaming about Nick. She swept the sand from the stairs and opened her front door to empty it away. A large brown envelope was lying on the mat. It didn't have her name on it. She carried it back upstairs and opened it. It was a wad of information about fertility and sperm banks and donors. Patrick must have printed it out and given it to Nick to deliver. Thank goodness it was well-sealed. She wouldn't have wanted Nick to see this. She pushed it back in the envelope. She wasn't ready to research this stuff yet – didn't know if she really wanted to. It wasn't the right time. Maybe . . . if she finally gave up on relationships . . . perhaps she would read it.

She made some lunch and then decided to go for a walk to while away the afternoon. She dropped a note in Nick's door on the way, inviting him for a walk and supper. She wandered through the Botanic Gardens, sitting on different benches, watching people studying the plants or each other. She kept looking at her watch, the day seemed endless. She decided to go back home and start preparing for the evening. She smiled; it would be just her luck if Nick was working late again tonight.

Evie had just arrived back with the kids when she got home. Sophie joined her for a cup of tea.

'Haven't seen much of you lately,' Evie said.

'No, busy time at work.'

'I always feel a sense of sadness this time of year – when the holidays arc over and everything starts to wind down.'

'I can't imagine you being sad, Evie.'

'I like the sun. That's why Kyp and I go away to Greece for a while to get some more of it. And we like the kids to keep in touch with the other half of their roots.'

'It will seem strange when you go. I expect it's very quiet here in the winter.'

'Apart from the sea, yes. I don't expect you'll stay here all alone though, will you?'

'Well, Nick will be here.'

'Depends when he goes.'
'Goes?'
'Didn't he tell you? He's decided to go back to New Zealand.'
Sophie felt her heart drop like a stone inside her. 'I thought he was going to stay. He said—'
'Yes, I know. I don't know why he's changed his mind.'
'When did he tell you?'
'Last night.'
'Last night? I thought he was out.'
'Well, he was here, looking up flights on the kids' computer. He seemed quite down. Kyp and I were surprised. He's been so much more cheerful lately – ever since his holiday with Neptune.' She smiled. 'At one time, we thought you and he might get together. Kyp's a real matchmaker. I kept telling him that it was far too soon. Nick's been through a hell of a lot, as you know.'
Sophie nodded bleakly. Her mind was desperately trying to invent reasons why Nick would be looking up flights to New Zealand that didn't involve him leaving. Perhaps he was doing it for someone else – someone at work. Perhaps his mother-in-law wanted to visit him.
'And I told Kyp,' Evie was saying, 'after your near miss with Peter, why would you want another man?'
Jack and Mila came rushing up from the beach, wanting food. Evie got up. 'Sorry, got to feed the brats. Let me know if you find out anything. I'm concerned for Nick.'

Sophie staggered back to Sea Spray, her mind numb with pain. Why? Why would he go back now? He said he wanted to stay, that Blue Slipper Bay was feeling like home. He had work here and friends. And she thought he meant her! How stupid she'd been. She'd concocted a fantasy relationship in her head. And all he'd wanted was friendship. That's what he'd said. Someone to talk and walk with. She reminded herself that he'd never made any moves towards her. She'd always been the one to throw herself hysterically at him. He probably saw her as a silly woman – having a drama with an ex-husband. She felt her face grow red with embarrassment. She wished she hadn't put that note through his door. She didn't know how she was going to face him later and act normally.

Nick picked up the note that had been slipped under his door. A walk and supper with Sophie. A couple of days ago he would havc been overjoyed. But now, he couldn't read anything into it that wasn't there. A drink and supper with a friend. Would she want to talk about her plans to have a child by an unknown man? He'd delivered the information early this morning, first sealing it in an envelope that he'd begged from Jane. He didn't want Sophie to know that he knew the contents. How could he sit and listen to her without betraying his emotions?

He'd thought through all this yesterday, wondering

if he would be able to watch Sophie expand with pregnancy, perhaps help her move into a small house in Ventnor, bump into her pushing a buggy along the esplanade. Maybe he couldn't make this place his home after all. He'd gone along to Kyp and Evie's last night and looked up flight times and prices to New Zealand. He was being impetuous, he knew. He didn't really want to go, but he didn't want to stay either. He'd stayed out late, watching television with Kyp, wanting to avoid her. Later, he'd lain in bed, tossing and turning, wondering if he should offer himself as a father for her child. But, that wasn't what he wanted. He didn't want to be a sperm donor; he wanted to be a lover, a husband, maybe a real father – he couldn't think about that yet.

He read Sophie's note again. He would have to face her. Maybe he should return her miracle box – he'd kept it a long time. But he wanted to hold onto it for a bit longer – he wasn't finished it with yet and it gave him such comfort. He showered and dressed and stood outside on the path, staring at the sea, trying to psyche himself up to meet her.

'Nick.' He looked up. She was leaning over her balcony. His heart gave a lurch. 'Are you coming up?'

He walked up the stairs. She was standing by the window, looking strangely formal. She smiled. 'Thought I was never going to get to see you again,' she said.

Nick was confused, unsure what she meant. 'Sorry?'

'You know, ships that pass in the night?'

'Oh, right. Yes, we have been busy, both of us.'

'Do you want to walk, or are you too tired after your hard day?'

'To tell you the truth, I am a bit.'

She stood looking at him, as if waiting for him to say something else. 'Sit down, then,' she said. 'I'll get us a drink.'

Nick sat, immediately wishing that he'd said yes to the walk. He was finding it hard to think of anything to say. Sophie brought in a tray of drinks and crisps and set it on the table. She poured two glasses and handed one to him.

'Thanks for delivering the envelope,' she said. 'I assume it was you.'

'Patrick asked me,' he said, bracing himself. Was she going to talk about it?

'How's the building going at Wraith Cove? I hear it's been frenetic.'

'Yes, boots tramping all over the place. I'm going to have to start the garden over again, I reckon. When they've gone.'

'Gone?'

'Well, some of them will be going back to their universities in a few weeks. Patrick has taken the reins now. He's really interested in the restoration work. Jane's glad to have him.'

'As well as you?'

Nick nodded. Sophie was looking at him

differently. Her face seemed serious. Perhaps he should tell her that he was thinking of going away. But he felt guarded, as if he were waiting for her to open up and then he would feel free to do the same. There was a growing feeling of unease between them. Whatever had happened to their vow to be honest with each other?

'How's Jill?' he found himself saying, trying to veer away from anything too personal.

'Struggling.' He saw her bite her bottom lip as if she were keeping something back. 'They're trying to hold it together for the children's sake.'

'Do you think they'll be able to?'

'They might. The children are very important to them. They are firm believers in quality parenting. Jill always wishes her mother hadn't been so easy going and Ash's parents are a bit on the Victorian side – the opposite extreme.'

'What do you think?'

'About what?'

'Shared parenting?'

Sophie sighed; a shadow seemed to pass over her face, as if she were troubled.

'Every situation's different, isn't it? It's the best possible scenario I suppose. Two caring parents must be good for any child. But reality isn't like that, not any more. Perhaps it never was.' She got up. 'I'll go and put the spaghetti on.'

'Sophie,' Nick couldn't cope with this. He couldn't sit through a meal with her, suppressing his feelings and being dishonest. 'Do you mind if

I give supper a miss? I'm absolutely whacked. I think I'm going to have an early night.'

She turned to look at him. Her face seemed full of distress, as if she were going to cry. He wanted to take those few steps towards her, take her in his arms and tell her how much he loved her. He wanted her to prevent him from running away.

'Okay,' she said. 'If that's what you want to do.'

'Another time,' he said, hardly able to bear the look of hurt and puzzlement on her face.

She nodded. Nick turned away and left.

CHAPTER 33

On her way to work the following morning Sophie didn't notice the sea or if there were any ships out there. She didn't notice whether the sun was shining or whether the wind was blowing. She didn't feel cold or hot. All she felt was misery. Nick didn't love her. He was going away to the other side of the world – as far away as he could possibly go. He didn't even love her sufficiently to tell her why he'd decided to do this. She wasn't even a good enough friend for that. Perhaps he felt free again after expressing his grief. Perhaps he wanted to spread his wings and fly away from a place as confining as Blue Slipper Bay and this little island. There must be exciting prospects enticing him once more. A single male with no ties. The world was his.

When she got to work she realised she'd forgotten she was meant to get in early so that Rachel could go and have a financial chat with Chas. Aidan had been yanked out of his pit once again and was stumbling around looking rough.

'Sorry,' Sophie mumbled, tying on her apron. Fortunately the café was quiet.

'Can I go back to bed?' Aidan yawned.

'Clear off,' Sophie said.

'You're full of love and light this morning. Mum is furious with you.'

'Is she? Why?'

'For being late. She wanted to tell you something important.'

'What?'

'Dunno. Goodnight.'

The weather turned drizzly. A few customers wandered in for coffee and to read their papers. Sophie blundered around, wiping a cloth over anything she came into contact with. She wondered when Nick planned to go. Would he stay until the weather cooled down here so that he could fly from summer to summer? Or would he just take off? She might get home one day to find him gone. Tears welled up into her eyes. She brushed them away with the cloth. Audrey wouldn't approve of her disregard for hygiene. She put the cloth in the bin and took a fresh one from the cupboard. Perhaps she should return to London after all. She didn't feel drawn back there, but did she want to stay here now? She mustn't let this passion for Nick spoil everything. She loved it here – but then again she had so many difficult feelings about Jill to contend with now. Nonetheless, she still had Rachel and Blue Slipper Bay and a share in other people's children. Perhaps it was just as well that Nick was going. She could then decide whether to go ahead with the single parent idea. But it was no good. Trying to talk herself out of the pain she was feeling was just not working.

Rachel arrived back late morning.

'Forgot I was meant to be early,' Sophie mumbled.

'I wanted to speak to you,' Rachel said. 'Let's get these people served and we'll talk.'

Her face looked serious; she kept glancing at Sophie as they kept up their pleasantries for the customers.

'Right,' she beckoned Sophie behind the cake cabinet, out of view of most of the café. 'Never have sons. They fuck you up.'

'Aidan? What's he done?'

'No, Patrick. I'm so angry with him. I asked him to look up that information for you on the web – you know?'

'Yes, I got it. Nick left it. I haven't read it yet.'

'But I didn't know he'd taken his computer to Wraith Cove. The idiot downloaded some sleaze – just came with it, so he says! He printed it out for the benefit of his pond-life friends and they were all having a laugh when Nick walked in. Patrick told him it was for his neighbour and asked Nick to deliver it. I'd meant him to give it to me.'

Sophie felt puzzled. 'I didn't see anything sleazy. It was sealed up in an envelope.'

'Patrick says he took the porn stuff out. But Nick was obviously angry with him for being so insensitive towards you. There were some pretty ribald remarks going around. Patrick hadn't realised that you were a good friend of Nick's.'

'Nick must have rescued my information and

put it in an envelope for me. Is that what you're saying?'

'He must have. Patrick is so sorry. He was very worried about the effect it might have on you if it got around. He wants to see you to apologise. And so he should – the dick-head.'

Sophie stood still, thinking about the implications of all this. So, Nick knew what was in the envelope when he left it outside her door. Even if he hadn't read it he must have heard what Patrick was saying and he must at least have noticed what he was sealing up. She had been the butt of smutty student innuendo and Nick must be thinking . . . what must he be thinking? That she was planning to have a baby by a sperm donor. That she wasn't interested in having a man in her life, another relationship. After the Peter debacle, she had decided to go it alone. Was that why he was so distant last night? Was he waiting for her to tell him? Or did none of this matter anyway? Perhaps it was none of his concern.

Rachel was looking at her. 'I'm so sorry about all this, Sophie,' she said. 'I could kill Patrick. He's usually quite responsible. I've also discovered that he's been on holiday with Rose. So Ash might kill him first – but then again . . . Oh, dear, you must be worried about what Nick might be thinking.'

Sophie nodded. 'It doesn't matter, Rachel. Nick's going back to New Zealand anyway.'

'But he can't be.'

'He is. Evie told me.'

'Have you told him how you feel about him?'

'No. I couldn't bring myself to. I don't think it's reciprocal.'

'But of course it is. You must feel it. I can tell just by looking at him looking at you.'

'But—'

'Tell him, Sophie. You've got nothing to lose now.' She reached behind Sophie and yanked at her apron strings. 'Go home. Go and tell him.'

'He'll be at work,' Sophie said.

'Go to Wraith Cove, then.'

'No,' she snapped, grabbing her apron back. 'I haven't got my car with me.' She rushed out to greet a couple of new customers, nearly pushing them into their chairs. 'What can I get you?' She smiled, inanely, shoving menus into their hands.

She managed to stay out of Rachel's range by circulating amongst the tables. She didn't want to think about any of this right now. If she stopped to imagine Nick listening to a group of youngsters making lewd remarks about her, she might burst into tears. She could hear the type of thing they would say. She was certain that Nick wouldn't hold her responsible for the pornography but he would know everything else. At least he'd had the decency to find an envelope.

The door burst open and Jill walked in.

'Right,' she said to Sophie. 'Get your coat. We're going.' She walked round the counter and spoke to Rachel. She picked up Sophie's bag, grabbed her arm and hefted her out of the café. 'Get in the car.'

'What's going on?' Sophie asked, frightened. 'Is there an emergency?'

'Rachel phoned me to come and get you. She said you were behaving in a distracted manner and someone ought to bang your head against Nick's.'

'I don't want to talk to you. Rachel would never have phoned you if she knew what you'd done.' She glared at Jill. 'I don't want your advice. I'm not a child,' she added, thinking her voice sounded extremely childish.

'Do your seat belt up,' Jill commanded. 'I know you're not a child. And this isn't about you and me. But I agree with Rachel, you should talk to Nick.' She put her hand on Sophie's. 'The trouble is, you've both been clobbered by life and you're both afraid of being hurt – or causing pain – again. Am I right?'

Sophie pulled her hand away, but nodded, tearfully.

'So, now you're both caught up in some sort of stalemate, full of misunderstandings. You might both end up regretting it.'

'But, what can I possibly say to him that won't put him on the spot? He hasn't given me any reason to believe that he feels the same.'

'Let's just put it down to female intuition.'

'Which female exactly?'

'Me, Rachel, Evie, Jane – not to mention some non-verbal communication from Marguerite.'

Sophie sat back in her seat. This was getting

ridiculous. Was everybody talking about her behind her back?

'This is a small island,' Jill said, starting the car. 'Besides, I've got an awful lot of reparation to do to earn back your friendship.'

Jill dropped her at the entrance to the hotel grounds. The earth was full of tyre tracks. There didn't seem to be anyone around. Sophie walked over to the portable cabin. The door was open and cigarette smoke drifted out. She didn't think Nick would be in there. She walked over to the stable block which was looking smart under its new tiled roof. She could hear the sound of hammering and went round to the back of the building. A man looked up and pushed his cap back.

'Looking for someone?' he asked.

'Is Nick around?'

'Nick? Oh, he's gone.'

'Gone where?'

The man shrugged. 'He left a couple of hours ago.'

Nick stood on the path looking at the sea. There was a storm on its way. He wanted to swim before it came any closer. He'd left work early, knowing that he wasn't doing a good job. He didn't want to talk to anyone. He knew that the only thing that could clear his mind and relieve his tension would be a hard swim. The tide was in, already covering the deserted beach. Dark clouds were grouping on the horizon to the west. He could smell the rain carried on the strengthening wind. He'd put on his wet suit. No sense taking any risks and getting too chilled out there.

He jumped down from the path onto the beach and ran straight into the water, feeling its familiar cold slap. He let out a gruff shudder of sound, scooping handfuls of water over his face and head. His hair would hold the water, chill him. He must shave it again when he got back. He began to swim, concentrating on the feel of his body, his muscles working. He felt back to his former strength now. It felt good, here he was, just him and the surge of water, pitted against each other. No space left to think of anything other than this primal urge to move forward. He took a deep breath and plunged beneath the waves, deadening the sound of the wind and water, bubbles escaped from his lungs, surrounding his head. He stayed under until he felt something might burst. He was suddenly reminded of the day he tried to drown himself, when Neptune and Marguerite had rescued him. This was different. He didn't want to die now. He knew he could live with the pain and survive.

He burst through the surface, gasping. He lay on his back, carried by the swell of the water. Everything seemed clearer now. He should talk to Sophie; tell her how he felt. He should be honest with her instead of running away. Didn't their friendship deserve that? And then she would know, and it might free her to reveal her plans to have a child. He couldn't tell whether they might still be friends after his confession of love. It would be bound to change things. But then that would have to be the next decision – whether to go away or stay here. He had to live the experience if he wanted to find out.

He looked back towards the shore. He'd swum a long way. He could see the waves spraying up against the path. The sky looked heavier, the wind moaning. He should head back. His arms and legs ached but he felt he could almost let the sea carry him in. He glanced up; the shore was coming closer. He could see the three cottages quite clearly. His heart warmed with love for Blue Slipper Bay. What a refuge this had been to him. Even if he decided to leave, he would want to come back from time to time.

There was someone standing on the path. They should take care; rogue waves could sweep right over without warning on spring tides like this. He wiped his eyes and peered. The person was waving. Perhaps it was a nervous holiday maker trying to warn him to get out of the sea. And then his vision cleared and he recognised Sophie. His heart bounded. What was she doing?

'Take care,' he shouted, knowing the wind would whip his words away from her. He tried to swim faster; she shouldn't be standing there. He attempted to wave a warning, but she waved back.

And then, as he watched she started to walk down the slip-way. A wave washed over him and he had to clear his eyes again. Sophie was nowhere in sight. My God, had she been swept into the sea? He knew she couldn't swim very well. He swam as if he were going for gold. His lungs and throat burned. He felt his feet strike the rocks. He scanned the sea. Where the hell was she? And then he saw her; she was clinging to one of the wooden posts at the side of the slip-way.

'Hold on,' he yelled. He half swam, half waded towards her. Her hair was plastered over her face, she couldn't push it back because she using both arms to hang on. He caught hold of her roughly and swept her hair back. 'What the hell do you think you're doing?' he said, his voice shaking with fear.

'I was coming to rescue you.'

A wave slapped Nick hard in the back. He prised Sophie's hands from the post and, keeping firm hold of her, managed to get them both up onto the slip-way.

'You were what?' he shouted, above the wind.

'I thought you were drowning.'

'Drowning!' Water was dripping down her face. Nick wondered if she was crying. He half carried her towards Sea Spray, threw open the door and supported her up the stairs. Her legs were shaking and buckling on every step. He sat her down at the top and dripped into her bathroom and grabbed towels. He wrapped them around her.

She was shivering, her teeth chattering. She was looking down at her shaking hands.

'You need a hot shower,' he said.

She thought he was drowning. She didn't think about what she was doing. She knew if she could just get close enough to him, she would be able to help him.

When the builder at Wraith Cove had said that Nick had gone, she'd panicked. She thought he had really gone, that he might be heading for the ferry, for the airport. She should have let Jill wait for her in the car. Jill wanted to, but Sophie didn't want her there, interfering in her relationship with Nick. And then she'd had to run all the way back to Blue Slipper Bay along the road and down the steep path. She'd searched for him everywhere and then she'd spotted his sandals outside Fair Wind.

Sophie coughed, her throat felt raw from the yelling and the salt water. She was still huddled on the floor just inside the sitting room door. Nick was turning on the shower. He helped her to her feet and guided her towards the bathroom. This was the second time he'd had to do that recently. He must regard her like a helpless child.

'Stand under that hot water. I'm going next door to get changed.'

She peeled off her clothes. They were plastered with sand and bits of sea debris. She left them in a heap and stepped under the shower. It stung but felt wonderful. All she could think was that

Nick was safe. She didn't care if he didn't want her. She just felt an overwhelming sense of relief that he was still alive. She dried herself and put on her dressing gown.

Nick had carried in a pile of logs and was on his knees lighting the woodburner. He looked up at her, frowning.

'How are you feeling?'

'Okay. A bit shaky, but otherwise—'

'Promise me you'll never do anything so stupid again.' His voice was stern. 'The sea is much too rough to go paddling today.'

'I wasn't paddling, I—'

'No, I know. But you're not a strong swimmer, Sophie. You could easily have been swept out to sea.'

'But you—'

'I know the sea well. But I don't take risks.' He gestured towards the window. 'Do you hear that wind? I wouldn't go out there now.'

He wasn't listening to her. He was treating her as if she'd just been silly. He didn't realise she thought he was drowning. He continued to kneel on the floor, glaring at her. She started to shiver with shock and a feeling of overwhelming despair. Tears started to roll down her face and her body started to heave with sobs.

'But I thought you were going to die,' she wailed. 'I thought that if I could wade out a bit I could grab you as the waves washed you in.'

'Oh, Sophie,' Nick said. 'I wasn't—'

'How was I to know?' she yelled. 'You told me you'd almost drowned before, and Neptune and Marguerite rescued you.'

'But that was—'

'And I didn't want you to die without knowing that I love you,' she cried.

The room went silent apart from little crackling noises from the logs. Wisps of smoke curled outwards from the fire. Well, I've done it now, she thought. He's probably kneeling there, planning his escape to New Zealand.

Nick got up slowly and came to sit beside her on the sofa. He took her hands in his. He's going to try to let me down gently, she thought. 'So, when are you going?' she asked, looking down at his hands, scoured clean by the sea.

'Going? Going where?'

'New Zealand.' She couldn't meet his eyes, didn't want him to pity her. A silence fell and seemed to go on for ever.

'If I go, would you come with me?' he said, softly.

'Go with you?' She looked up at him then. He was gazing at her intently. Little pinpoints of flame were reflecting in his eyes from the fire.

'Sophie, did you mean what you just said? It isn't just shock?'

She shook her head. She couldn't deny it, not now. 'I've known it for ages – ever since I got clear about Peter – but I've been frightened to tell you in case I lost you – as a friend. Maybe I have now.'

'That's just what I've been scared of.'

'Losing me as a friend?' She tried to smile. 'I'm sure I—'

'No, I mean, I've wanted to tell you that I love you too, but I've been petrified I'd frighten you away.'

Sophie wondered if she had drowned after all and this was happening in some after-life experience. She put out a hand to touch his face. He felt real enough. He closed his eyes and pressed her palm to his lips.

'Oh, God, Sophie,' he whispered, 'I love you so much.' He put his arms around her and held her close. She could feel his heart beating and smell the sea in his hair.

'I didn't scare you away then, with my subversive literature?' she said, wrapping her arms around his back. 'It was Rachel's suggestion – information only.' He moved his mouth against her neck and she felt something inside her finally go into meltdown.

'I thought it meant that you'd decided to go it alone and didn't want me,' he murmured.

'And I thought you were going back to New Zealand because you didn't want me.' Her body no longer contained any bones. They slid down onto the hearth rug still clinging together, so that they were in contact from head to toe. 'Do you think . . . just maybe . . . we've been a little too sensitive?' she whispered.

CHAPTER 34

Jill lay listening to thc familiar sounds that inhabited Cormorants at night. The little creaks and cracks of the old house settling, creeping on its slow journey seawards – like a glacier. Ash was beside her, snoring lightly. No sounds from the children's rooms. Rose's was empty anyway – she had told Jill and Ash, quite firmly, that she was spending the night in Patrick's caravan. Ash had flexed his finger joints and said nothing.

Jill thought about Stephanie asleep in the attic room – Sophie's old room. Jill had been glad to have her mother around the last few days while all the turmoil was settling. Stephanie had been firm and practical, almost as if she were setting parental boundaries for Jill that were long overdue. Jill felt safe in her presence as she never had as a child. Stephanie also distracted Tom and Fleur from their war, and they were delighted to have their Grandma from Africa to tell them stories.

Jill thought about Sophie, hoping she was tucked up in bed at Blue Slipper Bay with Nick. She didn't know if Sophie would ever be able to forgive her for her deception and betrayal. Jill knew that

Sophie would no longer trust her or ask her advice about anything. And that was a good thing. All Jill wanted was to hold on to some contact with her. At least she had done the right thing, taking her to find Nick. It hadn't been easy to agree with Rachel's plan when she phoned. Jill imagined that Sophie might throw a cup of coffee over her this time. But she knew it would be a first step.

She couldn't bear to think of life without Sophie. Sometimes she felt she loved her more than anyone she had ever been connected with – except maybe Tom and Fleur.

She thought about Peter and the destructive need they'd had of each other. Well, at least that was over. She pictured the little plastic envelopes containing a piece of skirt that she had cut up, and the strands of hair that she'd ripped out of his head. All gone now – she'd watched them shrivel in the flames. She had no more secrets hidden anywhere. Had she atoned for her sins enough? Or was there penance still to come? She was going to have to work hard to earn back the love of those she loved.

Ash turned over in his sleep. She felt the curve of his spine against her arm. Jill envisioned the smooth white vertebrae and mentally began sorting them into pairs.

Sophie felt herself drifting into sleep. She was exhausted but didn't want to let go in case she should wake up and find out that she'd been dreaming. She just wanted to lie in the firelight for ever, feeling the joyful, astonishing pressure of Nick's arms around her, the feel of his fingers tangled in her hair. How could she ever have thought she would have been able to let him go without a fight? What an amazing man he was – his devastating past so at odds with his gentle soul. And that slow smile of his, and his wise considering eyes. She'd have thrown herself in front of the jumbo jet on the runway if she'd had to.

She thought if she were a religious person, now would be the time to offer thanks. A sudden memory of Tiggy broke into her mind – his small brown face smiling. She realised that he'd been like a good parent, accepting her childish feelings, validating her wordless knowledge that underneath the harshness of life something glowed. He understood why she might feel an affinity with the dead and the graveyard. He hadn't thought she was a macabre little girl who needed to see a doctor. He had simply confirmed her experience. And it had served her well. She may have had parts of her in the deep freeze but she had never – could never – burn out. There was something indestructible at the very ground of her being. Was that what Jill saw in her and couldn't let go? Was that what Nick was looking for? Was it the alchemist's gold underneath the dross? She could feel it now – a soft shining brilliance to dissolve into – like sinking into a warm bath – except it wasn't wet, just glowing. She didn't think she was different from anyone else and heaven knows she ignored that feeling most of the time. But she always knew it was there – because Tiggy had told her it was the truth.

She knew she would be able to talk about this with Nick. He would know what she meant. She sighed and let go.

Nick propped himself up on one elbow to look at Sophie to reassure himself that he hadn't been dreaming. She was asleep. She must be exhausted after her confrontation with the sea and the hours they'd just spent delighting in each other's bodies. He'd lost track of time, it was almost dark. The fire gave just enough light to illuminate Sophie's beauty. He gently smoothed her hair back from her face. An amber earring glowed among her curls. How good it felt to be touching her like this, at last.

He felt a surge of fierce protectiveness rise up inside him. He desperately wanted to keep her – and himself – from pain and harm. But he also recognised that he had to let go of that desire. He'd matured through his experiences and knew he must accept his human life with all its implications of impermanence and unpredictability. He could only be his best and honest self with this newfound love. And maybe love itself was part of something permanent and more astounding than he yet realised.